Taiwan's
Democracy
Challenged

Taiwan's Democracy Challenged

The Chen Shui-bian Years

edited by
Yun-han Chu, Larry Diamond,
and Kharis Templeman

LYNNE
RIENNER
PUBLISHERS

BOULDER
LONDON

Published in the United States of America in 2016 by
Lynne Rienner Publishers, Inc.
1800 30th Street, Boulder, Colorado 80301
www.rienner.com

and in the United Kingdom by
Lynne Rienner Publishers, Inc.
3 Henrietta Street, Covent Garden, London WC2E 8LU

Library of Congress Cataloging-in-Publication Data
Names: Chu, Yun-han, editor.
Title: Taiwan's democracy challenged : the Chen Shui-bian years / edited by
  Yun-han Chu, Larry Diamond, and Kharis Templeman.
Other titles: Chen Shui-bian years
Description: Boulder, Colorado : Lynne Rienner Publishers, Inc., [2016] |
  Includes bibliographical references and index.
Identifiers: LCCN 2015043556| ISBN 9781626374034 (hardcover : alk. paper) |
  ISBN 9781626374041 (pbk. : alk. paper)
Subjects: LCSH: Chen, Shuibian, 1951- | Democracy—Taiwan. |
  Taiwan—Politics and government—2000–
Classification: LCC DS799.847 .T7714 2016 | DDC 951.24905—dc23
LC record available at http://lccn.loc.gov/2015043556

British Cataloguing in Publication Data
A Cataloguing in Publication record for this book
is available from the British Library.

Printed and bound in the United States of America

The paper used in this publication meets the requirements
of the American National Standard for Permanence of
Paper for Printed Library Materials Z39.48-1992.

5 4 3 2 1

Contents

Tables and Figures

Tables

Figures

Acknowledgments

We are grateful for the assistance of many individuals and institutions who have helped to make this book possible. In particular, we would like to thank the Taipei Economic and Cultural Office (TECO) in San Francisco for its support of the Taiwan Democracy Project at Stanford University over the past decade. As the leaders of the Taiwan Democracy Project, Larry Diamond and Kharis Templeman would like to offer special thanks to the current director general of the TECO San Francisco Office, Joseph Ma, and to the past director, Bruce Fuh, as well as Vice Consul Sabine Chen and her predecessor in that role, Daniel Lin, for their commitment to the activities and conferences of our program. It has been our pleasure to engage them and their colleagues in the TECO office.

The Taiwan Democracy Project is a part of the Center on Democracy, Development, and the Rule of Law (CDDRL), which is in turn one of the research centers within the Freeman Spogli Institute for International Studies (FSI) at Stanford. For most of the period during which this book was produced, Larry Diamond directed CDDRL, but we would like to thank the current CDDRL director, Francis Fukuyama, for his support and interest in the program, as well as the current director of FSI, Ambassador Michael McFaul.

Throughout the long and productive life of the Taiwan Democracy Project, we have benefited from the administrative support of Alice Hazelgrove, who helped to arrange the conference from which this book originated, and who provided her ever-cheerful and efficient support of the activities of the program as we worked to complete the manuscript.

We want to thank Lynne Rienner for her creative assistance in helping to structure, frame, and title the book, and for her enduring commitment to quality and affordable publishing of scholarly books in this challenging era for academic publishing. We are also grateful to Steve Barr of Lynne Rienner Publishers for his excellent management of the editorial process, to Tara Joffe for copyediting, and to Robert Swanson for assembling the detailed index. We would also like to thank Bernadette St. John, of St. John and Associates, for her assistance preparing footnotes and references.

Finally, we would like to thank all of the authors in this collection for their patience and commitment as we saw this ambitious project through to completion.

Yun-han Chu
Larry Diamond
Kharis Templeman

1

Taiwan's Democracy Under Chen Shui-bian

*Kharis Templeman, Larry Diamond,
and Yun-han Chu*

On March 20, 2000, Chen Shui-bian was formally inaugurated as president of the Republic of China, or Taiwan. His assumption of power marked several historic firsts. It was the first peaceful transfer of power in the island's history, and it ended more than fifty years of continuous rule by the Chinese Nationalist Party, the Kuomintang (KMT). It was also a triumphant moment for Chen's Democratic Progressive Party (DPP), Taiwan's principal opposition party since the inception of competitive politics. Having started in the 1970s as a motley collection of regime opponents with widely divergent goals, the DPP had been transformed into a party committed to and capable of winning popular elections.

Eight years later, on May 20, 2008, Chen Shui-bian left office under much less happy circumstances. A cloud of ethics issues hung over his head, and he was soon detained and then convicted of corruption charges. His once-ascendant DPP was defeated, divided, and demoralized, having lost the presidency while retaining less than a quarter of the seats in the legislature. A resurgent KMT recaptured full control of the central government, as Ma Ying-jeou won the presidential election in a landslide, with his party picking up 72 percent of the legislative seats under a new, more majoritarian electoral system. In many ways, the KMT appeared, at the end of the Chen era, to be more dominant than at any point since Taiwan's transition to democracy.

The first transfer of executive power is a crucial time for democratic consolidation, opening new opportunities for positive reforms that were previously blocked by the old elite, as well as generating new challenges as everyone adjusts to the new distribution of power and different roles in

1

the political arena. The chapters in this book explore various aspects of this process of reform, adjustment, and conflict during the eight years of the Chen Shui-bian presidency.

Taiwan's Democracy in Comparative Perspective

By any measure, Taiwan has become one of the most liberal and robust democracies in Asia. Since it completed its transition to democracy with a free and fair direct election of the president in 1996, Taiwan has continually been rated by Freedom House as a "free" country, with a liberal score of at least 2 on each of the 7-point scales of political rights and civil liberties (where 1 is most free and 7 is most authoritarian). After standardizing four different democracy measures (including the average Freedom House score on political rights and civil liberties) on a scale of 1 to 10, there is a relatively consistent picture in which Taiwan has more or less sustained over the past decade and a half the democratic progress it made in the 1990s. In 2004, Taiwan's score on the Polity IV scale of democracy rose to the maximum score of 10 and has remained there since. Its standardized Freedom House score rose to about 9 in 2000, with the election of Chen Shui-bian, and has essentially remained there since, though with some oscillation within categories. Although *The Economist* magazine's Democracy Index and the World Bank's voice and accountability measure show somewhat lower scores of about 7.5, they both have remained relatively steady for a number of years. The overall data suggest that democracy in Taiwan has been consolidated— and as a relatively liberal democracy, too—as Figure 1.1 shows.

Since Freedom House began releasing its subcategory scores in 2005, Taiwan's performance on the different dimensions of political rights and civil liberties has also been relatively consistent. From 2005 through 2013, Taiwan scored a 10 or 11 (and since 2008, consistently an 11) out of 12 on electoral process; consistently a 15 out of 16 on political pluralism; and a 9 (and since 2009, a 10) out of 12 on functioning of government (which includes control of corruption). On the four categories of civil liberties, two scores held more or less constant (associational rights at 11 out of 12 and individual rights at 13 out of 16) and two declined slightly after 2008 (freedom of expression, from 16 out of 16 to 14 in recent years, and rule of law, from 15 to 14 out of 16). Overall, political rights have varied from 34 to 36 out of 40 total points and civil liberties from 51 to 55 out of 60 points.

These various data show that Taiwan is not a perfect democracy. During the Chen Shui-bian era, Taiwan's democracy was challenged on several

Figure 1.1 Democracy Indicators for Taiwan, 1996–2012

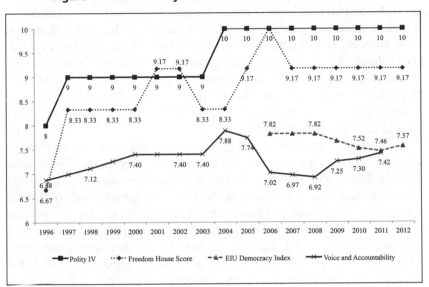

Sources: Polity IV Dataset; Freedom House; *Economist* Intelligence Unit; World Bank World-wide Governance Indicators.

Notes: 1. Freedom House Score = Political Rights + Civil Liberties (2–14). 2. The original Freedom House scores are inverted and standardized on a 0–10 scale. 3. The data for the following years are missing and replaced with the mean value of their neighboring years: EIU Democracy Index (2007, 2009); World Bank Voice and Accountability (1997, 1999, 2001).

fronts, which are detailed in this book, and it has continued to face challenges since. In fact, *The Economist* lists Taiwan as a "flawed democracy," ranking not only behind many European third-wave democracies but even (quite implausibly, in our view) behind India and South Africa.[1] Taiwan's democracy could and should be less corrupt and more accountable, with more protection for not only the rule of law but also individual and associational rights. Yet, when the metric is not the ideal or the performance of the older, mostly liberal Western democracies, but rather the performance of other third-wave democracies, Taiwan has been doing quite well. Only in the European Union and in Chile and Uruguay are there such democracies with somewhat higher levels of political rights and civil liberties.

During the presidencies of Chen and his successor, Taiwan has been one of the three most liberal democracies in Asia, with an average score on the twin Freedom House scales of at least 2 since the completion of the transition in 1996, and a score of 1.5 (or better) since 2004. Only the other two industrialized democracies of Asia—Japan and South Korea—

have done as well (see Table 1.1). On the total category scores for political rights and civil liberties, Taiwan clusters closely with Japan and South Korea on political rights and is slightly more liberal than South Korea on civil liberties. Taiwan trails slightly on political rights and lags a bit further behind on civil liberties when compared with three of the most successful democracies of Eastern Europe and Latin America—the Czech Republic, Poland, and Chile. Overall, the quality of democracy in Taiwan is about as high as anywhere in Asia but not as high as in the most successful third-wave democracies.

A somewhat more volatile picture emerges upon examination of the quality of governance in Taiwan over time. Since 1996, the World Bank Institute has produced annual measures of six dimensions of the quality of governance. Here, we examine the four measures having to do with the quality of the state: government effectiveness, regulatory quality, rule of law, and control of corruption.[2] Overall, governance has improved notably in Taiwan since the transition to democracy was completed in 1996, but the trend has been far from linear. In general, the four measures of state quality improved between 1996 and 2000 (the final term of President Lee Teng-hui) but then declined notably during the second term of President Chen Shui-bian. Reflecting the scandals of Chen's last years in office, the decline was particularly sharp in rule of law and control of corruption. During the first term of President Ma Ying-jeou, each measure rebounded. By 2012, the rule of law reached its peak level of 2004, at about the 83rd percentile globally, but the improvement in control of corruption was weaker. Regulatory quality traced a similar trajectory, dipping sharply in Chen's second term and then rebounding by 2012 to its peak level from the year 2000, the 86th percentile globally. Government effectiveness remained more stable between 2004 and 2012, oscillating between the 82nd and 86th percentiles (see Figure 1.2). In sum, throughout its democratic years, Taiwan

Table 1.1 Average Combined Scores on Political Rights and Civil Liberties in East Asian Democracies, 1996–2012

	1996	2000	2006	2012
Taiwan	2.0	2.0	1.0	1.5
Japan	1.5	1.5	1.5	1.5
South Korea	2.0	2.0	1.5	1.5
Mongolia	2.5	2.5	2.0	1.5
Indonesia	6.0	4.0	2.5	2.5
Philippines	2.5	2.5	3.0	3.0
Thailand	3.0	2.5	3.0	4.0

Source: Freedom House.

Figure 1.2 World Bank Governance Indicators, 1996–2012

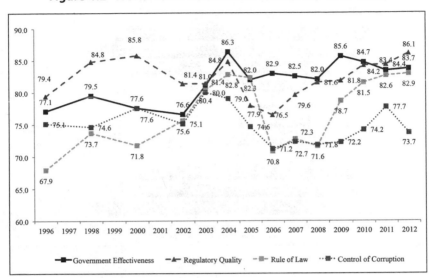

Source: World Bank, Worldwide Governance Indicators, interactive dataset, http://info.world bank.org/governance/wgi/index.aspx#reports.

has manifested relatively good governance, though it deteriorated during the latter years of Chen Shui-bian's presidency and then improved under the presidency of Ma Ying-jeou.

Taiwan's quality of governance compares favorably with most other East Asian democracies, trailing only Japan and performing slightly better than South Korea and markedly better than other East Asian democracies. Figure 1.3 traces the trends since 2000 in the average level of the four measures of governance, which we summarize as "state quality." As shown in another recent study, the quality of governance in Taiwan has been more or less equal to that in most of the better-governed third-wave democracies of Europe and Latin America, among which only Chile and Spain have done slightly better.[3] By 2012, governance in Taiwan had surpassed even that in the Czech Republic and Poland, not to mention the less economically developed democracies of East Asia, as shown in Figure 1.3.

What has all of this meant for economic performance in Taiwan? Since the transition to democracy was completed in 1996, Taiwan's economic performance has generally been good, with the exception of two short periods of economic contraction—2001, the first full year of Chen Shui-bian's presidency, and 2008–2009, when Taiwan's economy fell victim to the global financial crisis. For most of Chen's presidency, economic

Figure 1.3 State Quality in East Asian Democracies, 2000–2012

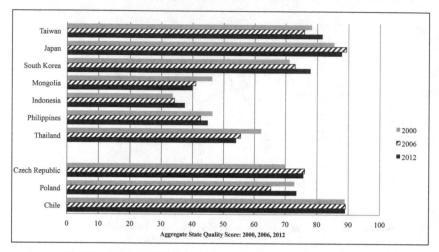

Source: World Bank, Worldwide Governance Indicators.

growth was quite respectable—well above 4 percent—for a maturing economy. Because of the global recession, however, economic performance during Ma's first term was much more volatile. Figure 1.4 shows the trends in economic growth and unemployment from 1996 to 2012. Unemployment has been much more stable since 2000, in the range of 4 to 5 percent. From 2000 to 2012, economic growth in Taiwan averaged 3.9 percent annually, considerably better than Japan, better than the Czech Republic and Poland, not as good as South Korea and Chile, and well behind Malaysia and Singapore (Figure 1.5). Like most emerging-market or newly industrialized countries to which it might be compared in Asia, Europe, and Latin America, Taiwan's economic growth rate slowed markedly (by about a third) in the 2000s, as compared with in the 1990s.

Finally, we can assess the health and performance of democracy in Taiwan through the eyes of its own citizens. Chapters 4 and 5 examine trends in public opinion in Taiwan, but here we briefly put this in comparative perspective. As shown in Table 1.2, satisfaction with the way democracy is working in Taiwan declined sharply between 1996 and 2001, probably reflecting the severe divisions around the election of Chen Shui-bian and then the decline in economic performance early in his term. However, democratic satisfaction then improved in each of the following two surveys, and by 2010 it had reached, and even slightly exceeded, the level in 1996, with a little more than two-thirds of the public reporting satisfaction. Similarly, the proportion of the public perceiving Taiwan's political system to be more or less fully democratic

Figure 1.4 Taiwan's Annual Gross Domestic Product Growth and Unemployment Rate, 1996–2012

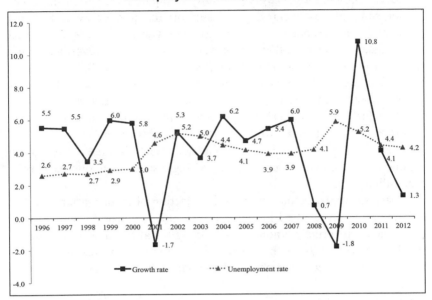

Source: Directorate-General of Budget, Accounting and Statistics, Executive Yuan, Republic of China.

Figure 1.5 Average Annual Percentage Growth in Gross Domestic Product, 2000–2012

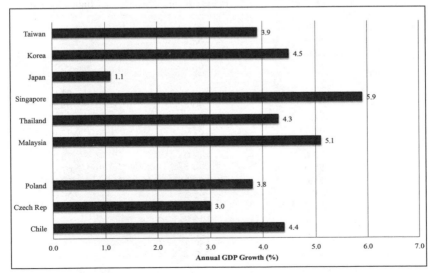

Source: World Bank; Directorate-General of Budget, Accounting and Statistics, Executive Yuan, Republic of China

increased significantly between 2006 and 2010, from 50 to 60 percent. As Table 1.3 shows, these levels generally compared well with the other democracies of East Asia. Explicit support for democracy as the best political system has been somewhat more equivocal in Taiwan, at least on some measures, than in other democracies in the region. Nevertheless, the trend across the three surveys, from 2001 to 2006 to 2010, has shown a steady increase in democratic support. Moreover, Taiwan roughly equals its two liberal democratic peers, Japan and South Korea, and all three together far exceed other Asian publics in the extent of rejection of all authoritarian alternatives to democracy. Roughly three-quarters of the population in each of these three countries reject all three authoritarian regime options posed to them: rule by a single strongman, one-party rule, and military rule.

Despite some fluctuation, popular rejection of authoritarian rule has become more entrenched in Taiwan over time. Repeated surveys show that none of the principal nondemocratic regime alternatives has appealed much to the public. As with the democracy support measures, rejection of authoritarianism became more emphatic with each new survey in Taiwan,

Table 1.2 Overall Assessment of Democracy: Taiwan and East Asia, 1996–2011

Country	Survey Year	Satisfaction with the Way Democracy Works in the Country	See the Country to Be a Full Democracy, or a Democracy with Minor Problems
Taiwan	1996	67.2	—
	2001	53.4	—
	2006	56.5	50.2
	2010	68.3	60.8
Japan	2007	45.2	56.1
	2011	55.8	61.6
South Korea	2006	46.8	59.2
	2011	59.5	66.6
Philippines	2005	37.0	45.4
	2010	47.1	55.7
Thailand	2006	79.0	78.3
	2010	79.1	67.2
Mongolia	2006	63.5	58.3
	2010	47.5	50.9
Indonesia	2007	58.9	41.4
	2011	56.9	47.1
Average	2005–2007	55.3	55.6
	2010–2011	59.2	58.6

Source: Asian Barometer.
Notes: Satisfaction = "very" or "fairly" satisfied. The other response alternatives in the last column are "a democracy with major problems" and "not a democracy."

Table 1.3 Support for Democracy in East Asia: Taiwan in Comparative Perspective, 2001–2011

Country	Survey Year	Agree Democracy Is Always Preferable	Want the Country to Be Democratic	Think Democracy Is Suitable for the Country	Believe Democracy Is Capable of Solving Society's Problems
	2001	40.4	72.2	59.0	46.8
Taiwan	2006	47.2	83.4	67.9	54.8
	2010	49.9	84.9	73.8	59.4
Japan	2007	62.2	88.8	75.2	65.9
	2011	61.7	71.8	71.9	68.5
South Korea	2006	43.2	94.4	78.0	54.2
	2011	65.6	82.2	82.4	70.2
Philippines	2005	50.4	69.4	55.2	55.6
	2010	54.2	62.1	62.1	55.3
Thailand	2006	73.0	84.9	82.7	66.5
	2010	68.3	85.5	85.5	75.5
Mongolia	2006	39.7	94.4	84.4	77.0
	2010	48.4	97.0	87.7	74.6
Indonesia	2007	64.3	86.4	79.8	76.2
	2011	58.6	72.0	71.4	70.0
Average	2005–2007	54.3	86.0	74.7	64.3
	2010–2011	58.1	79.4	76.4	67.6

Source: Asian Barometer.
Notes: The "Want" question used the following question in Wave II: *To what extent would you want our country to be democratic now?* (with 1 meaning completely undemocratic and 10, completely democratic). The following question was used in Wave III: *Where would you want our country to be in the future?* (with the same scale). We calculate the aggregate percentages of 6 and higher.

another sign of deepening democratic consolidation. However, the strength of popular objection to nondemocratic rule varies from one regime alternative to another, depending on the country's political legacy. In Taiwan, single-party rule and civilian dictatorship were historically viable options, in contrast to military rule, which is thus always the most widely rejected alternative.

The Legacy of the Chen Shui-bian Era: A Closer Look

The Chen Shui-bian era left a complicated legacy for Taiwan. On the positive side, his two terms coincided with significant and probably irreversible moves away from Taiwan's authoritarian past. As shown in Figure 1.1, the quality of democracy improved by three different measures during the first few years of his presidency. The mere fact that he was the first non-KMT president to hold office was a crucial step on the road to a consolidated democracy. The DPP's presence in the presidential office accelerated the process of differentiating the ruling party from state interests and resources, which had long been opaquely intermingled under the previous KMT regime. Chen's presidency also generated new impetus for reform of the military, police, judiciary, and other legacy institutions from the martial law era, and it strengthened the role that civil society organizations played in formulating national policies. In addition, the era coincided with a continued expansion and deepening of the norms of critical speech and vigorous public discourse, providing a stark contrast to the continued and increasingly sophisticated state censorship in the People's Republic of China (PRC). Elections, too, were often close and fiercely contested, yet were among the fairest and best-administered in all of Asia—the scourge of vote buying that had tainted many elections in the 1990s had become less effective and less prevalent and was prosecuted more consistently by the Ministry of Justice.

On the negative side of the ledger, Taiwan's economy was significantly weaker during the Chen years than in any period during the previous four decades. Recessions hit in 2001 and 2008, wage growth for the median worker remained stagnant, and unemployment among college graduates rose significantly. Interpreting this slowdown in growth and assigning responsibility for it are difficult tasks: economic growth inevitably decelerates as countries reach advanced levels of development, and Taiwan's heavily export-dependent economy typically suffers during recessions in the United States. Nevertheless, by the end of the Chen era, the widespread impression in Taiwan was that the island's economy had underperformed, especially relative to peer states such as South Korea and Singapore; the KMT presidential candidate, Ma Ying-jeou, built his successful campaign around this theme. What is certain is that a wide array of economic reforms languished during the Chen years, while the DPP administration devoted a great deal of time and energy to a controversial national referendum law, a quixotic bid to win UN membership, and an effort to draft a new constitution that antagonized both the United States and the PRC and ultimately went nowhere. The one set of constitutional reforms adopted during Chen's time in office created a more powerful but smaller and more majoritarian legislature—a decidedly mixed outcome for the island's democracy.

In addition, media coverage of politics and public discourse in Taiwan became more polarized, frenzied, and scandal driven than ever. Taiwanese politics increasingly took the form of a permanent election campaign: political rhetoric became more inflammatory and contentious, as President Chen resorted to ethnic and identity appeals to try to shore up his support, and the KMT and its splinter parties repeatedly challenged the political legitimacy of the DPP administration and its policies. Relations with the People's Republic of China were also fraught with challenges from the day President Chen took office, though two-way trade continued to expand rapidly, as did investment by Taiwanese in mainland ventures. These relations became much worse after Chen's narrow and controversial reelection in 2004, to which Beijing responded by adopting its own provocative Anti-Secession Law, which threatened the use of "non-peaceful means" against Taiwan. Thus, for most of Chen's presidency, cross-Strait relations remained at a standstill. Relations with the United States also became increasingly strained during the latter half of Chen's tenure, particularly over the DPP's repeated efforts to jettison the state's symbolic ties to mainland China.

Finally, Chen's legacy is badly tarnished by the series of corruption scandals that erupted in his second term, as well as his subsequent conviction and imprisonment. In 2006, Chen's son-in-law, wife, and several close personal aides were indicted for embezzlement of public funds, and Chen himself was accused of embezzlement, bribery, and misappropriation of a special diplomatic fund for personal expenses. The revelations sapped public support for the Chen administration, fueled intense hostility from the KMT and much of the island's media, and further eroded public trust in government institutions. In response, the KMT-led opposition demanded Chen's resignation; when it did not come, they initiated multiple recall motions in the legislature, supported large anti-Chen street demonstrations, and, in general, refused to cooperate with the DPP-led government. Although DPP legislators united to block the recall motions from passing, many party members became openly critical of the president as well. By the time Chen Shui-bian left office, his approval rating was well under 20 percent, and he was widely reviled among the public.[4]

Nevertheless, appraisals of the Chen Shui-bian era have been disproportionately colored by the scandals that embroiled his last years in office and by his subsequent imprisonment. The ugly headlines and incendiary political rhetoric of the era have overshadowed subtler but more important political changes that occurred, both good and bad, in Taiwanese politics and society.

Focus of This Book

The chapters that follow explore many of the key developments that make up this complicated legacy. Together, they cover four major aspects of Taiwan's democratic development:

- Elections, the party system, and public opinion
- The performance of democratic institutions
- State-business and state–civil society relations
- National security and cross-Strait relations

Part 1: Politics and Public Opinion

The chapters in the first section of the book cover elections, the party system, and public opinion during the eight years of the Chen Shui-bian administration.

Elections and the Party System. Chen Shui-bian's election as president ushered in a new era of party realignment and greater partisan electoral competition at all levels of government. The election that brought Chen to power in 2000 was a turbulent and unpredictable affair. The stage was set for a competitive contest when President Lee Teng-hui was term-limited out of office, sparking a battle within the KMT to succeed him. The KMT member with the best combination of name recognition and personal popularity was James Soong, the former governor of Taiwan Province. Yet President Lee openly opposed Soong's nomination, instead favoring the sitting vice president, Lien Chan. Lee's preferences won out, and the KMT duly put forward the less popular Lien as its presidential nominee. In open rebellion, Soong declared his own independent campaign for president in July 1999, and the race was on. In the presidential election in March 2000, Chen Shui-bian came out on top but won only 39.3 percent of the vote. Soong polled close behind, winning 36.8 percent. And Lien Chan, the KMT's official nominee, came in third, winning an extraordinarily low 23.1 percent—the worst performance by a KMT presidential candidate in Taiwan's history (see Figure 1.6). As a result, Chen took office as a minority president who owed his victory to a serious split among KMT supporters.

Chen's victory was followed by a period of upheaval in the KMT and a significant realignment of Taiwan's party system. Soong attempted to capitalize on his strong showing in the election by forming his own party, the People First Party (PFP), which more than a dozen sitting KMT legislators joined. President Lee Teng-hui was forced out of his role as chair of the KMT, and shortly after turning over the presidency to Chen, Lee founded his own party, the Taiwan Solidarity Union (TSU), taking another chunk of KMT members with him.

One can get a sense of the dramatic effect the 2000 election had on the party system by looking at the legislative election results. Figure 1.7 shows the district-level vote shares of Taiwanese political parties from

Figure 1.6 KMT vs. DPP Share of Presidential Vote, 1996–2012

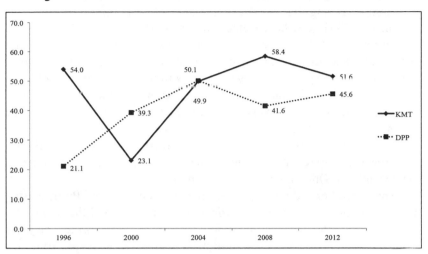

Source: Central Election Commission, Republic of China.

**Figure 1.7 KMT vs. DPP Vote and Seat Share
in Legislative Elections, 1995–2012**

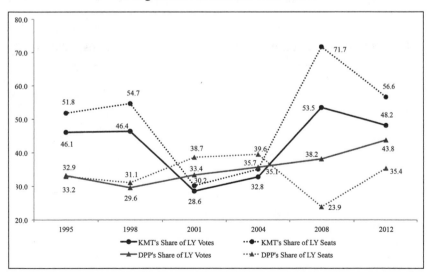

Source: Central Election Commission, Republic of China.
Note: LY—Legislative Yuan.

the elections in 1995 through 2012. The fragmentation of the KMT's support base following the 2000 presidential election is immediately apparent: in the 2001 legislative election, the upstart PFP and TSU both demonstrated that they were viable parties able to win a significant share of the vote. Rather than two significant parties, Taiwan now had four. From their founding, the TSU was allied with the DPP, and the PFP with the KMT—groupings that quickly became known as the Pan-Green and Pan-Blue camps, respectively—so-called for the primary color of the leading party in each. Following the 2001 election, control of the Legislative Yuan was closely split between the two rival alliances (see Figure 1.8). Together, the KMT, PFP, and a single New Party legislator formed a shaky coalition with a nominal two-seat majority.

This period ended with the 2004 presidential election. Putting aside their falling-out in the previous campaign, Lien Chan and the KMT successfully negotiated to have Soong join the party's ticket as the vice presidential candidate, with Lien running a second time in the top slot. Because the two together had won 60 percent of the vote in the 2000 election, this immediately made them the favorites in 2004, and Chen faced an uphill battle to retain power. Polling throughout the months leading to the March 20, 2004, election consistently showed the Lien-Soong ticket ahead, with their lead ranging from 5 to 15 percent, though some polls showed the race tightening in the last few weeks. The

Figure 1.8 Pan-Blue vs. Pan-Green in Legislative Elections, 1995–2012

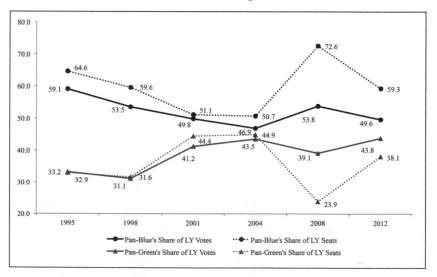

Source: Central Election Commission, Republic of China.

campaign was thrown into confusion the day before the election, when President Chen and Vice President Annette Lu were shot and lightly wounded during a campaign rally. To the credit of Taiwan's electorate and institutions, the election went ahead the next day, and voting and ballot counting proceeded relatively smoothly.

The final tally showed a surprising, razor-thin victory for President Chen—50.11 percent, compared to 49.89 percent for the Lien-Soong ticket, a margin of about 29,500 votes out of almost 13 million cast. Although Chen won reelection, his victory was controversial from the moment it was announced. For one, the Pan-Blue camp immediately raised suspicions about the March 19 shooting incident, suggesting that it had been staged to win President Chen sympathy votes and to prevent military and security personnel from going to the polls by putting them on high alert. Pan-Blue protesters held large rallies in several major cities and in front of the Presidential Hall, and Lien Chan publicly called the election results unfair, raising questions not only about the assassination attempt but also about the number of invalid votes cast: over 300,000, or more than ten times Chen's margin of victory. A recount of all ballots cast eventually shrank the difference to about 23,000 valid votes but did not change the result.

As Shelley Rigger reviews in Chapter 2, the narrow and contested result of the 2004 election produced new strains on Taiwan's democracy, roiling both party camps and leading to a new era of partisan warfare over even mundane issues, which ended only with the DPP's defeat in 2008. Sizable elements of the Pan-Blue camp never accepted the result as legitimate. For his part, President Chen took a more confrontational approach toward national identity issues at the beginning of his second term, proposing a China-to-Taiwan "name rectification" campaign and a new constitution and attempting to rally what seemed to be a rising tide of Taiwanese nationalism to the DPP. The DPP appeared to many observers, especially to party elites themselves, to be on an inexorable ascent, fueled by steadily increasing public support for a separate and independent Taiwan.

As Rigger documents, however, this view turned out to be a misreading of public opinion. While Taiwanese *identity* was indeed rising among the electorate, support for *formal independence* was not: the majority of the public continued, instead, to endorse the option of maintaining the cross-Strait status quo and increasing economic exchanges with the PRC. As a consequence, the next legislative election in December 2004 produced a setback for the Pan-Green camp, which had overestimated its electoral support and nominated too aggressively. Although the DPP retained its position as the largest party, the Pan-Blues together won enough seats to consolidate their majority in the Legislative Yuan. In hindsight, the 2004 presidential election was a high-water mark for the Pan-Green camp: it is the only time to date that the DPP has ever won a majority in an islandwide election. The next three years saw a significant decline in the party's fortunes. Cooperation between the Pan-Blue majority in the legislature and the DPP-controlled Executive Yuan was rare even before the first of the corruption scandals involving President Chen broke in 2006. For the rest of his term, Chen Shui-bian was under political siege, and the DPP was on the defensive. The DPP itself was wracked by factional conflict between its more moderate and fundamentalist wings, which the fundamentalists aligned with President Chen largely won; the slate of candidates the party put up in the 2008 legislative elections included many ideologues with little appeal outside a narrow segment of deep Green supporters.

By 2008, the DPP had been sapped of much of its popularity, and its defeat in both the presidential and legislative elections seemed inevitable. Rigger argues that every conceivable variable pointed in the direction of a large KMT victory. Ma benefited from the incumbent party's poor performance, the population's weariness with gridlock, the KMT's powerful local organizations, the voters' longing for economic rejuvenation, and Ma's own personal popularity. Especially important was the cascade of scandals that broke in Chen's second term, robbing the DPP of its image as a corruption fighter. From the viewpoint of party competition, Rigger asserts, the outcome of the 2008 presidential election indicated that the KMT had successfully repositioned itself to be more responsive to public opinion, whereas the DPP had not made the same shift and still attempted to "lead" public opinion toward its Taiwanese nationalist ideology.

The 2008 election for the Legislative Yuan also marked a significant break from the previous electoral patterns. Starting in 2008, a fundamental difference was the electoral system. Through the 2004 election, Taiwan had used the unusual and widely criticized single nontransferable vote (SNTV) system to elect its legislature. SNTV features multimember electoral districts in which voters cast a ballot for a single candidate, and multiple candidates win a seat. This system has well-documented shortcomings, particularly in its effects on political parties: It increases the incentives for intraparty competition for votes, encourages the development of factions within larger parties, and tends to reward candidates who stake out relatively extreme positions over more moderate ones. In addition, for parties and voters, it creates difficult coordination problems that are not present in most other electoral systems. A reform movement to replace the SNTV system gained steam during the Chen years, and over the objections of the smaller parties, the DPP and KMT eventually approved a switch to a mixed-member parallel system—one of the only significant institutional reforms to pass with both major parties' support during the Chen Shui-bian era.

Under the new electoral system, about 65 percent of legislators are elected from single-member districts, 5 percent from special aborigine districts elected using SNTV, and the rest from proportional representation using a closed national party list. At the same time, the size of the legislature was cut in half, from 225 members to 113. The reform had the effect of making Taiwan's electoral system significantly more majoritarian, putting the smaller TSU and PFP at a tremendous disadvantage. What the DPP did not anticipate—though a number of political scientists did—is that it would also dramatically reduce the DPP's representation in the legislature after the 2008 election. Despite capturing more than 38 percent of the district vote, the DPP won only 24 percent of the seats in the legislature, as compared to the KMT's 72 percent of the seats with only 54 percent of the vote. The electoral reform thus presents two puzzles: Why did the DPP perform so poorly under the new system? And why did the party support changing to an electoral system that so badly damaged its own short-term electoral prospects?

Jih-wen Lin takes up these questions in Chapter 3. Using district-level election returns, he argues that the DPP would have won about 40 percent of the seats under the old system had it been in place in 2008, and the KMT would have won, at most, 55 percent. The reason for the new system's disproportionality was the lack of safe seats for the DPP: in relatively few districts did the party have a clear majority of supporters. By contrast, the KMT enjoyed majorities in a large set of districts in northern Taiwan, the east coast, the offshore islands, and the aborigine constituencies, where the DPP's support was weak or nonexistent. The switch to single-member districts thus increased the structural bias in legislative elections in favor of the KMT. On the second question, Lin argues that the DPP misread the trends in popular support in the electorate at the time of the reform. The party expected rising Taiwanese identity to translate into greater partisan support for DPP candidates and, thus, an advantage in majoritarian elections. Moreover, the DPP had generally fared better in single-member races for county and city executives than it had in multi-member races, including winning an outright majority for the first time in the 2004 presidential election. As a consequence, it significantly overestimated the number of district seats it was likely to win under the new system, expecting that a more majoritarian electoral system would help it consolidate the non-KMT vote behind its own candidates and allow it to become the majority party in the legislature.

Trends in Public Opinion. The conventional story of public opinion in the Chen Shui-bian era is that Taiwan became significantly more polarized around the "national question": Should Taiwan seek independence, pursue unification with the mainland, or retain the "status quo" for the foreseeable future? That is certainly the impression one gets from looking at the media and public political discourse of the era. Yet public opinion data suggest a more complex story. In Chapter 4, Eric Chen-hua Yu argues that there is, in fact, only weak evidence of increasing polarization on this question during the Chen era. Yu draws a distinction between "polarized" opinion, in which large blocks of citizens support positions that are diametrically opposed and distant from one another, and what he terms "divided" opinion, in which citizens identify strongly with different political parties but do not actually support positions at the ideological extremes.

Yu finds that the association between partisanship and policy preference is actually relatively weak, especially for Pan-Green supporters. Moreover, the increasing partisan acrimony in the Chen era is a result, he argues, not of greater ideological polarization among the electorate at large but of a re-sorting of political elites into the two major groups based on their policy preferences: the party camps are more neatly divided on the national question, but the public has not become noticeably more polarized. Yu's empirical findings suggest cause for optimism about Taiwan's democratic consolidation: the Taiwanese public is actually not any more divided on the unification/independence issue than prior to the Chen era, and a large majority of the electorate continues to support maintaining the status quo in cross-Strait relations.

Nevertheless, survey data also provide some reason for concern. As Yun-han Chu, Min-hua Huang, and Yu-tzung Chang discuss in Chapter 5, support for democracy and perceptions about the quality of governance in Taiwan are strongly colored by partisan affiliation. Drawing from two waves of the Asian Barometer Survey collected in 2006, during the Chen administration, and 2010, when the KMT's Ma Ying-jeou was president, the authors find that strong partisans of each camp rate the quality of governance significantly lower when the other party is running the government. More concerning, strong partisans also demonstrate significantly less support for democracy when the other major party is in power. Chu, Huang, and Chang argue that the long-standing divisions over Taiwan's "national question" have aggravated the normal tensions between winners and losers present in all democracies, attenuating popular support for democracy among the losing camp and posing a long-term challenge to Taiwan's democratic consolidation.

Part 2: Democratic Institutions in Action

One of the greatest uncertainties at the beginning of the Chen era was how executive-legislative relations would function. According to the Republic of China (ROC) constitution, the Legislative Yuan is responsible for lawmaking, including approving all government budgets, whereas the Executive Yuan is responsible for implementation. The two bodies are arguably the most important democratic institutions in Taiwan. Thus, an assessment of government performance necessarily begins with an examination of the relationship between the two. In Chapter 6, Shiow-duan Hawang examines the evolution of this relationship since Taiwan's transition to democracy, identifying three distinct periods of government: first, unified KMT control before the election of Chen Shui-bian as president in 2000; second, divided government from May 2000 until January 2002, when the DPP controlled the presidency but held less than a third of the seats in the Legislative Yuan (LY); and third, severely divided government from February 2002 through January 2008, when the Pan-Blue coalition controlled a narrow majority in the legislature.

Hawang examines variation over the three periods in different legislative functions: lawmaking, control of the LY agenda in the Procedure Committee, and budgetary outcomes. By several measures, as expected, she finds executive-legislative relations to be most cooperative in the first period, under unified KMT control. In the second period, the Pan-Blue majority in the legislature made more frequent use of its ability to freeze or cut government budgets. The third period, in Chen Shui-bian's second term, appears, by most measures, to be the most antagonistic: the legislature initiated many investigations of the executive branch, blocked more than 80 percent of government-requested bills, and issued a large number of budget resolutions, limiting the way that government funds could be spent. Hawang's study confirms the impression that, by the end of the Chen era, relations between the Pan-Blue majority in the Legislative Yuan and the DPP-controlled Executive Yuan reached a level of dysfunction and discord unprecedented in ROC history.

The ROC constitution also gives special judicial and supervisory roles to two other institutions — the Judicial Yuan and the Control Yuan. In Chapter 7, Wei-tseng Chen and Chia-hsin Hsu investigate whether the promise of greater independence and robust supervision of these institutions over the other branches of government — what they term "horizontal accountability" — was realized during the Chen years. They evaluate the two institutions on four dimensions of accountability: independence, supremacy, technical capacity, and political accountability. Taiwan has made the most progress, they argue, in establishing the independence of these two institutions. The Judicial Yuan engaged in the investigation and prosecution of difficult, high-profile corruption cases during the Chen administration, including indicting the first lady and other prominent politicians of both political camps. The picture is less impressive with respect to supremacy, however: the ultimate power of the Judicial and

Control Yuans to compel enforcement of their legal decisions was limited, as government officials frequently ignored decisions by the two bodies. Moreover, the Control Yuan became a victim of partisan acrimony and was effectively moribund by 2005: the Pan-Blue majority in the Legislative Yuan refused to act on President Chen's nominees, and as a result, the body was left vacant through the end of Chen's second term. Prominent members of the judiciary were also threatened and salaries were cut by hostile legislators in response to unfavorable decisions.

Chen and Hsu argue that most judges were highly competent in their fields and frequently attempted to find compromise decisions that would tamp down partisan conflict. Nevertheless, the judiciary's institutional capacity as a whole was uneven during the Chen years, as judges struggled to issue consistent, high-quality legal decisions. Rulings in defamation cases were particularly problematic and often appeared to be influenced by political considerations. The courts also continued to wrestle with the tension between asserting their legal independence and responding to demands from social and political groups; in their struggle to navigate heightened partisanship, they largely abandoned efforts to remain politically and socially accountable. Overall, Chen and Hsu find that horizontal accountability in Taiwan significantly increased during the Chen Shui-bian era, though the lack of enforcement of judicial decisions and the effective suspension of the Control Yuan were worrisome developments.

In Chapter 8, the final chapter in this section, Yun-han Chu considers the status of constitutional reform at the end of the Chen Shui-bian era. The ROC constitution has been amended seven times since the Lee Teng-hui administration but still lacks the broad-based legitimacy enjoyed by constitutions in fully consolidated democracies. Chu argues that there have been two types of limitations in crafting a fully legitimate constitution: structural constraints and constraints resulting from the strategic choices of key players orchestrating constitutional change. Structurally, the international challenges of cross-Strait relations and sovereignty, the domestic problem of conflict over national identity, and the lack of a core commitment among domestic elites to the rule of law and constitutionalism have all presented formidable obstacles to the creation of a widely accepted permanent constitution. Strategically, elites orchestrating change have engaged in pact making over comprehensive constitutional reform, often driven by hidden agendas, short-term calculations, and improvised compromises. As a result, the extensive revisions have still not produced elite or public consensus as to what a final, acceptable, and fully legitimate constitution would look like.

The Chen years continued this pattern of proposed constitutional revisions for short-term political gain. At the beginning of Chen Shui-bian's second term, he made adopting a new "Taiwanese" constitution a top priority in a bid to strengthen his legitimacy after his highly contentious victory in the 2004 election. But pressure from the United States undercut Chen's efforts to rally his base behind the proposal, which appeared hopelessly unrealistic. In March 2006, Chen was forced publicly to admit respect for the status quo and the futility of the constitutional reform campaign.

Chu argues that the 2008 election outcome had the effect of halting the momentum of Taiwanese nationalism and temporarily suspending the debate over constitutional change. Instead, since the end of the Chen administration, there has been a new realization in Taiwan that the ROC constitution, however flawed, is here to stay, because the constitution is now hard to amend in practice. Chu notes that the ROC constitution represents a set of institutional and symbolic arrangements that relates organically to the realities of Taiwanese society, including its political legacies and complicated cross-Strait relations. He also advocates the idea that the constitution merely requires fine-tuning. Some changes are necessary, such as preventing the election of a minority president with a weak popular mandate, but radical change would ultimately do more harm than good.

Part 3: State-Society Relations

The third group of chapters explores various aspects of state-business and state-society relations during the Chen years.

One of the most positive aspects of this era was the creation of new space for civil society organizations to participate in governance. As Chang-ling Huang details in Chapter 9, civil society became an increasingly important channel for nonelectoral representation during the Chen Shui-bian era. The Executive Yuan had long made use of government commissions to serve as a forum for public discussion of regulatory policies. Traditionally, these commissions consisted only of government and business representatives; during the Chen years, however, they began to include representatives of civil society and to take on a more participatory role in developing policy. Huang examines three cases of confrontation between state and civil society organizations that played out in these commissions. The first focuses on the efforts of the civic members of an Executive Yuan commission on human rights to stop the Executive Yuan's instatement of a fingerprint requirement for state identification cards (IDs). The second case focuses on the actions of feminist advocates to stop the imposition of a new mandatory three-day waiting period for abortions. The third case tells the story of how members of an environmental commission boycotted their own meeting, sitting in front of the executive building to call attention to their lack of enforcement power and their inability to change environmental assessment practices.

Starting in 2001, the Chen administration created more commissions with more members, meetings, and interactions with other branches of government such as the Ministry of Foreign Affairs. Nevertheless, civil society organizations remained severely understaffed and underfunded, hindered by a large imbalance in resources and power when compared with the state. During the Chen years, the importance of ensuring the second-order accountability of civil society in Taiwan also became more apparent. Given the level of some nongovernmental organizations' (NGOs') cooperation with the government, there was an increasing need to ensure that NGOs were properly representing the people they claimed to be helping. Nevertheless, the increase in government engagement with civil society is one of the most positive legacies of the Chen Shui-bian era.

In addition to the increase in space for civil society, the Chen era was also noteworthy for the rising power of an independent, aggressive, and diverse media to influence and constrain state actions. Yet during the Chen Shui-bian years, it became increasingly apparent that the media's role in Taiwan's democracy was not an entirely positive one. As Chien-san Feng explores in Chapter 10, greater press freedom did not lead to an improvement in the public discourse or the accuracy and impartiality of news sources. Instead, newspapers, magazines, and especially television became increasingly sensationalized, scandal driven, and hyperpartisan. Although the media played an important watchdog role, they were not a neutral arbiter and did not have strong nonpartisan credibility with the public. Feng identifies three reasons the media largely failed to serve as a trusted, impartial source of information for Taiwan's citizenry: the legacy of decades of authoritarian control, a regulatory agency with neither the motivation nor the capacity to effectively monitor media, and the increasingly deep partisan divides within society. Chen Shui-bian's election offered considerable hope for improvement in the media environment on the island, and some progress was in fact made during the Chen years—for example, the KMT's financial and political stranglehold over television was loosened, and the number of Hakka- and Taiwanese-language television stations multiplied. The development of public service TV, however, was mostly disappointing. During his 2000 presidential campaign, Chen promised to expand public broadcasting, but after an initial burst of activity, the media reform movement remained stalled through most of Chen's time in office.

Feng argues that the Chen administration could have done much more to improve the media environment by working with civil society to implement higher-quality public television programming and revising outdated regulatory practices. For instance, government support for the public Taiwan Broadcasting System remained inadequate, and the Chen administration failed to win passage of laws that would regulate the media market and force media companies to operate more democratically and transparently.

Nevertheless, one positive effect of the more liberalized media environment was to raise the costs of political corruption, which by the late 1990s pervaded many corners of the central government. During the Cold War, the KMT regime developed and refined a classic form of state corporatism that gradually evolved into a system of party- and state-led capitalism. These clientelist networks and the attendant "black gold"—the combination of political corruption and organized crime—actually expanded in the wake of democratization, as Lee Teng-hui consolidated power in the Presidential Office and the KMT came under increasing electoral pressure. The ruling party became more reliant on clientelist practices as it incorporated and controlled large businesses, which in turn distributed funds to buttress the KMT's candidates in elections.

As James W. Y. Wang, Shang-mao Chen, and Cheng-tian Kuo detail in Chapter 11, the victory of Chen Shui-bian in 2000 upset the system, sparking frenzied efforts by KMT elites to defend their business interests. President Chen's top priority was to destroy party- and state-business networks while preserving the strong state. To this end, Chen replaced KMT appointees in big state-controlled businesses with DPP appointees. In Chen's first term, most of these appointees had technical expertise, and some state-controlled enterprises even showed improved efficiency and increased profits as a result. The KMT's party-controlled businesses, by contrast, fared poorly, turning into a liability for the party and eventually being sold at fire-sale prices. The KMT also sold its prominent headquarters directly opposite the Presidential Hall and moved to a more modest building a couple of miles away. The DPP had less immediate success ending patronage in local organizations, including the important county-level farmers' associations that had long served as key distribution points for resources to KMT-linked local factions. But Chen eventually managed to weaken KMT links to these associations as well by appointing DPP members to lead many of them.

State-business relations changed for the worse in President Chen's second term, however. Corruption in state-controlled enterprises surged, as he replaced many business advisers with less-qualified, pro-independence political appointees. Whereas under the KMT, corruption had taken place primarily at the institutional level, by the end of the Chen era, the authors argue, it had shifted to the level of individuals. One of the many ironies of this period is that the KMT began to advocate for increasing government transparency and tightening lax oversight procedures that it had routinely benefited from during its long time in power. As Wang, Chen, and Kuo note, the corruption scandals of Chen's second term demonstrated the continuing weakness of institutions of horizontal accountability and transparency in Taiwan—weakness that may have contributed to Taiwan's slower rate of economic growth during the Chen years.

One intriguing question is why the Chen administration, for the most part, failed to take over the KMT's extensive clientelist networks for its own political use. Chin-shou Wang takes up this question in Chapter 12, detailing both how the KMT system of patronage functioned and why it became largely defunct after the DPP's rise to power. As Wang notes, the clientelist system relied, to a surprising degree, on aspects of authoritarian rule to sustain it, including the lack of a viable opposition party, the absence of electoral competition between local factions, firm party-state control over the judiciary, the deep penetration of the state intelligence apparatus into local politics, and the absence of meaningful freedom of the press. Once these features of the regime changed, the system became unstable and ultimately unsustainable. Wang's analysis suggests that the DPP's attempts to replace the KMT's system with its own were doomed to failure from the start, because the same conditions that allowed the DPP to win power worked to constrain the party once it held the presidency.

Part 4: National Security and Cross-Strait Relations

Beyond the headlines, subtle but fundamental changes took place within the Taiwanese state during the Chen years. The reform of the security sector is at the top of this list. Taiwan had been under martial law for almost forty years; when that law was formally lifted in July 1987, the regime had an extensive domestic security apparatus that operated entirely beyond the reach of elected officials. A number of significant steps were taken during Lee Teng-hui's presidency to put security agencies and the military more firmly under democratic control. These steps included abolishing the Taiwan Garrison Command and ending the prosecution of civilians in military courts. Nevertheless, when Chen Shui-bian came to power, there remained serious concerns about how the military would respond to a new, non-KMT president whose party officially supported Taiwanese independence from China.

As Yi-suo Tzeng describes in Chapter 13, the legacy of KMT party control over the security forces presented a different kind of challenge for democratic consolidation in Taiwan at that moment. The pressing concerns about improving military professionalism, establishing the primacy of civilian over military leadership, and delegitimizing the idea of the military as an independent actor in domestic politics, as faced by many other young democracies, were less central in Taiwan. The relentless external threat posed by China led to an outward defense posture, which in turn contributed to the development of a strong tradition of military professionalism. In addition, the KMT's dense hierarchical party structure and system of political indoctrination had ensured that the military and intelligence agencies, though highly professionalized, were also fully subordinate to the party's top leadership. Thus, similar to many postcommunist countries with a history of party- rather than state-controlled armies, Taiwan faced a legacy of civilian politicians manipulating the security apparatus for partisan ends. Instead of getting the military out of politics, the challenge in Taiwan was getting politics out of the military.

President Chen's accession to office hastened efforts to "nationalize" the armed forces—that is, to transfer military loyalty and duty from party and national leaders to state and society. Tzeng notes that this nationalization policy helped the military avoid becoming too entangled in civilian political disputes, and despite a handful of controversies, the armed forces were generally effective at establishing and maintaining their standing as fully professionalized, nonpartisan, and democratically accountable institutions.

The picture is more mixed with respect to the intelligence agencies, however. By the end of the Chen administration, the procedures for domestic eavesdropping and other sensitive activities had still not been fully regularized, and the collection, distribution, and employment of intelligence for domestic political purposes, including in election campaigns, remained a significant concern. Nevertheless, Tzeng concludes on a positive note, arguing that the norms of political neutrality and accountability to civilian leadership have become well established in Taiwan and that a fully depoliticized and institutionalized security sector is no great way off.

Perhaps the most difficult challenge of the Chen Shui-bian era was managing relations with the People's Republic of China, which were strained even at their best. Chen's first election win in 2000 came as a shock to Beijing, which scrambled to develop a policy response to the rise to power of the pro-independence DPP. For his part, President Chen started his administration on a moderate note, promising in his inaugural address to uphold what quickly became known as the "Four Noes and One Without": provided the PRC expressed no intention to use military force against Taiwan, Chen would not (1) declare independence, (2) change the title of the country, (3) include the doctrine of special state-to-state relations in the ROC constitution, or (4) promote a referendum on unification or independence. In addition, the "One Without" was a pledge not to abolish the National Unification Council, a long-standing body set up in 1990 to promote reintegration of the Republic of China with mainland China. Yet by the end of his presidency, Chen had made public statements or taken actions that undermined all of these pledges.

Throughout his presidency, Chen's political space to maneuver in cross-Strait relations was quite limited. He faced three major structural constraints. The first was his limited popular and legislative support. Chen took office as a minority president, with over 60 percent of the electorate having voted for somebody else. Thus, he could not persuasively claim to have received much of a mandate to implement significant changes in cross-Strait ties. During Chen's first term, portions of the KMT publicly questioned his legitimacy to take unilateral actions even in domestic arenas, most notably with his appointment of a DPP premier. Moreover, Chen never succeeded in winning a legislative majority for his own party and, instead, had to face an uncooperative and often openly hostile Pan-Blue coalition in the Legislative Yuan for his entire time in office. As a consequence, the legislature effectively blocked most of his attempts to reshape cross-Strait policies.

Second, Chen was under some obligation to pro-independence activists in his own party. Many DPP members were committed to an ambitious nation-building project, including the active strengthening of a separate Taiwanese identity, and they expected the president to deliver on their long-cherished nationalist goals. Thus, Chen received consistent pressure to undertake controversial but mainly symbolic steps to change the names of the country and adopt a new constitution. When these steps appeared out of reach, supporters pushed a "name rectification" campaign to remove "China" from the formal titles of state-owned enterprises and government bodies. As Chen's support among the public at large deteriorated in his second term, he came to rely more and more heavily on the support of "deep Green" pro-independence legislators and activists to fend off impeachment attempts.

Third, Chen faced serious constraints on his freedom of action in foreign policy from both the People's Republic of China and the United States. The PRC steadfastly promoted its own unification project, and the United States remained committed to preserving the status quo in the Taiwan Strait and was wary of any steps that would provoke a reaction from Beijing and further complicate US-PRC relations. Thus, cross-Strait relations during the Chen years were deadlocked, caught between a Taiwan leader motivated for domestic reasons to pursue greater distance from the mainland, a Chinese leadership determined to oppose even symbolic steps to expand Taiwan's diplomatic space or drop links to the regime's Chinese past, and a US administration concerned about the actions of both.

Yet, despite this set of diplomatic face-offs, cross-Strait economic relations deepened during the Chen years. In Chapter 14, Tse-kang Leng demonstrates how the economic factor in cross-Strait relations has grown in importance through the last three Taiwanese administrations and how it has, in turn, changed Taiwan's domestic politics. Leng focuses on continuity and change in Taiwan's policy toward the so-called three links—direct commercial, postal, and transportation links with the PRC. In addition to the ideological clash over fostering closer ties to China, Leng notes there is also an important, and underappreciated, cleavage between more isolationist, protectionist-oriented groups and proglobalization ones in Taiwan that does not map neatly onto partisan divisions.

Taiwan's Democratic Future

In the years ahead, Taiwan's democracy will likely continue to be buffeted by many of the social and political stresses and institutional contradictions that plagued it during the Chen Shui-bian era. The presidency of Ma Ying-jeou, Chen's successor, resolved some of these challenges but neglected or exacerbated many others: deep social divisions and frustrations over rising inequality, the pace and direction of cross-Strait relations, trade liberalization more generally, and other economic and quality-of-life issues all appear to have little prospect of a swift, clear resolution in the near future. Yet the test of democratic consolidation is not whether democracy is able to fashion societal consensus around clear policy directions or even, for that matter, around effective policies. Rather, democratic consolidation requires a durable consensus about the institutional rules of the game. Through two transfers of power, an intensely disputed 2004 election, the scandal-plagued second term of Chen Shui-bian, and the surprising recurrence of legislative gridlock during Ma Ying-jeou's presidency, democracy in Taiwan has faced stressful tests. It may not have passed them with flying colors, but it has endured. Few people in Taiwan today would support a return to authoritarianism in order to resolve current political conflicts. Taiwan's democracy must improve in its functioning if it is to meet the expectations of its citizens and the demands of an increasingly competitive regional and world economy. But as it draws toward the end of its second decade, there can be little doubt that Taiwan's democracy is consolidated.

Notes

1. This is mainly because of relatively low scores on political participation and political culture, as well as the different way in which this index weights certain factors—in contrast to, say, Freedom House.

2. Each of these four indices reflects diverse sources of perceptions and assessments. Government effectiveness captures the quality of public services, policy formulation and implementation, and the professionalism and neutrality of the civil service. Regulatory quality measures the government's ability to formulate and implement sound policies that facilitate private-sector development. Rule of law measures not only the extent of crime and violence but also the quality of contract enforcement, property rights, the police, and the courts. Control of corruption is self-evident. Voice and accountability was examined in Figure 1.1 as a measure of democracy.

3. Larry Diamond and Gi-wook Shin, "Introduction," in *New Challenges for Maturing Democracies in Korea and Taiwan,* ed. Larry Diamond and Gi-wook Shin (Stanford, CA: Stanford University Press, 2014). See in particular Figure I.1.

4. For instance, a TVBS poll taken between May 9 and May 13, 2008, just before President Chen left office, recorded an approval rating of only 13 percent, with 69 percent disapproving.

2

Party Politics and Elections: The Road to 2008

Shelley Rigger

Consolidated democracies have political parties to aggregate and represent popular preferences; they also have party systems and electoral systems that hold governments accountable to voters. Evaluated on these grounds, Taiwan's 2008 elections reflected the country's continuing, but imperfect, progress toward democratic consolidation. Above all, the decisive defeat of Democratic Progressive Party (DPP) candidates in both the legislative and presidential elections showed that Taiwanese voters were capable of "throwing the rascals out" when government performance was poor.

In rejecting the DPP candidates, voters were holding the party accountable for the performance and policies of Chen Shui-bian's administration. Although not surprising, this outcome was not inevitable. Critics of Taiwan's democracy pointed to President Chen Shui-bian's reelection in 2004 as evidence that democratic accountability was not working. Many Taiwanese viewed his victory, which he had attained in the face of widespread dissatisfaction, as proof that the electoral system could be manipulated in defiance of popular will. The election results four years later put those fears to rest.

Although progress toward accountability was evident in 2008, the political parties' uneven adaptation to public opinion suggested that Taiwan's democratic progress still faced limitations. Between 2004 and 2008, the Kuomintang (KMT), or Chinese Nationalist Party, moved steadily to capture the center by shaping positions in response to popular preferences, whereas the DPP was mired in wrenching debates over ideology, loyalty, and strategy. The conflict between ideological purists and election-minded pragmatists erupted most destructively during the legislative primary in 2007, but it continued to fester right through to the end of the presidential campaign. Although the election results were undoubtedly influenced by widespread disappointment with the Chen administration's performance, the DPP's crushing defeats in the 2008 elections also reflected the party's failure to calibrate its message in response to popular preferences. Nonetheless, Ma Ying-jeou was barely settled into the presidential office in 2008 when the DPP's fortunes turned, as voters began to look to the Democratic Progressives to balance KMT power. DPP candidates won a string of by-elections around the country, and in 2010, the party held its own in the much-anticipated "supermunicipality" elections held at year's end.

The Overdetermined Election

With nearly every conceivable variable aligned in his favor, Ma's landslide victory surprised no one. He benefited from the incumbent's poor performance, the population's weariness with gridlock, the KMT's powerful local organizations, the voters' longing for economic recovery, and his own first-rate reputation. Especially important was the cascade of scandals that erupted in Chen's second term, robbing the DPP of its image as a corruption fighter. In retrospect, it is tempting to call Ma's landslide victory inevitable.

Few close observers would dare to make such a bold statement, however, not least because although most of these factors were already present in 2004, Chen Shui-bian did manage to win that year's election with the DPP's largest-ever vote share. Why was Frank Hsieh, the DPP candidate in 2008, unable to build on Chen's success?

The snowballing corruption scandal that began in 2005 and continued through Chen's second term was a critical factor in 2008. For almost two decades, voters had associated the DPP with corruption fighting and clean government. Losing that mantle deprived the party of a central element in its popular appeal. Ma's squeaky-clean reputation made the issue even more of a loser for the scandal-tainted DPP.

The scandal also put the DPP on the defensive, which gave Ma an opening to set the campaign agenda. He zeroed in on Chen's weak economic management. In 2004, however, when the KMT candidate had attacked Chen's economic record, his criticism had fallen flat, even though Taiwan's economy had performed poorly during Chen's first term. By 2008, after four years of much stronger economic performance, voters nonetheless responded well to Ma's economic complaints, especially his argument that the DPP's restrictive approach to cross-Strait engagement was damaging Taiwan's economic prospects.

Ma's credibility with voters also helped his policy agenda gain purchase. For years, opinion polls had shown Ma to be far more popular than Lien Chan. Ma had been one of Taiwan's most charismatic politicians and a more credible spokesman than Lien for moderate policies. In 2000, Lien led the KMT in a sharp rightward turn, which hurt him in 2004, because it validated DPP charges that Lien's enthusiasm for unification put him outside the mainstream. Yet, Ma was able to avoid the taint of pro-unification extremism (at least among centrist voters), so that when he campaigned on a moderate platform in 2008, voters believed him.

Candidate selection, party platforms, partisan alignment, incumbent performance, and economic conditions are all important factors for explaining the results of Taiwan's 2008 presidential election. From the standpoint of Taiwan's political parties, however, the most critical variables are the ones they can control: candidate selection and party platform. If parties want to win power and implement their programs, they have to choose attractive candidates who appeal to voters, and they have to design credible platforms that attract broad support. On the first point, Taiwan's major parties share a similar, mixed record. On the second point, the KMT was far more successful than the DPP.

Political scientists have long reported a gap between the preferences of Taiwan's voters and the strategies of political parties, especially those of the DPP. Public opinion has been noticeably centrist, and although both main parties' platforms have moved toward the center, campaign strategies and political rhetoric remained substantially more polarized than median voter theory would predict.[1]

In the run-up to the 2008 presidential election, the KMT moved decisively to appeal to centrist voters. It crafted a platform that captured, with remarkable fidelity, the complex, even contradictory, preferences of the mainstream electorate, and it selected a candidate whose commitment to those policies was credible to voters. The DPP, in contrast, was gripped by an internal struggle over whether to move to the center or to try to shift public opinion closer to its own ideology. The DPP presidential campaign never really settled on either strategy; top party leaders continued to contradict one another throughout the election season, and the DPP candidate, Frank Hsieh, never appeared fully in control of his own campaign. The discord within the DPP had important implications for Taiwan's democratic consolidation: if the Democratic Progressives continued to eschew the center, their party would be unable to challenge the KMT for national power, in effect restoring the one-and-a-half-party system Taiwan had in the early days of its democratic transition.

Although many of the factors and forces that drove the 2008 presidential election result were unique to that election and that year, the two major parties' responses to popular preferences have been evolving for decades. To win majority support, a party must understand the structure of public opinion. If opinion is polarized, it makes sense to appeal to one "pole" and push to maximize turnout among that group. If opinion is more normally distributed, appealing to the center is a better approach. The DPP has been debating this problem since before the party was formally founded, and it continued to do so after the 2008 election. Because the consequences of that debate were so grave, not only for the DPP but also for Taiwan's democracy, it is worth analyzing the debate in detail.

Locating Taiwan's Median Voter

The idea that Taiwan politics is polarized has great currency, including among many DPP strategists. The term *polarization* is used loosely in popular media to refer to political systems rife with conflict; however, political scientists use it more precisely to describe a bimodal structure of opinion in which preferences cluster at the extremes. One implication of this definition is that when opinion is polarized, the center is vacant. President Chen Shui-bian himself endorsed this characterization of Taiwan politics when he said there were no centrist voters in Taiwan.[2]

In January 2008, the Taiwan Foundation for Democracy hosted an international conference to compare polarized politics in Taiwan, South Korea, and the United States. The event rested on the assumption that Taiwan politics was deeply polarized, but some of the scholars who attended the conference challenged its premise. Sun Yat-sen University political scientist Liao Da-chi and Stanford University researcher Eric Yu argued that polarization was limited to political elites and that "the polarization of political officials is not necessarily a direct reflection of a similarly polarized mass electorate."[3]

Liao and Yu made an important point. The appearance of polarization in Taiwan politics was due mainly to the fierce competition among elites, which intensified during eight years of divided government. During the Chen administration, elite conflict took the form of a zero-sum competition for power between the DPP-led executive and a legislature dominated by the KMT and its allies (the so-called Pan-Blue coalition). In this setting, compromise was rare; verbal nastiness, common; and physical violence, not unheard of. To make matters worse, the focal point for the two sides' disagreements—that is, Taiwan's national identity—was an ideological issue on which Taiwan had little room for maneuvering, setting the stage for what Sigmund Freud called the "narcissism of small differences."

Among the public, evidence of polarization was harder to find—a fact political scientists had been at pains to point out for some time.[4] Since the early days of Taiwan's democracy, the percentage of Taiwanese who say they do not identify with any political party has always exceeded the percentage who identify with any of the existing parties; clearly, the public has not lined up in opposing camps, as the polarization hypothesis would suggest.[5] Likewise, on the issue cleavage that best defines the two camps, surveys find Taiwanese agnostic. Even during the Chen administration, when the government was making strenuous efforts to build support for Taiwan's independent sovereignty, Election Study Center surveys on the independence-unification issue consistently found a majority of respondents favoring the most moderate responses: "maintain status quo, decide later" and "maintain status quo indefinitely."[6]

Political scientist Yun-han Chu designed a survey to measure support for independence and unification under ideal circumstances. In 2006, he found that 29.8 percent of his respondents could accept independence but not unification, and 15.1 percent could accept unification but not independence. The largest group—33.3 percent—was willing to accept either outcome, and another 7.8 percent rejected both options.[7] Here again is evidence not of polarization, but of a range of opinions weighted toward the center.

The popular characterization of Taiwan politics as polarized includes the idea that opinion was distributed bimodally across a number of issues. This idea assumes that Taiwanese on the "Green" (DPP) side of the spectrum defined themselves as "Taiwanese," supported independence, voted for the DPP, and opposed closer engagement with mainland China, whereas those on the "Blue" (KMT) side took contrasting views on all these issues. In fact, however, Taiwan public opinion was not consistent across issues during the Chen Shui-bian era.[8]

Enthusiasm for immediate, de jure independence changed very little during the Chen years, rising from about 3 percent in 2000 to 6 percent by March 2008, whereas support for unification remained consistently below 4 percent. In those same years, however, the proportions of Taiwanese identifying as "Chinese," "Taiwanese," or "both Taiwanese and Chinese" changed dramatically. The proportion identifying as "Chinese" dwindled to about 5 percent, and the proportion identifying as "Taiwanese" rose to nearly 45 percent, effectively equaling the proportion calling themselves "both Taiwanese and Chinese."[9] However, as Taiwanese identity was gathering strength, enthusiasm for cross-Strait economic engagement also was rising sharply. Between 1992 and 2008, the percentage of Taiwanese who believed the pace of cross-Strait exchanges was too slow increased from 19 percent to 35 percent, with another 41 percent saying the pace was just right.[10] In the same period, support for tougher regulations on cross-Strait exchanges fell from 57 to 44 percent, whereas support for loosening the rules more than doubled, from 20 percent to 42 percent.[11] In 2008, three-quarters of Taiwanese supported transportation links across the Strait.[12]

Taken together, these various measures of public opinion demonstrate that there *was* a political center in Taiwan during the Chen Shui-bian era. It was characterized by a strong identification with Taiwan as a homeland, moderate views on the independence-unification issue, and reasoned support for cross-Strait economic engagement. Public opinion data simply do not support the claim that Taiwan society was polarized into warring camps. For politicians, the message should have been clear. As Robert Ross wrote, "The vast majority of Taiwan voters, regardless of identity, is deterred from challenging the status quo by mainland retaliatory threats. These findings further suggest that pragmatic Taiwan politicians seeking to maximize voter support would not promote a revisionist foreign policy."[13] One task facing political parties, then, was to offer policies that appealed to this center.

The KMT's Adjustment to the Median Voter

In March 2008, Ma Ying-jeou won a landslide victory, polling 58.45 percent of the vote overall and winning majorities in eighteen of the island's twenty-three municipalities. His success, along with his party's victory in the January legislative elections, conferred on the KMT leadership both a popular mandate and the institutional backing to implement a broad range of policy initiatives. Although the election results revealed voters' deep dissatisfaction with Chen Shui-bian, they also represented a significant affirmation of the KMT and its policies. The KMT's opponents in both races—mainly candidates of Chen's DPP—were at pains to distance themselves from Chen. There was no shortage of criticism for President Chen and his policies among his party brethren, and many DPP candidates (including the party's presidential nominee, Frank Hsieh) espoused positions closer to Ma's than to Chen's. Nonetheless, large majorities preferred KMT candidates in both elections. A key reason for the KMT's success was their decision to craft a platform that could attract centrist support.

The KMT's conversion to a median voter–seeking party began in the 1990s under President Lee Teng-hui, who recognized that the DPP's competitive strength was its credibility as a party representing the people of Taiwan. Yet the KMT's long-standing attachment to unification, along with the disproportionate representation of mainland-born émigrés in its top ranks, increasingly felt anachronistic and dated. Lifting restraints on free speech exposed the KMT to criticism on the grounds that its Chinese nationalist ideology was inappropriate for a democratic Taiwan. Rather than allow an outdated ideology to undermine his party's competitive ness, Lee pushed the KMT to embrace Taiwanese identity and a "Taiwan first" approach to policymaking. As Alexander Tan put it, "Lee and the mainstream faction effected the reorientation of the KMT from a mainlander party focused on reunification with China to a Taiwanese party focused on maintaining governing status in the island . . . and deepening its attachment and ties to Taiwan."[14]

Not everyone in the KMT, however, could accept the dilution of the party's core position. In 1993, several members of the KMT's conservative wing left to found the Chinese New Party (NP), which picked up the pro-unification torch, though it never attracted a wide following. In 2000, the KMT split again when two prominent politicians, Lien Chan and Soong Chu-yu (James Soong), ran against each other in the presidential election. Together, the two won more than 60 percent of the vote, but divided between the two, their share was not enough to defeat Chen Shuibian, who won the presidency with 39 percent.

After the presidential election debacle, Soong organized his followers into the People First Party (PFP). Although not as vocal as the NP in support of unification, the PFP was more assertively pro-China and anti-independence than the KMT. The PFP made a bigger electoral impact than the New Party, but its popularity was not sustained, and by 2008, the PFP was moribund; nearly all the successful politicians associated with it had returned to the KMT fold.

Ma Ying-jeou's presidential campaign followed Lee's mainstream approach. His platform promised to improve economic and political relations with the People's Republic of China (PRC), while preserving Taiwan's fundamental interests—most important, its de facto independence. Given the sensitivity of the issue and the (perceived) competitiveness of the race, the temptation to waver on the issue must have been intense at moments. Yet Ma never retreated from his core positions. In insisting on these positions, Ma sent costly signals to both the Taiwan electorate and the PRC government—signals that, had he misjudged public opinion, would have lost him the election or, if he had misjudged Beijing, would have undermined his presidency.[15]

Ma's determination to deepen economic engagement with the mainland was captured in one of his most high-profile platform planks—the call for a cross-Strait "common market." The common market idea, which originally was associated with Ma's running mate, Vincent Siew, attracted intense criticism from the DPP camp. According to Hsieh's campaign, Ma's policy would create a "One China market" that would flood Taiwan with low-wage, socially inferior mainland Chinese workers and dubious Chinese capital. (In the last week of the campaign, the Hsieh camp ran a newspaper advertisement showing three men urinating in public; the text read, "With a One China market, our public parks will turn into public toilets.") Ma also promised to open direct transport links between Taiwan and the PRC and lift investment restrictions that had driven many Taiwan companies to delist from the Taiwan stock exchange. Both ideas were popular with voters, but the DPP argued that Ma's eagerness for cross-Strait progress would blind him to Taiwan's interests.

On political engagement with Beijing, Ma's campaign advocated reopening dialogue based on the "1992 consensus,"[16] which is even more controversial than the cross-Strait common market. President Chen had attacked the concept relentlessly, and Hsieh, his would-be successor, did the same throughout the campaign. The DPP rejected the 1992 consensus both on procedural grounds, claiming it was a fraud that never actually happened, and on substantive grounds, arguing any formulation binding Taiwan to a One China framework would harm Taiwan's interests. Thus, it was risky for Ma to insist on this point, given the volume of attacks against the 1992 consensus from the DPP in the sixteen years since the consensus was (allegedly) concluded. Setting the consensus aside and focusing on other issues—or obfuscating the matter—would have been safer.

One might imagine that such calculations were unnecessary, given Ma's strong lead in the polls, but in fact, KMT leaders were never confident he would win. Their experiences in 2000 and 2004, when they had watched huge polling leads evaporate just weeks or even hours before the voting, combined with the enormous number of voters calling themselves undecided in preelection surveys, convinced KMT strategists to take nothing for granted. In the last days before the election, Ma's campaign staffers drove themselves to distraction imagining DPP's dirty tricks to "steal" the election, which is how they believed Chen had won in 2004. Nor were many foreign observers confident in predicting a Ma win. On March 21, the *New York Times* reported, "The suppression of Tibet protests by Chinese security forces, as well as missteps by the Nationalist Party, which Beijing favors, have nearly erased what had seemed like an insuperable lead for Ma Ying-jeou, the Harvard-educated lawyer who has been the front-runner in the race."[17] The fact that Ma refused to retreat from the 1992 consensus, even in this perilous political environment, underscored his determination to establish its legitimacy as the basis for dialogue with Beijing.

The DPP pointed to Ma's commitment to the 1992 consensus as one of many signs that the KMT candidate was more committed to unification than to protecting Taiwan's interests. Hsieh's campaign rallies rang with accusations that Ma and the KMT were preparing to "sell out Taiwan" to the PRC. To make their case, however, DPP speakers needed to ignore or dismiss the many public statements in which Ma warned Beijing to temper its expectations. These messages constituted a second costly signal—one that could delay or derail the progress on cross-Strait relations Ma needed to prove his mettle as president.

Ma never denied that the KMT's long-term preference was for unification, but he regarded unification as one of several options that Taiwan might adopt, rather than as an inevitable solution. As long as decisions about Taiwan's future resulted from a democratic process, Ma stated, he could accept any outcome. To reinforce this emphasis on democracy as the basis of his policy, Ma said there was no chance Taiwan would unify with a nondemocratic People's Republic of China. In addition, to qualify as democratic, the PRC government must meet specific, concrete criteria, including reversing its verdicts against the Tiananmen Square protesters of 1989.

Ma's campaign message regarding unification centered on two themes. First, he flatly stated that unification would not be a topic for dialogue during his term of office. This unequivocal statement, reiterated regularly throughout the campaign, put Beijing on notice that moving too quickly to press Taiwan on unification would backfire. It also reassured Taiwanese voters that electing Ma would not result in precipitous changes to Taiwan's status. Ma's second campaign theme was his "three noes" formula: no unification, no independence, no armed conflict. This statement offered reassurance to both the PRC and the Taiwan electorate, as it addressed the deepest fears of each side.

Just in case Beijing might miss the point, Ma added a stinging coda at the very end of the campaign. On March 18, with violence raging in Tibet, Ma issued a statement that landed on every one of Beijing's sore spots. The statement began, "The Republic of China is a sovereign independent democratic state. The future of Taiwan should be decided by Taiwan's 23-million people, and no intervention by the PRC is to be tolerated." After calling PRC premier Wen Jiabao's assertion that mainland Chinese people should have a role in determining Taiwan's status "not only rude, irrational, arrogant, and absurd, but also self-righteous," the statement described the crackdown in Tibet as "a savage and stupid act." Ma reiterated his support for Taiwan's reentry into the United Nations and urged Beijing to "open a dialogue with the Dalai Lama." Finally, as if to make sure that no sacred cow would escape the tirade unharmed, Ma concluded, "If the PRC continues its crackdown on the Tibetan people, and if the situation in Tibet continues to deteriorate, I will not, if elected President of the Republic of China, rule out the possibility to stop sending our delegation to the 2008 Beijing Olympic games."[18]

If Ma's campaign message to Taiwan's voters was that they should expect him to move aggressively toward tighter cross-Strait economic relations and to seek better political relations under the 1992 consensus framework, the message to Beijing was equally blunt: "Don't expect me to deliver Taiwan on a silver platter if I win." By making both messages plain and unequivocal, Ma earned credibility to move toward dialogue, while taking unification off the agenda.

What would the content of this vaunted dialogue be? Here again, the Ma campaign made its intentions clear. Ma's agenda for dialogue was rooted in an agreement that KMT chair Lien Chan and Chinese Communist Party (CCP) general secretary (and PRC president) Hu Jintao had reached in April 2005. The two leaders' joint statement reads, in part, "It is the common proposition of the two parties to uphold the 'Consensus of '92,' oppose 'Taiwan independence,'[19] pursue peace and stability in the Taiwan Strait, promote the development of cross-strait ties, and safeguard the interests of compatriots on both sides of the strait." The statement also called for enhanced economic cooperation, including "all-round, direct, and two-way 'three links'" and expressed the two sides' shared desire to "promote a formal ending to the cross-strait state of hostilities, reach a peace accord, and build a framework for the peaceful and steady development of cross-strait ties, including the establishment of a military mutual trust mechanism, to avoid cross-strait military conflict." The leaders agreed to "promote discussion on issues of participation in international activities, which concern the Taiwan public, after cross-strait consultations are resumed, including priority discussion on participation in the World Health Organization's activities." Ma's campaign emphasized this last point in its promise to work with the PRC to achieve a modus vivendi on Taiwan's international space.[20]

To call for dialogue while excluding the issue about which one's negotiating partner ostensibly was most eager to talk, as Ma did, would seem to guarantee failure, but the Lien-Hu agreement provided fodder for years of negotiations without ever raising the issue of unification. (The closest the agreement comes to mentioning unification is a call for a "virtuous circle of cooperation . . . so as to bring about brilliant and splendid prospects for the Chinese nation.") Using interim steps—that is, the economic agreements and peace accord—to facilitate dialogue, while0postponing the day of reckoning on unification, was an important part of the Ma Ying-jeou/ KMT approach to cross-Strait relations, as that approach could meet the expectations of both the Beijing leadership (which had signed onto it already) and the Taiwanese people.

Chu Yun-han's studies and other surveys of preferences on the independence-unification issue demonstrate the degree to which the mainland China policy, promoted by Ma Ying-jeou and his party during the campaign, aligned with popular preferences on the island.[21] As Chu put it,

> My analysis does not support the view that cross-strait relations are on the verge of a major departure from the status quo. While the prospect of peaceful reconciliation has turned more promising, a negotiated peace between the two sides is still far off. . . . Democratization has reinforced the Taiwanese quest to retain charge of the island's own future, making the threshold for constructing a winning coalition for reunification extremely high.[22]

If this is the case, it is not surprising that Taiwanese voters would endorse a policy aimed at promoting engagement and dialogue, while deferring a conversation about unification to the distant future.

The DPP's Policy Debates

In 2000, when Chen Shui-bian took over the executive function in Taiwan, the island appeared on the verge of consolidating a two-party-plus system in which the KMT and DPP would contend for national power, while fringe parties—the PFP, NP, and Taiwan Solidarity Union (TSU)— would provide consistent support to the two major parties. By 2004, however, the KMT's fortunes had deteriorated to the point at which some commentators wondered whether the DPP might soon come to dominate the political system.[23]

Just four years later, the KMT held a larger share of political power than at any time since democratic national elections had been instituted in the early 1990s; at the end of the Chen Shui-bian era, it was the DPP that faced an existential crisis.[24] The DPP's success in 2000 was something of a fluke, as Chen won with much less than a majority of support. To become a party capable of competing for a majority of votes, the DPP needed to use its years in government to increase its vote share by 10–15 percentage points. They were able to pull this off only once—in the 2004 presidential election, when Chen won a hair over 50 percent. In the other elections during Chen's presidency, the DPP fell well below 50 percent, and the DPP fell far short of becoming a party capable of competing for majority status.[25]

Under Chen Shui-bian's leadership (as president, 2000–2008, and party chair, 2007–2008), the DPP considered three options for increasing its vote share from 35–40 percent to 50 percent or more: making a heresthetic move aimed at altering the salience of various issues, adjusting the party's message to appeal to centrist voters, or using the power of government to convert voters to the DPP's point of view.

During the 1990s, the DPP successfully used heresthetic moves to change the basis of political competition in Taiwan. Rather than trying to compete with the KMT on its strong suits (e.g., economic policy, national security, competent government), the opposition activists who created the DPP brought forward new issues on which the KMT had no advantage. The most important of these were democratization and ethnic justice, or the idea that the Taiwan-born majority should enjoy equal rights with the mainland-born minority who had dominated public life since the 1940s. These issues were so popular that the KMT soon adopted them as its own; today, many historians and citizens, both inside and outside Taiwan, credit the KMT presidents Chiang Ching-kuo and Lee Teng-hui as the architects of Taiwan's democratization and nativization (*bentuhua*).

As the KMT increasingly represented itself as the champion of democracy and equality, the DPP was pushed to sharpen its positions even further. In 1991, the DPP voted to make Taiwan independence a formal goal—a move that energized DPP's core supporters but also gave the KMT powerful ammunition to use against the DPP. Beijing was threatening to use military force to stop Taiwan from becoming independent, making it easy for the KMT to portray the DPP as reckless and irresponsible. A 1998 DPP survey found that 24 percent of respondents believed the party's most prominent quality was "radical," and another 20 percent said "violent."[26] In the same survey, respondents tended to prefer the DPP on "soft" issues, such as social services, but gave the KMT higher marks on "hard" issues, such as economic management, national security, and foreign policy.

After the KMT leapfrogged the DPP on issues related to democratization, the Democratic Progressives came up with a new issue with strong voter appeal, one the KMT could not co-opt: anticorruption. Dafydd Fell's work on political advertising and issue-based politics shows that the DPP emphasized anticorruption throughout the 1990s, while the KMT rarely mentioned the issue.[27] The appeal worked well for the DPP, as Fell argued: "There is a clear pattern that on the two occasions the DPP suffered serious electoral setbacks in 1991 and 1996 it had failed to stress political corruption in its election advertising. In contrast, whenever the DPP centered its campaign on anti-corruption it achieved improved electoral results."[28]

Throughout the 2004 presidential election, the DPP continued to stress anticorruption, including accusations of personal corruption on the part of KMT politicians, KMT connections to organized crime, and improperly acquired KMT assets. Unfortunately, the DPP's ability to exploit the issue collapsed soon after Chen's reelection, when evidence of corruption within his administration began to surface. Over the course of Chen's second term, a snowballing series of scandals implicated not only many of his close advisers but also his son-in-law and wife and, ultimately, the president himself.

Thus, the corruption issue played a part in the 2008 election campaign but not in its traditional role of helpmate to the DPP. Instead, the KMT candidate was widely hailed as the face of clean government, while voters expressed deep cynicism and disappointment about the DPP's claims of incorruptibility. Both presidential candidates were investigated for corruption during the campaign. While Hsieh was never indicted, Ma was indicted, tried, and acquitted of all charges, a development that confirmed the views of the many Taiwanese who believed the charges were politically motivated from the outset. In a TVBS survey taken in September 2007, 40 percent of respondents said that of the two candidates, Ma was less likely to lead a corrupt administration, while only 22 percent said they thought a Hsieh government would be cleaner.[29]

The DPP attempted to raise other issues in addition to democracy, Taiwanese self-determination, and anticorruption. It toyed with a center-left agenda emphasizing environmental protection, foreign relations, social welfare, and workers' rights. In the end, though, these issues did not give the DPP the boost it needed. The KMT leapfrogged over the DPP to co-opt its most popular ideas, while other center-left ideas were downplayed because they split the DPP coalition.[30]

Changing the subject had worked for the DPP when the party could credibly claim to "own" popular issues. As those issues disappeared, however, it faced a different choice: to move its position closer to the voters or to try to move the voters closer to its position. Over the years the DPP shifted its positions on many issues in ways aimed at capturing moderate voters, but it never managed to displace the KMT as the party of the center. An important reason for this was the DPP's persistent image as aggressively, even recklessly, pro-independence.

The DPP first adopted independence as a platform plank in 1991, but the decision was controversial from the start. Senior party figures tried to distance themselves from the issue, but many DPP candidates, including the party's presidential nominee in 1996, continued to stress the issue. In

May 1999, the DPP Party Congress passed the "Resolution on Taiwan's Future," which stated,

> Taiwan is a sovereign and independent country. In accordance with international laws, Taiwan's jurisdiction covers Taiwan, Penghu, Kinmen, Matsu, its affiliated islands and territorial waters. Taiwan, although named the Republic of China under its current constitution, is not subject to the jurisdiction of the People's Republic of China. Any change in the independent status quo must be decided by all residents of Taiwan by means of plebiscite.

DPP officials characterized the resolution as a moderate gesture that would replace active pursuit of independence with defense of a status quo characterized by Taiwan's de facto independence. The resolution allowed the DPP to downplay the independence issue; but even then, individual candidates and campaigners could not always hide their enthusiasm for formal independence, and mass media played up their most inflammatory statements.[31] As Fell put it, "The DPP has not abandoned Taiwan independence but repackaged it."[32] The result is that, although the major parties' formal platforms converged, including on the all-important question of relations with the PRC, the public still viewed the DPP as favoring independence.[33]

Chen Shui-bian's first presidential campaign, waged in 1999 and early 2000, is a good example of a DPP effort to woo centrist voters. Candidate Chen stressed his qualifications as a moderate, eschewing references to independence and emphasizing his support for cross-Strait economic engagement, including direct transport links. In his first inaugural address, Chen issued his famous "five noes" promise, pledging not to move Taiwan toward formal independence. He even used the phrase "political integration" to describe how the relationship between the two sides might evolve after many years of economic and people-to-people ties.

Putting voters' minds at rest about his intentions before the election may well have helped Chen get the 39 percent of the vote he needed to defeat a divided KMT, but the five noes (and other conciliatory gestures he made early in his presidency) did not win over his critics both in the legislature and in Beijing. The PRC leadership declared it would "watch and wait," while the KMT and its legislative allies declared war on the executive. Moving toward the center helped Chen win the presidency, but governing was another matter. Nor was Chen willing to yield to demands he found unreasonable. Of the 1992 consensus, Beijing's precondition for reopening dialogue with Taipei, Chen said, "Acquiescing to the 1992 agreement is tantamount to ending the sovereignty of ROC [Republic of China]."[34]

Chen's qualifications as a moderate were wobbly to begin with, but they took a major hit in 2003 when he launched campaigns on behalf of two controversial political reforms: a popular referendum and a new constitution. Although the right to referendum was contained in the ROC constitution, there was no enabling legislation in place, and the concept had long been linked to independence. (Early independence advocates had promoted a plebiscite as the mechanism for realizing their goal.) As for a new constitution, this move, too, was widely viewed as a pro-independence stratagem, both because the content of a new constitution might redefine the state and because creating a new constitution struck many observers—especially those in Beijing—as dangerously similar to creating a new state.

Chen pushed both ideas hard during the 2004 presidential campaign. In November 2003, the legislature passed enabling legislation designed to block the president from calling provocative referendums. Chen wriggled through a loophole in the law and put forward two symbolic questions aimed at mobilizing pro-independence voters without giving Beijing a clear casus belli. The maneuver confirmed the judgment in Taiwan and elsewhere that Chen was no moderate.

Chen's abandonment of moderation was, in a sense, overdetermined. Trying to cooperate with his political opponents got him nowhere, so tactical moderation seemed useless. Within the DPP, support for independence remained strong, and Chen was under relentless pressure from his party's fundamentalist wing to do more for their cause. Once reelected, he had little incentive to cater to the center, so it was not surprising that he would favor his base. No one believed he was a moderate, so why keep up the pretense?

Still, even if Chen's decision to play to his ideological base was understandable, why did his party follow him? Given the president's abysmal popularity ratings, one might have expected his party to look elsewhere for its direction. Instead, the DPP closed ranks behind the president and took a sharp turn toward its fundamentalist wing. To explain this development, we must look to the DPP's organizational structure.

Before the DPP was founded, the political activists who had formed the core of Taiwan's opposition movement had been divided into two tendencies—one focused on ideology and policy and the other on electioneering.[35] Throughout most of the party's history, the existence of two blocs served a useful purpose; they were complementary forces within the party, performing different, but equally necessary, tasks. They argued over emphasis, and they fought over party leadership positions, but they recognized the useful symbiosis between them.

Over the years, "thinkers" in the DPP gravitated toward the New Tide faction. Although New Tide had once taken relatively extreme positions on the national identity issue (it was behind the effort to put a pro-independence plank in the party platform), more recently, New Tide has become an organizational vehicle for those favoring a pragmatic approach to the issue. Relations between New Tide and the DPP's pro-independence wing (the fundamentalists) deteriorated sharply, both because of the perceived loss of New Tide's purity and because of its strong influence over the party's decisionmaking apparatus. Although New Tide's stronghold was the party's national leadership, the fundamentalists and electoralists (whose views on the national identity issue vary widely) dominated the grassroots.

Chen's shift to a more confrontational orientation sparked a debate within the party. The fundamentalists supported his push for a new constitution and other gestures they believed would give greater latitude to pro-independence forces.[36] Meanwhile, the moderates worried that Chen's approach would undermine the party's chances in the December 2005 municipal executive elections. The conflict came to a head in October 2005, when Luo Wen-chia, the party's candidate for Taipei County executive, and New Tide leader Tuan Yi-kang announced the formation of a New DPP Movement. Luo and Tuan said the party needed to examine its flaws—a thinly veiled jab at the scandal-ridden Chen government—and return to its core values of democracy and good government.

The New DPP Movement won support from many DPP politicians, but it infuriated Chen, his advisers, and the fundamentalists. The new movement touched off an ideological and generational conflict, with many young politicians lining up with Luo and Tuan and the old guard closing ranks behind Chen. Within weeks, Chen and his supporters squelched the movement, but enforced unanimity could not repair the DPP's battered reputation. The election results confirmed Chen's critics' worst fears. The party won only six of the twenty-three municipal executive posts up for grabs, and its losses included some counties that had been considered DPP strongholds.

After the local election catastrophe, many observers thought Chen could not avoid a move to the center, but he defied them yet again. In a speech delivered on January 1, 2006, Chen unveiled a policy to tighten regulations on cross-Strait economic engagement. The speech focused on three themes—consolidating Taiwan consciousness, strengthening controls on cross-Strait economic ties, and promoting a new constitution—each of which seemed designed to appeal to hard-line Taiwan nationalists. The speech also stressed the risks of cross-Strait engagement and called for the government to step up its role as "gatekeeper" and avoid "taking shortcuts."

The speech defied mainstream views—elite and grassroots alike. Because the DPP's own postelection review had attributed the December defeat in large part to its failure to reach out to centrist voters through moderate policy positions, DPP legislators criticized Chen's speech. Said legislator Julian Kuo, "Although the opening of direct links has created dispute within the party, . . . I think that most DPP politicians are in support of the move." The strongest denunciations came from New Tide figures, such as legislator Lee Wen-chung, who told the *Taipei Times*,

> The government must face the reality that China is rising economically and politically. The nation must respond to the situation and try to reposition itself in an era of globalization. . . . I just don't think it is right for the president to continue the one-person decision-making model and leave everyone else out of the loop, especially in the wake of the party's resounding defeat in the December 3 local elections.

The 2005 municipal elections proved the DPP was in trouble. Efforts to bring the party to a more moderate position had failed, and the hard-liners' grip continued to strengthen. Relations between moderates and fundamentalists reached their nadir in mid-2007. During the legislative primary in that year, fundamentalists singled out a group of moderates—most affiliated with New Tide—whom they labeled the "eleven bandits." They accused the eleven of being soft on China, and some talk-radio hosts went so far as to call them traitors to Taiwan.

The only bright spot for the moderates during Chen's second term was Frank Hsieh's victory in the party's presidential primary. Hsieh had long advocated a pragmatic, flexible mainland policy. Still, in the context of DPP internal politics, Hsieh's nomination was problematic, because it came at the expense of the New Tide favorite, Su Tseng-chang. According to party insiders, Hsieh benefited from the fundamentalists' campaign to crucify the moderate legislative hopefuls. Once he had secured the nomination, Hsieh was unable to extricate himself from the hard-liners' influence; throughout the campaign, radical statements from Chen and others undercut his efforts to craft a moderate message.

The DPP's move away from a centrist position toward a hard-line, fundamentalist stance was the product of many forces, including factional conflict, as well as Chen's personal frustration with the failure of his early moderation. Equally important, I would argue, was the growing conviction among Chen and other hard-liners that the best way to execute the DPP's mission as a governing party was to use the power of the presidency to build support for its ideology. Lin Chia-lung, a DPP official and adviser to Chen Shui-bian, explained this strategy to me in an interview in 2005: "I think we should try to persuade people of our values, to influence them to agree with us, not just follow behind the voters. You need to have values and ideals."[37] This interpretation explains the Chen administration's doggedness in implementing its national identity agenda.

In the wake of the 2008 defeats, the DPP confronted a familiar dilemma: remake itself as a centrist party or seek a winning vote share among supporters of its traditional ideology. In May 2008, the Democratic Progressives elected as party chair Tsai Ing-wen, a moderate whose first political job was on Lee Teng-hui's mainland policy team, raising hopes that the pragmatists would prevail. But the competition was heated: Tsai's rival for the job, the eighty-one-year-old fundamentalist Koo Kwan-min, won almost 40 percent of the vote on the argument that insufficient ideological purity was to blame for the DPP's recent setbacks.

Conclusion

Ma Ying-jeou enjoyed so many advantages in the 2008 presidential election that his victory seemed almost preordained. He started out as a popular politician with a clean reputation, and again and again, his opponents' failings magnified his strengths. For many voters, the presidential election was an opportunity to express their disappointment or frustration with Chen Shui-bian's administration, and Ma was the inevitable beneficiary of that sentiment.

Frank Hsieh was not literally responsible for Chen's shortcomings, but the essence of democratic accountability is to punish (or reward) the successor for the predecessor's performance. To persuade voters to elect him, Hsieh and his party needed to construct a credible rationale for the party's past performance and an attractive vision for its future. In both cases, the DPP's internal conflicts undermined its efforts. Overcoming Chen's legacy and Ma's popularity was a daunting assignment, but resolving the DPP's internal contradictions proved even more difficult. Those conflicts were a leading cause of the party's defeats in 2008, and until they were resolved, they would continue to retard its progress. The party's successes in 2009 and 2010 proved that voters had not given up on it, but parlaying that support into a national majority in 2012 would require considerably more compromise than the DPP managed in the previous round of national elections.

Notes

1. Lin Chia-lung identified this pattern more than a decade ago in his PhD dissertation, "Paths to Democracy: Taiwan in Comparative Perspective" (Department of Political Science, Yale University, 1998).
2. "The KMT Must Transcend Blue and Green," *United Daily News,* January 28, 2008.

3. "Polarized Political Scene Not Good for Economy: Pundits," *Taipei Times,* January 27, 2008, 3.

4. See, for example, Eric Chen-hua Yu in this volume, or John Fuh-sheng Hsieh's characterization of Taiwan as a "mildly divided society" in his article, "National Identity and Taiwan's Mainland Policy," *Journal of Contemporary China* 13, no. 40 (2004): 480.

5. Election Studies Center, *Changes in Party Identification of Taiwanese as Tracked in Surveys by the Election Study Center, NCCU, 1992–2007* (Taipei City: National Chengchi University), http://www.esc.nccu.edu.tw/eng/data/data03-1.htm.

6. Election Studies Center, *Changes in the Unification-Independence Stances of Taiwanese as Tracked in Surveys by the Election Study Center, NCCU, 1994–2007* (Taipei City: National Chengchi University), http://www.esc.nccu.edu.tw/eng/data/data03-3.htm.

7. Chu Yun-han, "Taiwan's Politics of Identity: Navigating Between China and the United States," in *Power and Security in Northeast Asia: Shifting Strategies,* ed. Byung-Kook Kim and Anthony Jones (Boulder, CO: Lynne Rienner, 2007), 245.

8. For an extended discussion of these categories and the inconsistencies among them, see Shelley Rigger, *Taiwan's Rising Rationalism: Generations, Politics and "Taiwanese Nationalism,"* Policy Studies 26 (Washington, DC: East-West Center, 2006).

9. Election Studies Center, *Changes in the Taiwanese/Chinese Identity of Taiwanese as Tracked in Surveys by the Election Study Center, NCCU, 1992–2007* (Taipei City, Taiwan: National Chengchi University), http://www.esc.nccu.edu.tw/eng/data/data03-2.htm.

10. "The Pace of Cross-Strait Exchanges," Mainland Affairs Council, accessed April 7, 2008, http://www.mac.gov.tw/english/index1-e.htm.

11. "How Should Our Government Handle Taiwanese Investment on Mainland China?" Mainland Affairs Council, accessed April 7, 2008, http://www.mac.gov.tw/english/index1-e.htm.

12. "Should We Open Up Direct Transportation Links with Mainland China?" Mainland Affairs Council, accessed April 7, 2008, http://www.mac.gov.tw/english/index1-e.htm.

13. Robert Ross, "Explaining Taiwan's Revisionist Diplomacy," *Journal of Contemporary China* 15, no. 48 (2006): 453.

14. Alexander C. Tan, "Transformation of the Kuomintang Party in Taiwan," *Democratization* 9, no. 3 (2002): 157–158.

15. For more on "costly signaling" in international relations, see James D. Fearon, "Domestic Political Audiences and the Escalation of International Disputes," *American Political Science Review* 88, no. 3 (1994): 577–592.

16. The "1992 consensus" refers to talks between Taipei and Beijing in 1992, when the two sides agreed to set aside the problem of national sovereignty in order to discuss practical issues. In essence, they agreed that trying to find a mutually acceptable definition of each side's sovereignty would make a dialogue on the practical matters impossible; so, instead, they would agree that both sides believed in One China and leave the discussion there. The KMT describes the 1992 consensus as "One China, different interpretations," with the Taiwan side interpreting "One China" to mean the Republic of China. In short, the KMT holds that the two sides reached an agreement to disagree. The DPP has consistently held that no consensus was reached in 1992; it also rejects the idea that Taiwan is part of China under *any* interpretation.

17. Keith Bradsher, "China Tensions Could Sway Vote in Taiwan," *New York Times,* March 21, 2008.

18. Ma Ying-jeou statement, March 18, 2008, accessed April 5, 2008, http://www.kuomintangnews.org.

19. The Chinese Communist Party and the KMT differentiate between Taiwan independence, which is unacceptable to both, and the independence of the Republic of China. The KMT has always insisted that the ROC exists as an independent, sovereign state. In theory, ROC independence is unacceptable to the CCP, but it has not challenged the KMT on this point in many years.

20. The English translation of the KMT-CCP agreement from which these passages are excerpted is available at http://news.bbc.co.uk/2/hi/asia-pacific/4498791 .stm (accessed April 5, 2008). A complete Chinese text is available at http://news.sina .com.cn/c/2005-04-29/19065787389s.shtml (accessed April 7, 2008).

21. See Chu, "Taiwan's Politics of Identity"; Andy G. Chang and T. Y. Wang, "Taiwanese or Chinese? Independence or Unification? An Analysis of Generational Differences in Taiwan," *Journal of Asian and African Studies* 40, no. 1–2 (2005): 29–49; Rigger, *Taiwan's Rising Rationalism*; Gunter Schubert, "Taiwan's Political Parties and National Identity: The Rise of an Overarching Consensus," *Asian Survey* 44, no. 4 (2004): 534–554.

22. Chu, "Taiwan's Politics of Identity," 250.

23. A *Newsweek* article from March 8, 2004, captured the feeling of panic in the KMT even before it lost the presidential election. The article quoted Taiwan political scientists Lo Chih-cheng ("If they lose the election they'll be in real trouble. . . . This is the KMT's last stand") and Chu Yun-han ("Like the ANC in South Africa, . . . [the DPP] could become the dominant party for a generation"). George Wehrfritz and Tim Culpan, "Taiwan: The KMT's Fear Factor," *Newsweek International Edition,* March 8, 2004.

24. When Taiwan's national legislature, the Legislative Yuan, was first subjected to comprehensive reelection in 1992, KMT-nominated candidates won 63.0 percent of the seats with 53.0 percent of the votes. In 2008, KMT candidates captured 53.5 percent of the vote and 72.0 percent of the seats. In the first direct presidential election, held in 1996, KMT nominee Lee Teng-hui captured 54 percent of the vote. Ma Ying-jeou polled 58.5 percent in 2008.

25. For party vote shares in specific elections, see the figures in the introduction to this volume.

26. *Survey on Party Images in Taiwan* (Taipei: DPP Survey Center, July 23, 1998).

27. See Dafydd Fell, *Party Politics in Taiwan: Party Change and the Democratic Evolution of Taiwan, 1991–2004* (New York: Routledge, 2005).

28. Dafydd Fell, "Political and Media Liberalization and Political Corruption in Taiwan," *China Quarterly* 184 (2005): 883.

29. TVBS, "*2008 zongtong daxuan bannianqian mindiao*" [Survey six months prior to the 2008 presidential election], September 2007, http://www.tvbs.com.tw /FILE_DB/DL_DB/yijung/200709/yijung-20070920210903.pdf.

30. Dafydd Fell, "The Evolution and Role of Campaign Issues in Taiwan's 1990s Elections," *Asian Journal of Political Science* 9, no. 1 (2001): 87.

31. Ibid., 84.

32. Ibid., 89.

33. For discussions of party convergence, see Schubert, "Taiwan's Political Parties and National Identity," and Shelley Rigger, "Party Politics and Taiwan's External Relations," *Orbis* (Summer 2005): 413–428.

34. Quoted in Chien-min Chao, "Introduction: The DPP in Power," *Journal of Contemporary China* 11, no. 33 (2002): 607.

35. I am avoiding the use of the word *faction* here because although these tendencies overlap with factions to an extent, they do not conform perfectly to one another. In the DPP, *faction* refers to a formal, organized subgroup within the party;

there have been several election-oriented factions over the years. That said, the ideology and policy "tendency" overlaps very closely with the New Tide faction.

36. As Alan Romberg put it, the plans for a new constitution unveiled by Chen in his second term "[set] the stage for what could well become a free-for-all in which radical, independence-oriented draft amendments or even full texts would likely be put forward." Alan Romberg, "The Taiwan Tangle," *China Leadership Monitor* 18 (Spring 2006): 1–28.

37. Interview with the author, autumn 2005.

3

The Democratic Progressive Party in Majoritarian Elections

Jih-wen Lin

On January 12, 2008, Taiwan conducted its first election of members of the Legislative Yuan under the new mixed-member majoritarian (MMM) electoral system. Adopted by the National Assembly in June 2005, this system divides the 113 legislative seats into three parts: 73 seats are elected by the single-member simple plurality (henceforth called single-member) rule, 34 seats (with half reserved for women) are allocated by closed-list proportional representation (PR) in a nationwide district, and 6 are set aside in two multimember aboriginal districts. The seats of each part are counted separately, and each voter casts one ballot for a candidate and one for a party. The new legislative electoral system has made the single-member race a defining feature of Taiwan's elections, covering contests for the offices of president, legislator, county magistrate, and city mayor. Because this reform has reshaped Taiwan's party system, the results of the 2008 election provide important clues about the future of Taiwan's democracy.

With almost two-thirds of the seats elected from single-member districts, Taiwan's MMM is a highly disproportional system.[1] Scholars expected the new system to encourage strategic voting and to put the minor parties at a disadvantage.[2] The results of the 2008 election proved these expectations correct, but in a surprising way. As shown in Table 3.1, the Kuomintang (KMT) won 53.5 percent of the district vote and 51.2 percent of the PR vote, whereas the vote share of the Democratic Progressive Party (DPP) in the local and PR districts was 38.2 and 36.9 percent, respectively.[3] However, despite the 15 percent difference between the vote shares of the KMT and the DPP, the gap between their seat

51

Table 3.1 Vote and Seat Shares in the 2008 Legislative Election

	KMT	DPP	TSU	PFP	NPSU	Ind.
District vote share	53.50	38.17	0.95	0.29	2.42	3.98
District seats	61	13	0	1	3	1
PR vote share	51.23	36.91	3.53	0	0.70	0
PR seats	20	14	0	0	0	0
Total seats	81	27	0	1	3	1
Total seat share	71.68	23.89	0	0.89	2.65	0.89

Source: Central Election Commission, http://db.cec.gov.tw/histMain.jsp?voteSel=20080101A2.
Notes: KMT = Kuomintang; DPP = Democratic Progressive Party; TSU = Taiwan Solidarity Union; PFP = People First Party; NPSU = Nonpartisan Solidarity Union; Ind. = independent candidate; PR = proportional representation.

shares was much greater, with the KMT taking eighty-one seats in total and the DPP receiving only twenty-seven seats. This result created a ratio that is much greater than the "cube rule" would predict.[4]

What explains the DPP's electoral fiasco? To what extent do the results of the 2008 elections presage the DPP's performance in other single-member races? The answers are important not only for the DPP but also for the prospects for Taiwan's democracy. The probability of the opposition party winning in majoritarian elections affects how much the ruling party will be deterred from abusing its political power. By examining the DPP's performance in Taiwan's single-member elections, this chapter will show that the party still has a good chance of winning majoritarian elections, despite its performance in 2008. After all, the DPP did manage to win two presidential elections and a considerable number of county magisterial or city mayoral seats—all single-member elections—even though its vote shares did not vary much.

The track record of the DPP's electoral performance offers an explanation for why it endorsed the MMM system, under which its seat share shrank to less than a quarter. When the Legislative Yuan passed the electoral reform in August 2004, the DPP had already enjoyed a series of electoral victories—it won the presidential election in 2000; became the plurality party in the 2001 legislative election; took nine county magistrate seats, representing more than half the population of Taiwan, in the local elections of 2001; and claimed victory again in the presidential election of 2004. Such an uninterrupted upward swing gave the DPP leadership confidence that, by adopting a majoritarian-leaning system for legislative elections, the party had a good chance of consolidating the non-KMT vote behind its candidates and becoming the majority party in the Legislative Yuan.

The 2008 election proved this confidence misplaced. What was missing in the DPP reformers' calculations? How can the DPP's uneven performance in single-member elections over time be explained? To measure the stability of the DPP's vote-getting capability, this chapter begins by using the township as the unit of analysis and explores how much the DPP's vote share varied across these localities in different single-member elections. The next section examines why the DPP—the second-largest party since 2008—received a seat share that was much lower than its vote share in the 2008 legislative election.[5] A plausible answer lies in the way the DPP's votes were spread out, which deprived the party of safe districts.

Following this logic, the third section studies the stability of the DPP's performance in single-member races by calculating the correlation between the party's vote shares in different elections. The fourth section gives a detailed account of the 2004 presidential election—the case in which the DPP first garnered a majority of votes—and compares it with other single-member elections. This comparison reveals the swing constituencies in which both the DPP and the KMT have a history of winning majorities. A model is constructed to explain how the swing constituencies decide which party to support, and this model is confirmed by an empirical analysis of the relationship between the changes in the dependence on subsidies and the DPP's presidential vote shares. The last section discusses the prospects for the DPP's electoral fortunes and for Taiwan's democracy.

Where and How Was the DPP Defeated?

As stated earlier in this chapter, the electoral system used in Taiwan's 2008 legislative election is an MMM system comprised of separate plurality and PR tiers. The allotment of the PR seats is easy to estimate, because it essentially reflects the vote share of the political parties after excluding those that failed to reach the 5 percent threshold. In the tier in which seats are allocated by plurality rule, a party's performance is determined by the distribution of its votes across electoral districts. Thus, we can study the DPP's performance in the 2008 legislative election by the vote share it received in the seventy-three single-member districts.

The most challenging question is why the DPP, the second-largest party, received only 16.5 percent of the district seats, even though it obtained 38.2 percent of the district votes. Since most districts featured competition between the DPP and the KMT, explaining the DPP's misfortune also answers why the KMT could claim sixty-one of the seventy-nine plurality seats (77.2 percent), while winning only 53.5 percent of the district votes.

Some observers have ascribed the DPP's debacle to "unfair" districting under the new electoral system. As the critics of this system pointed out, the constitution requires each county to have at least one legislative seat, which creates huge differences between the numbers of citizens represented by each legislator. At one extreme, a legislator from Lienchiang County represents only 7,867 voters; at the other extreme, a legislator from Hsinchu County represents 357,385. It so happened that the DPP tended to be weak in overrepresented counties like Lienchiang. In six other counties, the DPP's vote share in 2008 was less than 30 percent, which meant it would have been unable to win even if the KMT had been divided and had two candidates running in the race. The DPP's electoral disadvantage in these counties contributed to the national disproportionality of the seats, which was permanently institutionalized in the new system unless the districts are redrawn in the future.

Nevertheless, unfair districting is insufficient to account for the DPP's poor performance. Under a majoritarian electoral system, the DPP still would not win any seats in these unfavorable districts, even if its vote share were 40 percent. A more likely culprit for the DPP's misfortune is the lack of safe districts. Examining the vote distribution can help evaluate this claim by showing the source of the DPP's problem in 2008 (see Figure 3.1). The median of the distribution was roughly 40 percent, suggesting that the DPP was about 10 percent short of a majority in most

**Figure 3.1 The Distribution of the
DPP's Vote Share in the 2008 Legislative Election**

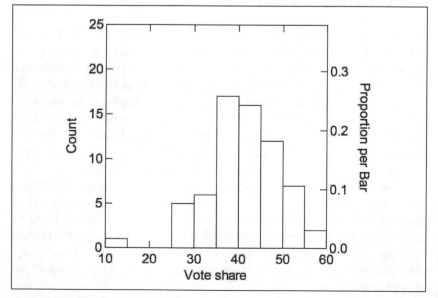

Source: Author's calculation.

districts. The KMT's pattern was the reverse, given the zero-sum competition between the two parties in almost all districts. Calculating the difference between the vote shares of each party in each district, we find the median to be between 10 and 20 percent. The distribution of the vote-share differences shows that the DPP enjoyed fewer safe districts than the KMT. In the districts where the KMT outperformed the DPP, the winner's average lead was 18.8 percent; in districts where the DPP won, the average margin was only 5.1 percent. These numbers indicate that even in its strongholds, the DPP could only marginally outperform the KMT, whereas the KMT was able to win landslide victories in many other districts. The KMT outperformed the DPP by more than 20 percent in twenty districts, whereas the DPP beat the KMT by more than 10 percent in only one district.[6]

If 10 percent represents the typical gap between the KMT and the DPP in 2008, how large is this in practical terms? Would it be possible for the DPP to make up this difference under other circumstances? The answers depend on the electoral system. Under PR, one party winning 50 percent and the other winning 40 percent of the popular vote may result in two parties receiving similar numbers of seats. Under a majoritarian system, however, a 10 percent difference can produce more divergent outcomes. If the difference in party vote share resulted mostly from a general dissatisfaction with the DPP's performance in government, then it is hardly permanent. After the change in ruling party, the DPP would have a good chance of winning back swing voters if they were to become disappointed with the KMT's performance. Another possibility, however, is that the difference between the DPP and the KMT was more ingrained and not sensitive to short-term changes in approval.

A simple method to determine which of these effects was stronger is to examine whether there was a regional pattern to the DPP's electoral performance. If the DPP lost to the KMT because of popular discontent with its governance, then the DPP's votes should have been more or less randomly distributed among the electoral districts, assuming a random distribution of voters' attitudes toward the ruling party. On the other hand, if there were a significant regional pattern to the DPP's electoral performance, its vote-getting capability might not vary much over time, because regional factors are less susceptible to short-term changes such as government performance.

In the 2008 legislative election, the distribution of votes had a clear regional pattern. All nine districts where the DPP garnered more than half the votes were in counties or cities of southern Taiwan, including Tainan City, Tainan County, Chiayi County, Kaohsiung City, and Pingtung County. Although the districts where the DPP performed poorly were less concentrated, many were located in northern Taiwan, such as Taipei City, Taipei County, and Taoyuan County. In seven districts, the DPP was so weak that it did not nominate a candidate at all.

Many factors potentially contribute to the regional pattern of a party's electoral strength. In Taiwan's context, an intuitive explanation for the DPP's stronger southern presence was the role played by national identity in electoral politics. As long as the Hoklo Taiwanese were more likely than other subethnic groups to embrace the idea that Taiwan should seek its own identity, the pro-independence DPP had a good chance of maintaining its turf in southern Taiwan, where the percentage of Hoklo Taiwanese was high. Nevertheless, the validity of this theory depends on how much it can explain two other facts: why the KMT had amassed solid grassroots support in other areas dominated by Hoklo Taiwanese, and why the DPP was less successful in central Taiwan, which was demographically similar to southern Taiwan. A clue to answering these questions can be found in the overall regional pattern of the DPP's electoral performance.

Table 3.2 tabulates the DPP's vote shares by region in recent single-member elections. Several patterns are noteworthy. First, the DPP indeed has been expanding its territory in southern Taiwan, as indicated by the majority of votes the party has consistently received there. Second, the DPP's vote shares in central Taiwan have varied greatly across elections, from as high as 53.15 percent in the 2004 presidential election to as low as 36.96 percent in the 2008 legislative election. Third and most

Table 3.2 The Percentage of the DPP's Single-Member Election Vote Shares by Region, 2000–2010

Region	North	Central	South	East	Offshore
President 2000	34.68	40.22	47.84	33.56	23.88
Magistrate 2001	43.18	41.43	51.40	37.19	23.01
President 2004	44.34	53.15	58.79	43.73	31.21
Magistrate 2005	38.82	43.11	50.73	28.91	27.66
Legislative 2008	34.70	36.96	60.84	33.10	22.90
President 2008	36.23	43.37	51.02	35.58	24.27
Magistrate 2009–2010	44.67	52.16	54.28	47.41	48.07
Average	39.52	44.34	53.56	37.07	28.71
Standard deviation	4.49	6.07	4.70	6.43	9.05

Source: Author's calculation.
Notes: North—Keelung City, Taipei County, Taipei City, Taoyuan County, Hsinchu County, Hsinchu City, Miaoli County; Central—Taichung County, Taichung City, Changhua County, Nantou County, Yunlin County, Chiayi County, Chiayi City; South—Tainan County, Tainan City, Kaohsiung County, Kaohsiung City, Pingtung County; East—Yilan County, Hualien County, Taitung County; Offshore islands—Penghu County, Kinmen County, Lienchiang County. The data exclude constituencies in which the DPP did not nominate any candidate.

interesting, the regional concentration of votes was most salient in the 2008 legislative election: in central Taiwan, the DPP obtained only 36.96 percent of the vote, which was 7.38 percent lower than the area's average, whereas in southern Taiwan, its vote share was 60.84, which was 7.28 percent *higher* than the area's average over the previous decade.

Together, these patterns reveal the likely mechanism behind the DPP's electoral performance—that is, a politically consolidated Taiwanese identity. The fact that voters in central Taiwan were more likely to support the DPP than those in northern Taiwan suggests that the greater the percentage of Hoklo voters, the better the DPP's performance.[7] However, subethnicity is by no means the sole explanation for the DPP's performance; it is even possible the correlation between subethnicity and vote distribution is spurious. In any case, the DPP's vote shares were much lower than the percentage of population that is Hoklo, and the KMT maintained a solid grassroots basis in the rural constituencies, many of which were in central and southern Taiwan. Clearly, extra incentives were needed for the DPP to garner votes by resorting to the voters' Taiwanese consciousness.

The DPP's performance in the 2008 legislative election provides an important clue: it gained 60.84 percent of the southern vote, in sharp contrast with its overall vote share of 38.17 percent. Given that the DPP controlled most of the southern county and city governments and that the size of the legislative districts under the new electoral system was smaller, the most likely cause of the DPP's anomalous performance in southern Taiwan in the 2008 legislative election was the party's control of the grassroots political machines, which helped it identify potential supporters and ply them with social, political, or even material incentives. The question is, could the DPP replicate the southern model and enlarge its territory to include other parts of Taiwan? The following sections provide some reflections on this question.

The Swing Constituencies

Although the DPP performed poorly in the 2008 legislative election, it had won the presidential election in 2004 by obtaining a majority of votes. The gap between these two elections leads to some general questions: Which election signifies the DPP's typical performance in single-member races? Does the type of election affect the party's performance? Is the party's electoral strength increasing or declining in the long run? In sum, what is the trend of the DPP's electoral performance? Because districts vary by elections, I evaluate the DPP's electoral strength at the township level—a level lower than the smallest district—so that a comparison can be made across elections.[8] Before calculating the correlation of the DPP's vote shares in these townships, however, I first show the trend of the DPP's electoral performance.

Figure 3.2 displays the DPP's vote share in different elections from the time it was founded in 1986 through 2008. The picture discloses several important messages. First, despite the ups and downs between elections, the long-term trend was gradually upward. Second, the DPP's performance was associated with electoral systems, as evidenced by the party's lower vote shares in the multimember elections for the National Assembly and the Legislative Yuan held before 2008 than in single-member ones held since then. Third, although the DPP's seat shares in the multimember elections were largely proportional to its vote shares, the results of the single-member elections were much less predictable. For example, in the county magistrate election of 2001, the DPP received 45.27 percent of the vote, taking nine seats and claiming a victory; in 2005, its vote share dropped by just 3.32 percent, but it lost three counties it had previously held, including the largest, Taipei County. In the 1996 presidential election, the DPP lost the election, receiving only 21.13

Figure 3.2 The DPP's Vote Share in Different Elections, 1986–2008

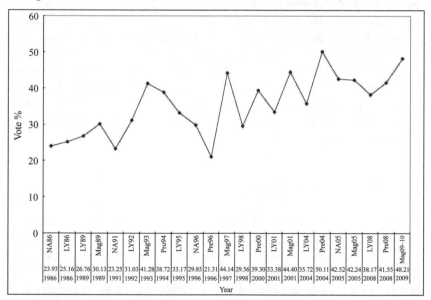

Source: Central Election Commission, http://db.cec.gov.tw/histMain.jsp?voteSel=20080101A2.
Notes: NA = National Assembly; LY = Legislative Yuan; Mag = county magistrate and city mayor; Pro = Taiwan provincial governor; Pre = president. Through 2009, the county magisterial elections data include city mayoral elections held in Taipei and Kaohsiung a year later. The 2009/10 data pool the results of the 2009 magistrate and the five 2010 metropolis elections.

percent of the vote; four years later, its vote share increased to 39.30 percent, and it won the election.

To project the DPP's electoral future, we need to examine whether the change in its vote shares at the aggregate level resulted from the party's performance at the local level. This analysis also allows for identification of the townships in which the DPP's vote share increased or decreased most significantly. The following analysis starts from the presidential election of 2000—the year marking a momentous rise in the DPP's vote share—and examines how much the party's performance varied in different elections. As shown in Table 3.3, the stability of the DPP's electoral strength at the township level was quite remarkable. The correlation coefficients among the nationwide single-member races, including the legislative and presidential elections, are all significant, suggesting that data from the 2000 presidential election can be used to predict what would happen ten years later if the correct parameters are available. The correlation coefficients of the county magistrate elections and the legislative elections held under the old electoral system are weaker but still statistically significant.

It should be noted that a significant correlation coefficient does not show how the elections are correlated. It is possible that the same correlation coefficient results from linear correlations, with different intercepts indicating the opposite direction of vote-share change. It is even possible for a nonlinear relationship to produce a statistically significant linear correlation coefficient. To deal with these problems, the exact relationship among different elections must be specified. The following analysis uses the 2004 presidential election, when the DPP received a high vote share across the island, as the benchmark and examines how that share

Table 3.3 The Correlation Between the DPP's Vote Shares in Different Elections, 2000–2008

	Pre00	Mag01	LY01	Pre04	LY04	Mag05	Pre08	LY08	Mag09/10
Pre00	1.00	0.78	0.74	0.98	0.63	0.85	0.99	0.79	0.87
Mag01		1.00	0.66	0.78	0.54	0.74	0.77	0.66	0.60
LY01			1.00	0.72	0.68	0.58	0.72	0.62	0.65
Pre04				1.00	0.63	0.85	0.99	0.77	0.88
LY04					1.00	0.55	0.63	0.53	0.46
Mag05						1.00	0.86	0.76	0.69
Pre08							1.00	0.79	0.90
LY08								1.00	0.69
Mag09/10									1.00

Source: Central Election Commission, http://db.cec.gov.tw/histMain.jsp?voteSel=20080101A2.
Notes: Pre = president; Mag = county magistrate and city mayor; LY =Legislative Yuan.

differs from the DPP's shares in other single-member elections. Such a comparison can reveal the "swing constituencies"—namely, the townships in which the majority of votes "swung" between the DPP and the KMT across different elections. This leads to the questions: Were the swing constituencies urbanized areas dominated by middle-class voters, or were the DPP's lost votes randomly distributed among different townships, signifying widespread discontent toward the party? And, is it possible that the swing constituencies were predominantly rural, suggesting that the DPP's misfortune may have had less to do with policy voting than with the party's weak grassroots bases?[9]

I first compare the 2004 presidential election and the 2008 *legislative* election, which featured the party's best and worst national electoral performance in the single-member races, respectively.[10] After plotting the DPP's vote shares in these two elections, an interesting pattern emerges (Figure 3.3). Not surprisingly, the vote shares in these two elections share a strong positive correlation. However, the relationship does not appear to be linear. Data points in the middle of the range are mainly below the line representing the equality of the vote shares in these two elections, but the extremely high or low vote shares did not change much between these two elections. The townships in the lower-right part of the graph can thus be seen as the swing constituencies in these two elections—that is, voters

Figure 3.3 The DPP's Township Vote Shares in the 2004 Presidential Election and the 2008 Legislative Election

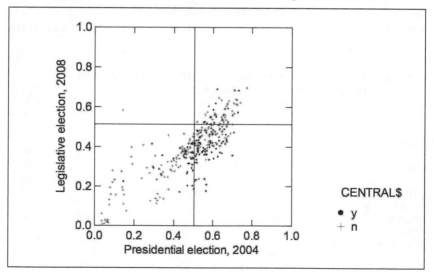

Source: Author's calculations.

in these townships cast a majority of votes for the DPP in the presidential election of 2004 but not in the legislative election of 2008.

To see if the same pattern can be applied to the presidential elections, Figure 3.4 plots the DPP's township vote shares in the 2004 and 2008 presidential elections. The same pattern appears: the farther a data point is from the two extremes, the more likely it is to be below the equality line. Moreover, the pattern comes out in a much clearer way, because a comparison between the two presidential elections controls for many intervening variables. Other comparisons yield similar results, suggesting that the same mechanism is at work.

An important question immediately follows: What commonalities did the swing constituencies share? A clue lies in their location. Measured by the percentage of votes lost by the DPP between the 2004 presidential election and the 2008 legislative election, the top twenty townships in which the DPP's vote share declined were predominantly located in central Taiwan. To be more specific, eight of them were in Changhua County, seven in Yunlin County, and three in Chiayi County. Central Taiwan also included most of the swing constituencies if the 2008 presidential election is used to calculate the twenty townships in which DPP's vote share declined the most: seven of them were in Nantou County, and six were in Taichung County. The counties mentioned in these two

Figure 3.4 The DPP's Township Vote Shares in the 2004 and 2008 Presidential Elections

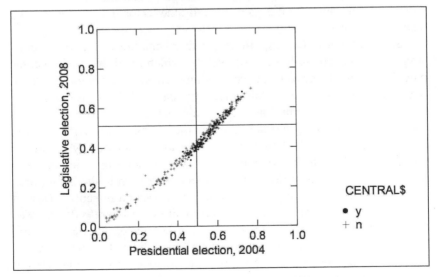

Source: Author's calculations.

comparisons are the same five counties that constitute "central Taiwan" in Table 3.2.[11]

This pattern also applied to the lower administrative level. Among the townships that had given Chen Shui-bian a majority of votes in the 2004 presidential election, sixty-six of them no longer gave majority support to the DPP's candidates in the 2005 county magistrate election, the 2008 legislative election, or the 2008 presidential election. Out of these sixty-six townships, thirty-nine (59.1 percent) were in central Taiwan, even though this area accounts for only 29.46 percent of Taiwan's electorate. The next section considers the nature of these swing constituencies.

The Advantages and Disadvantages of the Governing Party

The preceding analysis shows that the likelihood of a DPP resurgence was strongly affected by its capacity to garner majority support in Taiwan's swing constituencies. It also shows that these constituencies were more likely to be located in central Taiwan than in other areas. The key question is why the electoral results in these constituencies varied more than elsewhere. An intuitive answer lies in the political tendency of the residents of the swing constituencies: the closer the number of voters who support different parties and the greater the percentage of undecided voters, the more likely they are to constitute a swing constituency. Such an explanation can hardly be wrong, because a party's vote share in a constituency is the aggregated outcome of individual choices. But this explanation is insufficient, for it does not specify the factors responsible for the change in a voter's choices.

Several theories can explain the voting behavior of the swing constituencies. One possibility is issue voting, which requires voters to compare the policy platforms of the competing parties. Issue voters tend to be well-informed and independent and, thus, have a higher probability of living in cities than in rural areas. For this reason, issue voting does not look like a convincing explanation for the swing in the DPP's votes, because the degree of urbanization in central Taiwan was by no means the highest in Taiwan. In fact, the top twenty townships in which the DPP lost the most votes from the 2004 presidential election to the 2008 presidential election not only were predominantly located in central Taiwan (seventeen out of twenty) but also were mainly peripheral villages. For less informed voters, vote decision is often influenced by local leaders, who have their own preferences about which candidate to support. A reasonable assumption is that the vote choice of local leaders who are not loyal activists of a particular party is affected by the resources they can receive from a candidate or his/her party. Once their decision is made, local leaders will use their social connections to garner votes for the candidate they intend to support.

This explanation fits central Taiwan well. This area was renowned for the active role played by local factions in elections, the results of which are usually determined by the factional competition for resources.[17] The question is, when would local leaders stand by the nominees of the DPP, which was far less resource-rich than the KMT? Given that the functioning of Taiwan's local government was highly dependent on the financial support of the central government and that most local leaders lived on government-granted resources or privileges, the best time for the DPP to boost its support in the swing constituencies was when it controlled the central government, which occurred only between 2000 and 2008.

Yet, the relationship between the central government and local leaders was more complicated than an exchange of money for votes. Local leaders had little incentive to garner votes for a candidate who was unlikely to win, even if he/she received their support, because an unpromising candidate could not credibly deliver the resources the local leaders demanded. In this situation, a local leader's best strategy was to jump on the bandwagon of the rival candidate, who, by definition, had a much greater chance of winning the election.

If this theory holds, it would be expected that the DPP would win the swing constituencies when votes there were sufficient to make the party win an election that helped it control the government; in return, the swing constituencies would receive particularistic goods from the DPP government. Conversely, this relationship collapsed when the DPP had little chance of winning, even if it obtained the swing votes.

As explained in the appendix, these hypotheses can be derived from a game-theoretic model. To test these hypotheses, the best case is the presidential election—the ultimate competition for political power. The key elements of this test are the DPP's odds of winning and the allocation of financial resources among the local governments. The odds of winning are reflected in opinion polls, and the allocation of financial resources can be approximated by the subsidies delivered by the central government to each county and city. The central government collected a heavy portion of taxes, making it necessary for most local governments to balance their revenues and expenditures through the subsidies provided by the central government. For the same reason, subsidies were also vital for local leaders who depended on government resources to survive.

As for how the provision of subsidies is to be operationalized, some notes should be addressed here. First, the unit of analysis should be county and city rather than a smaller administrative unit, because the county and city governments are legally defined as the recipients of the subsidies provided by the central government. The county and city governments then allocate the subsidies to lower-level administrative units (e.g., townships). Second, according to Taiwan's law on the allocation of financial revenues and expenditures, the central government, in order to reach specific goals of development, is obliged to provide local governments with aid and subsidies. Given that the allocation of subsidies is supposed to consider the demographic profile of a county or city and that local governments have unequal financial capabilities, the contribution of subsidies is signified not so much by how much a local government receives from the central government as by its dependence on these subsidies. Therefore, this chapter uses the following formula to indicate a local government's dependence on subsidies:

$$\frac{\text{Annual Expenses} - \text{Annual Subsidies}}{\text{Annual Revenue}}$$

The value of this formula can be positive or negative; the smaller the value, the greater the dependence of a local government on the subsidies. Third, to control for the demographic variables of the counties and cities, I measure the dependence on subsidies by the rate of change, rather than by the absolute amounts of those subsidies.

In line with the aforementioned operationalization, the subsequent analysis examines how the allocation of subsidies affected the DPP's performance in the presidential elections of 2004 and 2008. For the 2004 presidential election, the dependent variable is the rate of change in the DPP's county and city vote shares from 2000 to 2004, and the independent variable is the rate of change in the administrative units' dependence on subsidies from 2001 to 2004. The analysis of the 2008 presidential election follows the same model, using the rate of change in the vote share of each county and city from 2004 to 2008 as the dependent variable and the rate of change in subsidy dependence from 2005 to 2007 (the DPP lost the presidential election in March 2008) as the independent variable. The change in subsidy dependence should have had a positive effect on the growth of the DPP's presidential vote share when the party's odds of winning were high, but not so when the DPP was unlikely to win the presidential election.

The DPP's odds of winning in the two presidential elections can be gauged by the opinion polls and the commonly recognized important events that swayed the voters' choices. In the 2004 presidential election, the DPP nominated as its candidate Chen Shui-bian, the incumbent president. Chen was only challenged by the Pan-Blue camp, which selected the KMT's Lien Chan as the presidential candidate and the People First Party's James Soong as the vice presidential candidate. It was difficult for Soong to team up with Lien because both had run in the 2000 presidential election, when Soong had garnered 12 percent more of the vote than Lien. According to the opinion polls on the popularity of the two presidential candidates, this presidential election was a neck-and-neck race.[13]

The limited gap in opinion polls between the two presidential candidates made several events critical in the outcome of the election. The election was marked by Chen Shui-bian's attempt to enhance his popularity by initiating a defensive referendum on cross-Strait relations. Designed to consolidate the Taiwanese consciousness of the DPP's potential supporters, attitudes toward this referendum did share a correlation with the choices voters made.[14] Another commonly held belief is that the assassination attempt that took place right before Election Day changed the mind of some voters and helped Chen win the election. To what extent the assassination attempt changed voters' minds is a debatable issue, but it is obvious that this event, even if helpful to the DPP, would not have changed the result of the election had the popularity gap between Chen Shui-bian and Lien Chan been large.

These conditions disappeared after Chen was reelected. A major change was the KMT's new presidential candidate. As a two-time loser in presidential elections, Lien Chan was unlikely to run again. Instead, the loyalists of the Pan-Blue camp bet their future on Ma Ying-jeou, a member of the KMT elite who had defeated Chen Shui-bian in the 1998 Taipei City mayoral election. Unlike Lien Chan, Ma at that time had been a popular politician supported by many non-KMT voters. The DPP's predicament was exacerbated by Chen Shui-bian's plummeting popularity. Chen's second term saw an escalating clash between the pro-independence Pan-Green camp and the anti-independence Pan-Blue camp. In response to the Pan-Blue's criticism that the March 19 assassination attempt had been staged, Chen delivered radical pro-independence signals to consolidate his core supporters.[15] Chen's strategy, however, diminished the DPP's ability to appeal to centrist voters.

Chen's credibility was further tarnished by scandals surrounding his family and staff members. In May 2006, Chen's son-in-law was accused of insider trading, and his wife was charged with obtaining gift coupons from a department store in exchange for settling its ownership problem. A month later, Chen himself was accused of using fake invoices to claim government expenses. Unsurprisingly, the DPP's approval rate dropped as a result of these events.

Another problem that troubled the DPP was the nomination of the presidential candidate—Chen was unable to run again, and other contenders looked equally unpromising. Eventually, Frank Hsieh, the former mayor of Kaohsiung City, won the primary, but only after a highly contentious and divisive intraparty battle. In the opinion polls, Hsieh lagged behind Ma by at least 15 percent, and there was no sign of a narrowing gap.

Given the noticeable disparity between the DPP's electoral fortunes in these two presidential elections, the local leaders should also have made different decisions about whether to help the DPP. Using counties and cities as the unit of analysis, Figure 3.5 displays a scatter plot of the change in subsidy dependence from 2001 to 2004 and the growth of the DPP's presidential vote shares from 2000 to 2004. The figure shows clearly that, during this period, the growth of the DPP's presidential vote share in the island's counties and cities was significantly correlated with the increase in the dependence on subsidies.[16] More specifically, the coefficient of the change in subsidy dependence is –1.79 (standard error is 0.23), indicating a significant impact of this factor on the growth of the DPP's presidential vote shares.[17]

Figure 3.5 Changes in the Dependence on Subsidies versus Changes in the DPP's Presidential Vote Share, 2000–2004

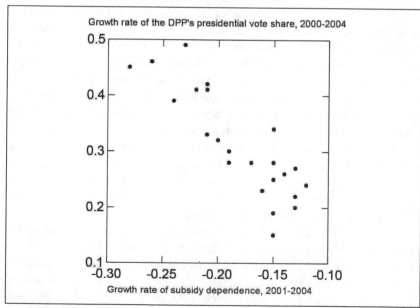

Source: Author's calculations.
Note: Kinmen and Lienchiang are excluded.

After 2004, the dependence on subsidies no longer explains the change in the DPP's presidential performance. Using the same model, the change in subsidy dependence becomes statistically insignificant. It is thus likely that, after Chen Shui-bian was reelected, some local leaders shifted their support to the KMT, despite receiving favorable subsidies from the central government. This possibility also helps explain why the DPP suffered a serious setback in the 2005 county magistrate election, even though its vote share dropped by only 3.32 percent. This magistrate election was held in conjunction with the elections for the county council members and the township governors, where the KMT typically performed much better than the DPP. This "three in one" election helped grassroots leaders at different levels integrate their vote-getting networks and deliver unified support to the KMT's candidates, which explains why a slight decrease in the DPP's vote share deprived the party of a significant number of magistrate seats. Most likely, the DPP's electoral misfortunes in 2008 were caused by a similar process.

The DPP's Electoral Future and Its Impact on Taiwan's Democracy

This chapter has provided evidence that the DPP bumped up against a ceiling on its electoral growth during the Chen Shui-bian era. On the one hand, the unresolved dispute over national identity gave the DPP a firm and stable electoral base as a pro-Taiwan party. On the other hand, the DPP's independence-leaning platform prevented it from winning the support of voters who worried about the consequences of strained cross-Strait relations. President Chen attempted to break through this ceiling using two tactics: emotional appeals to Taiwanese consciousness and distribution of material resources to local leaders. These strategies worked in the 2004 presidential election but quickly declined in effectiveness afterward. The 2008 elections demonstrated the limits on the DPP's electoral base.

The DPP's electoral prospects were further constrained by the new electoral system for the Legislative Yuan elections. Had the 2008 legislative election occurred under the old single, nontransferable vote in multimember districts, the DPP could have retained at least 40 percent of the legislative seats, and the KMT, at most, 55 percent.[18] Under Taiwan's new MMM system, however, a party receiving 49 percent of the vote could end up with no district seats at all if it failed to win majority support in any constituency. Born as an anti-authoritarian and pro-independence party, the DPP had yet to build a solid grassroots foundation even by the end of the Chen era. As a result, very few districts could be seen as safe for the DPP, especially when the party did not hold incumbency advantage at the central government level.

If the electoral bases of Taiwan's political parties do not change much in the near future, they must seriously consider the impact of the current electoral system on Taiwan's democratic prospects. Because the DPP held less than a quarter of the legislative seats between 2008 and 2012, it was deprived of many powers that minority parties have typically held in the Legislative Yuan, including initiating motions for a vote of no confidence in the premier, the impeachment of the president, or the removal of the speaker of the Legislative Yuan. In addition, the DPP just barely had enough votes to reject a proposal to amend the constitution.[19] Yet going back to the street to challenge the legitimacy of the entire system does not look like a feasible alternative—after all, the DPP had been in charge of this system for eight years.

At the end of the Chen Shui-bian era, the KMT had again become the ruling party leading a unified government, and it would ultimately have to be accountable to voters for what the government did. But the drastic decline in the number of effective players in Taiwan's political system made it hard to predict the new government's behavior. The KMT could actually pass any law or execute any policy it wished, unless the party itself were divided.[20] Once the KMT controlled all the key branches of government, decisionmaking became more efficient but not necessarily fairer.

These changes fundamentally transformed the way democracy was practiced in Taiwan, forcing electoral reformers to consider whether the KMT's renewed dominance could be counterbalanced by the improvements made by the new electoral system. To the disappointment of some reformers, the financial resources, including vote buying, devoted to the 2008 legislative campaign were allegedly higher than before, contradicting the reformers' presumption that a single-member district election would reduce the cost of campaigns. This was not a surprise, given the worse odds of winning that the candidates had to face after the total number of seats in the legislature was halved. Nevertheless, this legislative election did bring about some important changes. Because the new system shrank most electoral districts and increased the winning threshold, election campaigns became much more local—and thus less ideological.

The most significant transformation induced by the new electoral system was probably the growing importance of undecided voters without strong partisan attachments to either camp. Especially critical were voters living in the swing constituencies, because they had a good chance of deciding the overall results of elections. As discussed earlier, many of the swing constituencies were located in central Taiwan, where the population was predominantly Hoklo and the influence of local factions was strong. If the DPP's Chen Shui-bian once claimed victory in these constituencies by delivering particularistic goods to their leaders but later lost their support, the same logic applied to the KMT. As indicated by the county executive and city mayor elections in 2009 and 2010, Ma Ying-jeou paid a high price when he attempted to reduce the KMT's reliance on local factions: it was not accidental that the KMT mayoral candidate in the Taichung metropolis almost lost the election, even though he had been leading in the opinion polls. Very likely, this same set of local factors also determined the performances of the KMT and the DPP in the legislative and presidential elections in 2012, and it will probably affect the outcome of the 2016 elections as well.

Appendix: A Game-Theoretic Model of Incumbent Advantage

The following model depicts the strategic interaction between the central government and a local leader in the face of an upcoming presidential election. The central government moves first and has two strategies: to provide the local leader with favored subsidies or not to do so. If the central government does not give the local leader any favored subsidy, the payoff of the central government is v, or its vote share without the help of the local leader, and the payoff of the local leader is 0. If the central government chooses to provide the local leader with favored subsidies, and the local leader decides to help the government acquire votes, the government receives $v + m - c$, and the local leader gets b, where m stands for the government's votes added by the local leader; c, the financial cost of the favored subsidies; and b, the local leader's payoff for helping the government, which increases with v. If the local leader accepts the favored subsidy but does not help the government garner votes, the government's payoff is $v - c$, and the local leader's payoff is 0. (See Figure 3A.1.)

It is obvious that v, m, and c are greater than 0 and m is greater than c. For the local leader, b is greater than 0 if supporting the government can help the ruling party's candidate win the election. If local support cannot help the government win this election, the local leader will antagonize the opposition party's nominee, who is going to win the election, and make b less than 0. The larger v is, the more likely it is that the governing party will win the election; thus, the subgame perfect equilibrium of this game is determined by b in two ways. First, when v is so high that b is greater than 0, the government will give the local leader favored subsidies, and the local leader will help the government; second, when v is small enough to make b less than 0, the local leader will not help the government, and the government will not provide the local leader with

Figure 3A.1 A Game-Theoretic Model of Incumbent Advantage

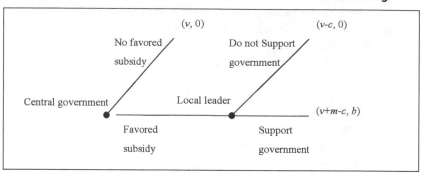

favored subsidies. These results suggest that the greater the strength of the government, the more likely the local leader will support the government.

Notes

1. Although many young democracies adopted mixed-member electoral systems, very few were as disproportional as Taiwan's new system. On the recent change in the electoral system and the peculiarity of the East Asian experiences, see Benjamin Reilly, "Democratization and Electoral Reform in the Asia-Pacific Region," *Comparative Political Studies* 40, no. 11 (2007): 1350–1371.

2. Maurice Duverger, *Political Parties: Their Organization and Activity in the Modern State* (New York: Wiley, 1963), 217.

3. For more detailed results of this election, see the website of the Central Election Commission at http://www.cec.gov.tw. The Commission is responsible for announcing the official outcome of Taiwan's elections.

4. The cube rule states that cubing the ratio of votes received by two major parties yields the ratio of seats they win in a single-member simple plurality election. According to this rule, the ratio of the KMT's seats to the DPP's seats in the 2008 legislative election should have been 2.75, which is much smaller than the actual ratio of 4.69. Another shocking result of this legislative election was that the other small parties received almost no seats at all.

5. According to Duverger, *Political Parties* (217), the single-member simple plurality system favors the two-party system because votes for the minor parties will be strategically shifted to the two largest parties.

6. This was the second district in Chiayi County.

7. The chances of a mainlander living in northern Taiwan are much higher than those of the other subethnic groups. By this logic, residence is an effective predictor of one's vote choice. For a study on the relationship between the DPP's vote share and subethnicity, see Yung-ming Hsu and Chang-ping Lin, "'Nanfang zhengzhi' de zai jianyan: zongtong xuanpiao de fenliang huigui fenxi" [Reexamining "Southern Politics" in Taiwan], *Journal of Electoral Studies* 16, no. 1 (2009): 1–35.

8. To be more exact, the units are the subdivisions of a county or a city. Their official titles are village (*xiang*), town (*zhen*), city (*shi*), and administrative district (*qu*).

9. It is logically possible for the DPP's lost votes to be concentrated in the strongholds of the Pan-Blue camp. However, this probability is small, because the DPP's vote shares were already low in these places. It is also unlikely that the DPP lost its support in its own strongholds. In a single-member district election, the core supporters of a party usually vote for the nominees of this party insofar as they are more preferable to those nominated by the opposition parties.

10. To avoid confusion, the analysis excludes townships in which the DPP did not nominate any candidate in the 2008 legislative election when the comparison involves this election.

11. This chapter follows the definition of *regional division* commonly used by Taiwan's government agencies.

12. For the relationship between Taiwan's local factions and elections, see Ming-tong Chen, "Local Factions and Elections in Taiwan's Democratization," in *Taiwan's Electoral Politics and Democratic Transition: Ruling the Third Wave,* ed. Hung-mao Tien (Armonk, NY: M. E. Sharpe, 1996); Chia-hung Tsai, "Policy-Making, Local Factions, and Candidate Coordination in Single Non-Transferable Voting: A Case Study of Taiwan," *Party Politics* 11, no. 1 (2005): 59–77; and Chung-li Wu, "Local Factions and the Kuomintang in Taiwan's Electoral Politics," *International Relations of the Asia Pacific* 3, no. 1 (2003): 89–111.

13. For example, see http://www.tvbs.com.tw/news/poll_center/index.html?dd=2011/1/12 for the polls conducted at different periods.

14. An empirical study shows that, in the 2004 presidential election, a correlation existed between a voter's attitude toward the referendum and his or her vote choice. See Chia-hung Tsai, Yung-ming Hsu, and Hsiu-tin Huang, "Liangji hua zhengzhi: jieshi Taiwan 2004 zongtong daxuan" [Bi-polarization of politics: Explaining the 2004 presidential election in Taiwan], *Journal of Electoral Studies* 14, no. 1 (2007): 1–31.

15. For an analysis of Chen's cross-Strait remarks and their impact, see Jih-wen Lin, "The Institutional Context of President Chen's Cross-Strait Messages," *Issues and Studies* 44, no. 1 (2008): 1–31.

16. For two reasons, the scatter plot excludes Kinmen and Lienchiang, two sparsely populated offshore islands. First, they were not a part of Taiwan Province and were treated in special ways under the budgetary laws. Second, on these two islands, the number of voters was so small and the DPP's vote shares so low that a tiny change in the number of votes could produce a significant change in vote shares.

17. As expected, out of the nine counties and cities that increased their dependence on subsidies from 2001 to 2004, six were in central Taiwan. Thus, the growth of the DPP's presidential vote share was also enhanced by the DPP's control of the county or city government, but the impact is statistically insignificant.

18. The old legislative election electoral system was a semiproportional system, which gave small parties a much greater chance of winning seats than under the majoritarian systems.

19. In Taiwan, an impeachment of the president must be approved by two-thirds of the legislators, and a proposal to amend the constitution must receive support from at least three-quarters of the legislators.

20. Gridlock usually results from the competition between two equally powerful political forces, whereas the freedom of a decisionmaker is maximized when he or she is the only veto player.

4

Partisanship and Public Opinion

Eric Chen-hua Yu

Taiwan's party system has undergone considerable transformation since the first transfer of power in 2000 from the Kuomintang
(KMT) to the Democratic Progressive Party (DPP). After the KMT lost
power for the first time, political competition in Taiwan took on a new
character. Two new parties—the People First Party (PFP) and the Taiwan
Solidarity Union (TSU)—split from the KMT in late 2000 and won a significant number of seats in the 2001 legislative election. Although the
DPP and KMT remained the two largest parties in the Legislative Yuan
(LY), neither enjoyed a majority. Three minor parties—the PFP, the TSU,
and the New Party (NP), another KMT splinter party established in the
mid-1990s—jointly held more than a quarter of the seats in LY, not only
giving them leverage over the two major parties but also allowing them
to have a real impact on policymaking. The 2000 presidential election
appeared to be a critical election that led to a political realignment, producing a moderate multiparty system at the beginning of the DPP era.[1]

Yet, a true multiparty system never became fully institutionalized.
The transformation from a multiparty configuration into two party
"blocs" in fact took place right after the 2001 election, when the KMT
began close cooperation with the PFP and NP, and the DPP started coor-
dinating its strategies with the TSU. These two party blocs quickly
became known as the Pan-Blue (KMT, PFP, and NP) and Pan-Green
(DPP and TSU) camps. The minor parties faded further in influence after
the 2004 presidential election, in which the KMT-PFP joint presidential
ticket still came up short against President Chen Shui-bian, the DPP
incumbent candidate endorsed by the TSU. In the 2004 legislative and

73

2005 municipal executive elections, support for all three minor parties declined considerably as both the PFP and NP gradually integrated themselves into the KMT and as the TSU failed to distinguish itself from the DPP. The outcome of the 2008 election effectively ended the multiparty configuration, as only the two major parties—the KMT and DPP—obtained seats in the Legislative Yuan.[2]

When commentators and pundits saw this multiparty political competition harden into two distinct, deeply antagonistic party groups, they labeled it "polarization." The implication of that term was that Taiwan's political divisions not only ran deep within the mass public but also were based on clear ideological fault lines.[3] Scholars have long agreed that Taiwan's significant political divisions are mostly unidimensional and aligned based on different conceptions of national identity.[4] The notion of Taiwan's national identity usually consists of two closely related, but distinct, concepts: ethnic consciousness (or ethnic identity) and preferences toward Taiwan's future relations with the People's Republic of China (PRC).[5] The first is usually broken into three categories: "Chinese," "Taiwanese," or "both." The second is also normally classified into three broad categories: "unification with China" (unification), "maintaining the status quo" (status quo), and "Taiwanese independence" (independence). Along the perceivable identity spectrum, the Pan-Blue camp is positioned on one side of the spectrum and stands for a "Chinese" or "both" identity and supports unification or the status quo. The Pan-Green camp, however, is positioned on the other side of the spectrum and stands for Taiwanese identity and Taiwan independence. Because the intracamp party lines were blurred but the intercamp competition was severe after the 2000 election, the multiparty configuration established after 2000 fit well into a framework of two-party competition.

In the Legislative Yuan, voting patterns generally track this convergence toward two major party blocs. As Shiow-duan Hawang shows in Chapter 6 of this volume, the likelihood of Pan-Blue legislators voting against their Pan-Green counterparts increased significantly after Chen Shui-bian took office as president. The rise in legislative cohesiveness, as measured by party unity scores, also indicates that almost all legislators, regardless of their party affiliation, became more likely to vote in agreement with their party during the Chen Shui-bian era than they were before. As party lines drew apart and hardened at the elite level, the mass media also frequently noted how politicians had successfully taken positions toward the ideological extremes to appeal to voters. The referendum issue in the 2004 presidential election, for example, functioned as a useful campaign tool for both parties to consolidate their bases.[6] Although some evidence showed that political parties became more polarized during the Chen Shui-bian era, many scholars and popular media commentators assumed that this elite-level polarization also reflected the polarization of the mass public.

But did Taiwan's electorate really become more polarized? If so, what issues triggered the growth of mass polarization? If not, how can we understand the development of Taiwan's mass partisanship during the Chen era? In addition to national identity, what other issue cleavages might have influenced the underlying structure of Taiwan's party system or contributed to further polarization? The purpose of this chapter is to answer these questions by examining the dynamics of partisanship, national identity, and issue cleavages in the electorate during the DPP era.

Two concepts need to be clarified before proceeding further: divided electorate and polarized electorate. Pundits and scholars routinely conflate these two concepts, leading to analytical confusion. In a two-party system, the term *divided electorate* suggests that it is possible to draw a clear line separating one political grouping from the other. But a divided electorate does not necessarily imply polarization. Two types of relationships between partisan divisions and ideology are possible:[7]

1. *A divided but not polarized electorate:* A clear line divides the general public into two distinct groups differentiated by partisanship. Either ideological overlap between the two parties still exists, or the majority of the general public still holds a moderate, centrist position on the ideological spectrum, despite the divide between the parties themselves. Suppose there exists an ideological scale such that 0 indicates "liberal" and 1.0 indicates "conservative." The upper panel of Figure 4.1 demonstrates this type of relationship between partisanship and ideology.

2. *A divided and polarized electorate:* The electorate is clearly divided along partisan lines. But, in addition, party supporters themselves hold views at the relative extremes of the ideological spectrum, with little ideological overlap between partisans of opposite blocs. The term mass polarization implies a bimodal distribution of opinions. When the electorate is highly polarized, the ideological middle ground vanishes, and voters tend to cluster at the extremes, rather than hold views toward the center. The lower panel of Figure 4.1 illustrates this divided and polarized pattern.

The distinction between division and polarization is clear: The former concept suggests a close alignment between partisanship and ideology. Divisions are caused by one (or multiple) cutoff line(s) on the ideological spectrum and have nothing to do with the distribution of preferences. Polarization, by contrast, simply refers to the formation of

Figure 4.1 Two Distributions of Mass Opinion

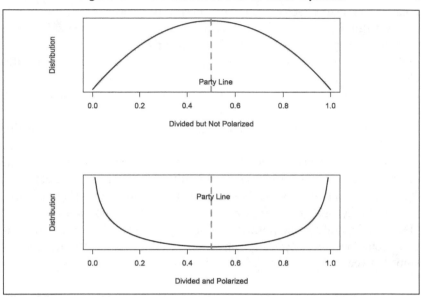

Source: Drawn by the author.

bimodal distributions of ideological preferences, as well as the disappearance of ideologically moderate views.

The rest of this chapter uses this distinction between partisan division and partisan polarization to take a new look at longitudinal survey data. The next section examines the evolution of mass partisanship and national identity in Taiwan in order to evaluate whether Taiwan's electorate became significantly more polarized during the Chen Shui-bian era. Following that, I look at the relationship between partisanship and national identity to explore how and in what ways Taiwan's electorate was divided during this period. The next section looks at other issues not related to national identity and considers whether any of these issues was relevant to Taiwan's partisan alignments. The chapter concludes with a discussion of some avenues for future research.

The Evolution of Mass Partisanship and National Identity

The major proposition behind the claim that mass public opinion in Taiwan was polarized during the Chen Shui-bian era was that the ideological middle ground had disappeared. If the electorate had been polarized, then voters would have moved toward the extremes of the ideological spectrum, fleeing the center, and the political parties would have followed suit. However, as this section shows, this is not an accurate description of trends in public opinion during the Chen Shui-bian era.

Figure 4.2 illustrates three trends (smoothed using nonparametric regression) of mass "partisanship" between 2000 and 2008 — that is, the proportion of survey respondents who expressed support for the Pan Blue or Pan-Green camp or who identified as independents. Assume for a moment that Taiwan's configuration of political parties captured the full range of public opinion on the national identity question. If polarization had been occurring during this period, then support for the Pan-Blue and Pan-Green camps should have increased, while the proportion of independent voters should have decreased. Yet the trends shown in Figure 4.2 are quite different: There was no divergence between partisan and independent respondents. The share of independents, though fluctuating somewhat, remained relatively steady for the 2000–2008 period. On average, 41 percent of respondents self-identified as independent voters during that time. Although overall support for the Pan-Blue camp appeared to increase, it did so at the expense of support for the Pan-Greens, not independents. In fact, the proportion of independent voters appears to have increased toward the end of Chen Shui-bian's second term, rising to a record 46 percent in 2007.

Figure 4.2 Trends in Mass Partisanship in Taiwan, 2000–2008

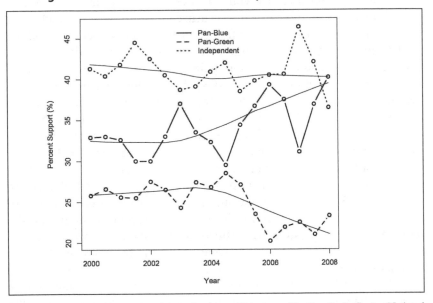

Source: Trends in Core Political Attitudes Among Taiwanese, Election Study Center, National Chengchi University, Taiwan.

In short, the relatively large and steady proportion of independent voters suggests that there was no partisan polarization in the DPP era at the level of mass public opinion. The middle ground of the electorate, represented by independent voters, never disappeared during this period. In addition, the bases of the two opposing party camps did not change in any dramatic way after 2000, with support for the Pan-Blue and Pan-Green blocs fluctuating around 35 percent and 25 percent, respectively, of the electorate.

It is worth noting that the absence of polarization along the *partisan* spectrum does not necessarily indicate the absence of polarization along *identity* lines. Although self-reported national identity is often taken as a proxy for partisanship itself in Taiwanese public opinion research, it is logically possible that respondents retained only weak or nonexistent partisan attachments at the same time that their national identity attachments were becoming increasingly fixed and mutually exclusive. That is, there could still be polarization along the national identity spectrum, even in the absence of partisan polarization.

If public opinion were not polarized along partisan lines during this period, then the next step is to examine the trends in the two most widely used measures of national identity to see whether polarization increased on this dimension. First, I look at Taiwanese attitudes toward ethnic consciousness and ethnic identity, which are typically measured by the following survey question: "Do you consider yourself to be only Chinese, only Taiwanese, or both?" This measure posits "Chinese" and "Taiwanese" identities as the two extremes of the identity spectrum and the dual identity ("both") as the moderate option. If mass attitudes about national identity had become more polarized during the Chen Shui-bian era, then there should be a relatively symmetric increase in respondents identifying with either the exclusive Taiwanese or Chinese categories and a decrease in those identifying as both Taiwanese and Chinese. Yet the results shown in Figure 4.3 indicate an asymmetric pattern: a steady increase in those identifying only as Taiwanese and a steady decline in those identifying only as Chinese. The share of respondents identifying as both, in fact, never declined substantially during this period, fluctuating around the 45 percent mark through the entire Chen Shui-bian era. In sum, mass attitudes in Taiwan did not become more polarized on the national identity question but instead shifted steadily away from one extreme—an exclusively Chinese identity—to the other—an exclusively Taiwanese one.

The second measure of national identity can also be thought of as a policy question: "In the future, should Taiwan seek unification with the People's Republic of China, de jure independence, or maintenance of the

Figure 4.3　Trends in National Identity in Taiwan, 2000–2008

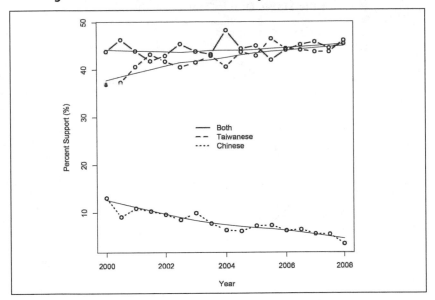

Source: Trends in Core Political Attitudes Among Taiwanese, Election Study Center, National Chengchi University, Taiwan.

status quo?" This question has been the single most salient political issue in Taiwanese politics ever since the pro-independence Chen Shui-bian took office in 2000. The independence-versus-unification question is not only the most fundamental domestic political issue, it also has grave consequences for the security balance in the Taiwan Strait, because the PRC has vowed to use military force against Taiwan if it declares formal independence.[8]

The most commonly used measure to understand Taiwanese public opinion on the unification-independence issue is a 6-point scale.[9] To simplify presentation, I use a measure that condenses the scale into three categories: "lean independence," "maintain the status quo," and "lean unification." Figure 4.4 shows the trends in these independence-unification preferences between 2000 and 2008.

Again, if public opinion had been diverging on the unification-independence issue during the Chen Shui-bian era, there should be an increase in preferences for both lean independence and lean unification and a decline in preferences for maintaining the status quo. Yet Figure 4.4 shows a decline in support for unification (i.e., lean unification) but gradual increases in support for both independence and the status quo (i.e., lean independence and maintain status quo). It is clear that voters in

Figure 4.4 Support for Independence, Unification, or the Status Quo in Taiwan, 2000–2008

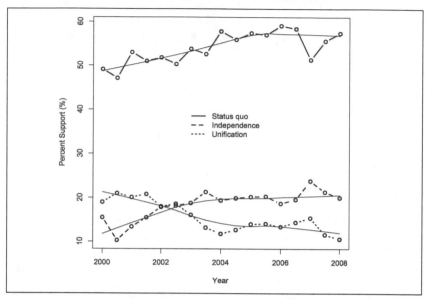

Source: Trends in Core Political Attitudes Among Taiwanese, Election Study Center, National Chengchi University, Taiwan.

Taiwan no longer considered unification with China to be the default outcome for future cross-Strait relations, as they had in previous generations. For an increasing number of Taiwanese during this period, becoming a formally independent country was a viable and desirable option for the future.

Yet Figure 4.4 also shows that the centrist, moderate option—maintaining the status quo—remained the choice of a majority of Taiwanese. Again, because the "middle ground" of public opinion never vanished, we cannot conclude that the general public became more polarized along the unification-independence spectrum. Nevertheless, by the end of the Chen Shui-bian era, support for unification had gradually declined to less than 15 percent. At least in the short term, unification ceased to be a viable option for most Taiwanese. In fact, even the PRC government in Beijing did not pursue this option but simply tried to prevent Taiwan from moving toward de jure independence during this period.[10] Similar to trends in national identity, the entire distribution of mass preferences on the unification-independence issue appears to have shifted away from one extreme (unification) and toward the other (independence).

Party Sorting Along National Identity Lines

The questions about political polarization in Taiwan echo those in the United States, where there has been a lively debate about the nature and causes of increasing partisan polarization in Congress and elsewhere in Washington, DC. One counterintuitive argument made by Morris Fiorina and his colleagues is that elite level political polarization has not been driven by a movement toward the political extremes at the mass level, but instead by partisan sorting—that is, wide-scale party switching by individuals that produces a tighter fit between political ideology and party affiliation.[11] In other words, party supporters have re-sorted themselves more consistently along ideological lines, but the distribution of policy preferences in the electorate as a whole has not changed a great deal.

Is *party sorting,* rather than *polarization,* a more accurate label for the changes in Taiwanese politics during the Chen Shui-bian era? Chen's election initiated a period of increasingly sharp differentiation between the two party camps. As President Chen continued to win support from almost all voters who self-identified exclusively as Taiwanese and those who favored Taiwanese independence, and repelled almost all who identified as Chinese and favored unification, the positions of the DPP and KMT became much more clearly defined than before the 2000 election.

Figure 4.5 shows the trends in national identity, broken out by partisan identification between 2000 and 2008. The relationship between partisanship and national identity gradually changed over this period in two key ways. First, the proportion of respondents who self-identified exclusively as Chinese decreased among partisans of not only the Pan-Green but also the Pan-Blue camp. By 2008, less than 10 percent of Pan-Blue supporters considered themselves to be only Chinese, suggesting that Chinese identity ceased to play a meaningful role in determining support for the Pan-Blue camp.

Second, during this period, the proportion of Pan-Blue supporters who held a dual Taiwanese-Chinese (i.e., "both") identity increased from 60 to 70 percent, while the proportion that held an exclusively Taiwanese identity decreased slightly from 25 to 22 percent. By contrast, the proportion of Pan-Green supporters who held an exclusively Taiwanese identity increased from 52 percent in 2000 to 78 percent in 2008, whereas the proportion holding a dual identity declined from 43 to 23 percent. These trends suggest an increasingly strong relationship between partisanship and national identity during the Chen Shui-bian era. As two-thirds of Pan-Blue supporters held a dual national identity and three-fourths of Pan-Green supporters held an exclusively Taiwanese identity, by 2008,

Figure 4.5 Trends in National Identity by Partisan Camp, 2000–2008

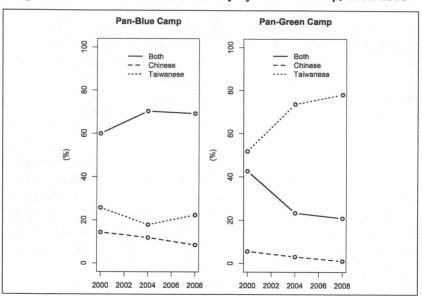

Source: 2000, 2004, and 2008 Pre-Presidential Election Telephone Survey Data, Election Study Center, National Chengchi University, Taiwan.

the supporters of the two party camps appeared quite different from each other on this dimension.

Figure 4.6 suggests that a similar sorting phenomenon occurred in the relationship between partisanship and attitudes toward the unification-independence issue. Specifically, the proportion of Pan-Green supporters who preferred Taiwanese independence increased from 38 percent in 2000 to 50 percent in 2008. By contrast, the proportion of Pan-Blue supporters who preferred independence, already quite low, declined from 9 to 5 percent during that same period. In addition, the proportion of Pan-Green supporters who preferred the status quo decreased from 55 to 44 percent. Although the proportion of Pan-Blue supporters who preferred the status quo also declined from 80 to 73 percent, this decline might have been due to an increase in the proportion of Pan-Blue supporters who preferred unification with the PRC from 11 to 22 percent. It is possible that some of the Pan-Blue supporters who used to favor the status quo might have changed their views to support unification with mainland China during this period. The exact reasons for this change, however, are beyond the scope of this study.

In short, as more than 90 percent of Pan-Blue supporters favored unification with the PRC or the status quo by 2008, the Pan-Blue camp

Figure 4.6 Support for Independence, Unification, or the Status Quo by Partisan Camp, 2000–2008

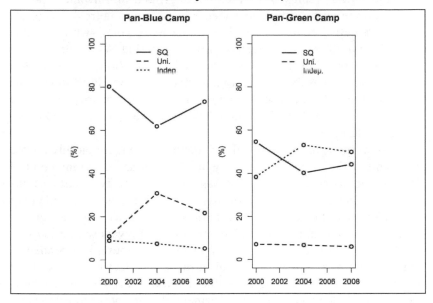

Source: 2000, 2004, and 2008 Pre-Presidential Election Telephone Survey Data, Election Study Center, National Chengchi University, Taiwan.
Notes: SQ = status quo; Uni. = unification; Indep. = ndependence.

clearly became a more cohesive anti-independence bloc. On the other hand, despite an increase within the Pan-Green camp over this period, support for Taiwanese independence remained far from universal among Pan-Green partisans. Even at the end of the Chen Shui-bian era, only a slim majority of Pan-Green supporters favored outright independence then or in the future, and support for the status quo remained strong. Contrary to the conventional wisdom that the Pan-Green camp represented a unified bloc of pro-independence partisans, its supporters were in fact split almost equally into pro-independence and anti-independence (or at least "not pro-independence") groups.

An important caveat to this conclusion is that the meaning of the status quo option is ambiguous, and respondents with opposite partisan leanings probably would offer different definitions of it. For example, one person might argue that the status quo means, "Taiwan is already a sovereign nation," while another might view the status quo as "a divided Chinese nation." Regardless of the meaning, however, the KMT appeared to have more success labeling itself as a status quo party during the Chen Shui-bian era, and it used the term to consolidate and convert opposition to the pro-independence movement into electoral support. If we think of the status quo as representing the middle ground in Taiwanese public opinion on the unification-independence issue, then Figure 4.6 suggests that the Pan-Blue camp managed to attract more voters who held this view than did the Pan-Green camp during this period. As Shelley Rigger argues in Chapter 2 of this volume, the KMT's ability to win over moderate voters, as well as the failure of the DPP to reposition itself toward the middle of the political spectrum on this issue, was probably one of the key determinants of Ma Ying-jeou's landslide victory in the 2008 presidential election.

In short, partisanship and national identity were more closely related at the end of the Chen era than they had been at any previous point in Taiwan's democratic history. The supporters of the two party camps appeared to have sorted themselves based on their attitudes toward either ethnic identity or the independence-unification issue, with the vast majority of Pan-Green supporters self-identifying as Taiwanese and the vast majority of Pan-Blue supporters opposing Taiwanese independence. Although the party-sorting mechanism made the electoral bases of the two camps appear increasingly distinct from one another, these differences did not reflect a significant movement of moderates toward the ideological extremes. Although mass public opinion in Taiwan's electorate at the end of the Chen Shui-bian era was divided along partisan lines, it was not significantly more politically polarized.

Partisanship and Policy Preferences

A separate but equally compelling question is whether this partisan sorting along national identity lines also contributed to greater differentiation between the two camps on other policy issues. To answer this question, this section considers three issues that were the subject of extensive debate in Taiwan during the Chen Shui-bian era: the level and nature of cross-Strait economic exchanges, the relative importance of environmental protection versus economic development, and the level of social welfare. The first issue is unavoidably linked to the independence-unification issue and has been controversial since at least 1996, when President Lee Teng-hui introduced his "No haste, be patient" policy regulating economic relations between the two sides of the Taiwan Strait. The second and third issues tap into potentially crosscutting "new politics" and "social justice" issues, which first drew significant public attention in the late 1980s and the early 1990s.[12]

Drawing from different surveys over time, I construct three dichotomous variables to measure public preferences toward these three issues — specifically, whether to decrease or increase economic exchanges with mainland China, whether to stress environmental protection or economic development, and whether to increase or decrease social welfare provided by the government. The actual wordings of the survey questions are summarized in the appendix to this chapter.[13]

Figure 4.7 shows changes from 2003 to 2007 in the attitudes of Pan-Blue supporters, Pan-Green supporters, independent voters, and all respondents on the issue of cross-Strait economic exchanges. The proportion of Pan-Blue supporters who supported an increase in economic exchanges between Taiwan and mainland China grew dramatically, from around 55 percent in 2003 to more than 90 percent in 2007. Although this dramatic rise might be, in part, a product of the differences of question wordings, the trend is strong enough to suggest that the partisan re-sorting occurring over this period coincided with a growing consensus among Pan-Blue supporters in favor of increasing economic exchanges with the PRC.[14]

**Figure 4.7 Support for Increasing Cross-Strait
Economic Exchanges by Partisan Camp, 2003–2007**

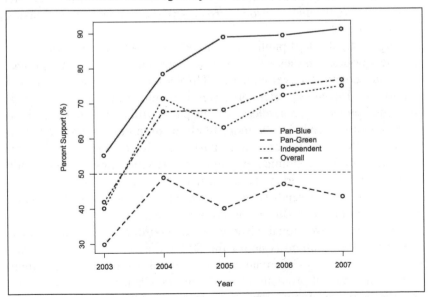

Sources: 2003 Taiwan's Election and Democratization Studies; 2004 and 2005 Survey Project of Cross-Strait Relations and National Security, Duke University; 2006 and 2007 Survey Project of Policy Preference and Political Behavior, Election Study Center, National Chengchi University.

By contrast, the Pan-Green camp also exhibited a split on this issue. Support for increasing cross-Strait economic exchanges among Pan-Green supporters fluctuated between 40 and 50 percent over this period. In 2007, 44 percent of Pan-Green supporters favored an increase in exchanges, with 56 percent opposed. Indeed, Pan-Green supporters were consistently more likely to oppose increasing exchanges than their Pan-Blue counterparts. At no point did more than half of Pan-Green partisans support increasing exchanges. Nevertheless, neither was there a convergence of opinion toward opposing economic exchanges across the Strait. As Figure 4.7 shows, Pan-Green supporters maintained divergent views on this aspect of cross-Strait relations. It is likely that party sorting did not lead to convergence of opinion here because Chen Shui-bian and the Pan-Green camp never articulated a consistent position on this issue.

Because the economic relationship with the PRC was the primary campaign issue in the 2008 presidential election, it is worth noting that, at least since 2004, the majority of self-identified independents favored increasing cross-Strait economic exchanges. When Ma Ying-jeou emphasized the importance of increasing cross-Strait economic ties and linked this issue with Taiwan's economic future in the global era, he articulated a policy position that appealed not only to Pan-Blue supporters but also to the vast majority of independent voters. Ma's success in priming this issue was largely due to broad, cross-partisan support for increasing cross-Strait exchanges.

Figure 4.8 displays public opinion between 2000 and 2007 on one of the "new politics" issues—the trade-off between environmental protection and economic development.[15] Throughout this period, a sizable majority of Taiwanese voters preferred economic development to environmental protection, regardless of their party affiliations. However, Pan-Blue supporters tended to be more likely to support economic development than their Pan-Green counterparts, and this difference grew over time. Support for economic development over environmental protection among Pan-Blue supporters increased from 44 percent in 2000 to 72 percent in 2007. These trends suggest that prodevelopment voters gradually moved toward the Pan-Blue camp during this era.

Although conventional wisdom is that environmental protection has been a long-term salient issue for the DPP,[16] the data actually show that the majority of Pan-Green supporters favored economic development over environmental protection throughout the Chen Shui-bian era. Support for the prodevelopment position among Pan-Green supporters fluctuated mostly in the range of 50 to 60 percent over this period, starting from 49 percent in 2000. This finding reflects the fact that the DPP government tended, in practice, to favor developmental policies at the

Figure 4.8 Support for Economic Development over Environmental Protection by Partisan Camp, 2000–2007

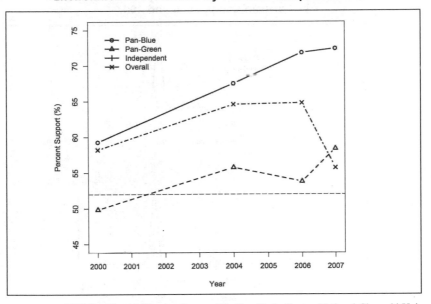

Sources: 2000 Presidential Election Survey, Election Study Center, National Chengchi University; 2004 Taiwan's Election and Democratization Studies; 2006 and 2007 Survey Project of Policy Preference and Political Behavior, Election Study Center, National Chengchi University.

expense of environmental protection.[17] In short, Pan-Blue supporters developed a greater degree of consensus in favor of economic development than did their Pan-Green counterparts.

The third issue concerns the level of government social services. Because only two waves of survey data are available, it is not possible to construct any longitudinal measures to show long-term trends in public opinion on this issue. Instead, I use distributions of the public opinion measures to highlight the differences between the two party camps in Chen Shui-bian's second term. Because the form of response for this question is dichotomous, the respondents were forced to make a choice between the two positions—0 stands for less social welfare service, and 1 stands for more social welfare service. I then transformed the opinion measures into beta distributions in the 0 to 1 probability range.

Figure 4.9 displays the beta density functions of the two party camp supporters and of independent voters on the social welfare issue.[18] The x-axis indicates the probability (range from 0 to 1) of choosing less welfare service. The upper panel shows the data collected in 2006, while the lower panel presents the data for 2007.

Figure 4.9 Probability Densities of Support for Government vs. Individual Responsibility for Social Welfare by Partisan Camp, 2006 and 2007

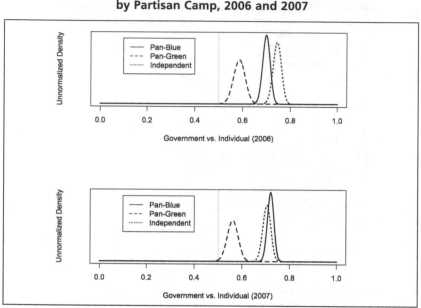

Source: 2006 and 2007 Survey Project of Policy Preference and Political Behavior.

The idea of a larger welfare state did not enjoy much support among either Pan-Blue or Pan-Green supporters. On average, 71 percent of Pan-Blue and 57 percent of Pan-Green supporters were in favor of less welfare spending during this two-year period. Due to the lack of measures that could be used to highlight any long-term dynamic change, it is not possible to evaluate whether any kind of partisan sorting took place on this issue over time. Yet it appears that Pan-Blue supporters, once again, were more in agreement than Pan-Green supporters on the social welfare issue: if 0.5 is the position with the least intraparty consensus, then the distribution of Pan-Blue supporters is significantly farther from this line than that of the Pan-Green supporters in each panel.

It is interesting to note that independent voters were also likely to reject the idea of higher taxation and a larger welfare state: around 73 percent of them believed that individuals should take care of themselves. Because the distribution of independents and Pan-Blue supporters overlaps in both panels, the preferences of independent voters appear to be more closely aligned with the Pan-Blue than the Pan-Green camp on the social welfare issue.

The empirical evidence shown in this section suggests that the Pan-Blue camp was, by the end of the Chen Shui-bian era, more homogeneous than the Pan-Green camp with respect to their supporters' preferences toward the issues of cross-Strait economic exchanges, environmental protection, and social welfare. In addition, the trends in attitudes toward cross-Strait economic exchanges and environmental protection are consistent with party sorting among Pan-Blue supporters: their partisanship and policy preferences came into closer alignment over time. By contrast, Pan-Green supporters showed no convergence in attitudes on any of the three issue cleavages examined here. For Pan-Green supporters, the linkage between their party label and their policy preferences on these issues, if any, was relatively weak.

Conclusions and Future Research

Was Taiwanese politics deeply polarized along the fault line of national identity during the Chen Shui-bian era, as many scholars and pundits claimed? In terms of mass public opinion, the answer is no. The middle ground of public attitudes on national identity and cross-Strait policy never vanished; a considerable proportion of the general public still held moderate, centrist positions when Chen Shui-bian left office.

Yet, partisanship and national identity were more closely related at the end of the Chen Shui-bian era than they had been in the past. Supporters of the two party camps became more consistent in their national identity and in their views about the preferred direction to take cross-Strait relations. By 2008, most Pan-Green supporters identified solely as Taiwanese, whereas most Pan-Blue supporters opposed Taiwanese independence. The most plausible explanation for these trends is mass-level sorting: many individual voters switched political camps to bring their existing preferences into greater alignment with their preferred political party. However, there is no evidence to suggest that moderate, independent voters declined in number or moved toward the political extremes. Taiwan's electorate became more divided along partisan lines during this period but not more polarized along ideological ones.

The partisanship and policy preferences of Pan-Blue supporters also converged on other issue dimensions beyond national identity questions, including the level of cross-Strait economic exchanges, the relative importance of economic development versus environmental protection, and the preferred level of social welfare. The findings discussed in this chapter consistently demonstrate that, by the end of the Chen era,

Pan-Blue partisans shared broad agreement on all of these issues. By contrast, there is little evidence of a similar convergence of partisanship and preferences within the Pan-Green camp. The views of Pan-Green supporters were close to evenly split on increasing cross-Strait economic exchanges, favoring economic development over environmental protection, and seeking a larger welfare state. It seems plausible that this lack of agreement within the DPP's base—in particular, about cross-Strait policy—played a role in the party's disastrous performance in the 2008 legislative and presidential elections. When Ma Ying-jeou pursued closer economic ties to the PRC, the Pan-Green camp faced the prospect of a shrinking electoral base, because a significant share of Pan-Green supporters actually favored aspects of President Ma's cross-Strait policies. The key for a DPP political recovery appeared to be recognizing and responding to these trends in public opinion, and then adjusting the party's approach toward cross-Strait relations in order to broaden its appeal.

The findings of this study also raise some possible avenues for future research on the development of mass partisanship in Taiwan. First, if political polarization has not occurred at the mass level, why and to what extent has it apparently emerged at the elite level? Pundits and commentators frequently cite anecdotal stories, such as severe verbal and physical confrontations among lawmakers in the Legislative Yuan, to substantiate the claim that Taiwanese elites are highly polarized. Yet there are few empirical studies that attempt to systematically measure the extent to which polarization exists at the elite level or to document changes in elite polarization over time. The degree of elite responsiveness to mass publics has long been an important subject for students of democratic theory. If polarization is only occurring among political elites, but not in the population at large, then the implication is that Taiwan's political system is becoming less responsive and less accountable to the citizenry—a worrying development if true.

Second, although this study has emphasized that party sorting is the mechanism producing greater partisan divisions in the absence of greater polarization of public opinion, it has not addressed a number of relevant questions. For instance, why did party sorting at the mass level occur in the first place? Why was there a difference between Pan-Blue and Pan-Green partisans in the degree of convergence of opinion on key policy issues? How does the mechanism of party sorting operate at the individual level, and what are its possible implications for Taiwan's future party system? In particular, has a divided electorate helped consolidate partisan competition and institutionalize the party system, or has causality run in the other direction? Perhaps the institutionalization of the party system drove voters to re-sort into two more homogeneous party camps. To answer these questions, more investigation is needed into the interaction between political elites and the electorate.

Third, it is striking to remember that in the 1990s, distributional justice issues appeared at one point to be rising in salience enough to crosscut the traditional divide between the KMT and DPP over national identity questions.[19] Yet social welfare and related policy questions never emerged to divide the two major political camps; instead, national identity has remained the most significant cleavage in Taiwanese politics.[20] The existence of crosscutting cleavages helps produce multiple and evershifting majorities in the electorate and, thus, benefits the development of stable democracy.[21] If partisan sorting continues, it is possible that all significant new issues will become subsumed within the existing ideological divides of the party system, and elections will not produce these "evershifting majorities" but will instead result in contests more akin to zerosum games. Thus, the relationship between the party-sorting mechanism and the development of new issue cleavages in Taiwan also deserves additional scholarly attention.

Appendix: Questions About Issue Cleavages

Cross-Strait Economic Exchanges

2003 Taiwan's Election and Democratization Studies (TEDS)
> Some people think, "Taiwan should develop closer economic relations with Mainland China." Other people think, "Taiwan should try to reduce its economic reliance on Mainland China." Which one do you agree with more?

2004 and 2005 Survey Project of Cross-Strait Relations and National Security, Duke University. (Principal Investigator: Emerson M. S. Niou)
> Some people think, "Taiwan should develop closer economic and trade relations with mainland China in order to facilitate economic development in Taiwan." Other people think, "Taiwan should reduce its economic and trade relations with mainland China in order to prevent damage to Taiwan's national security." Which one do you agree with more?

2006 and 2007 Survey Project of Policy Preference and Political Behavior, Election Study Center, National Chengchi University. (Principal Investigator: Chia-hung Tsai)
> Should we decrease or increase trade with mainland China?

Importance of Environmental Protection and Economic Development

2000 Presidential Election Survey, Election Study Center, National Chengchi University. 2004 Taiwan's Election and Democratization Studies (TEDS)

Regarding the question of economic development versus environmental protection, some people in society emphasize environmental protection, while others emphasize economic development. On this card, the position that emphasizes environmental protection is at 0 on a scale from 0 to 10, and the position that emphasizes economic development is at 10. About where on this scale does your own view lie?

2006 and 2007 Survey Project of Policy Preference and Political Behavior, Election Study Center, National Chengchi University. (Principal Investigator: Chia-hung Tsai)

Should we stress environmental protection, or should we stress economic development?

Social Welfare Service

2006 and 2007 Survey Project of Policy Preference and Political Behavior, Election Study Center, National Chengchi University. (Principal Investigator: Chia-hung Tsai)

Should the government be allowed to collect more tax in order to provide more social welfare service, or should the government collect less tax and let an individual take care of him/herself?

Notes

1. Huo-yan Shyu, "Partisan Territorial Lines Redrawn in Taiwan: A Comparison of the Electoral Bases of the DPP, KMT, and PFP" [in Chinese], *Soochow Journal of Political Science* 14 (March 2003): 83–134.

2. Most NP and PFP candidates ran under the KMT banner in the 2008 legislative election. In contrast, the TSU did not coordinate well with the DPP and ended up winning no seats. In addition to the 109 partisan members, four legislative members were elected as independents. However, they coordinated and worked with the KMT party caucus on most issues.

3. Chia-hung Tsai, Yung-ming Hsu, and Hsiu-tin Huang, "Bi-Polarizing the Politics: Explaining the 2004 Presidential Election in Taiwan" [in Chinese], *Journal of Electoral Studies* 14, no. 1 (2007): 1–31.

4. Andy G. Chang and T. Y. Wang, "Taiwanese or Chinese? Independence or Unification? An Analysis of Generational Differences in Taiwan," *Journal of Asian and African Studies* 40, no. 1–2 (2005): 29–49; Szu-yin Ho and I-chou Liu, "The Tai-

wanese/Chinese Identity of the Taiwan People in the 1990s," *American Asian Review* 20, no. 2 (2002): 29–74; John Fuh-sheng Hsieh, "Ethnicity, National Identity, and Domestic Politics in Taiwan," *Journal of Asian and African Studies* 40, no. 1–2 (2005): 13–28; Jih-wen Lin, "The Politics of Reform in Japan and Taiwan," *Journal of Democracy* 17, no. 2 (2005): 118–131; Huo-yan Shyu, "National Identity and Partisan Vote-Choices in Taiwan: Evidence from Survey Data Between 1991 and 1993" [in Chinese], *Taiwanese Political Science Review* 1 (1996): 85–128; Nai-teh Wu, "Identity Conflicts and Political Trust" [in Chinese], *Taiwanese Sociology* 4 (December 2002). 73–118.

5. Chi Huang, "Dimensions of Taiwanese/Chinese Identity and National Identity in Taiwan: A Latent Class Analysis," *Journal of Asian and African Studies* 40, no. 1–2 (2005): 51–70; Shelley Rigger, *Taiwan's Rising Rationalism: Generations, Politics, and "Taiwanese Nationalism"* (Washington, DC: East-West Center, 2006).

6. Yung-ming Hsu, Chia-hung Tsai, and Hsiu-tin Huang, "Referendum: New Motivation to Forge Taiwan's National Identity" [in Chinese], *Taiwan Democracy Quarterly* 2, no. 1 (2005): 51–74; Tsai, Hsu, and Huang, "Bi-Polarizing the Politics."

7. The conception used here is borrowed from the literature on polarization in American politics. Fiorina and his colleagues argued that polarization and divisions are not the same thing; one should separate them conceptually before studying political polarization. See Morris P. Fiorina, Samuel J. Abrams, and Jeremy C. Pope, *Culture War? The Myth of a Polarized America* (New York: Longman, 2006); Morris Fiorina and Matthew Levendusky, "Disconnected: The Political Class Versus the People," in *Red and Blue Nation? Characteristics and Causes of America's Polarized Politics*, ed. Pietro Nivola and David Brady (Stanford, CA: Brookings/Hoover Institution Press, 2007).

8. Brett Benson and Emerson M. S. Niou, "Public Opinion, Foreign Policy, and the Security Balance in the Taiwan Strait," *Security Studies* 14, no. 2 (2005): 1–16.

9. The coding scheme is as follows: (1) seeking (declaring) independence as soon as possible, (2) maintaining the status quo now and seeking (declaring) independence later, (3) maintaining the status quo indefinitely, (4) maintaining the status quo now and deciding what to do later, (5) maintaining the status quo now and seeking unification later, and (6) seeking unification with China as soon as possible. A recent methodological debate has been about whether it is appropriate to use a single-dimensional scale to measure public preferences on this issue. Some scholars have proposed conditional preferences or a two-dimensional scale to measure Taiwanese public opinion toward the independence-unification issue. This debate is beyond the scope of this chapter; for more details, please see Nai-teh Wu and Shiau-chi Shen, "Ethnic and Civic Nationalism: Two Roads to the Formation of a Taiwanese Nation" (paper presented at the Conference on US and Cross-Strait Relations Since the Taiwan Election, University of Illinois at Urbana-Champaign, October 6–7, 2002); and John Fuh-sheng Hsieh and Emerson M. S. Niou, "Measuring Taiwanese Public Opinion on the Taiwan Independence Issue: A Methodological Note," *China Quarterly* 18, no. 1 (2005): 158–168.

10. Rigger, *Taiwan's Rising Rationalism*.

11. Fiorina, Abrams, and Pope, *Culture War?*; Fiorina and Levendusky, "Disconnected."

12. Shing-yuan Sheng, "Issues, Political Cleavages, and Party Competition in Taiwan: From the Angles of the Elites and the Public" (paper presented at the Annual Meeting of the American Political Science Association, Chicago, IL, August 30–September 2, 2007).

13. I use various surveys to construct two variables that measure attitudes toward the cross-Strait economic exchanges and environmental protection issues over time.

Different question wordings and measurement scales may contribute to some level of incompatibility of the time series.

14. The wording of the 2003 question linked economic reliance on China as a possible scenario for increasing political ties with mainland China. The 2004/05 question emphasized Taiwan's national security as the primary reason for not increasing cross-Strait economic ties. The 2006/07 question did not include any preconditions or possible consequential scenarios; it asked the respondents specifically about cross-Strait trade ties rather than about the broader economic relationship between the two sides of the Strait.

15. The 2000/04 question asked respondents to position themselves on an 11-point scale, where 0 indicates environmental protection and 10 indicates economic development. I transformed the data into a dichotomous measure, in which the respondents who placed themselves between 0 and 4 were categorized as supporters for environmental protection and those between 6 and 10 were categorized as supporters for economic development. The respondents who placed themselves exactly at the middle on the scale (i.e., 5) were randomly assigned to either category. The 2006/07 question directly asked respondents to choose a side between the two.

16. Ming-sho Ho, "Taiwan's State and Social Movements Under the DPP Government, 2002–2004," *Journal of East Asian Studies* 5, no. 3 (2005): 401–425.

17. Ming-sho Ho, "Weakened State and Social Movement: The Paradox of Taiwanese Environmental Politics After the Power Transfer," *Journal of Contemporary China* 14, no. 43 (2005): 339–352.

18. I characterize each party's response to the question as a beta distribution, with the parameters α= number answering "1" and β= number answering "0."

19. Yun-han Chu and Tse-min Lin, "The Process of Democratic Consolidation in Taiwan: Social Cleavage, Electoral Competition, and the Emerging Party System," in *Taiwan's Electoral Politics and Democratic Transition: Riding the Third Wave,* ed. Hung-mao Tien (Armonk, NY: M. E. Sharpe, 1994), 79–104; Chia-lung Lin, "Taiwan's Democratization and Party System Change: Electoral Linkage of Elite and Mass," *Taiwanese Political Science Review* 4 (2000): 3–55.

20. Dafydd Fell, "Inter-Party Competition in Taiwan Since the 1990s," *China Perspectives* 56 (November/December 2004): 3–13; Hsieh, "Ethnicity, National Identity, and Domestic Politics in Taiwan."

21. E. E. Schattschneider, *The Semi-Sovereign People* (Hinsdale, IL: The Dryden Press, 1975).

5

Polarized Politics and Support for Democracy

Yun-han Chu, Min-hua Huang, and Yu-tzung Chang

Democracies are designed to create unequal outcomes through electoral competition: for some to win, others have to lose. In the past two decades, political scientists have begun to pay closer attention to the consequences of this inequality for the legitimacy of democratic political institutions and systems. The efficacy and ultimately the survival of democratic regimes can be seriously threatened if the losers do not accept defeat.

In a pathbreaking study of this "losers' consent" across democracies around the globe, Christopher Anderson and his colleagues found that losing generates ambivalent attitudes toward political authorities. Although there tends to be a gap in support for the political system between winners and losers, it is not ubiquitous. Anderson and his colleagues painted a picture of political actors whose experience and incentives to accept defeat are shaped both by who they are as individuals and by the political environment in which loss is given meaning.[1] They also found that the nature of representative democratic institutions, as measured by Arend Lijphart's consensus-majority index of democracies, mediates the relationship between a person's status as part of the political minority or majority and his or her satisfaction with how the system works. Specifically, they found that losers in systems that are more consensual display higher levels of satisfaction with how democracy works than do losers in systems with majoritarian characteristics.[2]

But what about in Taiwan? It is of both theoretical and practical relevance to examine how presidential election results have shaped citizen evaluations of the performance of Taiwan's democratic system and, ultimately, their support for the legitimacy of democracy. Although the analytical framework proposed by Anderson and his colleagues is a good starting point, it remains too crude and too generic to understand the phenomenon of losers' consent in Taiwan in much depth. Not only has the winner-take-all nature of Taiwan's semipresidential system tended to aggravate the difference in attitudes toward the political system between the losing camp and the winning camp, but also at least four other important factors are at play.

First, the difference in attitudes can be affected by the nature of the primary social cleavage that divides the two camps. If a cleavage involves intrinsically undividable and nonnegotiable issues, such as national identity or religious beliefs, it is far more difficult for the losing camp and winning camp to converge on accepting the system's performance and legitimacy. Second, the gap could be worsened by the way the incumbent exercises the power of office. If the governing elite abuses the power of incumbency for partisan gain or to maximize its chance of winning again, and if it does so in an utterly unlawful and undemocratic way, it is unlikely that the losing camp will acquiesce to the election's outcome or the legitimacy of the system itself. Third, it also depends on how the constitutional design resolves the issue of "competing mandates" under divided government. If the losing camp in a presidential race becomes the winning camp in the subsequent legislative election, but the constitutional design does not automatically award them with some formal role in the government, then the losing sentiment can be compounded by the feeling of being grossly deprived and mistreated winners. Fourth, the attitudinal gap between the losing camp and winning camp could be aggravated if there exist serious disputes over the fairness of the election itself. Unfortunately, in the case of Taiwan, all these unfavorable factors were significant and profoundly affected politics after the first transfer of power in 2000.

Based on two waves of the Asian Barometer Survey (ABS) conducted in 2006 and 2010, this chapter systematically assesses the phenomenon of polarized politics and its political consequences in terms of perceived quality of governance during and after the Chen Shui-bian era. The results indicate that Taiwan's deep political divides repeatedly attenuated popular support for democracy among the losing camp during this period—and thus posed a serious challenge to Taiwan's democratic consolidation.

The next section establishes the case that this worrisome pattern was rooted in Taiwan's national identity crisis and was aggravated by the political gridlock under divided government brought about by the first transfer of power. Polarized politics emanated from a clash between a minority Democratic Progressive Party (DPP) president and a Kuomintang

(KMT)–controlled Legislative Yuan and then spilled over into all issue areas. The most visible impact of this contagion was the development of partisan-laden perceptions of quality of governance. The dispute over the fairness of the 2004 presidential election simply poured more salt into the political wound. Political polarization in Taiwan reached its peak around 2006, when President Chen provoked an escalation of tension in the Tai wan Strait; the effects lingered on even after Ma Ying-jeou won the 2008 presidential election in a landslide.

The third section employs survey data to show that the perception gap between the Pan-Green and Pan-Blue camps became even wider during Chen Shui-bian's second term. In particular, we analyze how partisan antagonism and perceived quality of governance affected the level of support for democracy. The data also suggest that the second transfer of power only slightly narrowed the perception gap between the winning and losing political camps. As a mirror image of Pan-Blue partisans under Chen Shui-bian, Pan-Green supporters registered much higher levels of political discontent and frustration under Ma and expressed a much lower level of belief in the democratic legitimacy of the political system. Toward the end of the chapter, we provide a synthetic analysis, with the help of a causal model, which takes into account relevant explanatory variables other than partisan antagonism.

The Escalation of Political Polarization

The Fallout from the 2000 Presidential Election

The first transfer of power after the 2000 presidential election set in motion a nasty political confrontation between the so-called Pan-Green camp, consisting of the DPP and the Taiwan Solidarity Union (TSU), and the Pan-Blue camp of the KMT, the People First Party (PFP), and the New Party (NP). The increasing political polarization of this era stemmed from Chen Shui-bian's lack of majority support in the Legislative Yuan (LY) and his unwillingness to share power with the opposition. It also brought many undesirable consequences for Taiwan's young democracy. More specifically, it eroded the contending political elites' commitment to due process and shook their faith in the openness and fairness of the political game. The political struggle frequently devolved into a "race to the bottom," and partisans of both camps viewed the battle for control over the state apparatus as a zero-sum game.

Given that he was first elected with only a minority of the popular vote and that he faced a hostile Pan-Blue majority in the legislature, Chen

Shui-bian and his top aides were anxious to consolidate their hard-won but shaky hold on power. This worry only grew after the KMT regrouped, survived the 2001 legislative election, and later on began threatening to bring impeachment proceedings against President Chen. It proved impossible to resist the temptation to use whatever means were available, including some of the dubious political practices of the previous regime, to enhance the DPP's control over the executive and turn it to political advantage. In practice, this meant removing a large number of bureaucrats and appointees with KMT backgrounds from "strategic" positions and replacing them with loyalists, redistributing government subsidies away from civic organizations and associations sympathetic to the KMT and toward "Green" ones, and applying sticks and carrots to peak corporatist organizations and trade unions to convert their political orientation. It also included conducting unlawful surveillance on political opponents (including rival factions within the DPP);[3] selectively prosecuting or auditing KMT-affiliated precinct captains, local factions, and political donors until they either cut their ties with the Pan-Blue camp or switched sides; soliciting large sums of political donations from big businesses, in order to outspend the deep-pocketed KMT, and rewarding them with lucrative business deals or soft loans from the state-controlled banks; forming a cartel among progovernment advertisers to punish unfriendly media;[4] and substantially expanding the advertisement budgets under various ministries and state-owned enterprises and then strategically and centrally dispensing them to induce friendlier coverage from the mass media.[5] The KMT fought back like a wounded lion, wielding the most potent weapon the party still enjoyed—its legislative majority—to its logical and confrontational extreme.

Under Chen Shui-bian's tenure, the intensity of the political struggle eventually deteriorated into a total breakdown of mutual trust, fed by a vicious cycle of tit-for-tat battles among the two camps, whose politicians were often politically rewarded for their deplorable behavior, underhanded political tactics, and unlawful practices by their die-hard supporters. For both the so-called deep Green and deep Blue voters, the stakes in the struggle for power were simply too high for them to be gracious losers. It was a battle between two seemingly irreconcilable emotional claims about Taiwan's statehood and the national identity of the Taiwanese people. Both sides feared that the other side would use the power of the state to impose its ideological agenda to irreversibly change cross-Strait relations and reshape national identity. The deep Green voters vehemently opposed the possibility of a return of the KMT-PFP alliance to power, fearing that Pan-Blue leaders would undo the state-sponsored cultural program launched by Lee Teng-hui, take measures to accelerate cross-Strait economic integration beyond the point of no return, and "sell out" the interest of Taiwan in a hypothetical future cross-Strait political negotiation. The deep Blue voters vowed to stop the political ascendance of the DPP-TSU alliance, fearing that Pan-Green leaders would put an end to the Republic of China and replace it with a "Republic of Taiwan," purge the state's remaining connections to its mainland Chinese past, and sooner or later ignite a deadly military conflict in the Strait with their "reckless" pursuit of Taiwan independence.[6]

The Collateral Damage from the 2004 Election

The buildup of distrust, hostility, and paranoia gave the March 2004 presidential election many unfortunate characteristics. The race was viewed by many die-hard supporters of the two camps as a kind of final showdown after two inconclusive electoral battles—the March 2000 presidential election and the December 2001 LY election—as well as four years of endless political furors and fistfights. The campaign involved all-encompassing social mobilization by both sides. Frenetic efforts by both camps prompted millions of enthusiastic supporters to march in the streets to show their solidarity and support for their respective political camps. For many voters, their emotions were stretched nearly to nervous breakdowns by this tumultuous, exhausting, sensational, and protracted campaign. The whole society became excessively politicized and polarized, and partisan acrimony penetrated into every aspect of social life. The campaign was littered with examples of political rumor mongering, mischievous plots, and unsubstantiated character attacks.

Even the integrity and independence of the Central Election Commission came under suspicion during this election campaign, something that had never happened during Taiwan's transition to democracy.[7] The damage to the popular faith in the fairness of Taiwan's democratic game was considerable. Postelection surveys show that the March 2004 election failed to pass the fairness test in the eyes of Taiwan's electorate. Comparable surveys indicated that the previous two presidential elections had enjoyed solid popular affirmation of its legitimacy, even among the losing camp: 82.6 percent of respondents considered the 1996 presidential election to be fair, and 80.7 percent said the same about the 2000 election. In comparison, only 47.3 percent of eligible voters felt the same way about the 2004 election. Furthermore, this assessment diverged sharply between the winning and losing camps: among Pan-Blue supporters, only 10.0 percent thought the election was fair, while 85.6 percent of Pan-Green supporters thought so.[8]

In a most dramatic way, the partisan acrimony surrounding the 2004 presidential election left Taiwan's democracy badly scarred. Taiwanese society was deeply divided over the outcomes of the election, as well as the story behind the bizarre shooting incident that took place a day before the election. The frenzy and extraordinary circumstances under which this election took place revealed many worrisome trends, some of which had deeper roots in the political soil and which continued to afflict Taiwan's fragile democracy even after President Chen left office.

The Political Crisis of 2006

In the second half of President Chen's second term, political polarization reached new heights as he became embroiled in the worst political turmoil of his presidency. The political firestorm that engulfed Chen was triggered by an insider trading scandal involving his son-in-law and was then fed by a series of corruption allegations implicating his top aides, his wife, and him. Throughout 2006, President Chen faced repeated attempts by the opposition in the LY to recall him from office, an open revolt by political heavyweights in his own party, and mounting popular support for his ousting. Hundreds of thousands of angry citizens participated in waves of demonstrations led by Shih Ming-teh, a former DPP chair, calling on Chen to step down. Crimson-clad demonstrators, known as the Red Shirt Army, haunted the president everywhere he went. Chen's crisis reached a point of no return on November 4, when the prosecutor indicted first lady Wu Shu-chen on corruption and forgery charges in connection with the handling of the state affairs fund. Chen Shui-bian was also suspected of graft and forgery and would be indicted as soon as he stepped down and was no longer entitled to presidential immunity.[9]

As President Chen circled the wagons to fend off waves of popular protests, he became ever more dependent on the unwavering support of the deep Green end of the political spectrum. To galvanize this core constituency, he took ever-riskier strategies and kept making provocative gestures. He instructed his loyalists to use explicitly ethnocentric language to demonize the Red Shirt Army. He even mobilized his loyalists to march in the street and fight with anti-Chen demonstrators. He also did everything conceivable to bolster his pro-independence credentials in the eyes of independence advocates. For example, he accelerated state-sponsored de-Sinicization programs, such as revisions to school textbooks. Periodically, he intentionally set off alarm bells by issuing provocative statements about symbolic national identity issues, such as his announcements of plans to abolish the National Unification Guideline and the National Unification Council, to draft a new constitution and hold a popular vote on it by 2007, to revise the constitutional provision on the country's territory and jurisdictions, and to freeze the current constitution and make a transition to a "Second Republic." Each time, his spokesmen were forced to backpedal after the US government asked for clarification. But he kept coming back to this survival tactic over and over again.

Chen's provocative moves reached a climax toward the end of 2007. He launched an all-out propaganda campaign promoting the so-called UN for Taiwan referendum. In responding to a protest by eighteen Pan-Blue county executives and city mayors who threatened not to comply with the DPP-controlled Central Election Commission's ruling on the "one-stage" balloting procedure for the referendum and presidential election, Chen publicly suggested the possibility of imposing martial law or postponing the LY election if political unrest threatened law and order in Taiwan.[10]

Despite increasing popular resentment toward his presidency, Chen's strategy to strengthen long-term partisan attachments to the DPP by seeking to highlight ideological issues still worked to a remarkable extent. At every critical juncture, Chen managed to mobilize sufficient popular support by stoking inflammatory issues of national identity, ethnic divides, and historical grievances.[11] For example, he successfully directed the Kaohsiung mayoral campaign during September and December 2006 and helped the DPP candidate Chen Chu win the election by a slim margin (0.14 percent), despite a gloomy political climate. Winning this crucial battle pretty much took the heat of the Red Shirt Army demonstration off his back and saved him from an open revolt from within the DPP, which would have demanded his resignation.

After the Second Transfer of Power

Little controversy surrounded Ma Ying-jeou's landslide victory in the 2008 presidential election. Nevertheless, the second transfer of power did not significantly ameliorate the political divisions between the Pan-Blue and Pan-Green camps. Although the intensity of the partisan political struggle receded somewhat, mutual trust among elites on either side of the divide remained low. The Pan-Green camp felt increasingly threatened by the political implications of the acceleration of cross-Strait economic exchanges under Ma Ying-jeou and attempted to slow it down. The Pan-Green politicians tried all kinds of disruptive strategies in the legislature to block the KMT government's cross-Strait legislative initiatives.

In theory, President Ma enjoyed the benefits of presiding over a unified government with a large, single-party, KMT majority in the LY; however, his administration paradoxically also suffered from "divided government syndrome." Although he served as the KMT chair for three consecutive terms beginning in 2005, Ma was still not able to forge a unified party. He isolated himself by excluding most senior KMT leaders from the government decisionmaking process. The KMT's Central Standing Committee was downgraded to little more than a talking shop. The same style of leadership also appeared in his rule of the country as president, which was widely criticized by news commentators and opinion leaders, and undermined his political support even among KMT politicians. Ma relied almost exclusively on a narrow set of advisers in his inner circle to set policy, and his insulation from broader input and criticism led to a political predicament similar to what Chen Shui-bian had faced. Ma could not fully implement his policies as quickly as he expected, and at times, KMT lawmakers even opposed legislation introduced by the Executive Yuan. Put simply, President Ma failed to incorporate other KMT leaders into a power-sharing structure; as a consequence, he was never able to fully secure the effective support of the KMT-controlled Legislative Yuan.

At the same time, the economic onslaught from the global financial crisis derailed much of Ma's initial economic reform agenda. Although Taiwan's economy did show signs of recovery in 2010, the general public did not feel much improvement in their personal economic situation. On the contrary, most middle-class families were still experiencing wage stagnation, and the double-digit youth unemployment rate refused to decline. As a result, popular discontent with Ma's leadership quickly escalated. The Ma administration's capacity and efficiency were criticized, and he was blamed for failing to improve the lot of struggling workers and lower-income families.

The Pan-Green camp tended to judge the performance of the Ma Ying-jeou administration even more harshly. In particular, Pan-Green politicians regularly attributed Taiwan's sluggish economic performance to the island's growing economic dependency on the People's Republic of China (PRC), pointing to capital flight to mainland China and the exodus of export-oriented manufacturing activities. The pro-DPP mass media bombarded their audience with anecdotes that cast Ma Ying-jeou's cross-Strait policies in the worst possible light. Behind these hostile attacks was a growing anxiety and frustration within the Pan-Green camp over its fading hopes for Taiwanese independence and their unpleasant but unavoidable daily encounters with mainland Chinese tourists and visitors, who arrived on the island in large numbers and quickly replaced Japan as Taiwan's number one source of tourist income. At the end of the day, the Pan-Green crowd harbored a deep worry that Ma would sell out Taiwan by opening the door for the Chinese Communist Party's (CCP's) political infiltration and thus undermine Taiwan's sovereignty by endorsing the so-called One China principle.

Measuring Political Polarization over Time

The political experience of polarized politics under the presidency of Chen Shui-bian and Ma Ying-jeou imposed great social and economic costs on Taiwanese society. Politicians of both camps repeatedly boosted their political careers by skillfully playing to their partisans, polarizing the electorate in a bid to win support. It is important to know to what extent elite polarization contributed to divergent attitudes toward the quality of democracy and support for democracy between partisans of both camps. This section delves into this question by examining two waves of the ABS.

Here, *political polarization* is defined as the effect that partisan attachment has on other mass-level political behaviors and attitudes. To detect whether a society has polarized politics, we draw on survey results to measure the degree to which behavioral or attitudinal traits diverge based on partisan attachment. Operationally, we propose a partisan polarization index (PPI), which is the difference in percentage between self-identified Pan-Blue and Pan-Green respondents' positive responses to questionnaire items. The value of the index ranges between -1 and 1; at the two extremes, a respondent's political behavior and attitudes are totally polarized and can be perfectly explained by partisanship. When the PPI index exceeds 0.15, the difference is significant and possibly a sign of political polarization.

Before attempting to measure political polarization, however, we must identify the key issue dimensions in Taiwanese politics around which it might vary. Several issues have become focal points during previous elections or in the daily public discourse: (1) national and ethnic identity, (2) constitutional reform, (3) the quality of democratic governance, (4) economic stagnation, and (5) partisan antagonism and legislative gridlock. These five dimensions are interrelated and are divided along partisan lines. For example, during the period under consideration, most Pan-Green supporters opposed the KMT government policy that promotes greater integration with the PRC in political, economic, social, and cultural arenas. They insisted that Taiwan was an independent nation-state and that the problems of democratic governance, economic stagnation, political antagonism, and legislative gridlock resulted from a deficient constitutional design. What was required was a new constitution to replace the old system inherited from the pre-1949 nationalist government. Likewise, Pan-Blue supporters, standing on the other side of the dispute, attributed all of Taiwan's political problems to the failure of the Chen administration and the DPP's uncompromising position on Taiwan independence. As a result, the most powerful factor shaping people's position on these intertwined dimensions was their partisan attachment, which showed clearly in their vote choice.

In the second- and third-round Taiwan ABS (conducted in 2006 and 2010, respectively), several batteries of questionnaire items tap into these issues, especially the quality of democratic governance. Because quality of democratic governance is an all-embracing concept, the Asian Barometer employed a full array of items to capture the relevant dimensions. We include as many items as possible and categorize them into ten distinctive dimensions to reflect people's subjective evaluation of democratic governance. The ten dimensions are trust in political institutions, regime evaluation, competition, freedom, equality, rule of law, corruption, vertical accountability, horizontal accountability, and responsiveness. Table 5.1 shows all the included items and their basic descriptive statistics.

Items that show a PPI larger than 0.16 or smaller than –0.16 are highlighted in Table 5.1. A positive PPI suggests that more Pan-Blue respondents agreed with the question than Pan-Green ones, and a negative PPI suggests the opposite. As the table shows, ten items showed clear signs of polarized politics in both waves of the ABS Taiwan surveys, and eight more items did so in at least one wave. These eight indicators were spread out over all ten dimensions, suggesting that partisan antagonism during this period spilled over into every possible aspect of democratic performance, from trust in political institutions and regime evaluation to competition, freedom, rule of law, and corruption. At the peak of the partisan confrontation during Chen's second term, sixteen items showed a substantial winner-loser gap, according to our 2006 survey. During Ma Ying-jeou's second term, twelve items still differed substantially between the supporters of the two camps.

In particular, if we adopt a slightly higher standard by PPI greater than 0.2 or less than –0.2, seven items consistently showed a larger winner-loser gap: trust in the president and trust in the national government, under the category of trust in political institutions; overall economic evaluation and satisfaction with the incumbent government, under regime evaluation; transparency of government information, under vertical accountability; perceived government responsiveness, under responsiveness; and effort of controlling corruption, under corruption. The results exhibit a clear pattern: respondents in the winning camp tend to give substantially better evaluations of democratic governance. Pan-Green voters were much more positive toward the Chen Shui-bian administration and its performance in the 2006 survey, whereas Pan-Blue voters in the 2010 survey showed greater support for the Ma administration and its performance.

Table 5.1 Perceived Quality of Democratic Governance in Taiwan, 2006 and 2010

Label		Questionnaire items	2006 ABS				2010 ABS			
2006	2010		Blue	Green	Total	PPI	Blue	Green	Total	PPI
Democratic performance—Institutional trust										
[q007]	[q007]	Trust in prime minister or president	**14.6**	**50.9**	**30.9**	**−36.2**	**54.9**	**13.3**	**38.2**	**41.6**
[q008]	[q008]	Trust in the courts	28.6	39.6	33.6	−11.0	39.1	23.0	32.7	16.1
[q009]	[q009]	Trust in the national government	**24.9**	**54.9**	**38.4**	**−30.0**	**49.9**	**18.0**	**37.2**	**31.9**
[q010]	[q010]	Trust in political parties	13.9	21.6	17.4	−7.7	20.2	12.4	17.1	7.8
[q011]	[q011]	Trust in Parliament	22.8	18.4	20.8	4.4	26.9	13.0	21.5	13.9
[q012]	[q012]	Trust in civil service	52.1	62.1	56.7	−9.9	55.6	46.3	52.0	9.4
[q013]	[q013]	Trust in the military	53.2	65.9	58.9	−12.7	51.3	46.6	49.5	4.7
[q014]	[q014]	Trust in the police	43.8	52.7	47.8	−9.0	54.5	41.7	49.5	12.9
[q015]	[q015]	Trust in local government	53.7	60.4	56.8	−6.7	57.4	53.6	55.9	3.8
[q016]	[q016]	Trust in newspaper	30.7	27.1	29.1	3.6	25.4	26.0	25.6	−0.6
[q017]	[q017]	Trust in television	33.0	29.0	31.2	4.1	28.5	30.8	29.4	−2.2
[q018]	[q018]	Trust in the election commission	**45.3**	**70.2**	**56.5**	**−24.9**	**62.3**	**58.4**	**60.8**	**3.8**
Regime evaluation										
[q001]	[q001]	How would you rate the overall economic condition of our country today?	**27.6**	**59.2**	**42.0**	**−31.6**	**45.6**	**24.9**	**37.4**	**20.7**
[q093]	[q089]	On the whole, how satisfied or dissatisfied are you with the way democracy works in Taiwan, Republic of China?	**53.0**	**69.5**	**60.3**	**−16.5**	**78.0**	**61.2**	**71.4**	**16.8**
[q094]	[q090]	In your opinion how much of a democracy is Taiwan, Republic of China?	47.0	60.5	53.0	−13.5	69.8	56.3	64.5	13.5
[q095]	[q092]	Where would you place our country ten years ago?	23.4	13.0	18.7	10.4	54.3	50.0	52.6	4.3
[q099]	[q095]	How satisfied or dissatisfied are you with the Chen Shui-bian/ Ma Ying-jeou administration?	**6.3**	**43.0**	**22.8**	**−36.7**	**59.2**	**13.2**	**41.2**	**46.1**
Quality of democracy—Competition										
[q043]	[q037]	On the whole, how would you rate the freeness and fairness of the last national election?	**28.9**	**83.3**	**53.4**	**−54.4**	**91.3**	**78.6**	**86.4**	**12.7**

(continues)

Table 5.1 Cont.

Label		Questionnaire items	2006 ABS				2010 ABS			
2006	2010		Blue	Green	Total	PPI	Blue	Green	Total	PPI
[q105]	[q099]	Political parties or candidates in our country have equal access to the mass media during the election period.	64.4	70.8	67.3	-6.4	78.6	69.5	75.1	9.1
[q114]	[q111]	How often do your think our elections offer the voters a real choice between different parties/candidates?	50.9	58.7	54.4	-7.8	61.8	58.0	60.3	3.8
Quality of democracy—Freedom										
[q110]	[q106]	People are free to speak what they think without fear.	**68.6**	**85.0**	**76.0**	**-16.4**	80.1	72.9	77.3	7.3
[q111]	[q107]	People can join any organization they like without fear.	77.4	86.7	81.6	-9.3	86.5	77.4	83.0	9.1
Quality of democracy—Equality										
[q108]	[q104]	Everyone is treated equally by the government.	**35.0**	**53.5**	**43.5**	**-18.5**	31.0	20.8	27.0	10.2
[q109]	[q105]	People have basic necessities like food, clothes, and shelter.	57.5	72.1	64.2	-14.6	66.2	56.8	62.5	9.4
Quality of democracy—Rule of law										
[q103]	[q098]	People have the power to change a government they don't like.	60.8	67.6	63.9	-6.8	60.3	60.5	60.4	-0.1
[q113]	[q110]	How often do national government officials abide by the law?	**32.1**	**49.4**	**39.9**	**-17.3**	**47.4**	**26.8**	**39.3**	**20.7**
Quality of democracy—Vertical accountability										
[q104]	[q108]	Our current courts always punish the guilty, even if they are high-ranking officials.	**37.5**	**55.2**	**45.6**	**-17.6**	42.7	29.5	37.5	13.2
[q106]	[q100]	Between elections, the people have no way of holding the government responsible for its actions.	68.6	59.7	64.6	8.8	53.3	66.6	58.5	-13.3
[q112]	[q109]	How often do government officials withhold important information from the public view?	**64.5**	**42.3**	**54.6**	**22.2**	**48.9**	**69.0**	**56.8**	**-20.1**

(continues)

Table 5.1 Cont.

Label		Questionnaire items	2006 ABS				2010 ABS			
2006	2010		Blue	Green	Total	PPI	Blue	Green	Total	PPI
Quality of Democracy—Horizontal accountability										
[q107]	[q101]	When the government breaks the laws, there is nothing the legal system can do.	67.5	47.7	58.7	19.8	44.3	57.3	49.4	-12.9
[q115]	[q112]	To what extent is the legislature capable of keeping the government in check?	51.0	64.6	57.1	-13.6	63.3	34.1	51.8	29.3
Quality of democracy—Responsiveness										
[q116]	[q113]	How well do you think the government responds to what people want?	26.3	52.9	38.3	-26.6	51.9	24.1	40.8	27.8
[q102a]	[q097]	How likely is it that the government will solve the most important problem you identified?	38.6	39.4	39.0	-0.8	45.5	29.3	39.1	16.2
Quality of democracy—Corruption										
[q117]	[q116]	How widespread do you think corruption and bribe taking are in your local/municipal government?	69.6	63.1	66.7	6.6	62.5	70.0	65.5	-7.3
[q118]	[q117]	How widespread do you think corruption and bribe taking are in the national government?	74.2	6.9	66.6	17.3	56.7	74.5	63.6	-17.8
[q119]	[q119]	Have you or anyone you know personally witnessed an act of corruption or bribe taking by a politician or government official in the past year?	28.4	24.3	26.5	4.1	24.0	31.1	26.8	-7.1
[q120]	[q118]	In your opinion, is the government working to crack down on corruption and root out bribes?	58.0	79.1	67.7	-21.1	81.7	58.7	72.7	23.1

Source: Asian Barometer Taiwan Survey Wave 2 (2006) and Wave 3 (2010).
Notes: ABS = Asian Barometer Survey; PPI = partisan polarization index. All figures are the percentage of positive responses.

In particular, Pan-Blue voters in 2006 were less trustful toward the president (14.6 percent vs. 50.9 percent), the national government (24.9 percent vs. 54.9 percent), and the Central Election Commission (45.3 percent vs. 70.2 percent); much more negative in their evaluations of the country's economic conditions (27.6 percent vs. 59.2 percent for so-so or better); and much less satisfied with the Chen administration (6.3 percent vs. 43.0 percent). In addition, they rated the freeness and fairness of the 2004 presidential election much more negatively (28.9 percent vs. 83.3 percent), were much more likely to believe that the government withheld important information (64.5 percent vs. 42.3 percent), and were less likely to think that the government was responsive (26.3 percent vs. 52.9 percent) and working to crack down on corruption and root out bribes (58.0 percent vs. 79.1 percent). Similarly, Pan-Green voters in 2010 were less trustful toward the president (13.3 percent vs. 54.9 percent) and the national government (18.0 percent vs. 49.9 percent), much more negative in their evaluations of national economic conditions (24.9 percent vs. 45.6 percent for so-so or better), much less satisfied with the Ma administration's performance (13.2 percent vs. 59.2 percent), and much less willing to believe that national government officials followed the law (26.8 percent vs. 47.4 percent) or were able to keep the government in check (34.1 percent vs. 63.3 percent). In addition, they were much more likely to believe that the government withheld important information (69.0 percent vs. 48.9 percent) and were less likely to think that the government was responsive (24.1 percent vs. 51.9 percent) and working to crack down on corruption and root out bribes (58.7 percent vs. 81.7 percent).

A striking commonality is that Pan-Blue voters in 2006 and Pan-Green voters in 2010 were much more negative in their evaluations of democratic governance compared to those identified with the party in power. Most items that show significant partisan divergence were centered on the president (Chen in 2006 and Ma in 2010) and on the government outputs people believed the two presidents should deliver, such as better economic conditions, political transparency, and government responsiveness. However, it is also obvious that idiosyncratic factors played important roles in the two eras. For Chen's presidency, Pan-Blue voters never stopped questioning the integrity of the 2004 presidential election. Fewer than 30 percent of Pan-Blue voters thought that the 2004 election was free and fair, and fewer than 50 percent trusted the Central Election Commission. These two numbers indicate that a major challenge for Chen's second term was to recover some of the political legitimacy he had lost in the protracted controversy over the election.

On the other hand, the two remaining items that show significant PPI scores indicate a deep apprehension among Pan-Green supporters that Ma had monopolized governing authority without any checks and balances, because his party controlled both the presidency and a majority in the legislature. Fewer than 30 percent of Pan-Green supporters thought that national government officials followed the law, and fewer than 35 percent thought the legislature was capable of keeping the government in check. These results suggest deep concern among Pan-Green partisans that Ma would sell out Taiwan by pursuing a pro-unification policy, thus causing irreversible damage to Taiwan's sovereign status.

There remain a few items under trust in political institutions on which respondents' perceptions do not appear to be biased by their partisan inclinations, such as trust in political parties, trust in the legislature, trust in television, and trust in newspapers. Unfortunately, this cross-party agreement was because a large majority of survey respondents, regardless of their partisan attachments, considered *all* of these institutions to be untrustworthy. The only solace in these results is the somewhat respectable level of trust that both Pan-Green and Pan-Blue partisans had in the military, the police, the civil service, and the local government, which were the core components of the permanent state. However, even the courts were not immune from the damaging effects of partisan antagonism.

As for the evaluation of the overall performance of the democratic system, the winner-loser gap was consistently above 0.16 or below –0.16 across the two surveys. Nevertheless, the overall level of satisfaction with democracy improved between 2006 and 2012.

Implications for Support for Democracy in Taiwan

A central question about the protracted political polarization that characterized the Chen Shui-bian era in Taiwan is whether it contributed to a decline in popular support for democracy. To answer this question, however, we must first determine how support for democracy typically evolves over time in new democracies before delving into a causal analysis. Given the availability of relevant data from various sources, we can make both longitudinal and cross-sectional comparisons. The instrument for measuring support for democracy comes from asking people whether they agree with this statement: "Democracy is always preferable to any other kind of government" (sometimes referred to as the "preferability of democracy"). This question is available in the 1998 Taiwan Social Change Survey (TSCS); the 2001, 2006, and 2010 ABS; and the 2003, 2008, and 2012 Taiwan Election and Democratization Study (TEDS). Altogether there are seven waves of surveys covering most of the period following the conclusion of Taiwan's transition to democracy in 1996.

These time-series data provide an important set of reference points to trace how the level of support of democracy has evolved over the years.

Table 5.2 shows that support for democracy dropped significantly between 1998 (64.1 percent) and 2001 (42.8 percent); a reasonable speculation is that the transfer of power in 2000 and the resulting political uncertainty eroded the popular foundation of democratic legitimacy. This figure hovered toward the low end of the range between 2001 and 2008, and although it gradually bounced back after 2008 (49.9 percent in 2010) and reached 52.2 percent in 2012, it was still far below its level in 1998. It appears that political polarization contributed to a significant decline in support for democracy, and well into the Ma Ying-jeou era, Taiwan's democratic legitimacy had still not fully recovered.

Is the level of support for democracy in Taiwan dangerously low in the East Asia context, especially after the first transfer of power? If we examine the survey results from the three-wave ABS surveys, Taiwan was indeed one of the few countries that suffered from a very low level on the preference for democracy measure. As can be seen in Table 5.3, Taiwan ranked the second lowest among the eight countries in the first-wave ABS surveys, and the fourth lowest among the thirteen countries in the second- and third-wave ABS surveys. Taiwan consistently recorded a lower level of democratic legitimacy over the past decade than most other East Asian countries.

In addition, an interesting comparative pattern emerges from these surveys. Taiwan, South Korea (for the first two waves), and Hong Kong

Table 5.2 Support for Democracy in Taiwan, 1998–2012

Response category	1998 (TSCS)	2001 (ABS)	2003 (TEDS)	2006 (ABS)	2008 (TEDS)	2010 (ABS)	2012 (TEDS)
Authoritarian government can be preferable, or it does not matter whether we have a nondemocratic or democratic regime.	32.1% (577)	47.6% (674)	48.4% (810)	46.6% (739)	45.5% (867)	45.5% (725)	41.7% (762)
Democracy is preferable to any other kind of government.	64.1% (1,152)	42.8% (605)	44.2% (739)	47.2% (749)	44.4% (846)	49.9% (796)	52.2% (953)
Don't know, no answer, decline to answer, or missing	3.8% (69)	9.6% (136)	7.5% (125)	6.3% (99)	10.1% (192)	4.6% (74)	6.1% (111)
Total	100% (1,798)	100% (1,415)	100% (1,674)	100% (1,587)	100% (1,905)	100% (1,595)	100% (1,826)

Source: Taiwan Social Change Survey (1998); Asian Barometer Taiwan Survey (2001, 2006, 2010); Taiwan's Election and Democratization Study (2003, 2008, 2012).

Note: The figures in the parentheses are the number of respondents.

Table 5.3 Support for Democracy in East Asia: Taiwan in Comparative Perspective, 2001–2010

Country	Survey year	Agree democracy is always preferable	Want our country to be democratic	Think democracy is suitable for the country	Believe democracy is capable of solving society's problems	Which is more important: democracy or economic development?
	2001	40.4	72.2	59.0	46.8	23.6
Taiwan	2006	47.2	83.4	67.9	54.8	24.4
	2010	**49.9**	**84.9**	**73.8**	**59.4**	**20.9**
Japan	2007	62.2	88.8	75.2	65.9	50.6
South Korea	2006	43.2	94.4	78.0	54.2	32.3
Philippines	2005	50.4	69.4	55.2	55.6	25.4
Thailand	2006	73.0	84.9	82.7	66.5	48.2
Mongolia	2006	39.7	94.4	84.4	77.0	32.2
Average	2005–2007	52.6	85.9	73.9	62.3	35.5

Source: Adapted from Table 1 in Yu-tzung Chang, Yun-han Chu, and Chong-min Park, "Authoritarian Nostalgia in Asia," *Journal of Democracy* 3 (2007): 70.

(for the last two waves) recorded very low levels of democratic preference. The common features of these three societies included a strong Confucian cultural inheritance, a long record of strong economic performance under authoritarian rule, and recent short-term political turbulence. By contrast, most of the Southeast Asia countries had democratic preference levels near or above 55 percent. Japan also had a relatively high democracy preference level of over 60 percent for all three waves.

Although many factors contribute to these cross-national survey results, some important comparative elements might supplement the longitudinal data and help explain the Taiwan case. First, traditional Confucian values, as many political culture theorists have pointed out, could explain, at least in part, the relatively lower levels of support for democracy, because the core cultural concept is maintenance of a hierarchical and harmonious social order based on the traditional family structure. It is probably not a coincidence that there are relatively low levels of support for democracy in Taiwan, South Korea, and Hong Kong, as all of them inherited Confucian cultural legacies despite their more liberal political environments. The lower levels of preference for democracy in these countries, as compared with other East or Southeast Asian countries, might be ascribed to the cultural influence of Confucianism.[12] Japan and Singapore were also influenced by traditional Confucian culture but probably not to the same extent: Singapore is a multiracial society located in Southeast Asia, and Japan has historically been on the outskirts of the so-called Confucian cultural sphere of influence.

Confucianism might explain some variation in the cross-sectional data, but it cannot possibly account for the longitudinal variance because the cultural factor remains constant. Another possible factor influencing the level of support for democracy is socioeconomic conditions, which can fluctuate wildly over a relatively short period. After the first transfer of power, Taiwan suffered a severe and unprecedented economic downturn, which occurred at the same time as the decline in the level of support for democracy captured in the longitudinal data. Furthermore, this correlation is not present in the South Korean and Hong Kong cases, which both recorded fairly strong macroeconomic performances during the same period. In fact, Taiwan even had a negative growth rate in 2001, and as Wang, Chen, and Kuo argue in Chapter 11 of this volume, political uncertainty created by the first transfer of power almost certainly contributed to this economic downturn.

Finally, the series of tumultuous political events that occurred over this period in Taiwan led to deep political distrust and antagonism between the Pan-Blue and Pan-Green camps. Hong Kong, though politically not a democracy, nevertheless also went through a politically turbulent period, with public conflicts over civil liberties (Article 23 of the Basic Law), electoral reform (for selection of the chief executive and the Legislative Council), and patriotic education (introduction of a moral and nationalist curriculum to promote Chinese identity). All three issues were closely linked to Hong Kong's future democratic prospects. In South Korea, Roh Moo-hyun's victory in the presidential election held in 2002 shook the incumbent elite and transformed the political landscape that had existed since the beginning of democratization. Although his victory marked a new era in South Korean politics, he was also a polarizing political figure—much like Chen Shui-bian in Taiwan—who was impeached by the National Assembly and suspended from office. He then formed a new party (the Uri Party), which won a majority of the seats in the 2004 parliamentary election, and he finally was reinstated as president by a Constitutional Court decision that overturned the impeachment.

The preceding discussion suggests that cultural inheritance, economic performance, and controversial political events all contributed to the low level of support for democracy in these three East Asian countries. In a Confucian society, where affluent living standards are taken for granted, people will expect the government to deliver a decent economic performance and a stable political environment. When any of these expectations is not met and a country's overall prospects deteriorate, the Confucian cultural element, which links the concept of hierarchical social order with better economic performance and political stability, will lead to a decline in support for democracy.

We apply the second-wave ABS dataset to test this argument in Taiwan. To operationalize the hypotheses, we need additional contextual knowledge. We use the subjective evaluation of quality of governance as a measure of whether government performance in the economic and political arenas meets public expectations. We expect that the better the quality of governance that people perceive, the higher their level of support for democracy.[13] Nevertheless, given the most significant feature of Taiwanese politics during the Chen Shui-bian era was political polarization and a large partisan gap in perceptions of quality of governance, it is highly likely that partisan attachment is a confounding variable in this relationship and that the correlation between perceived quality of governance and support for democracy is spurious. We propose a simple structural equation model to evaluate this potential spurious correlation problem.

Research Design

The goal of our research design is to test whether political polarization in Taiwan affects the causal inference about the relationship between perceived quality of governance and the level of support for democracy. Conceptually, we hypothesize a positive relationship between perceived quality of governance and the level of support for democracy. This relationship is modeled in a structural equation analysis, in which the dependent variable is support for democracy, the main explanatory variable is perceived quality of governance, and both are controlled with demographic and socioeconomic variables. To test for a possible spurious relationship, we modify the model by treating perceived quality of governance as an intervening variable and add the exogenous explanatory variable of partisan attachment, which is hypothesized to be simultaneously associated with the perceived quality of governance and the level of support for democracy.

We use data from the second and third waves of the Taiwan ABS for the statistical analysis. In terms of operationalization, the dependent variable of support for democracy is recoded into a binary variable from responses to the question, "Democracy is always preferable to any other kind of government." The intervening variable of perceived quality of governance is a latent construct measured by the three items related to evaluations of the overall economic condition, the Chen administration, and government responsiveness. These three indicators reflect the most contentious issues in the political context of Taiwan during the Chen Shui-bian era: the economy, satisfaction with the president, and evaluations of governance performance. The exogenous explanatory variable is partisan attachment, which is measured by respondents' self-reported vote choice—a better measurement than self-reported partisanship, due to the smaller number of missing-value observations.[14] For controls, we only include four basic demographic and socioeconomic variables: age, gender, education, and income. Descriptive statistics for each variable can be found in the appendix.

We analyze a logistic path-effect model by using Mplus 6, applying the built-in structural equation analysis function with categorical dependent variables. The dependent and intervening variables are both specified with four control variables. If the relationship between perceived quality of governance and the level of support for democracy remains unchanged when partisan attachment is added into the model, we can rule out the spuriousness hypothesis. Otherwise, we need to seek other explanations to assess democratic legitimacy under the phenomenon of political polarization.

Empirical Findings

The results of the structure equation analysis are presented in Table 5.4, and Figure 5.1 presents the path effects. All the models have good fit statistics (CFI > .90, TLI > .90, RMSEA < .06), so there is no need to revise model specification.[15] The decrease in sample size after adding partisan attachment into the models is due to the significant number of missing-value observations. Although multiple imputations can be done before the analysis, we regard the reliability of this variable's information as more important than advanced methodological considerations; therefore, we do not conduct multiple imputations.

For the 2006 ABS dataset, provided that incumbent partisan attachment is not specified in the model (Model I), the results show that perceived quality of governance is positively correlated with the level of support for democracy. In other words, people tended to be more supportive of democracy if they evaluated the quality of governance more positively. This result is consistent with the hypothesis that good government performance is needed to sustain support for democracy over the long term. In addition, male, older, and better-educated respondents tended to be more supportive of democracy. As for factors that explain the perceived quality of governance, female and better-educated respondents tended to be more critical. The three measures of perceived quality of governance are all significant, but satisfaction with the Chen administration appears to be, by far, the most the powerful one to tap into this latent concept. In addition, the explanatory power of the model for the two dependent variables is quite modest: the model only explains 13 and 6

Table 5.4 Support for Democracy: Structural Equation Analysis Results, 2006 and 2010

	2006 ABS		2010 ABS	
	I. Not specifying partisan attachment	II. Specifying partisan attachment	III. Not specifying partisan attachment	IV. Specifying partisan attachment
Support for democracy *on*				
Perceived quality of governance	**.20****	**.16***	−.08	−.01
Incumbent partisan attachment	—	.01	—	−.16**
Income	.07	.06	.02	.01
Education	.31**	.31**	.16**	.17**
Male	.09**	.07	.07*	.07
Age	.18**	.21**	.19**	.20**
Perceived quality of governance *on*				
Incumbent partisan attachment	—	**.56****	—	**.55****
Income	.00	.00	.07	.02
Education	−.21**	−.14**	.12*	.01
Male	.10**	.07*	−.01	−.01
Age	.04	.01	.04	−.01
Perceived quality of governance *by*				
Overall economic evaluation	.59†	.62†	.56†	.51†
Satisfaction toward the government	.94**	.97**	.81**	.95**
Evaluation of government responsiveness	.63**	.61**	.73**	.66**
R square				
Support for democracy	.13	.11	.04	.06
Perceived quality of governance	.06	.36	.02	.31
Overall economic evaluation	.35	.39	.31	.26
Satisfaction toward the government	.89	.94	.66	.89
Evaluation of government responsiveness	.40	.37	.54	.43
Fit statistics				
CFI	.93	.95	.96	.95
TLI	.84	.90	.90	.90
RMSEA	.05	.04	.04	.05
N	1,420	1,170	1,447	1,236

Source: Asia Barometer Survey II and III. Program: Mplus 6.

Notes: Entries are standardized coefficients from a path-effect model. Significance level: *$p \leq 0.05$; **$p \leq 0.01$. † default item for the latent construct.

percent of the variance for the level of support for democracy and perceived quality of governance, respectively. Finally, education played an important role, though with countervailing path effects. On the one hand, better-educated people tended to be more critical and less supportive of democracy through the intervening effects of unfavorable evaluations of the quality of governance. On the other hand, the strong direct effect of

education on support for democracy swamped the relatively small intervening path effect just mentioned.

As Figure 5.1a shows (Model II in Table 5.4), if we specify partisan
attachment as the main exogenous variable, the evidence for the hypothesis
is mixed. On the one hand, perceived quality of governance does have a
strong and positive relationship with support for democracy, even if partisan attachment is held constant. This indicates that the perception of quality
of democratic governance can explain some of the variation in the level of
support for democracy. On the other hand, the path coefficient with the
greatest magnitude is for the path between partisan attachment and perceived quality of governance, suggesting that the way people evaluated
quality of governance was highly subjective and extraordinarily influenced
by their partisan attachments. Based on these findings, we can clear away
concern about a spurious relationship, but we still have to recognize that
the escalation of political polarization drove people's partisan-laden
perceptions of government performance and thus affected the level of
support for democracy. Because the perception of the quality of democracy is specified as a powerful intervening factor in our model, this
explanation is not complete without tracking back to the original cause of
polarized politics: the national identity cleavage and the resultant electoral competition and party antagonism. In this sense, the effect of perceived quality of governance on support for democracy could lose most
of its power once political polarization is significantly ameliorated.

We compare the results of Models III and IV by running the same
model with the 2010 ABS dataset. If partisan attachment to the incumbent is not added into the model, we find some important differences
from the results of Model I in 2006. First, perceived quality of governance was not significantly related to level of support for democracy in
2010, indicating that respondents' evaluation of government performance,
regardless of whether the evaluation is impartial or biased, cannot explain
their attitudes toward the legitimacy of democracy. Second, respondents'
level of education was positively associated with perceived quality of
governance. This result differs from the negative relationship found in
Model I, suggesting that better-educated people tended to be more positive, rather than critical, in evaluating government performance. A plausible explanation is that the KMT was the incumbent party in 2010, and its
supporters, on average, had a higher level of education than Pan-Green
supporters. Therefore, both findings could be confounded if we do not
include incumbent partisan attachment in the model. Interestingly, the
demographic factors that appear to explain democratic legitimacy in
Model III are the same as those in Model I. In addition, the measurement
model for the latent construct of perceived quality of governance is equally
valid, though with more weight given to the evaluation of governance

responsiveness and less to satisfaction with the Ma administration. This indicates that our structural equation model can nicely explain the 2010 ABS dataset and that people shifted their concerns from discontent with the president, which dominated in 2006, to greater apprehension about government responsiveness in 2010.

If the variable of incumbent partisan attachment is added into the model (Model IV), the negative relationship between education and perceived quality of governance vanishes, and Pan-Blue partisanship better explains perceived quality of governance under the Ma administration. This result is similar to the finding in Model II that Pan-Green partisanship better explains perceived quality of governance under Chen. However, perceived quality of governance still does not explain level of support for democracy, while Pan-Blue partisanship is associated with a lower level of support. These results suggest that political polarization after 2008 hardened into a more static form within public opinion. As Figure 5.1b shows, although partisan attachment to the incumbent party is associated with divergent perceptions of government performance, respondents did

Figure 5.1 Path Effects of Partisan Attachment on Democratic Legitimacy

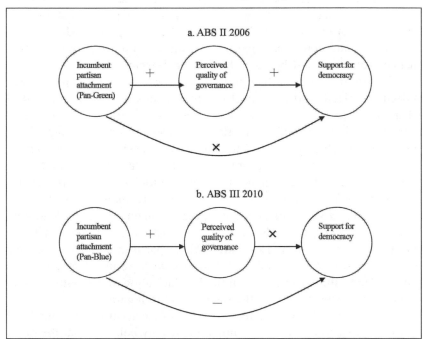

Note: Only the results of path effects between partisan attachment, perceived quality of governance, and support for democracy are reported.

not reduce their support for democracy in 2010, unlike in 2006. However, the lingering effect of partisan-laden resentment remained significant, suggesting that discontent with government performance continued to spill over into frustration with democracy itself. Put more simply, everybody knows that partisan rivalry shaped popular evaluations of government performance during this period, and even some supporters of the incumbent party were not satisfied with the government. However, they tended to blame the opposition for this poor performance and to rationalize their frustration with the thought that something had to be wrong with the democratic system in order to prevent their preferred party from achieving satisfactory governance outcomes when it was in power.

Conclusion

Democracy is not just about elections, and support for democracy should never depend on the personal charisma of leaders or on partisan interests. Maintaining a well-functioning democracy requires broad public support for the principle of democracy, even if actual government performance is not satisfactory. However, over the long run, the foundations of support for democracy can be eroded if many people perceive the quality of democratic governance to be poor and unresponsive to popular demands. This chapter set out to analyze the relationship between perceived quality of governance and democratic legitimacy under the political polarization that characterized the Chen Shui-bian era in Taiwan.

The findings suggest that politics in Taiwan during this period was indeed polarized, and its impact has persisted well beyond the end of Chen Shui-bian's time in office. The partisan confrontation that occurred at the beginning of Chen's first term as president was at first triggered by intense electoral competition. While partisan animosity continued to grow as the conflict between the president and the legislature—and more broadly between Pan-Green and Pan-Blue politicians—escalated, political polarization was initially confined to disagreements about how the president should share the power with the legislature under divided government. However, after Chen refused to share executive power with the Pan-Blue majority in the Legislative Yuan, partisan animosity became even more severe, and political contests were reduced to zero-sum games. Once that occurred, political polarization led to attempts to manipulate the institutions of the state for partisan gain.

Although there was no direct evidence of electoral fraud in the 2004 presidential election, Pan-Blue supporters deeply believed that the many legally questionable campaign tactics adopted by President Chen had undercut the legitimacy of the outcome. They suspected not only the

Central Election Commission of being complicit in Chen's effort to win reelection, but also the whole government apparatus, including the National Security Bureau, the courts, and the military—all of whom were implicated in a concerted effort to bend the rules in favor of the DPP.[16] But none of these allegations was convincing to Pan-Green supporters, and most viewed the complaints as simply a replay of the past four years of political confrontation, with Pan-Blue politicians and supporters simply unable to accept that they had lost. In their mind, President Chen's reelection with an absolute majority of votes, no matter how slim the margin (50.1 percent vs. 49.9 percent), had reaffirmed Chen's legitimacy and strengthened his rightful grip on power. Following the 2004 election, these two opposing views colored debates over most other issues as well.

A serious consequence of the political polarization that emerged in Taiwan during the Chen Shui-bian era was the rise of a partisan gap in perceptions of the quality of democratic governance. Under normal circumstances, citizens should be able to provide an impartial evaluation of government performance, uncolored by partisan bias. However, Taiwan was deeply polarized along partisan lines during the Chen era, and heightened partisanship hindered the ability of citizens to evaluate government performance fairly, without reference to which party held power. This polarization gave rise to a deep apprehension about Taiwan's democracy because of the threat it posed to government accountability and responsiveness.

Empirical evidence in this chapter supports this causal account. To be sustained over the long run, democratic legitimacy requires performance legitimacy. However, it is what people perceive, rather than what the government really delivers, that matters. In a society like Taiwan's—which has come through intense partisan struggle and been overburdened with many structural problems, including a deep conflict over national identity, cross-Strait rivalry, and institutional gridlock in a semipresidential system—the perceived quality of governance has become an all-encompassing concept that reflects citizens' overall evaluation of the government. The prolonged political polarization of this period contributed to the formation of lasting partisan biases, which continue to color perceptions of the quality of governance in Taiwan even today.

Ma Ying-jeou's landslide victory in the 2008 presidential election held out the promise of arresting or even reversing the decade-long growth in political polarization in Taiwan. However, in President Ma's first term, Taiwanese society remained deeply divided by partisanship, and the lingering impact of political polarization remained strong. Yet people also seemed to become more aware of their partisan biases and became more able to separate their views about the legitimacy of democracy in a broad sense from perceptions of the quality of democratic governance under the current administration. This empirical finding should serve as a warning—not only do people not appear to evaluate their government through impartial thinking, but even an evaluation biased by partisan attachments does not affect their assessment of the legitimacy of democracy. Instead, partisan attachments continue to shape people's views about the political system, marginalizing concerns about accountability and responsiveness. This evolving trend under political polarization poses the toughest challenge for Taiwan's democratic consolidation.

Appendix

Table 5A.1 Variable Information

Variable	Measurement items	Recoding scheme	Scale	Range
Support for democracy	Which of the following statements comes closest to your own opinion? 1. Democracy is always preferable to any other kind of government. 2. Under some circumstances, an authoritarian government can be preferable to a democratic one. 3. For people like me, it does not matter whether we have a democratic or a nondemocratic regime.	1>1; 2 to 3>0	Binary	(0,1)
Overall economic evaluation	How would you rate the overall economic condition of our country today?	1 to 3>1; 4 to 5>0	Binary	(0,1)
Satisfaction toward the government	How satisfied or dissatisfied are you with Chen Shui-bian's/Ma Ying-Jeou's government?	1 to 2>1; 3 to 4>0	Binary	(0,1)
Evaluation of government responsiveness	How well do you think the government responds to what people want?	1 to 2>1; 3 to 4>0	Binary	(0,1)
Partisan attachment[a]	Do you identify yourself as a supporter of the Pan-Green or Pan-Blue camp?	Pan-Green>1 Pan-Blue>2	Nominal	(1,2)
Income	Level of income	Original coding	Ordinal	(1,5)
Education	Level of education	Original coding	Ordinal	(1,5)
Male	Gender	1>1; 2>0	Binary	(0,1)
Age	Age group	Original coding	Ordinal	(1,5)

Notes: a. Partisan attachment is recoded into a group dummy called "incumbent partisan attachment." In the 2006 survey, "incumbent partisan attachment" refers to the Pan-Green identity; in the 2010 survey, "incumbent partisan attachment" becomes the Pan-Blue identity.

Notes

1. Christopher J. Anderson, André Blais, Shaun Bowler, Todd Donovan, and Ola Listhaug, *Losers' Consent: Elections and Democratic Legitimacy* (Cambridge: Cambridge University Press, 2005).

2. Christopher J. Anderson and Christine A. Guillory, "Political Institutions and Satisfaction with Democracy: A Cross-National Analysis of Consensus and Majoritarian Systems," *American Political Science Review* 91, no. 1 (March 1997): 66–81.

3. In a 2004 survey of 104 members of the Legislative Yuan, 47 percent said they believed their phones were regularly (and illegally) bugged by the security apparatus. *Xin Xinwen* [The Journalist], September 23, 2004, 40.

4. On the potent threat to freedom of the press posed by the formation of the Taiwan Advertisers' Association, see the news analysis by Tsai Bai-hui and Liu Po-Chi, *Xin Xinwen* [The Journalist], April 29, 2004, 60–63.

5. For instance, Star TV abruptly canceled the contract of the political program *Sisy's News,* presented by independent legislator Sisy Chen, a longtime critic of President Chen, allegedly due to pressure from the presidential office and a secret agreement that the government would buy advertising from Star TV. See Reporters without Borders, "Taiwan—2004 Annual Report" (Paris: Reporters Without Borders, 2005), in *The 2004 Global Press Freedom World Tour.*

6. Yun-han Chu, "Taiwan's Democracy at Turning Point," *American Journal of Chinese Studies* 11, no. 2 (May 2005): 901–924.

7. A few independent members of the Central Election Commission resigned to protest the Executive Yuan's blatant meddling in the balloting procedures in order to tie the controversial referendum vote to the presidential ballot about a month before the election. See *China Times,* February 7, 2004, A2.

8. The 1996 and 2000 postelection surveys were conducted by a research team led by Fu Hu and Yun-han Chu of National Taiwan University. The 2004 postelection survey was conducted under the auspices of the 2004 Taiwan Election and Democratization Survey (TEDS) Project. All three surveys were sponsored by the National Science Council.

9. See *Taipei Times,* November 5, 2006, 1.

10. President Chen spoke about "the possibility of imposing martial law or postponing the legislative election" at a large-scale campaign rally in Taipei County on November 25, 2007. Chen was responding to eighteen Pan-Blue county executives' and city mayors' threat to boycott the "one-stage" balloting procedure, which was believed to be designed by DPP top officials and later approved by the Central Election Commission to favor the Pan-Green camp's candidates in the upcoming legislative election in January 2008 ("Chen's Threat to Impose Martial Law," *United Daily Evening News,* November 26, 2007, 3). However, the next day, Chen immediately denied that this was what he meant and blamed the media for misquoting him. (See "Chen Blamed the Media's Mudslinging," *Apple Daily,* November 27, 2007.)

11. For example, one of Chen's favorite campaign slogans was, "This election is about choosing between Taiwan and China; if you choose Taiwan then you should vote for the DPP. Otherwise, you can vote for the KMT and choose China."

12. For an extended discussion of Asian political culture, especially Confucianism, see Lucian Pye, *Asian Power and Politics: The Cultural Dimensions of Authority* (Cambridge, MA: Belknap Press, 1985).

13. For previous work on this hypothesis, see Anderson and Guillory, "Political Institutions and Satisfaction with Democracy," and Anderson et al., *Losers' Consent.*

14. If we use the self-reported partisan attachment, 40.4 percent (641) of all cases have a missing value. But if we use vote choice, instead, the percentage falls to 34.7 percent (550). In addition, vote choice in terms of supporting Pan-Blue or Pan-Green candidates is virtually evenly split—50 percent (518) versus 50 percent (519)—but the split for self-reported partisan attachment is 63.7 percent for Pan-Blue versus 36.3 percent for Pan-Green. We think the former figure is a better measurement of partisan attachment than the latter, which is apparently biased toward the Pan-Blue camp.

15. The TLI statistic in Model I is slightly lower than .90 (.84). This fit statistic is usually acceptable, because most of the time TLI is lower than CFI, given that CFI and RESEA are good enough.

16. Many Pan-Blue supporters believed that the March 19 shooting incident and other election tricks could not possibly have happened without the full cooperation of the whole government—especially the military and national security system.

6

Executive-Legislative Relations Under Divided Government

Shiow-duan Hawang

At the beginning of Chen Shui-bian's first term as president, a key source of uncertainty was how executive-legislative relations would change. Until that point, the Executive Yuan and Legislative Yuan had always been under control of the same political party, the Kuomintang (KMT). Although Chen's victory in the 2000 presidential election ended KMT control of the presidency, the former ruling party retained a legislative majority either outright or in coalition with its ally, the People First Party (PFP), throughout Chen's time as president. Thus, President Chen's inauguration ushered in the first period of divided government in Taiwan's history and, with it, a new, more confrontational era in executive-legislative relations.

When President Chen took office, it was not clear how much control the legislature would be able to exert over the cabinet, due to the Republic of China's (ROC's) unusual institutional structure.[1] The ROC constitution provides for a cabinet, the Executive Yuan, which is headed by a premier who is supervised by, but nominally independent from, the president. Constitutional revisions in the 1990s were intended to establish a semipresidential regime, with a popularly elected president and a separately constituted legislature sharing power over the cabinet. Under the revised constitution, legislators enjoy a number of important oversight powers, including the right to interpellate the premier, hear reports about administrative policies and regulations, pass or reject bills proposed by the executive, and review and freeze or cut government budgets. Nevertheless, the crucial decision about political control over the premier was resolved in favor of the president: the premier is appointed and can be dismissed by the president without the consent of the Legislative Yuan (LY). The LY does have the power to remove the premier through a vote of no confidence, but this action then gives the president the right to dissolve the legislature itself and call new elections. In practice, this feature has deterred attempts by the majority coalition in the legislature to oust a premier, and it has ensured that Taiwan functions much more like a presidential regime than a semipresidential one.

The consequences of this institutional design for executive-legislative relations became clear in the first year of the Chen administration. At first glance, President Chen's initial appointments to the Executive Yuan were consistent with the idea of a power-sharing coalition. Stating that he would be a president of the whole country, not the president of the Democratic Progressive Party (DPP), Chen's first cabinet included members of all major political parties; about one-third were members of the KMT, including the new premier, Tang Fei, who had been the minister of defense in the outgoing cabinet. Nevertheless, the lack of an investiture requirement meant that the legislature had no formal role in influencing appointments to the cabinet, nor did it have any way to prevent the president from removing ministers at will. Inevitably, the Executive Yuan was caught between a president eager to implement fundamental changes to a wide range of executive policies and a legislature controlled by a party suspicious of the president's legitimacy and hostile to his agenda.

Tensions between Premier Tang and President Chen soon came to a head over the issue of nuclear power: DPP party activists had long pushed to cancel the construction of a fourth nuclear power plant, which the previous KMT administration had initiated. When Chen came out publicly in favor of canceling the project, Premier Tang resigned rather than carry out the change. He had lasted fewer than five months in office, the shortest tenure of any ROC premier. To replace Tang, President Chen appointed a DPP member, Chang Chun-hsiung, who immediately announced that the nuclear plant project would be canceled. Despite fierce condemnation by the KMT, that party did not attempt to use the only formal tool at its disposal—the vote of no confidence—to oust Premier Chang, rightly fearing that it would lose seats in the next election. The experiment with a multiparty "government for all the people" had ended; from that point forward, the president's tight control over the Executive Yuan was assured, despite the presence of an opposition majority in the legislature.

This chapter examines the consequences of divided government for politics during the Chen Shui-bian era. It investigates how the policymaking process was affected by the greater need for cross-party cooperation under divided government, and it compares variations in lawmaking and budgetary outcomes with the period of unified KMT control of the government that preceded the Chen administration.

The Consequences of Divided Government

Previous research on the impact of divided governments is mixed and inconclusive, drawing heavily on observations from the United States. Researchers have attempted to measure the impact of divided government on the policymaking process in terms of a variety of measures, such as the approval of nominations and treaties, the frequency of high-publicity investigations, the passage of bills, and the use of vetoes.

One key debate in this literature is the degree to which legislative productivity is affected by divided government. An executive without majority support from the legislative branch presumably will be unable to win approval for a larger share of the bills that it proposes. Yet some studies in the United States find no major differences between periods of unified and divided government on this measure.[2] For instance, in a widely cited study, David Mayhew compiled a list of every major congressional investigation of alleged executive misbehavior from 1946 to 1990 in the United States.[3] His evidence is not strong enough to support the hypothesis that Congress increases its high-publicity investigations during times of divided government. As for legislation, during the nine periods of unitary government over the same time frame, an average of 12.8 major laws were passed, whereas an average of 11.7 laws passed during the thirteen periods of divided government. Mayhew concluded that "on average, about as many major laws passed per Congress under divided control as under unified control."[4]

Other researchers have reported similar results. Like Mayhew, Charles Jones found no difference in legislative productivity between periods of divided and unified government.[5] Looking at budget deficits, Senate confirmations of presidential appointments, Senate approval of treaties, and presidential vetoes, Morris Fiorina also found very little evidence to support the argument that presidents experience greater difficulty during divided government.[6] The only impact Fiorina did find was an increased number of vetoes corresponding to the proportion of congressional seats controlled by the opposition party.

In contrast, some scholars have argued that divided government does make life harder for the president and leads to gridlock and policy stalemate. Benjamin Ginsberg and Martin Shefter, for example, claimed that when the president's party does not control the majority in the Congress, elections no longer decide who wins.[7] Instead, partisan competition carries over into the institutional arena. Each party attempts to use all means at its disposal to undermine the influence of the other; as a consequence, the judiciary, the national security apparatus, and the mass media become instruments of political combat.

In a similar vein, Gary Cox and Samuel Kernell argued that partisan considerations become the most important factor in executive-legislative interactions under divided government.[8] Party differences then exacerbate the effects of formal separation of powers, eventually leading to intense institutional conflict. Under these circumstances, policy changes only result after prolonged bargaining among different veto-wielding institutions. Likewise, congressional committees, acting as oversight bodies, tend to cause more trouble for the executive branch when it is run by a president of the opposite party than when it is run by a member of their own party. Moreover, if total legislative productivity does not measurably differ, major laws, at least, are passed more frequently under unified party control than under divided control.[9]

In general, if divided government produces partisan gridlock, then it is reasonable to expect fewer bills to pass. Some quantitative studies of divided government have found evidence of this. For example, studies by Kelly, Coleman, Howell, and their colleagues argued that Mayhew used an inappropriate retrospective way to define *important legislation*.[10] Using a concurrent evaluation of the legislation, their results indicate that fewer pieces of important legislation pass under divided government than under unified government. Additional evidence is provided by Edwards, Barrett, and Peake, who compared the failure of potentially important legislation under divided and unified government from 1947 to 1992; their results also indicate that the legislation is more likely to fail under divided government than under unified government.[11]

In Taiwan, a small literature compares executive-legislative relations in unified and divided government. The earliest studies of this topic focused on the local level of government. In several cases, the DPP won mayoral seats, while the city council remained dominated by the KMT. However, a city council's power over legislation is weak, and the political climate at the local level is very different from that in the Legislative Yuan, making it problematic to draw inferences about the central government from these studies. Research on divided government at the national level started after Taiwan's first party turnover, when the DPP, for the first time, controlled the presidency but did not have a majority of seats in the legislature. One of the first studies was by Chung-li Wu and Chang-chih Lin, who used legislative debates about controversial issues, annual government budget cut rates, law enactments, and legislators' interpellation of executive officials as indicators of legislative performances. The results of their findings are mixed: debates about controversial issues and the size of the reduction in the central government's budgets are significantly different; however, laws passed and legislators' questions were not obviously different under divided versus unified government.[12]

In another study, Wan-ying Yang used the relative number of laws supplied and demanded, the delay of law enactments, the decrease in party line voting, and the degree of dependence on interparty bargaining to solve party conflict to show that conflict is common under both unified and divided government.[13] Shing-yuan Sheng, by contrast, found that during eras of divided party control, bills proposed by the Executive Yuan took longer to pass than bills proposed by opposition party members.[14] She concluded that if the party of the executive branch did not control a majority of seats in the legislative branch, it was difficult for it to lead in the policymaking process. In my article I focused on the interaction between the Executive Yuan and the Legislative Yuan—in particular, on the review of the budget and executive-proposed legislation.[15] All the results support the same conclusion: the DPP government faced serious challenges from the opposition parties because it did not control a majority in the LY.

In a different study using roll-call votes in the LY, Hawang and Chen found additional evidence that confrontations between the ruling and opposition parties have occurred more frequently under divided than under unified government. In addition, under unified government, party confrontations have been less frequent when the ruling party has controlled a large majority of the seats.[16] Under divided government, party confrontations have happened more frequently when the number of seats of the ruling party is closer to that of opposition parties. Confrontation increases with every increment of change from unified government with a large margin for the ruling party, to unified government with a small margin of seats, to divided government with a large margin, to divided government with a small margin.

Most research on the impact of divided government has focused on how many laws are passed, how many laws are vetoed, how many investigations are conducted, how many nominations or treaties are rejected, and how great a percentage of budgets were cut. However, researchers have not found a consistent effect of divided government on legislative productivity. There are two problems with relying on productivity as a measure of divided government's impact. First, it is difficult to determine what is meant by *important* or *innovative legislation*. Different researchers have based their findings on different samples of legislation. Second, comparisons of legislative outputs have not explored how the demand for legislation varies over time.

This chapter uses somewhat different measures of budgets, agenda control, and legislation to examine whether there is significantly different executive-legislative interaction under different types of government.

Research Method

To improve the robustness of research findings, legislative-executive interaction should be measured in a variety of ways. Lawmaking and annual budget decisions unquestionably involve the most dramatic and important form of legislative-executive interactions. Thus, this chapter examines their interactions with regard to budget review and deliberation over legislation. Bills, including the budget and all other legislation, are first sent to the Procedure Committee, which determines the order in which bills are deliberated in the Yuan Sitting, which is the earliest formal stage of the legislative process.[17] Where agenda setting takes place defines the opportunities for success in terms of legislative outcomes. The Procedure Committee's role is the focus of this study, because that committee controls whether a proposed bill will be placed on legislative agenda.

The budget review measures include both the annual budget cut rate and the total number of budget resolutions. The data on the annual budget cut rate are taken directly from the website of the Directorate-General of Budget, Accounting, and Statistics of the Executive Yuan. Budget resolutions are drawn from *Annual Central Government Budget Review Reports*. With regard to the Procedure Committee, I use the number of bills blocked or delayed by the committee according to the written records of the Procedure Committee's meetings. As indicators of legislative deliberation, I use the success rate of the incumbent party on roll-call votes, the patterns of cross-party alliance, and party unity scores.[18]

To examine whether legislative-executive relations function differently under different types of government, I divided the study into four periods. The first is the period of unified government from February 1, 1996 (first session of the Third LY) until May 19, 2000. During this time, one party—the KMT—held the presidency, the post of premier, and the majority in the LY. The second period is from May 20, 2000 (third session of the Fourth LY) to January 31, 2002 (sixth session of the Fourth LY). This period of divided government had a DPP president and premier, but the DPP controlled less than one-third of the seats in the LY. The third period is from February 1, 2002, to January 31, 2008. The composition of the legislature changed dramatically in 2002. In that year, the DPP became the largest party in the LY when the KMT split into three parties: the PFP, the Taiwan Solidarity Union (TSU), and the remaining KMT. During this period, no party had a majority in the LY. Although the DPP held the largest number of seats, it lacked a majority even in coalition with its ally, the TSU. Instead, the KMT allied with the PFP and several nonpartisan legislators to maintain nominal control of the chamber. The fourth period starts on May 20, 2008, when the KMT regained the presidency and captured an overwhelming majority of seats in the LY.

I expected that during the first and fourth periods, executive-legislative relations would be more cooperative, whereas during the third period, relations would be more antagonistic. During the second period, the ruling DPP held less than one-third of the seats in the LY. To get its proposals passed, the administration would have had to be more low-key and cooperative; therefore, I expected that the confrontation between the executive and legislative branches would be less than that of the third period but higher than that of the first and fourth periods.

Budget Review and Budget Resolutions

Budgets are the very foundation of government administration. Examining and amending budgetary bills is the most effective way for the Legislative Yuan to oversee government administration. In accordance with Article 63 of the ROC Constitution, the Legislative Yuan has the power to review budgetary bills. However, the legislature faces significant constitutional constraints on its ability to draft budget laws. First, only the Executive Yuan can propose and submit the budgetary bill. Moreover, this agenda-setting power is reinforced by Article 70 of the constitution, which states, "The Legislative Yuan shall not propose to increase expenditures above the budgetary bill presented by the Executive Yuan." If the legislature wants to increase the amount of any item of expenditure or create a new item in the budget, it must obtain the consent of the executive branch in advance. The legislature's budgetary authority is also reduced by Judicial Yuan Interpretation 391, which ruled that the Legislative Yuan cannot add, delete, or reapportion the amount of individual items within each government agency or among different government agencies, even if it does not change the overall budget number.

Nevertheless, the legislature does have the power to reduce, if not eliminate, funding for individual agencies, and the Executive Yuan is bound to accept the cuts. Table 6.1 indicates the average budget cuts by the LY from 1993 to 2008. During the first period of unified government, the total budget cut rate ranged from a low of 0.93 percent to a high of 3.88 percent. The average cut rate was 1.79 percent. The high cut rate in

1994 was due to the second-term legislators being the first popularly elected legislators in more than forty years; as such, they were especially anxious to wield their powers. During the second period, from 2000 to 2002, legislators set a record by reducing the administration's budget proposal by 5.04 percent. At first glance, this gives the impression that budgets were cut more during periods of divided government. However, during the legislative election in 2001, the DPP ran a series of campaign advertisements that accused the opposition of "barbarian behavior" for reducing the budgets for items such as children's welfare, an e-learning initiative, flood control, and local construction projects. This campaign had some resonance with the general public. In response, the opposition parties readjusted their strategies: instead of directly reducing the individual budgets, they used budget resolutions to impose extra conditions and constraints on the administration for how the money was to be used. As a consequence, the average budget cut rate for the third period dropped to only 1.56 percent.

Budget resolutions accompany the budget report and are promulgated by the president. In 1997, the Budget Law was revised to require the Executive Yuan to obey the budget resolution. Budget resolutions have varied, in both number and content, with the party in control of the executive. As Table 6.2 shows, the number of budget resolutions increased dramatically, from 98 to 191, after the DPP government submitted its first budget proposal to the LY for review. Although the number dropped in the 2002 budget review, this decrease probably occurred because legislators were busy with their reelection campaigns, as the number went up again as soon as the election was over. During the Chen administration, the overall trend in the number of budget resolutions was upward, declining only at the end of every three-year cycle due to the legislative elections. The average number of budget resolutions was 61.0 in the first period, 147.5 in the second, and 503.7 in the third. When the number of seats became more evenly balanced between the two rival camps, partisan conflict escalated; thus, the number of budget resolutions went up abruptly in the third period, despite the DPP's seat gain. During the period of unified government, legislators would express some suggestions through the resolutions but with no binding demands. During the periods of divided government, however, the opposition parties found ways to constrain the government by using budget resolutions. For example, many resolutions froze certain parts of budgets, requiring related administration staff to write a detailed plan and report to the related committee. In the 2005 annual government budget, for instance, a total of 212.9 billion in new Taiwan dollars (NT$) was frozen through 206 separate resolutions, covering 13.4 percent of the total government budget.

Table 6.1 Proportion of Legislative Yuan–Imposed Budget Cuts by Year, 1993–2010

Type of government	Year	Average yearly budget cut rate (%)
Unified government	1993	1.40
(first period)	1994	3.88
	1995	2.15
	1996	1.75
	1997	1.34
	1998	1.46
	1999	1.42
	2000	0.93
Divided government	2001	2.03
(second period)	2002	5.04
Divided government	2003	1.41
(third period)	2004	1.22
	2005	1.67
	2006	1.74
	2007	2.13
	2008	0.80
Unified government	2009	1.10
(fourth period)	2010	1.15

Source: Directorate-General of Budget, Accounting, and Statistics, Executive Yuan (2008), http://www.dgbasey.gov.tw/dgbas01/dgbas01.htm.

Table 6.2 Number of Legislative Yuan Budget Resolutions, 1997–2008

Type of government	Year	Number of budget resolutions
Unified government	1997	27
(first period)	1998	39
	1999	80
	2000	98
Divided government	2001	191
(second period)	2002	104
Divided government	2003	327
(third period)	2004	397
	2005	262
	2006	592
	2007	865
	2008	579

Sources: Various issues of *Annual Central Government Budget Review Reports*.

As one senior official from the Directorate-General of Budget, Accounting, and Statistics said, "In the past, though there was quarreling and debating during the budget review, we did not worry because we all knew when the vote was counted, the incumbent [government] would eventually win. But now opposition parties use all kind of methods to boycott the government's budget; budget resolutions and additional resolutions are some of the methods they use."[19]

The DPP government's difficult position and its intense confrontation with the opposition parties were further demonstrated by the fate of the 2007 fiscal year budget. The Chen administration's budget bill was referred to the legislature in September 2006. According to Article 51 of the Budget Law, the legislature is supposed to review and pass the budget plan no later than December of the previous year—that is, at the end of December 2006. However, the bill was delayed for 197 days. The delay was due to the KMT's decision to hold up the budget bill in order to get the DPP's agreement on the KMT's proposed amendment of the Organic Law of the Central Election Commission, restructuring it to create a Pan-Blue majority.

The Pan-Blue–controlled Procedure Committee put the Organic Law of the Central Election Commission at the top of the legislative agenda, ahead of the budget bill. After several months of confrontation, including fighting, shouting, and shoe throwing, KMT chair Ma Ying-jeou finally ordered the KMT caucus to allow the budget bill to be reviewed ahead of the commission bill and to pass it before the end of the legislative session. The LY finally passed the 2007 central government budget on June 22, 2007, but froze NT$62.0 billion of the total budget. Premier Chang Chun-hsiung claimed that the delay of the bill's passage had hurt the economy, hindering the launch of NT$70.6 billion of new public investment and infrastructure projects. He also pointed out that the delay could result in a slowdown of economic growth of an estimated 0.25 to 0.30 percentage points.[20]

In short, there is no evidence of meaningful differences in the size of budget cuts during unified versus divided government. However, the dramatic increase in the number of budget resolutions demonstrates that opposition legislators found other ways to exert control over government policies and to make life difficult for the executive branch during the Chen administration.

Agenda Control and Deliberation over Legislation

The constitution gives the Executive Yuan the right to initiate a government bill; the Legislative Yuan then has the power to revise the bill or propose a new bill under the same title. Executive bills enjoy no priority over private bills, thus leaving the Executive Yuan little constitutional power to intervene in the legislative agenda, especially when the government does not enjoy a majority of seats in the LY.

A proposed bill is first sent to the Procedure Committee, which consists of nineteen members assigned in proportion to each party caucus's share of seats in the legislature. (Each party caucus must have at least one member.) The Procedure Committee will decide whether the bill satisfies all procedural rules and is in compliance with the powers and functions of the Legislative Yuan. If there is no problem, the committee will forward the bill to the appropriate committee for review and decide the order in which bills will be reviewed. If the government wants to push legislation to be passed as soon as possible, it must persuade Procedure Committee members to place it in a priority position on the agenda.

In a study of the Third to Fifth LYs (1996–2005), Hawang found that whenever the incumbent party did not control the Procedure Committee, more confrontation took place in the committee.[21] It is no surprise that these confrontations became more severe when the DPP became the incumbent party, because it did not control a majority in the LY. On several occasions, every proposal sent from the Executive Yuan was blocked in the Procedure Committee. At one time, 50 different bills from the Executive Yuan were frozen, and more than 100 proposals were sent back from standing committees to the Procedure Committee. Vice Speaker Chiang Pinkun termed this "mutually destructive behavior."[22] The result of the conflict was long delays of legislation and a bad public image for the Legislative Yuan. Moreover, the pace of legislative action lagged far behind the expectations of the Executive Yuan. For example, during the third session of the Fifth LY, the Executive Yuan proposed 102 priority bills for either amendment or enactment.[23] Of these, only sixteen were passed, and twenty-eight remained stalled in the Procedure Committee.[24]

Table 6.3 provides more evidence of the Procedure Committee's role in the legislative process under unified versus divided government. During the Second Legislative Yuan, bills were rarely blocked or delayed by the Procedure Committee. In the first through third sessions of the Third LY (1996–1999), the ruling KMT did not fully control the committee, and there was a slight increase in the number of bills being blocked or delayed. But when the ruling party regained a majority in the Procedure Committee, the number declined again. In the first through third sessions of the Fourth LY (1999–2002), during a period of unified government, the Procedure Committee blocked only thirteen bills, as Table 6.3 shows. By contrast, during the period of divided government starting in 2000, the committee started to wield its gatekeeping power again, and 253 bills were blocked. The number of bills indefinitely stalled in the Procedure

Table 6.3 Number of Bills Blocked or Delayed by the Procedure Committee, 1993–2008

Term and session	Type of government	Number of meetings	Frequencies of bills blocked or delayed
2-1	Unified government	44	0
2-2	(first period)	29	0
2-3		37	1
2-4		32	1
2-5		35	1
2-6		21	9
Subtotal		197	12
3-1	Unified government	22	26
3-2	(first period)	30	21
3-3		26	26
3-4		22	18
3-5		22	4
3-6		11	2
Subtotal		133	97
4-1	Unified government	12	3
4-2	(first period)	18	4
4-3		33	6
4-4	Divided government	29	135
4-5	(second period)	18	112
4-6		13	6
Subtotal		123	268
5-1	Divided government	19	36
5-2	(third period)	17	105
5-3		15	289
5-4		18	542
5-5		24	640
5-6		16	533
Subtotal		109	2,145
6-1	Divided government	12	172
6-2	(third period)	19	367
6-3		19	504
6-4		17	719
6-5		17	754
6-6		16	695
Subtotal		67	3,211

Sources: The data are counted from the written records of the Procedure Committee's meetings.

Committee increased to 2,145 bills during the third session of the Fifth LY; of these, 698 had been proposed by the Executive Yuan. The situation became even worse during the Sixth LY (2005–2008), when the number of stalled bills increased to 3,211. Two problems with the Procedure Committee are that none of its meetings are open to the public, and unlike other standing committees, it does not keep any written public records. If citizen participation and transparency are a way to keep the legislature more accountable and responsible, the Procedure Committee certainly has far to go.

From the previous discussion, it is clear that there is a significant difference in the Procedure Committee's role under unified versus divided government. When the KMT has controlled both the executive and the legislature, the work of the Procedure Committee has been routine, and it has usually set the agenda according to the Executive Yuan's demands. By contrast, during periods of divided government under the Chen administration, Procedure Committee members became the focus of media attention. The Committee became the place where bills went to die: its members regularly stalled or killed bills that the opposition parties disliked without any public discussion or debate.

Moreover, even if proposed bills make it out of the Procedure Committee and are sent to the floor or standing committees for review, there is no guarantee they will pass. Sheng, for instance, found that an executive branch–initiated bill was likely to be passed much more easily and faster under unified government than under divided government.[25] Another indicator of legislative efficiency is the success of roll-call votes on government-initiated bills. Roll-call data can be used not only to calculate a rate of success when the incumbent party had a clear position on a vote but also to examine the patterns of cross-party alliances and party unity scores.

Table 6.4 shows the results of the roll-call votes, which did not account for most of the legislative decisions in the LY. Nevertheless, differences can be observed across periods of unified versus divided party control. During the first two sessions of the Fourth LY (1999–2000)—a period of unified government—the ruling KMT prevailed on 98 percent of the 177 roll-call votes on which it took a position. By contrast, during the third to sixth sessions of the Fourth LY (2000–2002), when the ruling DPP held less than one-third of the seats, it prevailed on only about a third (33 of 96). During the Fifth LY (2002–2005), when the DPP became the largest party but was still short of a majority, the party's success rate on roll-call votes remained only about one in three, or 32.9 percent. This dropped precipitously during the Sixth LY (2005–2008), when a mere 16 percent of bills were passed. The contrast with the post-2008 period is stark: after the KMT again became the ruling party and gained a supermajority, it won every single roll-call vote in the Seventh LY (2008–2012).

Table 6.4 also shows that during unified government, there were fewer votes in which each party took a clear position than during divided government. During unified periods, the KMT took a clear position on 78 percent of the votes, but during the divided government periods, the ruling

Table 6.4 Number and Success Rate of Roll-Call Votes by Type of Government, 1999–2009

Type of government	Session	Number of roll-call votes	Incumbent party	Frequency and percentage of incumbent party success on roll-call votes	Frequency and percentage of incumbent party failure on roll-call votes	Frequency and times incumbent party had clear position
Unified	4-1	85	KMT	79 (97.53%)	2 (2.47%)	81
government	4-2	139	KMT	98 (98.99%)	1 (1.01%)	99
(first period)	Subtotal	224	KMT	177 (98.33%)	3 (1.67%)	180 (78.3%)
Divided	4-3	1	DPP	0 (0.00%)	0 (0.00%)	1
government	4-4	52	DPP	11 (22.00%)	39 (78.00%)	50
(second period)	4-5	31	DPP	13 (41.94%)	18 (58.06%)	31
	4-6	15	DPP	9 (60.00%)	6 (40.00%)	15
	Subtotal	99	DPP	33 (34.38%)	63 (65.63%)	96 (97.0%)
Divided	5-1	72[a]	DPP	24 (33.33%)	47 (65.28%)	71
government	5-2	20	DPP	7 (35.00%)	13 (65.00%)	20
(third period)	5-3	65	DPP	16 (24.62%)	49 (75.38%)	65
	5-4	130	DPP	26 (20.00%)	104 (80.00%)	130
	5-5	101	DPP	40 (39.60%)	61 (60.40%)	101
	5-6	75	DPP	39 (52.00%)	36 (48.00%)	75
	Subtotal	463	DPP	152 (32.90%)	310 (67.10%)	462 (99.78%)
Divided	6-1	16	DPP	8 (50.00%)	8 (50.00%)	16
government	6-2	77	DPP	2 (2.60%)	75 (97.40%)	77
(fourth period)	6-3	62	DPP	11 (17.74%)	51 (82.26%)	62
	6-4	23	DPP	4 (17.39%)	19 (82.61%)	23
	6-5	91	DPP	19 (20.88%)	72 (79.12%)	91
	6-6	13	DPP	1 (7.69%)	12 (92.31%)	13
	Subtotal	282	DPP	45 (15.96%)	237 (84.04%)	282 (100%)
Unified	7-1[b]	49	KMT	48 (100.00%)	0 (0.00%)	48
government	7-2	263	KMT	261 (100.00%)	0 (0.00%)	261
(fifth period)	Subtotal	312	KMT	309 (100.00%)	0 (0.00%)	309 (99%)

Source: Author's calculations from roll-call votes in various issues of *Li Fa Yuan Kuan Pao.*
Notes: a. In the first session of the Fifth LY, one roll-call vote ended in a tie, so it is not counted as either a success or a failure. b. In the first session of the Seventh LY, in one case both KMT and DPP held the same position, so this vote is not counted as either a success or a failure. All 49 roll-call votes occurred after the KMT returned to power.

party had a clear position on almost all the roll-call votes. This shift is consistent with the claim that party confrontation became more common from 2000 to 2008.

Tables 6.5 and 6.6 show the results of different types of party alliances and party unity scores. By contrast, during the periods of divided government, especially during the third period, the Pan-Blue and Pan-Green coalitions were relatively unified and strongly opposed to one another, leaving little room for other types of coalitions to form. Party

Table 6.5 Frequency of Interparty Alliances by Roll-Call Votes, 1997–2008

A. First period: First and second sessions of the Fourth LY (1999–2000)
Major parties: KMT, DPP, and TSU

Type of alliances	Frequencies	Percentage
DPP vs. KMT + NP	28	12.5%
NP vs. DPP + KMT	28	12.5%
KMT vs. DPP + NP	56	25.0%
DPP vs. KMT	17	7.6%
DPP vs. NP	6	2.7%
KMT vs. NP	5	2.2%
Nonpartisan voting	84	37.5%

B. Second period: Third through sixth sessions of the Fourth LY (2000–2002)
Major parties: KMT, DPP, PFP, and NP

Type of alliances	Frequencies	Percentage
DPP vs. KMT + NP + PFP	47	47.5%
DPP + PFP vs. KMT + NP	3	3.0%
DPP + PFP vs. NP	2	2.0%
DPP vs. KMT + PFP	6	6.1%
DPP vs. NP + PFP	11	11.1%
DPP vs. NP	7	7.1%
NP vs. PFP	2	2.0%
Nonpartisan voting	21	21.2%

C. Third period: Fifth LY (2002–2005)
Major parties: KMT, DPP, PFP, and TSU

Type of alliances	Frequencies	Percentage
DPP + TSU vs. KMT + PFP	289	63.4%
DPP vs. KMT + PFP□most members of TSU were absent□24		5.3%
DPP vs. KMT + PFP + TSU	21	4.6%
DPP + PFP vs. TSU	2	2.17%
DPP vs. PFP	2	0.4%
TSU vs. KMT + PFP + DPP	63	13.8%
Nonpartisan voting	24	5.3%

Sources: The roll-call votes were collected from various issues of *Li Fa Yuan Kuan Pao*.

voting is defined as, at a minimum, a majority of one party voting in opposition to a majority of the other party.

Another way to compare differences between unified and divided government is to look at the kinds of cross-party alliances that formed most frequently. Table 6.5 displays all possible combinations of party alliances on roll-call votes. Overall, during the period of KMT control before 2000, party discipline among different parties was looser, there was less party confrontation, and voting coalitions varied across different

Table 6.6 Party Unity Scores, 1993–2012

Term	Type of government	DPP	KMT	NP	PFP	TSU
Second LY (1993–1996)	Unified (first period)	75.5%	63.2%	—	—	—
Third LY (1996–1999)	Unified (first period)	88.5%	70.9%	75.0%	—	—
Fourth LY (1999–2002)	Divided (second period)	94.8%	71.4%	69.9%	78.7%	—
Fifth LY (2002–2005)	Divided (third period)	94.4%	80.1%	82.5%	91.3%	86.5%
Sixth LY (2005–2008)	Divided (third period)	93.5%	91.4%	NA	85.8%	93.5%
Seventh LY (2008–2012)	Unified (fourth period)	85.1%	72.6%	NA	NA	NA

Sources: The Second LY data are from Li-Shang Hwang, "Incentives and Cohesion of Congressional Parties: The Second Legislative Yuan" (master's thesis, Soochow University, 1999).

Data on the Fourth through Seventh LY terms were calculated by the author. The data on the Seventh LY only include the first two sessions.

Notes: NA stands for not applicable. NP only has one seat in the Sixth LY, but no seat in the Seventh LY. TSU has no seat, while PFP only has one seat in the Seventh LY.

types of legislation. In a quarter of roll-call votes, opposition parties (that is, the DPP and the New Party [NP]) allied together against the incumbent KMT; in 12.5 percent of votes, the KMT allied with the DPP against the NP; and on another 12.5 percent of roll-call votes, the KMT acted with the NP in opposing the DPP. On cross-Strait relations issues, the KMT typically voted with the NP, whereas on environmental issues (including the fourth nuclear power plant budget), the NP and DPP joined together to oppose the KMT. With regard to certain economic development and local issues, the KMT allied with the DPP. There were 37.5 percent of votes that had no partisan division.

After the KMT became the opposition party in 2000, there was an interesting change of alliance patterns. The modal pattern of party alliance was the incumbent DPP versus all three opposition parties—the KMT, PFP, and NP—which constituted 47.5 percent of the votes. On five different occasions, the PFP allied with the DPP, but the KMT no longer ever allied itself with the DPP. Nonpartisan votes declined to 21.2 percent of the total. Party-line voting dramatically increased during Chen Shui-bian's second term, as nonpartisan votes declined to only 5.3 percent of the total. The modal pattern of cross-party alliance during this period was Pan-Green (DPP with TSU) against Pan-Blue (KMT with PFP), which made up 63.4 percent of all roll-call votes. Again, the KMT did not ally itself with the DPP except under special circumstances—for instance, when the TSU raised relatively radical proposals, such as cutting the salary of legislators in half and setting more limitations on cross-Strait marriages.

In addition to the increasing stability of the Pan-Blue and Pan-Green alliances, legislative party cohesion also increased during the Chen era. Cohesion is usually measured through average party unity scores, which are calculated as a percentage of each individual legislator's votes cast in agreement with his or her party's position. For example, if there were 100 party votes and one legislator had 70 votes in accord with his or her own party, then that legislator's personal party unity score would be 70 percent. When the KMT still dominated the legislature in the Second LY (1993–1996), both the DPP and KMT party unity scores were not particularly high; but as the smaller party, the DPP usually had higher party unity scores. The DPP's party unity scores increased further after President Chen took office in 2000, reaching as high as 94.8 percent. By contrast, the KMT's unity scores remained much lower during the first year of Chen's first term. Sharp partisan divisions and higher party unity within the Pan-Blue camp became more apparent after the 2001 legislative election, in which the DPP became the largest party in the legislature, although it was still short of a majority. With the seats held by the two camps closely balanced, the unity scores of all parties also increased—from 71 to 80 percent for the KMT, 79 to 91 percent for the PFP, and 70 to 82 percent for the NP. This kind of disciplined, party-line voting continued in the Sixth LY (2005–2008), when the party unity scores of the KMT reached as high as 91 percent (Table 6.6). Once the KMT returned to power in 2008, these figures went down to 85.1 percent for the DPP and 72.6 percent for the KMT.

Before the turnover of ruling parties in 2000, legislators would sometimes berate government officials in legislative hearings and criticize government bills; but this kind of behavior typically did not prevent bills from passing or constrain the behavior of executive agencies. Once President Chen took office, however, there was no reason for the Pan-Blue opposition parties to give the ruling DPP a free pass. The DPP government lost many important votes, including one enacting the Act of the Special Commission on the Investigation of the Truth About the March 19 Shooting Incident and another on the Organic Act of the National Communications Commission. Moreover, many important bills drafted by the Executive Yuan were either delayed or blocked in the Procedure Committee, including the Military Procurement Act, the Anti-Corruption Bureau Organization Law, and the Organic Act of National Human Rights Commission. Even the nominations of members of the Control Yuan were blocked.

Yet another issue in executive-legislative relations is the passage of legislation opposed by the Executive Yuan. The premier has the authority to block bills and return them to the Legislative Yuan for further consideration. However, the 1997 reforms lowered the required threshold for overriding a veto by the premier from a two-thirds supermajority to an absolute majority of all LY members. In this situation, the president and premier have to accept legislative resolutions that win majority support in the LY. Since the Chen administration never controlled a majority in the Legislative Yuan during its two terms in office, it was rarely able to sustain a veto of any bill passed by the legislature.

In light of the intense and consistent opposition of the legislative majority to the Executive Yuan's policies, it is worth revisiting why the opposition did not try to oust the premier through a vote of no confidence. The Legislative Yuan may propose a no-confidence vote against the premier of the Executive Yuan with the signature of more than one-third of its members. Should more than half of the total number of legislators approve the motion, the motion is passed, and the premier must resign. Nevertheless, because this then gives the president the option to dissolve the legislature and call new elections, the opposition parties were deterred from using this weapon to assert direct control over the Executive Yuan. Opposition legislators preferred not to risk using this power because of the extraordinary cost of running election campaigns and the high degree of uncertainty about the results of an election held as the result of a no-confidence vote.

This preference was clearly illustrated during the confrontation between the Executive Yuan and the Legislative Yuan over the fourth nuclear power plant issue, when the legislature chose not to vote out the premier. Instead, the opposition parties bottled up the nuclear plant legislation and treated Premier Chang as persona non grata, even refusing to let him enter the Legislative Yuan. This choice of action undoubtedly exacerbated the conflict between these two branches and contributed to the confrontational nature of executive-legislative relations that characterized most of the Chen Shui-bian era.

Conclusion

Chen Shui-bian's election as president in 2000 ushered in the first period of divided government in Taiwan's history, with a DPP president facing a legislature controlled by the KMT and its allies. President Chen could have let the opposition KMT form the cabinet, as has happened in France—the so-called "cohabitation" solution to divided government in a semipresidential system. However, this would have limited the president's authority to the areas of cross-Strait relations and national defense. After the resignation of President Chen's first premier, KMT member Tang Fei, Chen decided to go ahead and appoint a member of his own party as premier. However, because the administration did not have a majority in the legislature, it was almost inevitable that Chen's government would face a strong challenge from the opposition.

Previous research on the impact of divided government, both in the United States and in Taiwan, has produced mixed findings about its effects on policymaking. This chapter used new data and indicators to compare policy outcomes during different periods of unified and divided government in Taiwan. I found significantly different outcomes when one party controlled both the executive and legislative branches than when control was split. Budget cuts turned out not to be a good measurement of executive-legislative conflict, because opposition party members did not want to be accused of sabotaging the national budget. Instead, opposition legislators used a more sophisticated tool, budget resolutions, to exert control over the executive branch. The number of budget resolutions was low before 2000 during the first period of unified KMT control, higher during President Chen's first term in office, and the highest during his second term, as expected.

The Chen administration also was largely unable to control the legislative agenda. Between 2000 and 2008, thousands of bills prioritized by the Executive Yuan were either delayed or blocked in the Procedure Committee. My analysis of roll-call votes points to the same conclusion: the DPP government faced consistent obstruction from the opposition parties in the legislature, losing the majority of votes it faced, while enduring frequent confrontations with hostile legislators.

Since the 2008 legislative and presidential elections, Taiwan's politics have gone through another dramatic change. The KMT scored a sweeping victory over the DPP in legislative elections in January 2008, winning 81 of 113 seats, including 61 district seats, to secure a two-thirds majority. Other small parties were almost eliminated. Since legislators were first popularly elected in 1992, no party has ever held such a dominant majority in the LY. When the KMT candidate Ma Ying-jeou resoundingly defeated DPP candidate Frank Hsieh two months later by a margin of 17 percent, the KMT regained decisive control of both the executive and legislative branches.

Separation-of-powers systems like Taiwan's are designed to promote horizontal accountability—that is, to ensure that state institutions have the capacity to check abuse by other branches of government and public agencies. The most important check on the executive is the legislature, which performed this role aggressively during the Chen Shui-bian era. However, once the executive and legislative branches were again unified under KMT control, and the KMT enjoyed overwhelming dominance in the LY, the ruling party needed no support from any opposition parties to pass legislation and to launch new, far-reaching reforms. By contrast, the opposition parties have found few ways to challenge the power of the KMT government. The results of roll-call votes during the first session of the Seventh LY clearly show that the KMT won the votes it wanted (see Table 6.4). Thus, after the 2008 elections, there was reason to worry that a KMT-dominated majority in the LY would mean a setback for Taiwan's democracy.

Nor is this period of KMT dominance likely to end soon. Under the new electoral system first used in 2008, small parties have little chance of winning significant numbers of seats in the future. Unless small parties have support concentrated in certain regions, they will have no chance of winning any seats in the single-member districts. Although the party-list vote is meant to compensate for the disproportionality of the single-member-district vote, these proportional representation seats account for only about 30 percent of the LY; with a 5 percent threshold required to win legislator-at-large seats, it is not easy for small parties to gain any proportional representation seats either. In fact, in 2008, neither the TSU nor the NP reached the 5 percent threshold. In some constituencies, such as the offshore islands, the east coast, and aboriginal seats, the game is pretty much set in favor of the KMT. Unless the KMT has a very poor performance, even the largest opposition party, the DPP, is unlikely to win control of the LY. This structural advantage for the KMT in legislative elections poses a serious challenge to Taiwan's democracy. Moreover, it is not likely to be altered any time soon, given that the electoral system is now implanted in the constitution; amending the constitution requires both the support of three-fourths of LY members and approval in a referendum by an absolute majority of all eligible voters in Taiwan. It will simply not be possible to amend the system again unless the KMT voluntarily agrees to do so or comes under very strong public pressure. In short, whatever happens in presidential elections, the era of KMT dominance of the LY is likely to last a long time.

Notes

1. Jih-wen Lin, "Institutionalized Uncertainty and Governance Crisis in Post-Hegemonic Taiwan," *Journal of East Asian Studies* 3, no. 3 (2003): 433–460.
2. These studies include the following: Morris Fiorina, *Divided Government,* 2nd ed. (Boston: Allyn and Bacon, 1996); Charles Jones, *The Presidency in a Separated System* (Washington, DC: Brookings Institution, 2005); Keith Krehbiel, "Insti-

tutional and Partisan Sources of Gridlock: A Theory of Divided and Unified Government," *Journal of Theoretical Politics* 8, no. 1 (1996): 7–40; Keith Krehbiel, *Pivotal Politics: A Theory of US Lawmaking* (Chicago: University of Chicago Press, 1998); David R. Mayhew, "Divided Party Control: Does It Make a Difference?" *PS: Political Science and Politics* 24, no. 4 (1991): 637–640; David R. Mayhew, *Divided We Govern: Party Control, Lawmaking, and Investigations, 1946–1990* (New Haven, CT: Yale University Press, 1991); Mark P. Petracca, "Divided Government and the Risks of Constitutional Reform," *PS: Political Science and Politics* 24, no. 4 (1991): 634–637; J. Paul Quirk and Bruce Nesmith, "Explaining Deadlock: Domestic Policymaking in the Bush Presidency," in *New Perspective on American Politics,* ed. C. Dodd Lawrence and Calvin Jillson (Washington, DC: CQ Press, 1994).

3. See Mayhew, "Divided Party Control," 637–640.

4. See Mayhew, *Divided We Govern,* 639. In the second edition of his book (2005), Mayhew further reconfirmed his argument with a longer period of study.

5. Jones, *The Presidency in a Separated System.*

6. Fiorina, *Divided Government.*

7. Benjamin Ginsberg and Martin Shefter, *Politics by Other Means* (New York: Basic Books, 1990).

8. Gary W. Cox and Samuel Kernell, "Introduction: Governing a Divided Era," in *The Politics of Divided Government,* ed. Gary W. Cox and Samuel Kernell (Boulder, CO: Westview Press, 1991).

9. L. James Sundquist, "Needed: A Political Theory for the New Era of Coalition Government in the United States," *Political Science Quarterly* 103, no. 4 (1988): 613–635; N. Lloyd Cutler, "Some Reflections About Divided Government," *Presidential Studies Quarterly* 18, no. 3 (September 1988): 489–490.

10. Q. Sean Kelly, "Punctuated Change and the Era of Divided Government," in *New Perspectives on American Politics,* ed. C. Lawrence Dodd and Calvin Jillson (Washington, DC: CQ Press, 1994), 162–190; John J. Coleman, "Unified Government, Divided Government, and Party Responsiveness," *American Political Science Review* 93, no. 4 (1999): 821–835; William Howell, Scott Adler, Charles Cameron, and Charles Riemann, "Divided Government and the Legislative Productivity of Congress, 1945–94," *Legislative Studies Quarterly* 25, no. 2 (2000): 285–312.

11. George C. W. Edwards III, Andrew Barrett, and Jeffrey Peake, "Legislative Impact of Divided Government," *American Journal of Political Science* 41, no. 2 (1997): 545–563.

12. Chung-li Wu and Chang-chih Lin, "The Executive-Legislative Interactions at the Central Government Level Before and After the 2000 Presidential Election in Taiwan: An Examination of the Fourth Nuclear Power Plant Controversy and the Lawmaking Process" [in Chinese], *Theory and Policy* 16, no. 1 (2002): 73–98.

13. Wan-ying Yang, "Party Cooperation and Conflict Under Divided Government: The Fourth Term Legislative Yuan" [in Chinese], *Soochow Journal of Political Science* 16 (2003): 49–95.

14. Shing-Yuan Sheng, "The Influence of the Legislative Branch and the Executive Branch in the Process of Lawmaking: A Comparison of the Unified and Divided Governments" [in Chinese], *Taiwanese Political Science Review* 7, no. 2 (2003): 51–106.

15. Shiow-duan Hawang, "The Predicament of Minority Government in the Legislative Yuan" [in Chinese], *Taiwanese Political Science Review* 7, no. 2 (2003): 1–46.

16. Shiow-duan Hawang and Hung-Jiun Chen, "An Analysis of Party Interaction from Roll-Call Votes in Taiwan's Legislative Yuan: The Third Term to the Fifth Term of the Legislative Yuan" [in Chinese], *Journal of Social Sciences and Philosophy* 18, no. 3 (2006): 385–415.

17. Shiow-duan Hawang, "Divided Government, Agenda-Setting, and Procedure Committees" [in Chinese] (paper delivered at the Tenth Annual Taiwanese Political Science Association Conference, Taipei, Soochow University, December 2003).

18. The roll-call vote data are collected from the Legislative Yuan's written records, the *Li Fa Yuan Kuan Pao*.

19. Author's interview with one of the division heads of the Directorate-General of Budget, Accounting, and Statistics, Executive Yuan.

20. "Premier Urges Special Legislative Session to Pass Bills," *Taipei Times,* July 22, 2007, 3.

21. Before 1999, each standing committee assigned two members to the Procedure Committee, for a total of twenty-four members. The distribution of seats on the committee was not proportional to each party's share of seats in the LY; therefore, the distribution of party seats varied at each session. During the first through third sessions of the Third LY, the KMT failed to control the Procedure Committee, despite holding a majority of seats in the LY. When DPP took office in 2000, they never got more than 50 percent of the seats in the Procedure Committee. See Shiow-duan Hawang, "Divided Government, Agenda-Setting, and Procedure Committees."

22. *United Daily News,* May 14, 2002.

23. This number does not include those proposals that were not regarded as priority bills.

24. Shiow-duan Hawang, "An Overview of the Legislation Passed in the Third Session of the Fifth Term Legislature" [in Chinese], in *To See Through the Legislative Yuan: 2003 Report on the Supervision of the Congress,* ed. Chu Hai-yuan (Taipei: Asian Culture, 2004), 13–14.

25. Sheng, "The Influence of the Legislative Branch and the Executive Branch," 85–87.

7

Horizontal Accountability and the Rule of Law

Weitseng Chen and Jimmy Chia-Shin Hsu

At the end of Chen Shui-bian's second term as president, Taiwan's democratic development stood at a crossroads. On the one hand, two turnovers of power—one in 2000 and another in 2008—had fulfilled Samuel Huntington's minimal "two turnover" test of democratic consolidation. The rule of law had greatly improved. Constitutionalism was generally established. The overall level of protection of civil liberties and political rights was high enough to keep the country "liberal," according to Freedom House rankings, for well over a decade. Among the third-wave democracies, Taiwan was fortunate enough to have advanced to a liberal democracy.

On the other hand, Taiwan's political development experienced notable setbacks during this period. Throughout most of Chen Shui-bian's two terms in office, the minority Democratic Progressive Party (DPP) government faced a hostile, obstinate opposition in the legislature, led by the majority Kuomintang and People First Party (KMT-PFP) "Pan-Blue" alliance. The partisan struggle between the DPP and the Pan-Blue camp was fueled by and, in turn, worsened Taiwan's most salient political cleavage—namely, the split in national identity. Former president Lee Teng-hui aptly described this political conflict as an ongoing "democratic civil war."[1] Indeed, partisan conflict delayed, and oftentimes distorted, major reforms, as well as all other significant public policy debates. In short, although Taiwan's democratic regime managed to remain liberal, the quality and effectiveness of its democratic governance deteriorated.

Taiwan's inconsistent development of liberal democracy and the quality of democratic governance testify to how rough and twisted the

145

path to democratic consolidation can be, even for a young but relatively advanced liberal democracy. The momentum of liberalization gathered from the early stage of democratization may not always be conducive to consolidation. In addition, the underlying social conflict unleashed by electoral competition may prove to be the most daunting challenge to further democratic development. In other words, Taiwan's experience suggests that sustained liberalness does not necessarily indicate consolidation, even though "liberalness" is an extremely important dimension of democratic development. Democratic consolidation is a matter of solid legitimation of the democratic institutions or "rules of the game." Yet Taiwan's experience bespeaks a twist that is often underestimated. Democratic institutions are not just neutral rules of the game; rather, they embody the statehood to which all major political forces must pledge allegiance. Democratic rules of the game cannot be fully legitimated if governments continually suffer from a serious deficit of legitimacy of the national identity and ideology they seek to represent and promote. For Taiwan's democracy to be consolidated, the fundamental challenge is for existing democratic institutions to solve or neutralize the problems caused by deeply divided politics, while at the same time ensuring that they themselves are not torn apart by those problems.

This chapter deals with one dimension of democratic institutions: horizontal accountability and rule of law. We evaluate the development of Taiwan's Judicial and Control Yuans and their contribution to democratic consolidation from the first turnover of power in 2000 through the end of Chen Shui-bian's second term in 2008. The primary question we seek to answer is—By the end of the Chen era, did the Judicial Yuan and Control Yuan constitute a solid part of the democratic institutions that would sustain Taiwan's further consolidation? To address this question, we must also ask whether and how these two branches of government promoted horizontal accountability, how they were affected by Taiwan's deeply divided politics, and how they responded to these political cross-pressures.

Independence, Supremacy, Accountability, and Capability

For all new democracies, one of the most important tasks of consolidation is to develop institutions that can ensure horizontal accountability—that is, to resolve conflicts between other branches of government, monitor the behavior of public officials, and punish official malfeasance. These institutions must operate with sufficient independence to apply general rules in an impartial, consistent, and reasonably predictable manner. Yet the independence of judges, ombudsmen, or supervisors does not guarantee that their decisions will be respectfully accepted or implemented by other governmental branches. Hence "supremacy" should be distinguished from "independence" as a distinct analytical dimension of these institutions.[2] Supremacy means that the judiciary and other horizontal accountability institutions have obtained sufficient legitimacy and authority to command compliance, and the losers are restrained from attacking the institutions.

However, neither independence nor supremacy is an end in itself. The fundamental virtue of a horizontal accountability institution lies in its promise to fulfill social functions for which it is instituted. The debate is often framed as the tension between "independence" and "accountability." Whereas independence frees the judiciary and horizontal accountability institutions from undue intervention, accountability means that these institutions should be held accountable for their decisions.

In addition to accountability and independence/supremacy, to meet their social functions, the judiciary and other horizontal accountability institutions have to be capable. Being capable involves the ability to deliver high-quality decisions and conduct other judicial and semijudicial actions properly. Capability concerns factors such as the quality of judges and ombudsmen, the efficiency and reasonableness of trial and investigation procedures, the proper application and reasoning of the decisions, the ability of the judiciary and horizontal accountability institutions as a whole to deliver consistent opinions, and so on.

Taken together, these four dimensions—independence, supremacy, accountability, and capability—describe what is required for effective, legitimate horizontal accountability institutions to function in a democracy. In the following sections, this chapter explores and evaluates how Taiwan's judiciary and the Control Yuan have evolved and performed on these dimensions.

An Unusual Foundation: Rule of Law Without Democracy

Taiwan's development of accountability institutions is unusual in that the authoritarian state initiated the transition to a rule of law decades prior to democratization. To be sure, full independence and supremacy of the judiciary are not possible without democracy. The capability and accountability of the judiciary were also problematic due to the political constraints imposed on it in the predemocratic era. Administrative law litigation, for instance, did not fulfill its function to correct governmental wrongdoing until well after the transition to democracy.[3] Nevertheless, Taiwan's early rule of law development set in place relatively favorable conditions for the subsequent transition to and consolidation of democracy.

The timing of the development of rule of law matters to democratic consolidation in general and horizontal accountability in particular. Democratic politics inevitably creates winners and losers. Therefore, successful democratic consolidation relies on functional third-party mechanisms to solve disputes. Many of the reversals in young democracies witnessed today are partially attributable to the failure to establish legitimate dispute-resolution mechanisms between contending political forces.[4] For Taiwan, thanks to an early transition to a system of rule of law, a relatively functional legal system existed when Taiwan started democratizing in the second half of the 1980s. That system has played a critical role in the rocky process of democratization.

The authoritarian KMT party-state's rationale for improving the rule of law was instrumental in nature: it used the rule of law as a substitute for democracy. As suggested by empirical studies, economic development and democracy are highly correlated. Development raises people's demand for democracy, which guarantees more freedom, while democracy ensures accountability, provides checks and balances, and benefits development.[5] The KMT regime, however, separated rule of law from democracy and used it as part of its economic developmental strategy.[6]

Based on the colonial legacy of a transplanted civil law system introduced by Japan, the KMT implemented a number of dual-track legal reforms. It placed more focus on laws governing economic life than on laws protecting political and civil rights. On the one hand, a body of Westernized civil laws was introduced to improve investment, corporate governance, and property rights. It met the rising demand for rights protection made by the beneficiaries of rapid economic growth, including state-owned enterprises, foreign companies, and the growing middle class. On the other hand, those who received less benefits, such as labor, were relatively satisfied with the trickle-down economic effects, while expecting reforms promised by statutes that turned out to be more symbolic than effectual.[7]

Political factors, both domestic and international, accelerated the development of rule of law. Regular local elections served as an alternative law enforcement mechanism: political activists frequently used laws to challenge the KMT's policies in their campaigns.[8] International influence succeeded in pressing the regime to carry out legal reforms and pay more respect to human rights, because the KMT desperately needed international financial aid and security support, mainly from the United States.[9] Consequently, by the beginning of the transition to democracy, a functional court system and a relatively competent class of legal professionals were already extant, with nascent constitutionalism and increasing rights consciousness among the general public.[10]

During the political transition, the independence and supremacy of the courts greatly improved, with constitutionalism gradually taking root.[11] The capability of the judiciary increased, along with the quality of legal professionals.[12] According to Freedom House 2005, the control of judicial corruption became increasingly effective. In a 2006 survey of lawyers' views on judicial corruption and independence, a mere 3.8 percent of respondents expressed dissatisfaction with the integrity of judges and legal staffs, while only 4.7 percent cast doubt on judicial independence.[13] In addition, reformists within and outside the judiciary, including prosecutors, lawyers, and nongovernmental organization activists, frequently staged collective campaigns calling for judicial reforms. For instance, the Judicial Reform Foundation has, since the mid-1990s, regularly conducted a nationwide evaluation of judges and issued annual reports. Volunteers are recruited to sit in on court trials to evaluate each judge's performance. In addition, in 1999, an unprecedented Judicial Reform Rally, led by lawyers, also pressed the Judicial Yuan to hold a national Judicial Reform Conference, which resulted in a series of reforms in the early 2000s.

Thanks to all these achievements, Taiwan's judiciary attained a meaningful degree of legitimacy by 2000. However, the fierce partisan divide that ensued after President Chen Shui-bian took office dragged the judiciary into the center of political warfare. It put judicial legitimacy to the severest test by forcing judges to rule upon politically sensitive issues. In such cases, the judiciary was in danger of suffering reprisals from one of the contending political forces, with judicial supremacy undermined and capability strained as a result. Despite substantial progress to that point, the legitimacy enjoyed by Taiwan's judiciary on the eve of the 2000 power turnover could not, in every case, withstand the pressures that were to follow.

The following sections illustrate this danger by reviewing the performance of two major sections of the judicial branch—the Constitutional Court and the regular court system.

The Constitutional Court

The Constitutional Court of Taiwan, officially known as the Council of Grand Justices,[14] won critical acclaim during Taiwan's democratic transition as it steadily expanded its jurisdiction, accessibility, and power in the 1990s. However, the increasingly polarized nature of politics after 2000 inserted the Court into a political minefield. Increasingly, the Court was asked to arbitrate or mediate political disputes. Yet the more it got involved, the deeper in the mud the Court was mired, and the more its independence, supremacy, and even capability were strained.

As the institution standing at the apex of judicial power, the Constitutional Court confronted the challenge of how to ensure compliance with its constitutional interpretations, while retaining independence and supremacy. The Court used to face only one paramount party actor that determined its latitude for action — the KMT. After 2000, however, the Court had to deal with multiple major actors that looked to it to resolve their disputes. This new political game changed the ways the Court achieved its goals.

At critical moments in the transition to democracy, the Court used its constitutional powers to carry out fundamental reforms. The Court's monumental Interpretation 261 (1990), for example, ordered the old representatives in the Legislative Yuan, National Assembly, and Control Yuan, who had remained in office for over thirty years, to leave office by 1991. This interpretation cleared away the strongest bastion of the regime's old guard and ushered in an age of extraordinary judicial activism.

However, in 2000, when the Court responded to the overwhelming public outcry against the National Assembly's self-aggrandizement in Interpretation 499, the Court triggered a nasty backlash. In this interpretation, the National Assembly's constitutional amendments, including one extending the term of its own members, were declared unconstitutional. This interpretation provoked the National Assembly to the utmost degree, and proposals to abolish the Court were in the air.

The fundamental question raised by these two dramatic episodes is to what extent the Court could secure authority that stood on its own, rather than relying merely on support lent from other political forces. Interpretation 261, for instance, was less daring than it appeared in that it reflected the dominance of the KMT's reformist faction over the old guard.[15] Likewise, it could be said that the Court survived the crisis triggered by Interpretation 499 because it consciously sided with the ideals endorsed by the loose yet dominant alliance of the reformist wing of the KMT with the DPP.

Unfortunately for the Court, this politically decisive base of support ceased to exist once politics became more partisan and the cross-party political consensus broke down. After the change in ruling parties in 2000, the Court struggled to have the positive impact that it had had in the 1990s.

Strategic Ambiguity as Political Cover

At first, the Court adopted an approach of strategic ambiguity to avoid direct confrontation with either side in political conflicts, with the intent to play the role of a mediator promoting more deliberation between the political branches. In Interpretation 419 (1996), for instance, the Court refused to declare clearly whether Vice President Lien Chan could serve as the premier at the same time. It did so to avoid being directly involved in the conflict between the KMT president and premier and opposition parties such as the DPP and the New Party.

However, when the Court took a similar approach in 2000, it suffered from severe backlash from both sides for not helping to resolve the political standoff between the DPP-controlled Executive Yuan and the KMT-controlled Legislative Yuan. In Interpretation 520, the Court avoided a clear-cut answer about whether the executive's unilateral decision to stop construction of a nuclear power plant was unconstitutional. As a result, both the DPP and KMT claimed victory based on their partial and selective understanding of the interpretation. The nasty political conflict continued.

The backlash against Interpretation 520 showed that judicial ambiguity in a deeply divided political system would prolong, rather than solve, conflicts between the contending forces. Neither did it create more room for further deliberation and strategic maneuvering. As the deadlocks continued, judicial indecisiveness merely invited criticism of the Court from both sides—that is, strategic ambiguity ultimately put the Court in a dangerous position, endangering its authority and legitimacy.

Constitutional Decisiveness at the Risk of Political Backlash

The Court could have, instead, recognized the danger of ambiguity and decided to explicitly express its legal stance. However, this strategy was also inherently dangerous, as constitutional decisiveness would necessitate siding with one of the contending forces. The challenges then for the Court were how to protect itself against attacks from the losing party and how to ensure that the losing party would continue to comply with the Court's decisions.

One severe test for the Court came in the wake of the 2004 presidential election, which President Chen narrowly won after surviving an assassination attempt. The KMT and PFP alleged that the assassination was a conspiracy staged by Chen himself to attract popular sympathy. To bolster their claim, the Pan-Blue camp passed the Act of the Special

Commission on the Investigation of the Truth with Respect to the March 19 Shooting. The commission, with members appointed in proportion to the partisan distribution of seats in the Legislative Yuan, was granted exclusive jurisdiction over the investigation and extraordinary prosecutorial power to compel people to testify. The Court soon faced this unprecedented issue after the Executive Yuan and DPP legislators vehemently condemned the act as unconstitutional and filed a constitutional petition.

Similar to the role of the US Supreme Court in the 2000 presidential election dispute, the Court was in a position to overturn the election result by affirming the legitimacy of the commission, which was likely to endorse the opposition's accusation against the election result's legitimacy. Within two months, the Court held the commission overall constitutional, but it invalidated certain crucial functions that were significant enough to justify the Executive Yuan's resistance by withholding money, personnel, and documents. Justice Hsu Tsung-Li pointed out in a dissent that the majority opinion actually went out of its way to favor the commission's powers. Nevertheless, the Court's prudence did not earn it any gratitude from KMT and PFP legislators.

The Court did not get away with severe criticism this time; much worse, it had to fight against the actions taken by the opposition parties in revenge for the ruling. With clear retaliatory intent, the Legislative Yuan soon cut not only the budget of the Judicial Yuan but also the salaries of the grand justices, plus the budget for administrative matters such as computerization of the justices' conference room, overseas business travel expenses, vehicle renewal fees, and legal research expenses.[16] In response, the Court had to declare in Interpretation 601 (2005) that the retaliatory salary budget cut was unconstitutional. However, it was not able to save the budget for other administrative items.[17]

Despite the retaliation, the Court was not deterred from challenging the Legislative Yuan. For instance, in Interpretation 613 (2006), on the nomination and appointment powers for members of the National Communications Commission, the highest media regulatory organ, the Court declared certain controversial provisions unconstitutional and condemned the provisions as legislative self-aggrandizement. Nevertheless, to moderate the shock, the Court used the rather common technique of "invalidation with deadline" in an extraordinary way. The Court allowed the unconstitutional provisions to remain valid for more than two and a half years, until after the 2008 legislative and presidential elections. With this act, the Court was signaling to the Legislative Yuan that it did not want to be accused of aiding the DPP government; rather, its unconstitutionality finding was based on nonpartisan considerations. Perhaps due to this political prudence, this interpretation was met with vocal criticism but no retaliatory action from the Pan-Blue camp.

Overall Assessment and Explanations

During the eight years of the DPP administration, the Court was over loaded with political issues that placed its hard-won independence and supremacy under serious strain. Yet the Court showed surprising resilience, even though it did not come through this period politically undamaged. First, the Court's constitutional decisiveness, coupled with various tactics to moderate the impact of its decisions, did help break political deadlocks, although at the cost of some of its own authority. Second, the fact that the Court served as a responsible institutional mediator of last resort deterred the losing parties from launching political attacks against it that would cripple its legitimacy. Last, the Court showed impartiality that kept the rival parties in the legal system, because the party losing at one time still had hope of winning the next time.

One caveat should be noted. Despite its modest success, the Court was not able to command compliance in all politically sensitive cases. For instance, due to the Legislative Yuan's boycott of President Chen's nominees, the Control Yuan remained vacant until after Chen had left office, even though the Court declared the boycott "contrary to the constitution" in Interpretation 632 (2007). Both President Chen and the Legislative Yuan showed little interest in breaking the deadlock over nominees during this period. Out of pure political calculation, the contending parties decided not to comply with the Court's decision.

In the future, the constitution will continue to create difficult problems for the Court whenever one party controls the legislature and the other the executive. Without structural reforms through constitutional amendments, such bitterly divided politics will continue to drag the Court into the center of partisan political struggles. The Court's central role in this context may provide it with an opportunity to increase its power. However, under divided government, it is no less a danger than an opportunity.

Regular Courts

In addition to the Constitutional Court, the regular courts were repeatedly dragged into the political struggle between the two party camps. This section focuses on three types of politically sensitive cases: defamation cases related to the political speech market, election disputes, and the efforts of the prosecutorial system to curb political corruption.

Defamation Litigation in the Political Speech Market

The deep political divide has been both a cause and a consequence of Taiwan's pathological political speech market. The dysfunction of political speech is embodied most vividly in "the politics of rumors"—the grossly irresponsible use of unsubstantiated accusations and innuendo in the media against political opponents. Ironically, starting rumors proved to be one of the most effective weapons in political competition during the Chen Shui-bian era. National legislators, high-level government officials, party leaders, and political talk show hosts all tried, with varying frequency and accuracy, to inflict damage on political enemies through defamatory statements in public. Political elites from all parties scrambled to dig up dirt on each other, with or without substantial proof. Partisan media joined the battle by providing forums and discursive ammunition, appealing to a polarized and segmented citizenry. Taiwan's political culture was not mature enough to contain the abuse. Slanderous legislators won reelection and increased their approval ratings among partisans of their own camp, even if only one out of every ten accusations they made was ultimately substantiated. A politically divided citizenry chose what it wanted to believe, not what was worth believing. The truth-seeking function of the political speech market was seriously threatened.

Yet false statements of fact directed at specific individuals were among the few types of flaws in the political speech market that could directly be sanctioned by the judiciary. Not surprisingly, then, litigation became the primary means for defamed politicians to seek redress and clear their names. After 2000, high-profile defamation cases became one of the most common types of political litigation. Many party leaders, high-level officials and representatives, and famous media political talk show hosts became entangled in multiple defamation suits.

Throughout the Chen era, Taiwan's judiciary in general demonstrated commendable independence in these defamation suits. President Chen Shui-bian and former President Lee Teng-hui, as well as politicians of all political stripes, lost libel cases, either as plaintiffs or defendants. However, independence was but one virtue among many that would help the judiciary tackle the politics of rumors. Taiwan's judiciary also needed to develop proper legal doctrines and actively regulate the political speech markets when all other speech-market-checking institutions were failing. But the judiciary did not succeed in this regard.

The defamation laws in Taiwan were weakened in 2000 when the Constitutional Court issued Interpretation 509. The Court reinterpreted the criminal defamation provisions in the Criminal Code, ruling that defendants accused of defamation do not have to prove their previous statements to be true in order to be absolved of criminal punishment. The defendants are required only to produce evidence demonstrating that they have "substantial reasons to believe in the truth" of the statements in question. This interpretation was one of the most remarkable moments in the liberalization of the political speech market during Taiwan's transition to democracy.[18]

However, Interpretation 509 also generated great confusion about its actual meaning and scope. In the four years following the interpretation, different tribunals of the Supreme Court, which is Taiwan's highest court in the chain of regular courts but separate from the Constitutional Court, issued contradictory decisions about whether Interpretation 509 applies to the tort of defamation. In a headline-breaking case,[19] in which Vice President Lu Hsiu-lien sued the prominent news magazine *The Journalist* for falsely naming her as the source of a scandalous rumor about President Chen's extramarital affairs, the Third Civil Panel of the Supreme Court refused to apply Interpretation 509 to tort cases and found *The Journalist* liable for the defamatory report. In stark contrast, later in the same year, the Fourth Civil Panel of the Supreme Court ruled in the opposite direction, finding the defendant, a famous writer and political commentator named Li Ao, not liable for falsely accusing a prominent DPP legislator, Chang Chun-hung, of conspiring to "destroy" Li's talk show and the host TV network.[20] The inconsistency remained through the end of the Chen era and percolated to all levels of courts, which made the outcome of tort libel cases and the awarding of civil damages highly unpredictable.

Despite the doctrinal disorder, a relatively consistent pattern of judicial decisionmaking emerged across the various court levels. In both criminal and civil libel cases, judicial decisions usually relaxed the fault standards to an extraordinary degree, thus giving the defendants substantial freedom from tort or criminal liability. A large number of these decisions explicitly invoked the American doctrine of actual malice when the defamatory statements concerned public affairs. Yet when viewed closely, the standard of actual malice employed by Taiwanese courts was actually even looser than the US version.[21] The appropriation of this doctrine in practice created a radically speech-protective legal framework for defamation.

These interpretations of defamation laws reflected a judicial retreat from the courts' social function of promoting political truth and revealed the institutional weaknesses of Taiwan's judiciary. First, the courts explicitly invoked the doctrine of actual malice without an accurate understanding of its meaning, ignoring much research on US case law done in Taiwan's academic law circles. Second, the deep partisan divide of the time

gave the Supreme Court little incentive to try to resolve the legal inconsistencies among its separate panels, because a centralized, decisive ruling might generate political backlash against the court. The radically
speech-protective interpretation of defamation laws might, in fact, have
been the safest strategy for the courts to adopt. The alternative was to
take on the more difficult task of policing the speech market consistent
with Interpretation 509, which would have given the courts an active role
in regulating campaign speech.

During the democratic transition in the 1990s, members of the mass
media and legal reformists advocated the adoption of the actual malice
doctrine in order to liberalize the previously strict defamation regime—
thus, the further relaxation of the doctrine's meaning actually served a
reform purpose. The problem was that, throughout the Chen era, the
courts continued to use this politically correct rhetoric as convenient legal
cover to avoid being drawn into partisan political disputes.

The Judiciary's Severest Test: Election Disputes

The severest test for Taiwan's judiciary during the Chen Shui-bian era
turned out to be the dramatic 2004 presidential election. When the final
vote count revealed a close victory for President Chen, the Pan-Blue candidates Lien Chan and James Soong refused to accept the result. Half a
million Pan-Blue supporters took to the streets and demanded a full
"executive recount" or a new election. These demands went nowhere
because both lacked a statutory basis. As a consequence, the Lien-Soong
camp ended up accepting that the only way to overturn the election result
was through the courts.[22] This initial stage of forum shopping showed
that rule of law in Taiwan significantly constrained the strategic options
available to the Lien-Soong camp.

Lien and Soong eventually filed two suits with the Taiwan High
Court, exhausting all the options for electoral litigation prescribed by law.
One suit was against the Central Election Commission on the grounds
that the commission held the election in an unlawful manner.[23] The other
suit was filed against Chen Shui-bian and Vice President Lu Hsiu-lien on
the grounds that they had used unlawful means to coerce voters.[24]
Inevitably, these two suits were too fraught with explosive political consequences to be handled effectively by the judiciary.

The call for a comprehensive recount of more than thirteen million
votes was at the center of all the disputes. The volatile political environment following the election all but guaranteed that any inadvertent mis-
take in the recount process would trigger a political maelstrom. The more
daunting problem was whom to entrust to carry it out, as the group of peo-

ple to shoulder the task would have to be trusted by both camps, and they needed to be motivated not just to represent partisan interests but also to serve higher principles of impartiality and fairness.

After intense negotiations, the historic task fell to the legal profession, with both camps recruiting hundreds of lawyers to do the recount. This decision, urged on all parties by the presiding judges, proved to be wise. According to the accounts of participants, lawyers recruited by both camps showed reason and restraints, despite intense and continuous arguments and negotiations. One participant recalled that he worked with lawyers of the opposite camp who used to be fellow judicial reformists, and this bond between them ensured a relatively peaceful, though intense, process.[25] In contrast to the deep polarization of partisan supporters outside the courtroom, the professional identity shared by the lawyers inside provided a crucial bridge between the hostile camps.

During the trial, the courts withstood tremendous political pressure throughout a difficult, time-consuming process. The Lien-Soong camp repeatedly reproached the judges for failing to investigate the evidence thoroughly, and when the scheduled deadline for one of the decisions approached, Pan-Blue legislators threatened the court with budget cuts and demanded that it postpone its ruling, for fear that the ruling would negatively influence the upcoming Legislative Yuan election. On the eve of the verdict, speculation was in the air that Pan-Blue supporters would besiege the court.

In the end, both tribunals of the Taiwan High Court delivered their decisions in favor of the DPP.[26] The Lien-Soong camp appealed both cases to the Supreme Court, where both appeals were later denied. The deciding factor was that the recount did not overturn the original result. The courts adopted the strictest interpretation of legal text under the Act of Presidential Election and Recall in order to minimize controversy over their rulings.

This strategy is not surprising, because sticking to the text and the narrowest construal of the law gave the courts the most secure ground on which to resolve the controversy. Yet it did not save the courts from retaliation by the losing party. The Lien-Soong camp assaulted the courts, and the Legislative Yuan, which was controlled by the Pan-Blue camp, cut the High Court's budget by 10 percent in the following year.[27]

Despite the harm inflicted on the courts due to the deep polarization of political elites, Taiwan's judiciary continued to play the role of final arbiter in election disputes. For instance, in the high-profile Kaohsiung City mayoral election of December 2006, the KMT candidate sued the DPP mayor-elect for manipulating the result by spreading false rumors on the eve of the vote. The district court ruled in favor of the KMT candidate this time. The ruling was then overturned by the High Court. Both rulings triggered loud, scathing criticism from the losing side. Thanks to the broader legitimacy of the judiciary, however, the final ruling stood, and the DPP winner retained office.

The Prosecutorial System: Curbing Corruption

For the authoritarian party-state, the prosecutorial system was a crucial link in the regime's power network. As Chin-shou Wang details in Chapter 12 of this volume, the prosecutorial system offered crucial tools for disciplining the KMT's patron-client relationships and, thus, was indispensable to the maintenance of its clientelist networks.[28] Not surprisingly, the reform of Taiwan's prosecutorial system came later than did judicial reform; it was also destined to be a more difficult and treacherous undertaking.

Reform of the prosecutorial system culminated in revision of the Judicial Organization Act in January 2006. The revised act included three significant reforms. First, it gave official status to the Committee for Deliberation of Prosecutorial Personnel Matters, a goal of the reform-minded prosecutors who wanted to weaken the personnel appointment and disciplinary power of the minister of justice. Composed of nine members elected by all prosecutors and eight members appointed by the minister and the prosecutor general, the Personnel Committee has critical de facto power over the appointment of district chief prosecutors and job rotation decisions. Even though the deliberative results of the committee are not officially conclusive and are subject to the discretion of the minister, an unwritten norm developed that the minister should not ignore the committee's advice. This institutional design further shrinks the room for undue political intervention through personnel management.

The second reform was to change the appointment of the prosecutor general from a direct ministerial appointment to a presidential nomination with consent of the Legislative Yuan. This revision elevated the status of the prosecutor general and helped shield him or her from politically motivated interference from the minister. In theory, the minister of justice was left only with general policymaking power and would have little room for discretion in individual cases.

However, in practice the minister was still able to influence the direction of criminal investigations, since he retained the final power to appoint and remove district chief prosecutors. Given the highly polarized political climate, the DPP government came to be suspicious that some prosecutors were politically biased; therefore, the DPP's minister of justice at that time, Shih Mau-lin, resisted yielding authority over personnel appointments to the Personnel Committee.[29] In 2007, the minister tried to force through an unexpected change of chief prosecutors when the nine popularly elected prosecutors were absent from a Personnel Committee meeting. He met with vociferous protests from the district-level prosecutors and finally had to compromise with the elected members. The showdown powerfully demonstrated the political importance of control over personnel appointments in the ministry, and it illustrated the unresolved tension between prosecutorial autonomy and political accountability in the Taiwanese prosecutorial system.

The third major reform enacted in the 2006 revision was the establishment of a Special Investigation Division (SID) at the Supreme Prosecutorial Agency, which came into full operation in April 2007. The SID was charged with the special task of pursuing crimes of corruption committed by the highest-ranking officials, disturbance of national elections, and other serious white-collar crimes menacing social order. The establishment of the SID reflected the suspicion of the Pan-Blue-dominated Legislative Yuan toward the impartiality of ordinary prosecutors in the wake of the 2004 presidential election dispute. Closely watched by all parties and operating in a volatile political environment, this division proved indiscriminate in its investigations during the last year of the Chen administration. However, the SID was quickly sucked into the middle of several of Taiwan's fiercest political storms.

The first dramatic episode came in November 2006, when Taipei district prosecutor Chen Rui-ren indicted the first lady Wu Shu-chen and several core staff members in the president's office for embezzling from the National and Presidential Affairs Fund and supplying unrelated receipts to cover their withdrawals. President Chen was clearly implicated and was spared prosecution only because of presidential immunity from criminal investigation. This indictment sent unprecedented shockwaves through Taiwan's already-inflamed political climate. In an effort to limit the political damage, DPP legislators in turn accused KMT party chair Ma Ying-jeou, at that time still mayor of Taipei, of embezzling from the Special Fund for Head Officials, to which all local executives had access. The SID was then charged with investigating Mayor Ma, as well as head officials of all political stripes. As a result, almost all prominent politicians came under investigation for improper use of special funds, and Ma was later prosecuted. Thus, the SID unwittingly became one of the most destabilizing institutions in Taiwan's politics.

The underlying issue in all these cases concerned the longtime customary practice of appropriating soft budget funds, which would be illegal under a strict interpretation of anticorruption laws but was rarely pursued in the past. As then-premier Su Tseng-chang commented, it was a "historical common liability" of which all parties and politicians were guilty, and it should not be made a crime. Yet politics was so bitterly divided that there was simply no room for rational deliberation and the development of a collaborative, cross-party solution. The indictments had to stand because they were deadly weapons to be wielded in the political struggle.

As a result, the SID got bogged down investigating a huge number of special funds cases. To make matters worse, the prosecutor general initially failed to lay down consistent prosecution standards for the Special Fund for Head Official cases. As the SID investigated Mayor Ma and other local executive officials, district prosecutors in Tainan adopted an obviously looser standard in their investigation of the mayor of Tainan City than that used in Ma Ying-jeou's case; in the end, they decided not to prosecute the mayor. Contrary to common practice, the prosecutor general did not try to establish a consistent prosecution standard in these cases until late May 2008, when Ma Ying-jeou was inaugurated as president and the KMT officially took over both the executive and legislative branches. The unusual delay occurred because the prosecutor general feared being condemned as aiding a particular politician or political party.

The Control Yuan

The Control Yuan in Transition

Compared to the Constitutional Court and the regular courts, the performance of the Control Yuan has been much less impressive. Reflecting Dr. Sun Yat-sen's constitutional prescription for a "five power" government, Taiwan's Control Yuan is constitutionally equal in status to the Legislative Yuan, Executive Yuan, Judicial Yuan, and Examination Yuan. It historically served as one of the main organs ensuring horizontal accountability and, today, retains the authority to audit the budget expenditures of state agencies, impeach governmental officials for unlawful behavior, and censure state agencies on ill-managed policy matters.[30]

During the authoritarian era, the Control Yuan served as a functional monitoring institution under the KMT-led developmental state. That some members of the Control Yuan were liberal reformists and that the KMT also needed an internal mechanism to monitor the bureaucratic system contributed to the Control Yuan's effectiveness in its early years. At that time, the Control Yuan indiscriminately audited officials at different levels. For instance, prior to the 1980s, among the civil service officials impeached for violating laws and abusing discretions, middle-ranked officials accounted for 39 percent, whereas higher-ranked and lower-ranked officials accounted for 20 percent and 31 percent, respectively.[31]

Nevertheless, under the KMT party-state, the Control Yuan's effectiveness was selective and limited. The Control Yuan paid much closer attention to the financial and economic agencies than to others, such as the police, civil, and social administrations. Between 1948 and 1996, 44 percent of all impeachment cases were related to officials in charge of financial and economic affairs, while police administration cases accounted for only 4 percent; judicial affairs, 10 percent; land administration, 3 percent; and social administration, 0.6 percent.[32] In practice, a dual-track enforcement system, which had far more focus on economic affairs than others, existed in the operation of the Control Yuan. This dual-track enforcement reflected the KMT's strategy of using the Control Yuan as an instrument to monitor the bureaucracy for the sake of economic performance, while being reluctant to use it against organs charged with maintaining authoritarian hegemony and internal order.

During the transition to democracy, the Control Yuan was transformed from a semirepresentative institution responsible for exercising horizontal accountability to a semijudicial institution shouldering the same function. Prior to 1992, representatives of provincial councils elected the members of the Control Yuan, and an early Council of Grand Justices ruling (Interpretation 76) established that the Control Yuan was a house of the Parliament, along with the Legislative Yuan and National Assembly. However, a constitutional amendment in 1992 turned the Control Yuan into a semijudicial institution, with its members nominated by the president and approved by the Parliament (before 1993, by the National Assembly; after 1993, by the Legislative Yuan). This reform reflected both the rising status of the Legislative Yuan, which sought to monopolize the representative function, and the widespread demand that the Control Yuan be a more effective ombudsman free from political influence.

Throughout the transition to democracy, the powers of the Control Yuan remained the same in principle, and its capacity was actually reinforced with an expanded investigatory body of staff in 1998. The major shift in the Control Yuan's role resulted not from reform of its institutional structure but from changes in the broader political climate. The increasing rights consciousness among the general public during democratization gave rise to a rapid increase in petition cases to the Control Yuan during the 1990s and the 2000s, from an average of 7,150 cases annually in the 1990s to 12,870 in the 2000s. Although its institutional power remained unchanged, however, the Control Yuan did not succeed in building broad support for its continued existence.[33]

Challenges

Horizontal accountability is a way of institutionalizing mistrust in order for "the people" as principal to monitor "the government" as agent.[34] However, when the people are deeply divided and the logic of political conflict takes precedence over any constitutional consensus that may exist, this institutionalized mistrust can become distorted into a means of political struggle, and the monitoring institutions themselves end up sacrificed on the political battlefield. This happened to the Control Yuan, which became an institution that existed in name only from 2005 to 2008, when the opposition-dominated Legislative Yuan refused to act on President Chen's Control Yuan nominees. This standoff between Chen and the legislature grew out of the 2004 presidential election dispute and, thus, was not directly related to the Control Yuan's structure or role. Yet compared to the judiciary's resilience during this period, the Control Yuan's vulnerability reflected its inherent institutional weaknesses.

The ostensible reason for the standoff was the opposition Pan-Blue party's contention that President Chen's nominees were not politically neutral.[35] Yet this could hardly justify the wholesale boycott, because the Legislative Yuan could well have exercised its power to reject the nominees. Instead, the boycott became part of the KMT-PFP's strategy to undermine President Chen's authority in the wake of the 2004 presidential election dispute. In response, the DPP insisted on its constitutional power to appoint Control Yuan members and demanded that the Legislative Yuan exercise consent power. President Chen did not feel compelled to nominate alternatives acceptable to the Pan-Blue parties and, thus, solve the dispute, because the DPP's longtime stance had been to abolish the Control Yuan and transform the five-power constitutional structure to one with three branches like in the United States. As a result of this deadlock between the rival camps, the contested institution sat empty for most of Chen's second term, until Ma Ying-jeou assumed the presidency. From February 2, 2005, through July 31, 2008—three and a half years—the Control Yuan had no members and could not function.

The design of the appointment and consent process contributed to the deadlock. In a divided polity, with executive and legislative branches controlled by different parties, the executive branch has limited incentives to strengthen a horizontal accountability institution that might be used by the opposition party. The success of such an institution, therefore, depends partly on the goodwill of the executive leaders who are willing to promote good governance at the expense of their bargaining power with their rivals.[36]

In addition, the Control Yuan's powers as established by the constitution are limited. Its primary function is to authorize other bodies to sanction officials; actual disciplinary power is held not by the Control Yuan but by the executive branch, the courts, and the Commission on the Disciplinary Sanctions of Functionaries in the Judicial Yuan.[37] Although the Control Yuan can impeach public servants and issue orders to correct illegal or politically objectionable matters, the final sanction decisions are made by the courts and the relevant executive bodies after they receive the Control Yuan's decisions. Even though impeachment or corrective measures could be coexistent with criminal sanctions, the rigor and authority of the courts have, in practice, overshadowed the impeachment procedure.[38] The Commission on the Disciplinary Sanctions of Functionaries often suspends the trial of impeachment cases until relevant criminal procedures are complete. Similarly, an increasingly independent prosecutorial system is a far more effective corruption pursuer than the Control Yuan, because it possesses all the compulsory powers of investigation not available to the Control Yuan.[39] In short, democratization strengthened the judiciary but weakened the Control Yuan.

As a result, many political scientists and legal scholars in Taiwan have called for re-allocation of its authority to either the judicial system or the legislature. In fact, the way the Control Yuan has evolved indicates that it and the judicial system have functioned as substitutes for one another. Control Yuan statistics show that the number of impeachments and corrective measures in the 1950s and 1960s was higher than in the following two decades, as the judicial courts started taking root and playing a bigger role. Indeed, the overlapping and fragmented authority held by the Control Yuan, the Judicial Yuan, and the Legislative Yuan has probably increased the transaction costs of ensuring horizontal political accountability.

Judicial and Prosecutorial Independence in the Post-DPP Era

The KMT's landslide victories in both the presidential and legislative elections in 2008 put an end to the sharp clashes between the executive and the legislative branches of the central government. Even though elite politics remained polarized, the political struggle between the KMT and DPP became much less consequential. Given the KMT's renewed dominance of both the Executive and Legislative Yuans, the judiciary was mostly relieved from the burden of arbitrating or mediating interbranch conflict. However, the judiciary had to face troubles of a different kind, as governmental authority became more unified and centralized under President Ma and the KMT. This change provided observers with a great opportunity to assess whether the independence shown by Taiwan's judiciary during the DPP administration was more a matter of strategic guile than principled commitment.

The litmus test came quickly. On December 12, 2008, former president Chen Shui-bian was indicted on multiple corruption charges, including embezzlement of special presidential funds, money laundering, and bribery. According to the indictment, the amount of money siphoned off by Chen and his family totaled more than US$30 million. In addition to Chen, the dozen people indicted included his wife, son, daughter-in-law, former close aides, family friends, and retired government officials.

Given that Chen was the focus of Taiwan's politics of *ressentiment,* his corruption cases were destined to be politically charged. No matter how they ruled, prosecutorial and judicial decisions would inevitably ignite accusations of bias and political interference in the judiciary. Even before the trial, Chen's detention during the prosecutorial investigation stage aroused a storm of controversy due to the case assignment within the court. The three-judge panel of the Taipei District Court, headed by Judge Chou Chan-chun, decided to release Chen without bail on the grounds that the SID had not sufficiently demonstrated that Chen was a flight risk or a threat to tamper with evidence. This decision immediately provoked fierce criticism from the Pan-Blue camp, which mounted attacks on Judge Chou's impartiality, primarily on political talk shows.[40] After the prosecutors swiftly appealed, the High Court struck down Judge Chou's ruling and remanded it for another hearing at the district court level. However, Judge Chou and his panel made the same decision after the second hearing, opining that serious felonies should not be the only reason for detention and that the prosecutors did not convince the court the defendant would escape or tamper with evidence. In response to the District Court's second decision, the prosecutors appealed for a second time, the High Court overruled Judge Chou's ruling again, and the case was remanded for yet another hearing.

The back and forth between the two courts illustrates a long-standing question in Taiwan's criminal justice system—that is, whether the severity of crimes can, in itself, constitutionally be grounds for detention, both before and during a trial. However, Taiwan's polarized politics and distorted public sphere turned a great opportunity for legal reform into yet another partisan battle. More controversially, Judge Chou's panel was replaced through a case merger by another panel led by Judge Tsai Shou-hsun. Judge Tsai reversed Judge Chou's decision and ordered Chen detained. As the trial proceeded, Judge Tsai renewed the decision each time the legally prescribed two-month detention period was due to expire. Strikingly, Judge Tsai's decisions flew in the face of the spirit of Interpretation 653 of the grand justices, issued at about the same time on December 26, 2008. This interpretation emphasizes that detention "should be done prudently as the last resort of preservative proceeding. Unless the court is convinced that all legal requirements have been met, and that it is necessary to do so, detention shall not be taken."

The sudden change of panels in Chen's case raised serious doubts about the Taipei District Court's independence, because its timing was suspiciously convenient for the prosecution and the ruling KMT. The highly controversial timing of the change of panel and case merger, followed by rulings in accordance with the wishes of the Pan-Blue camp, almost certainly tarnished Taiwan's hard-won reputation for judicial independence.[41] Yet there are also good reasons to believe this episode did not represent a wider decline in judicial independence or even that it was as clear-cut a case of political inference as it might first have appeared. First, all judicial decisions are made by the panel as a whole, rather than by the chief of the panel alone. The chief judge is only delegated the power and responsibility to preside over the courtroom proceedings; he or she does not have the power to overrule the judgment of the other two judges. If someone wants to interfere with the panel's decision, all three judges, and not just the chief, have to be influenced. One of the authors interviewed several Taipei District Court judges about this case, and all of them said they had not heard rumors about undue political interference and would agree with the presumption that Judge Tsai's panel made the decision to detain Chen autonomously. Nor were such beliefs aired only by individual judges. A prominent reformist lawyer, Lin Yong-sung, stated in a 2009 public interview that "fewer and fewer people seriously suspect that judges can be interfered with by judicial administration officials."[42] These statements reinforced the impression among judges that, given the state of Taiwan's judicial system and the openness of the society after the end of the Chen era, it was very difficult, though not impossible, to coerce or threaten all three judges into making a decision they would otherwise not have made.

On the other hand, Taiwan's increasingly sensationalized, partisan, and hypercritical media exerted more and more negative influence over the judiciary during the Chen years, and fear of media condemnation might well have affected the ruling on his detention. As the well-known prosecutor Chen Rui-ren, who shocked the nation by indicting the then first lady Wu Shu-chen in 2006, remarked in 2009, "The judicial independence we talked about ten years ago is quite different from what it means today. Ten years ago, what we had to resist was political interference and bribery. That was what judicial independence meant back then. Now, the biggest challenge is how to be independent from the media."[43] To many observers, the fear of the media and the criticism they would receive in the forum of public opinion accounted not only for Judge Chou's panel's decision but also for Judge Tsai's repeated decisions to detain Chen. As a senior journalist speculated at the time, "Maybe the court does not want to be lambasted by social critics." Another judge, commenting on Judge Tsai's decision, argued, "Given the political atmosphere, to detain Chen would invite less social pressure than not to detain."[44]

In essence, the polarized media, exemplified by partisan political talk shows, has become a powerful new factor that has exerted great influence on judicial performance. This development is a bit ironic for a young democracy that is particularly proud of its freedom of expression and free media.

Conclusion

During the Chen Shui-bian era, Taiwan's polarized politics posed great challenges for horizontal accountability and the rule of law. With respect to the four dimensions for evaluating institutions of horizontal accountability and rule of law—independence, supremacy, capability, and political accountability—Taiwan's judiciary in general demonstrated a convincing degree of independence. Top governmental offices and high political influence did not shield politicians from being indicted or found liable in civil or criminal cases. All major political parties had their share of gains and losses in court cases and prosecutions. Taiwan's relatively developed rule of law and constitutionalism, together with its admirable degree of judicial independence, practically ensured that the judiciary would be called on to mediate political conflicts when they arose, even though the judiciary was still weak on other dimensions.

Yet the "judicialization" of partisan conflicts was inherently dangerous to the courts, and, as a result, the judiciary's supremacy was weakened. The losing party in political cases repeatedly attempted to take revenge on the courts by cutting judicial budgets and questioning judges' motives, thus challenging the legitimacy of judicial decisions. Nevertheless, the grand justices, for the most part, were not intimidated by the Legislative Yuan's actions and continued to issue independent rulings, regardless of the political consequences for each side.

The greatest cost to the judiciary of this period was to its political accountability. Accountability to the branches of government did not increase under the bitterly divided politics of the Chen years, because accountability to political branches in these circumstances meant yielding to partisan preference rather than responding to a broadly held set of preferences established through a deliberative and inclusive political process. As a result, the judicial and prosecutorial reforms enacted during this period largely neglected the need to make the courts and prosecutors more reasonably accountable to the other, popularly elected branches of government.

On the capability front, the Constitutional Court as an institution performed admirably in the decisiveness of its constitutional reviews, while skillfully finding ways to moderate the short-term political impact of its decisions and preempting criticism from partisans of both sides. Regular courts, however, continued to suffer from pervasive institutional weaknesses, including poor quality of legal reasoning, inaccurate comprehension of comparative legal doctrines, and doctrinal inconsistency. These weaknesses were magnified in politically charged cases, in which the courts were under tremendous political pressure. In defamation cases, for instance, the courts found shelter in the politically correct doctrine of actual malice and evaded the legally sound function of helping the speech market seek political truth. Similarly, the prosecutor general feared becoming a target in a partisan battle and, thus, shunned his duty to coordinate prosecution standards in the special allowance fund cases. The behavior of the regular courts left the application of law highly unpredictable and subjected individual prosecutors to intense political pressure.

The Control Yuan fared the worst of all accountability institutions during the Chen era. It became a direct casualty of the partisan warfare of the Chen years: in the wake of the contentious 2004 presidential election, it ceased to function when the Legislative Yuan refused to act on President Chen's nominees. The Control Yuan failed on all fronts—independence, supremacy, and capability. Although President Ma appointed new members and won confirmation for them in the legislature after he took office, the Control Yuan's serious institutional vulnerabilities remain. Unless its design is reformed and it is given the kind of systematic support and respect from legal professionals that the judicial system has, the Control Yuan will remain a weak, ineffective institution.

In the highly polarized politics that characterize many new democracies, judicial independence is likely to come into sharp conflict with institutional capability and political accountability. Despite some significant achievements, balancing these competing pressures will remain a major challenge for Taiwan in the post-Chen era. The KMT's return to power brought new—and in some ways surprising—challenges to horizontal accountability and the rule of law. But as Chen Shui-bian's indictment revealed, many judges and analysts felt that social pressure exerted by the aggressive and freewheeling mass media, and not direct political interference from elected officials, was what motivated many controversial decisions in this era. Unfortunately, the deep partisan divide prevented the judicial and prosecutorial system from making bolder moves to improve the institutions' capability and accountability. Despite making considerable progress and sustaining pockets of excellence, particularly in the Constitutional Court, Taiwan's accountability institutions as a whole remained a weak link in its democracy at the end of the Chen Shui-bian era.

Notes

An earlier version of this chapter appeared as Weitseng Chen and Jimmy Chia-shin Hsu, "Horizontal Accountability in a Polarised New Democracy: The Case of Post-Democratisation Taiwan," *Australian Journal of Asian Law* 15, no. 2 (2014): 1–19. It is reprinted here with the permission of the *Australian Journal of Asian Law*.

 1. Lee Teng-hui, *Xinshihdai taiwanren* [A new generation of Taiwanese] (Taipei: Quncehui, 2005), 34.

 2. Barry Friedman, "History, Politics, and Judicial Independence," in *Judicial Integrity and Independence,* ed. Andras Sajo and Lorry Rutt Bentch (Leiden, Netherlands: Martinus Nijhoff, 2004).

 3. Weitseng Chen, "Twins of Opposites: Why China Will Not Follow Taiwan's Model of Rule of Law Transition Toward Democracy" (paper presented at the World Congress of Constitutional Law at Oslo University, June 2014).

 4. Larry Diamond, *The Spirit of Democracy* (New York: Times Books, 2008).

 5. Daron Acemoglu and James A. Robinson, *Economic Origins of Dictatorship and Democracy* (New York: Cambridge University Press, 2006); Adam Przeworski, "Democracy and Economic Development," in *The Evolution of Political Knowledge: Democracy, Autonomy, and Conflict in Comparative and International Politics,* ed. Edward D. Mansfield and Richard Sisson (Columbus: The Ohio State University Press, 2004).

 6. Chen, "Twins of Opposites: Why China Will Not Follow Taiwan's Model of Rule of Law Transition Toward Democracy"; Jacques deLisle, "Chasing the God of Wealth While Evading the Goddess of Democracy: Development, Democracy, and Law in Reform-Era China," in *Development and Democracy: New Perspectives on an Old Debate,* ed. Sunder Ramaswamy and Jeffrey W. Cason (Hanover, NH: Middlebury College Press, 2003).

 7. Weitseng Chen, *Law and Economic Miracle: The Interaction Between Economy and Legal System in Taiwan After World War II* (Taipei: Angle Publishing, 2000); Sean Cooney, "The New Taiwan and Its Old Labour Law: Authoritarian Legislation in a Democratized Society," *Comparative Labor Law Journal* 18 (Fall 1996): 1.

 8. Chen, "Twins of Opposites: Why China Will Not Follow Taiwan's Model of Rule of Law Transition Toward Democracy."

 9. deLisle, "Chasing the God of Wealth While Evading the Goddess of Democracy; Cooney, "The New Taiwan and Its Old Labour Law," 1.

 10. Chin-shou Wang, "Judicial Independence Reform and the Breakdown of the Kuomintang's Clientelism," *Taiwanese Political Science Review* 10, no. 1 (2006); Tay-Sheng Wang and Wen-Liang Tseng, *The History of the Taipei Lawyer's Association in the 20th Century* (Taipei: Taipei Lawyer's Association, 2005); Thomas Ginsburg, *Judicial Review in New Democracies: Constitutional Courts in Asian Cases* (New York: Cambridge University Press, 2003); Jane Kaufman-Winn and Tang-chi Yeh, "Advocating Democracy: The Role of Lawyers in Taiwan's Political Transformation," *Law and Social Inquiry* 20, no. 2 (1995): 561.

11. Ginsburg, *Judicial Review in New Democracies*.

12. Heng-wen Liu, "A Study of the Judges and Prosecutors in Postwar Taiwan: An Observation Focused on Their Training Culture," *Journal of Humanities and Social Sciences* 40, no. 1 (2002): 125–182.

13. Data source: Judicial Yuan (2006).

14. The previous title of the institution is the Council of Grand Justices. However, in the constitutional amendment in 2000, the term *council* was deleted. As a result, the official title became the Grand Justices.

15. Ginsburg, *Judicial Review in New Democracies*, 147.

16. Hwei-chen Chiang, "An Unsatisfactory Constitutional Interpretation of Election Litigation: Post-Election Accounting?" *China Times,* January 13, 2005, A13.

17 After the budget cut, the DPP legislators soon responded with another petition to the grand justices about the constitutionality of the act of cutting the Court's budget. In Interpretation 601, the justices held that the salary budget cut violated Article 81 of the Constitution, which protects the salary of judges from being decreased without a statutory basis.

18. This interpretation also reflects the tremendous influence of American jurisprudence of the First Amendment on Taiwan's legal academia and the judiciary. In two significant concurring opinions to this interpretation, Justice Su Jyun-Hsiung and Justice Wu Geng both advocated, apart from the majority opinion, doctrines highly similar to the actual malice doctrine established in the US Supreme Court's *New York Times v. Sullivan*.

19. The Supreme Court Civil Decision, 93rd Bench, No. 851 (2004).

20. The Supreme Court Civil Decision, 93rd Bench, No. 1979 (2004).

21. It frees the defamer from liability when "the defamer did not utter the statement deliberately on total absence of grounds" (Supreme Court Decision No. 179, 1014, 775 [2004]). Extraordinarily, this interpretation deviates not only from the comparative legal source of US actual malice but also from the current statutory framework of liability of negligence in tort cases, and it is a radically loose interpretation of Interpretation 509 in criminal cases.

22. Hsu Shu-fen, *The Secret Code: A Record of the 2004 Presidential Election Lawsuits* [in Chinese] (Taipei: Qianwei Publishing, 2007).

23. The primary issues were whether the national referendum could be held on the same day as the presidential election and whether the variety of problems and flaws detected in the election management was significant enough to invalidate the election.

24. The nature of the suit was to dispute the legitimacy of the elected, such as whether the votes received were forged or accurately calculated and whether the elected used unlawful means to coerce and threaten voters or election staff. For example, (1) did the president violate the Act of Referendum by holding the defensive referendum, could it be held on the same day as the presidential election, and did the Central Election Commission's compliance with the president invalidate the presidential election? (2) Was the assassination attempt staged by President Chen himself? (3) Was the national security mechanism activated by the assassination part of a bigger conspiracy by the DPP to keep a substantial number of military and police personnel from voting, among whom KMT supporters presumably outnumbered those of the DPP?

25. Kao Yung-cheng, "Discussing Judicial Reform After the Century's Biggest Vote Recount," *Judicial Reform Journal* 51 (2004).

26. Taiwan High Court Article 93 No. 2, No. 4, Decision.

27. Lin He-ming, "On Judicial Yuan Budget, KMT and PFP Make a Scene, Greens Accuse Them of Retaliation," *United Daily News,* January 13, 2005, A4.

28. Wang, "Judicial Independence Reform and the Breakdown of Kuomintang's Clientelism."

29. During his five years in office, from 2000 through 2005, DPP Minister of Justice Chen Ding-Nan generally refrained from interfering in individual cases. However, although he was initially regarded by reformist prosecutors as a fellow reformist, Minister Chen did not want to forfeit his personal power completely to the Personnel Committee as the partisan divide deepened. See Chih-ming Chen, "The Prosecutoriate Is Only Half-Reformed," *Judicial Reform Journal* 51 (2004).

30. The 1992 Constitutional Amendment forbade Control Yuan members from serving simultaneously as members of Parliament and removed their power to impeach the president and vice president.

31. Data source: Standing Committee of the Control Yuan.

32. Ibid.

33. The DPP has consistently regarded the Control Yuan as outdated and unnecessary. It is not uncommon to find a negative impression among the general public that the Control Yuan is good only at "smashing the flies while avoiding the tigers."

34. Guillermo O'Donnell, "Horizontal Accountability: The Legal Institutionalization of Mistrust," in *Democratic Accountability in Latin America*, ed. Scott Mainwaring and Christopher Welna (New York: Oxford University Press, 2003), 34–54.

35. Chang-wen Chen, "On Control Yuan Nominees, Tell the President 'No,'" *United Daily News,* December 18, 2006.

36. For a relevant discussion about the interaction between the US president and the US Congress in models of veto bargaining that is similar to the nomination process for the Control Yuan members, see Charles Cameron, *Veto Bargaining: Presidents and the Politics of Negative Power* (New York: Cambridge University Press, 2000), 83–122.

37. Republic of China Constitution, Articles 97 and 98; Public Functionaries Discipline Act, Article 18.

38. This inability to enforce sanctions is by no means a new issue. As early as the 1950s, Control Yuan members frequently criticized the Executive and Judicial Yuans for ignoring the impeachment decisions made by the Control Yuan. Tao Pai-chuan, a prominent reformist as well as a Control Yuan member, once said, "The nature of the Control Yuan is simply to be a news reporter," since the Control Yuan did not have the "weapons" that other fellow institutions did. See Tao Pai-chuan, "United Daily News and the Control Yuan," *United Daily News,* September 16, 1955.

39. Due to such concerns about competence, the majority of President Chen's Control Yuan nominees were either senior attorneys or judges. However, this move triggered further debates: first, about whether this arrangement violated the Act for the Control Yuan's Organization, which requires that members come from a diverse variety of backgrounds given the diversity of the cases; and second, about whether to reorganize and redistribute the Control Yuan's power to the judicial branch, rather than turn the Control Yuan into another judicial organization, with incomplete judicial power.

40. In addition to deliberately overlooking the constitutional legitimacy of detention solely based on the severity of the alleged crimes, those attacks also ignored one obvious piece of counterevidence regarding Judge Chou's integrity. Judge Chou happened to be the presiding judge of the panel that ruled Chen Shui-bian's son-in-law, Chao Chien-ming, guilty of insider trading in 2007. Judge Chou gave Chao an unusually severe sentence of six years in prison.

41. Freedom House lowered Taiwan's score from 1 to 2 on civil liberties in its 2010 report, due to the apparent political interference in judicial functions in Chen Shui-bian's case.

42. Interview with Lin Yun-song, *Judicial Reform Journal* 72 (June 2009).

43. Interview with Chen Rui-ren, *Judicial Reform Journal* 72 (June 2009). See also the special issue on prosecutors and politics of *Taiwan Prosecutor Review,* which discusses the relationship between not only politics and prosecutors but also politics and the judicial branch in general, in which the media's negative influence is repeatedly highlighted: *Taiwan Prosecutor Review* 5 (January 2009). It should be noted that although in terms of chains of command, prosecutors belong to the executive branch, in Taiwan, prosecutors come into office through the same examination process as judges, and both go through the same early training for judicial officials. With respect to the salary system and protection of status, Taiwan's prosecutors prefer to think of themselves as "judicial officials in general," which gives them stronger protections against arbitrary removal or reduction of salary, rather than as officials in the executive branch. That is why, in many discussions, judges and prosecutors are treated similarly.

44. Hsi-ju Tian, "A New 'Judicial Politics' Era," *Judicial Reform Journal* 70 (March 2009).

8

Strengthening Constitutionalism

Yun-han Chu

To be effective, constitutions must relate organically to a society's reali-
ties; they must accommodate, even as they guide a country's basic inter-
ests. The most successful constitutions will intertwine civil society and
the state in ways that are most helpful to the permanent and aggregate
interests of the community.
—Alexander Hamilton, James Madison,
and John Jay, *The Federalist Papers*

In his first inaugural address, Ma Ying-jeou made a solemn pledge that he
would reestablish a robust tradition of constitutionalism by affirming the
authority of the Republic of China (ROC) constitution. In an established
democracy, a pledge like this would be viewed as pro forma and be likely
to go unnoticed, as it is usually taken for granted that all elected officials
are obligated to respect the authority of the constitution and abide by it.
In the context of Taiwan's democratic development, however, Ma's
pledge carried extraordinary significance. He was Taiwan's first popularly elected president to commit to maintaining and upholding the existing constitutional order as is, instead of altering or undoing it.

On Lee Teng-hui's watch, the ROC constitution had undergone six
phases of substantial revision. Most notably, with the introduction of the
popular election of the president in 1994, the elimination of the Legislative Yuan's (LY's) power to confirm the president's choice of premier in
1997, and the institutionalization of the National Security Council, the
basic design of the constitution system was shifted from parliamentarian-
ism to semipresidentialism.[1] Chen Shui-bian made the adoption of a new
constitution the top priority of his second term, and in his second inaugural

173

address, he openly pledged to have the new constitution ready by the end of his tenure. He probably would have pushed this agenda to its realistic limit had it not been for strong objections from Washington, DC, and the outbreak of a major political scandal in 2006, which dealt a fatal blow to his credibility and effectiveness.

The only reform that Chen Shui-bian managed to steer through the cumbersome constitutional amendment process on his watch was the passing of the Seventh Amendment in 2005. It was, however, as much a Kuomintang (KMT) initiative as a Democratic Progressive Party (DPP) one. The passage of this amendment also should be viewed not as an integral part of Chen's outlandish constitutional project but as an accidental sidekick. With the passage of this amendment, the size of the Legislative Yuan was drastically cut in half to 113 seats; the old single nontransferable vote (SNTV) system for electing LY members was replaced with a mixed system with a strong majoritarian bent;[2] the legislative term was extended from three to four years, making it possible to synchronize legislative and presidential elections; and the procedure for amending the constitution was made even more difficult by requiring not just a three-quarters majority in the Legislative Yuan but also the approval of at least half of all eligible voters in a plebiscite.

Ironically, these changes turned out to be extremely harmful to the DPP's political fortunes and its agenda. The changes to the LY electoral system contributed to the DPP's crushing defeat in the January 2008 legislative election, reducing its share of LY seats to less than a quarter, despite winning 38 percent of the district vote. In addition, the changes to the amendment procedure have virtually closed off any possibility for further alteration without traveling down an extraconstitutional route.

The second transfer of power in 2008 effectively marked the end of a protracted saga of constitutional engineering (or tinkering, if one will) stretching back to the beginning of Taiwan's democratic transition. Ma's landslide victory and the restoration of the KMT's electoral dominance appeared likely to take the debate over further constitutional change off the island's political agenda for a long while. The 2008 presidential election also decisively halted the momentum of Taiwanese nationalism and dampened the concomitant aspiration to replace the ROC constitution with a new, "bona fide Taiwanese" constitution through a plebiscite.

In this chapter, I attempt two analytical tasks. First, I explore why the political drive for a major constitutional overhaul at one point gathered significant momentum and why it came to an abrupt end. Second, I examine the implications of the political events leading to the second transfer of power for the strengthening of constitutionalism in Taiwan, an indispensable element of the consolidation of Taiwan's young democracy.

I begin my analysis with the legacy of politics of constitutional reform during Taiwan's democratic transition. I then analyze the reopening of the debate over the constitutional conundrum after the first transfer of power in 2000 and why the debate reached new heights during the 2004 presidential race. Next, I show how the momentum was halted as the politics of constitutional reform became inevitably entangled with the national identity cleavage and the political standoff across the Taiwan Strait. Finally, I argue that the second transfer of power inadvertently provided Taiwan with a historic opportunity to deepen the roots of constitutionalism.

The Legacy of the Politics of Constitutional Reform

The politics of constitutional reform was certainly not an enviable aspect of Taiwan's transition to democracy. After seven rounds of constitutional revision over a decade and a half, the constitutional order that existed at the end of the Chen Shui-bian era still lacked the kind of broad-based legitimacy that the working constitution in a consolidated democracy normally enjoys.

Over the course of the transition to democracy, the constitution-making process was complicated by some wrenching structural constraints that Taiwan's young democracy inherited, including an unsettled sovereign status in the international system, a deep division over national identity at home, the absence of a firm commitment among the contending elites to the rule of law, and the underdevelopment of constitutionalism. By constitutionalism, I mean the widely held belief that government can and should be legally limited in its powers and should abide by the norms and procedures prescribed by the constitution and relevant statutes. It also means that government authority depends on its observing these limitations and rules. The process was further complicated by the strategic choices of some key players, leaders, and political parties that orchestrated constitutional changes at key junctures in the island's democratic transition. The pact-making process was littered with their devious hidden agendas, short-term political calculations, and improvised compromises.[3] In the end, the emerging constitutional structure suffered from quite a few deficiencies.

At the most fundamental level, contending political elites and political parties were not able to reach consensus about what the final objective of constitution reform should be. For people who strongly believed in Taiwan independence, all the revisions undertaken within the framework of the ROC constitution were meant to be transitory. To them, the only acceptable final objective was the creation of a new constitution that would manifest the general will of the Taiwanese people and signify the island's independent sovereign status. For people who vowed to preserve and defend the existing state structure, however, the ROC constitution and all the political symbols it carried constituted the cornerstone of their political identity. To them, the amendments adopted at each round of constitutional revision were meant to be binding and lasting, at least until additional changes were demanded by a great majority of the people and realized through the amendment procedure prescribed by the constitution. They opposed any attempts to abolish the existing constitution through extraconstitutional means, such as a plebiscite, which happened to be the favorite option of Taiwanese nationalists. All of this means that the constitutional order that emerged after seven rounds of revision rested on a fault line between two colliding tectonic plates.

Next, the contending political elites held no strong consensus about the nature and logic of the government structure defined by the current constitution. When the representatives of the two major political parties—the KMT and the DPP—cooperated to craft the current government structure during the fourth round of revisions in late 1996 and early 1997, the newly amended constitution was sold to the public as an improved version of a semipresidential system featuring a dual-headed executive modeled after the French Fifth Republic. But this bipartisan understanding of the moment had no binding power and was not always shared by influential members within each party—and especially not by political figures who were not directly involved in the constitutional crafting process.[4]

More important, the system that emerged was different from the French system in some significant respects. First, when no candidate wins a majority on the first ballot, the French system requires the president to secure a clear-cut majority mandate through a runoff election. Under the revised ROC constitution, by contrast, the president was to be elected by a simple plurality with no minimum threshold. Thus, in Taiwan's system, a president could win office with a minority of the vote, with a weak popular mandate, and possibly without the support of a reliable majority in the legislature.

Second, under the French system, the president is obliged to appoint a premier with majority support in the parliament under a long-standing constitutional convention that requires an incoming premier to get a vote of confidence from the National Assembly. However, during Taiwan's fourth round of revisions, the old provision about Legislative Yuan confirmation of the premier was removed, and the president was thus given more leeway in appointing the premier. Nevertheless, both systems bestowed the Legislative Yuan with the power, through a vote of no confidence, to unseat a sitting cabinet to ensure that the government was ultimately held accountable to the legislature.

Third, whereas Taiwan's Legislative Yuan did not have a formal say in the appointment of the premier (and hence the formation of government), it was much more powerful than its French counterpart in steering the legislative agenda—and in crippling the government when the situation called for it. Unlike the French system, which empowers the cabinet to set the legislative agenda, the ROC constitution did not require that the legislature give priority to government bills; instead, the legislature controlled its own agenda. Neither the president nor the premier possessed the constitutional weapon of an executive veto to check legislative assertiveness. The cabinet could send back objectionable legislation and binding resolutions to the legislature for reconsideration. However, the legislature had the final say if the same bill was passed again with an absolute majority—that is, half of the total members plus one.

Fourth, the French system has more effective built-in mechanisms to break a potential deadlock between the president and the assembly during a period of "cohabitation." The president can try to reconstitute the parliament by dissolving the National Assembly, and the parliament can force out a cabinet that no longer enjoys the support of the National Assembly. Under Taiwan's system, however, the president could not dissolve the legislature on his own initiative. Instead, the president could call a new election only after the Legislative Yuan unseated the cabinet with a vote of no confidence.

With these significant departures from the French Fifth Republic system, it was difficult to predict how the system would function when the majority party in the Legislative Yuan was different from the president's party or when no party had a legislative majority. On the one hand, because the president could appoint the premier, the formal head of the government, without legislative confirmation, a minority president might be able to avoid a French-style cohabitation and take the risk of confronting a hostile majority in the Legislative Yuan. On the other hand, in its retaliation against the president, the majority in the legislature could choose to strangle the government piece by piece, rather than unseating the sitting cabinet and forcing a political showdown. By so doing, it would simply prolong the political gridlock and push off the showdown until the next legislative election.

In addition, the amendments of 1997 (also known as the fourth revision) left the constitution vague on two important issues. First, it was unclear whether the new amendments empowered the president to dismiss a sitting cabinet without the premier's own initiative; thus, it was unclear whether those amendments had changed the power relationship between the president and the premier in a fundamental way. Second, it was unclear whether the president enjoyed preeminence in the areas of national defense and foreign policy. With the introduction of the direct election of the president, it became unrealistic to expect a popularly elected head of state—especially one with majority support—to exercise self-restraint in these policy domains. These ambiguities opened the door for unprincipled politicians to twist the meaning of the constitution to suit the political needs of the day. This was not an issue under Lee Teng-hui, as he could exercise control over the premier and the KMT caucus in the legislature through his capacity as the KMT chair. However, well before the transfer of power in 2000, many constitutional scholars wondered how a non-KMT president would shape the cabinet and steer national policies without a power-sharing arrangement with the KMT, which by most accounts would (as it actually did until February 2002) maintain its majority in the legislature.

The Political Gridlock Under Taiwan's Semipresidential System

The historic transfer of power in 2000 was the first test of the newly adopted constitutional structure's coherence. From the very beginning, President Chen Shui-bian's governing capacity was severely circum-scribed by two facts: he was elected as a minority president, and the DPP controlled less than one-third of the seats in the legislature. Nevertheless, he refused the KMT's demand for party-to-party negotiations over a power-sharing scheme on the conviction that the KMT might never get its act together again after a humiliating defeat. He also rejected proposals to form a coalition government with the People First Party (PFP), which was created by James Soong after he lost the presidential election by a narrow margin. Instead, Chen appointed Tang Fei—a KMT member, former chief of the general staff, and the outgoing defense minister—to the premiership in the hope that Tang's mainlander and military background would soften the KMT's resistance and enhance the new government's credibility.

However, President Chen apparently had overestimated the power bestowed on the president by the constitution, as well as his chances of escaping the political imperative of cohabitation. The KMT regrouped much more quickly than Chen had expected. As soon as the KMT restored its organizational coherence by electing Lien Chan as its chair, the former ruling party started to flex its political muscle. Tang Fei soon lost favor with Chen when it became clear that the political value-added that the premier brought to the new government had rapidly evaporated.

After only four months in office, Tang Fei was forced to resign when he failed to work out a compromise between the KMT-controlled legislature and the president over the DPP's campaign pledge to halt the ongoing construction of the fourth nuclear power plant. Chen then stumbled into a political quagmire when he tried to outmaneuver the legislature by pushing his new premier, Chang Chun-hsiung, a veteran DPP legislator, to announce the cabinet's decision to suspend the construction without any warning signals and without the Legislative Yuan's formal consent. Chen's abrupt decision to scrap the nuclear power plant turned out to be a political fiasco. The business community was stunned because it seemed that Chen was not as pragmatic as they had anticipated. The decision also inspired his two previous opponents, Lien Chan and James Soong, to mend fences and form a united front, which then controlled an even more formidable voting bloc in the legislature.

To retaliate against Chen's unilateral action, the two major opposition parties declared Chen's decision reckless and unconstitutional and threatened to take drastic actions, including impeaching the president and introducing a motion to hold a recall election. From this point on, the confrontation between a combative president and a hostile legislature steadily escalated from a fierce competition over the steering wheel of the legislative agenda and national priorities to a nasty, costly, and protracted political war.

The saga of the political stalemate dragged on for the entire eight years of Chen Shui-bian's presidency. Neither the December 2001 nor the December 2004 LY elections changed Chen's political fortunes. Although the DPP made considerable electoral gains and replaced the KMT as the largest party in the legislature in 2001, the gains were not nearly enough to break the political logjam. Even with the help of the thirteen seats that the Taiwan Solidarity Union (TSU) won, the DPP government was still thirteen seats short of a working majority. With the steady hardening of the DPP-TSU alliance, known as the Pan-Green camp, and the KMT-PFP coalition (plus the majority of independents and the fading New Party), known as the Pan-Blue camp, the country was crippled by the nasty political battles between the two competing blocs for another three years. The "divided government" syndrome was prolonged by the outcome of the 2004 LY election, in which the Pan-Blue camp retained its majority. The light at the end of the political stalemate tunnel was three more years away.

Taiwan's electorate was appalled by the extremely nasty and seemingly endless political battles between the DPP government and the opposition and by the resultant political paralysis. The KMT-PFP coalition blocked virtually all major legislative bills introduced by the DPP government, questioned their hidden political agendas, and replaced the bills with their own versions. For its part, the Executive Yuan sometimes simply refused to implement some of the legally binding resolutions passed by the LY, accusing the opposition-controlled legislature of infringing on its executive power. In retaliation, the KMT-PFP coalition blocked more pending budget bills, and the vicious cycle went on.

Both sides exhausted all possible legal means to try to strangle one another. Most of the legal disputes ended up in the hands of the Council of Grand Justices, which became increasingly overburdened with highly politicized cases. On a number of occasions, the council avoided taking sides whenever possible and thus delivered its interpretations in vague language, which simply invited more partisan bickering and legal disputes. Another major battle erupted over the confirmation of the presidential nominees to three other branches—the Control Yuan, the Council of Grand Justices, and the Examination Yuan. The KMT-controlled LY blocked nominees who had what it thought to be dubious or substandard qualifications, and President Chen refused to nominate replacements, intentionally leaving many slots vacant. In the most dramatic case, in 2005, the LY sent back the whole slate of Control Yuan nominees, citing the controversial backgrounds of many candidates, and Chen then refused to submit new nominations. As a result, the Control Yuan was left empty and dormant for three years. In the end, the public tired of the blame games between the government and the opposition over who had been acting unconstitutionally and who was responsible for the total breakdown of mutual trust and the crippling political gridlock.

The most discouraging aspect of this political saga was the recognition that the existing institution arrangements were not equipped to produce a definitive resolution of the conflicts inherent to a semipresidential system. The only tie-breaking device under such circumstances turned out to be worthless. With the veiled threat of the dissolution of the legislature hanging over them, the KMT-PFP coalition never dared to initiate a vote of no confidence and take the risk of triggering a snap election. The reason was quite simple: the electoral uncertainty and the high campaign costs imposed by the SNTV system made legislators extremely reluctant to use the no-confidence vote, rendering this instrument of accountability virtually useless.[5]

The Debate over Constitutional Remedies

Throughout 2005 and 2006, the political stalemate spurred a heated debate over the inadequacy of the existing constitutional design and what was needed to fix the problem. The emphasis was on how the system could prevent the recurrence of the kind of costly political gridlock the island had suffered. Three basic approaches to making the constitutional structure more balanced and coherent were put forward during that debate. I shall label them the minimalist approach, the big bang approach, and the fine-tuning approach.

The minimalist approach was to seek a "good enough" remedy that would require only minimal surgical changes to the constitutional system. Proponents of this approach assumed that it would be difficult to get new amendments adopted and thus placed more emphasis on alternatives to formal constitutional revision. These alternatives included introducing new constitutional norms through consensus building among the political elite, compelling the Council of Grand Justices to deliver more constitutional interpretations to do away with ambiguities and inconsistencies, and introducing more detailed laws to eliminate uncertainty about who could do what. This approach dictated that political leaders should exhaust these alternatives first before resorting to amending the constitution. In stark contrast, proponents of the big bang approach thought the semipresidential system was not a viable option, as it was full of ambiguities and contradictions; therefore, they believed, the country would be better off by starting all over again and introducing either a purely presidential or a purely parliamentary system. The fine-tuning approach lay somewhere in between these two. Its proponents wanted to eradicate the loopholes and flaws in the existing system in a more systematic way, while acknowledging that a fine-tuned semipresidential system was realistically more achievable and could be as viable as either a purely parliamentary or purely presidential system.

As usual, the two major political camps were miles apart on this issue. By and large, the leaders of the Pan-Green camp were strongly in favor of the big bang approach, whereas the leaders of the Pan-Blue camp were strongly in favor of the minimalist approach. It was no coincidence that the big bang approach not only was congruent with the core objectives of the Pan-Green camp but also arguably suited the DPP's short-term political needs best. In a similar vein, the minimalist approach served the KMT better, both ideologically and politically. Many political scientists, however, considered the fine-tuning approach more desirable than the minimalist approach, while viewing the big bang approach as either too idealistic or too radical.

The prescription for implementing a fine-tuning approach was rather straightforward. Only two issues needed to be taken care of. First, the country needed to find ways to minimize the possibility of there being two competing popular mandates held by the president and the Legislative

Yuan. Second, the constitutional system needed more effective tie-breaking mechanisms to prevent protracted political gridlock from happening again. The proponents of the fine-tuning approach argued that these two problems could be dealt with by augmenting the existing constitution with several add-on provisions. First, the requirement of legislative confirmation should be restored so that future presidents would have to respect the wishes of the majority in the LY when appointing the premier. This device would, for all practical purposes, compel the president to accept a French-style cohabitation arrangement when the rival camp controlled the legislature. Second, the SNTV electoral system used to elect the legislature should be replaced with either single-member district plurality rule or proportional representation—or a combination of the two. This replacement would, in theory, reduce the uncertainty of incumbent LY members about getting reelected in a snap election (much like most incumbents in the House of the US Congress) and thus make the vote of no confidence a more credible tie-breaking device. Third, incoming presidents should be given the power to dissolve the legislature, and there should be a runoff election to ensure that every elected president could claim a majority mandate. Fourth, the term lengths of the president and of the legislature should be equalized, and the two elections should be synchronized to the fullest extent possible, thus making the occurrence of "divided government" much less likely.

The passage of the Seventh Amendment in 2005 paradoxically made the fine-tuning approach appear both more credible and less feasible. It appeared more credible because the approach's second and fourth prescriptions were basically incorporated into the amendment. The Seventh Amendment replaced the SNTV rules with a two-ballot system modeled after the current Japanese electoral system for the Lower House of the Diet. It also lengthened the term of the Legislative Yuan to four years so that it matched that of the president, making it possible to synchronize the two elections.[6] Thus, the proponents of the fine-tuning approach could argue that the process was already well under way. On the other hand, the Seventh Amendment made the legal hurdle for passing any future constitutional amendment formidably high. It now required first a three-quarters majority of the Legislative Yuan to adopt any draft constitutional amendment. Then the amendment proposal had to be formally approved through a plebiscite, with at least half of all eligible voters casting a yes vote.

Nevertheless, many politicians from the Pan-Green camp were not impressed by what was accomplished during the last round of constitutional revisions. They continued to argue that the constitutional tinkering of the past had proved to be inadequate and that only an overhaul of the constitutional design could set the country on a stable course of constitutional democracy for the long haul.[7] The only choice the country would have to make, according to them, was between a presidential system and a parliamentary system. In so doing, they argued, the ambiguity inherent in a mixed system could be done away with. As for which system was superior or more suitable for the country, the DPP and the TSU traditionally were strongly in favor of a US-style presidential system. However, toward the end of 2006, surprisingly more and more DPP and TSU political figures, who in the past had always been strongly in favor of strengthening the president's democratic legitimacy and aggrandizing this highest office of the land, "rediscovered" the merits of a parliamentary system. They echoed the view fervently espoused by Shih Ming-teh, a former DPP chair. Shih argued that Taiwan had been ill-served by the introduction of the direct election of the president, which had polarized the electorate, excessively politicized society, and produced an imperial presidency.

Most proponents of a big bang approach also advocated the abolition of the five-power government, which was based on the political theory of Dr. Sun Yat-sen. They wanted to replace it with a more typical three-power government. With this structure, the Control Yuan, which functioned as a nonpartisan body of ombudsmen and, to some extent, of independent prosecutors, and the Examination Yuan, which regulated the civil service and enforced the rules of merit-based recruitment and promotion, would be eliminated and their functions taken over either by the legislature or by independent nonpartisan commissions.

To justify the big bang approach, many DPP-affiliated legal scholars zealously promoted the view that the principle of popular sovereignty was so fundamental that it was above any positive laws, including the existing constitution. On that basis, it was intrinsically democratic for the people to replace the existing constitution with a new one through a plebiscite. They encouraged Chen Shui-bian not to be bound by the arduous constitution-amending procedures stipulated in the existing constitution but to convene an ad hoc constitutional assembly and send a draft constitution to a plebiscite by invoking this democratic first principle.[8]

The Pan-Blue camp, under the new leadership of Ma Ying-jeou, opposed the idea of another round of major constitutional change. They pointed out that the constitution had already been amended seven times over fifteen years. What the country urgently needed to do, instead, was enhance the stability of the constitutional order and strengthen the authority of the constitution as the highest law of the land. They argued that what Taiwan's new democracy was ostensibly lacking was not a perfect bundle of positive law but a tradition of constitutionalism, which could only grow over time and under a stable constitutional order. In particular, the KMT leadership registered its strong objection to an overhaul of the existing constitution, which it regarded as unnecessary and unrealistic.

Instead, the Pan-Blue camp asserted that the political gridlock the country had experienced for the previous six years could have been avoided had President Chen Shui-bian observed the letter and spirit of the existing constitution, which essentially was modeled after the French Fifth Republic according to a shared understanding between the KMT and DPP representatives who negotiated the basic framework during the fourth round of constitutional reforms. Although some KMT political figures acknowledged that it might not be a bad idea to reinstitute the old requirement of legislative confirmation to guarantee that an incoming premier enjoyed majority support in the LY, they argued that the existing system could be improved without further amendments to the constitution. First, the new electoral rules to be applied for the first time in the 2008 LY election would make the vote of no confidence a more credible mechanism for breaking the deadlock between the president and the legislature. Second, the system could be augmented by the introduction of a sensible constitutional norm by which all future presidents would openly pledge to respect the will of the majority party (or coalition) in the legislature in the appointment of the premier. To demonstrate his sincerity, Ma Ying-jeou publicly pledged that if, in the future, a KMT president were to face a DPP-controlled legislature, the KMT would follow the French precedent of cohabitation and ask the DPP to form the government.[9]

As always, this debate over constitutional reform was colored by partisan motivations. Many political commentaries questioned the hidden agenda behind the DPP's abrupt rediscovery of the merits of a parliamentary system. In particular, many KMT supporters suspected that the Pan-Green camp had suddenly become interested in promoting a parliamentary system simply due to the prospect of the KMT's return to power via Ma Ying-jeou's presidential victory in 2008, after the Pan-Blue coalition had captured almost two-thirds of the county governments in the December 2005 local elections. Looking through a partisan lens, KMT supporters strongly believed that the call for a return to a parliamentary system was just a shameless political ploy to pull the rug from under the feet of Ma Ying-jeou, who enjoyed a commanding lead in public opinion polls as a 2008 presidential hopeful.

Critics of the DPP government became even more skeptical after some DPP figures hinted that a 113-member chamber was not suitable for a parliamentary system, stating the size of the legislature should be restored to 200-plus, even though the DPP and the KMT had just voted for a constitutional amendment that cut the size of the LY in half. The critics suspected the DPP wanted to use the re-enlargement of the LY to sweeten the deal to lure some outgoing LY members to defect from the Pan-Blue camp when the DPP-initiated draft amendment came up for a roll-call vote on the legislature floor.

Coming from the opposite end of the power equation, the KMT had every practical reason to obstruct the DPP's initiative to overhaul the constitution. The KMT leadership did not want anything that might complicate its promising bid to take power. Taking the previous county executive elections as a bellwether event, the KMT anticipated a landslide victory in the 2008 LY election and a decisive win in the 2008 presidential race. They wanted nothing to stand in the way of victory.

Some editorials in leading newspapers also questioned the necessity of a constitutional overhaul if moving the existing system away from semipresidentialism and closer to parliamentarism was really the primary objective. These editorials argued that if the DPP leaders were really serious about returning to a parliamentary system, they should introduce two pieces of legislation immediately, without burdening the country with the formidable task of amending the constitution for the eighth time. The passing of just two key pieces of legislation, as the argument went, could credibly make the existing system function essentially as a parliamentary system. First, the legislature should abolish the National Security Council in order to block the only institutional channel through which the president could exercise his power in the domains of foreign policy, defense, and cross-Strait affairs.[10] Second, the legislature should modify its internal rules to ensure that the majority party (or the majority coalition) would hold exclusive steering power over all standing committees.[11] The latter change would make it imperative for the future president to appoint a premier with the support of the majority party (or coalition) in the legislature in order to avoid total paralysis of the executive.

These two measures would be enough to reinforce the parliamentary nature of the existing constitutional order, because the existing constitution still retained many essential features of a parliamentary system, even after seven rounds of amendments. For example, the constitution designated the premier, instead of the president, as the head of the government; the premier was entitled to form his cabinet and appoint all policy-level officials; the cabinet was held accountable to the Legislative Yuan (instead of to the president); only the cabinet, in the name of the Executive Yuan, had the legal power to introduce bills to the Legislative Yuan; most of the acts of the president required the countersignature of the premier; and so on.

Because the debate was dominated by partisan polemics, there was not much room for rational persuasion. Many political scientists and liberal-minded scholars, who otherwise might have preferred a parliamentary system to either a presidential or semipresidential one, chose to remain quiet, as they were reluctant to be drawn into the partisan tug-of-war over the issue of constitutional reform.

The Entanglement with the National Identity Cleavage and Cross-Strait Relations

Like most controversial political issues, this last round of the debate over constitutional reform became unavoidably entangled with the island's persistent divisions over national identity, as well as with the delicate balance in the Taiwan Strait.

Most advocates of an overhaul of the constitution marketed their political blueprint under the banner of a "new constitution movement," which echoed Lee Teng-hui's call for "New Constitution, New Nation." The creation of a new constitution that was truly "indigenous" and that would serve as the manifestation of the "general will" of the Taiwanese people had always been an ultimate goal of proponents of Taiwan independence, along with a new name for the country, a new national flag, and a formal declaration of independence. Prior to Chen Shui-bian's victory in 2000, most leading figures in the DPP had long vowed to abolish the existing constitution, which symbolized the imposition of the émigré regime's rule over Taiwan, because it was adopted by the Nationalists in mainland China with only the token participation of a few Taiwan-elected National Assembly deputies. Furthermore, for proponents of Taiwan independence, the existing constitution was a galling symbol of the unbroken political lineage passed down from the Chinese Republic founded by Sun Yat-sen to the current political system. In their view, Taiwan could not claim to be an independent state without severing this legal and historical bond. For this reason, most DPP leaders viewed the deal struck between the DPP and the KMT over constitutional amendments during and after the National Development Conference of 1996 as a tactical move, not a lasting accord.[12]

For that very reason, the Pan-Blue camp vehemently opposed any proposal to overhaul the constitution. It viewed the big bang approach as a deliberate effort to undermine the existing state structure and to remove all traces of the One China principle from the constitution. They also feared that once the One China pillar was eliminated, the tension in the Taiwan Strait would escalate to a boiling point.

After the DPP came to power in 2000, this unfulfilled aspiration continued to frustrate many DPP leaders and their die-hard supporters. They were especially antagonized by the constant reminders from Pan-Blue political figures that the One China principle was enshrined in the ROC constitution and prominently restated in the preamble of the section on constitutional amendments. The preamble declared that "all the following amendments are adopted to cope with the requirements of circumstances before the country becomes reunified."[13] In the words of Cheng-liang Kuo, a DPP legislator for the pro-independence constituency, it was like being "a Taiwanese nationalist soul locked inside a One China cage."[14]

Throughout President Chen's tenure, the pro-independence constituency relentlessly pushed for the adoption of a new constitution. They were unhappy with the "Four Noes and One Without" pledge made by Chen in his 2000 inauguration speech, and they believed he was under tremendous US pressure to uphold those assurances. President Chen also understood well that he had to periodically renew the DPP's longstanding commitment to deliver a new constitution to keep up the spirit of the pro-independence constituency. Thus, whenever Chen felt the need to galvanize his political base, he raised the prospect of pushing through a new constitution. When the campaign for his reelection bid picked up in the second half of 2003, Chen decided to use the new constitution as a major plank in his platform. To back up his promise, he appointed many strong advocates of a new constitution to an ad hoc drafting committee under the presidential office. He also openly pledged on the campaign trail that a new constitution would be enacted by 2006 (the twentieth anniversary of the DPP's founding) and would be fully implemented in 2008, in time for the next president.

President Chen's move drove expectations for a new constitution to new heights. Many of his followers truly believed that once Chen won reelection, Taiwan's "constitutional moment" would finally come. They believed that by then Chen would have nothing to fear, and he would care only about his legacy. Chen's campaign theme also earned some sympathetic ears among independent voters who had become fed up with the protracted political gridlock. To prevent President Chen from dominating the campaign agenda, however, the Lien-Soong campaign felt compelled to offer their own proposal for constitutional reform. They publicly announced that they were open to further constitution change, including a shift from a five-power system to a more typical three-power design. At this juncture in the 2004 presidential election campaign, it seemed that a constitutional overhaul was the "in" thing to do.

But the momentum for a new constitution turned out to be short-lived. The aspiration was once again dashed by a sudden escalation of tension in the Taiwan Strait. To preempt the possibility of Chen's move toward de jure independence during his second term, Beijing adopted an Anti-Secession Law in the second half of 2004. The Beijing leadership used this law to try to demonstrate its resolve and reinforce the credibility of its military deterrent.

Beijing's move prompted Washington, DC, to ramp up its crisis management measures. The George W. Bush administration twisted Chen's arm and forced him to reach out to James Soong and invite him to serve as a personal envoy to visit Beijing, where Soong conveyed Chen's assurance that he would maintain the status quo in the Taiwan Strait. At Soong's request, on March 26, 2006, President Chen also grudgingly signed a ten-point accord, in which he pledged in writing that he would treat the acceptance of the Republic of China as the common denominator in Taiwanese society. He also reiterated his "respect for the ROC constitution" and his "respect for the existing system." Chen also pledged that his constitutional reform proposal would not involve changes to the country's sovereignty or territory or to the status quo in the Taiwan Strait. Finally, he pledged that he would abide by the prescribed legal procedures for amending the constitution. These conciliatory statements amounted to a formal abandonment of the DPP's long-standing commitment to delivering a new Taiwanese constitution.

To make his public pledges even more convincing in the eyes of Washington, DC, and Beijing, Chen stated publicly that "the campaign to change the country's title and adopt a new constitution is self-delusional." The ten-point accord signed between Soong and Chen, as well as his disparaging comments about the "New Constitution, New Country" campaign, struck the Pan-Green camp like a lightning bolt. Many heavyweight elders in the pro-independence camp considered President Chen's about-face to be outrageous. As the pro-independence *Liberty Times* put it, Chen's reversal had "created the most serious ideological crisis within the party since its founding."[15]

This dramatic reversal on the part of Chen Shui-bian was a watershed event. It signaled the beginning of the end of the decade-long campaign to adopt a new country name and a new constitution. It sparked a new reckoning among the sympathizers of the new constitution movement that a breakaway from the existing constitutional order was simply not a realistic option for Taiwan. It threw cold water on the pro-independence constituency, which had been led to believe that a new constitution was within reach, with a heroic Chen Shui-bian at the helm, a paper tiger sitting on the Chinese throne, and a friendly George W. Bush in the White House. No matter how hard Chen and other DPP leaders tried to backpedal from the ten-point accord later on, the momentum of the Taiwanese nation-building crusade was lost. Although some presidential aspirants in the 2008 race, such as strong believers like Yu Shyi-kun, remained firmly committed to the cause and tried to prop up grassroots support for the movement, the enthusiasm of Pan-Green voters was nowhere near what it had been before.

Toward a More Resilient Constitutional Democracy

The constitution that Ma Ying-jeou and his government inherited after seven rounds of amendments was by no means flawless and well-designed. Taiwan's semipresidential system was still vulnerable to the recurrence of political gridlock under divided government, a scenario that Taiwan's electorate had suffered through for Chen Shui-bian's entire eight-year presidency. In addition, the new electoral system for the Legislative Yuan led to many unintended consequences, while delivering on few of its promises.[16]

At the beginning of President Ma's first term, the existing constitution appeared likely to stay. First, a great majority of Taiwan's electorate had clearly lost their appetite for any outlandish political reform agenda, including further changes to the constitution, regardless of the rationale. Ma took office with a clear-cut mandate that his government give first priority to economic revival and cross-Strait reconciliation, and he had little incentive to spend his limited political capital on amending the constitution. At the same time, the movement for a new constitution had evidently run out of steam. The new DPP leadership under Tsai Ing-wen was obliged to put this issue on the backburner.

Second, from a practical point of view, the danger of a recurrence of crippling political gridlock appeared quite unlikely for the foreseeable future. The KMT's electoral dominance was restored in the 2008 election, and the new electoral system was expected to help the KMT lock in its control of the Legislative Yuan for a long time. By contrast, the DPP had suffered two crushing defeats in a row, and its electoral base was threatened with further erosion under the KMT's open-door policy toward cross-Strait economic and cultural exchange. Therefore, the KMT had little incentive to respond to the call for further constitutional change, much less to initiate a new round of constitutional amendments on its own.

Third, within the DPP camp, there was a growing recognition that the campaign for a new constitution had passed its moment and that this plank in the platform could do little to help the party regain its electoral vitality. The only credible proposal for a constitutional amendment that the party could still pursue was how to revise the electoral rules for LY elections one more time in order to address the issue of disproportionality. However, many DPP politicians conceded that the KMT, with its comfortable absolute parliamentary majority and good prospects for locking in its electoral dominance for a long time, had no incentive to reopen the debate, despite Ma's token promise on the campaign trail that the KMT was willing to review relevant issues of constitutional reform in the second half of his first term.

Last but by no means least, the legal hurdle for passing any future constitutional amendment had become formidably high. It required first a three-quarters majority of the Legislative Yuan to approve a draft constitutional amendment. Then the draft had to be ratified via a plebiscite with at least half of all eligible voters casting a yes vote. This meant that any future amendments would require a strong bipartisan consensus and overwhelming support from the electorate. It took nothing short of a miracle, plus a gross miscalculation by the DPP, for the Seventh Amendment to be adopted in 2005, and that history appeared unlikely to repeat itself.

By the end of the Chen Shui-bian era, the ROC constitution had survived many crises and had finally established itself as a common political denominator not only for the great majority of the electorate but also, surprisingly, for the Washington-Beijing-Taipei triangle. In this sense, the existing constitution did function as a set of institutional and symbolic arrangements that related organically to Taiwanese society's realities, including all the historical legacies and the complicated relationship with mainland China that the island had inherited.

After the second transfer of power, all major political actors on the island had finally come to a point at which the possibility for further change to the constitution appeared virtually exhausted. They had little choice but to learn to live with an imperfect constitution. Making the existing constitution a living, active, authoritative legal document seemed to be the only feasible recipe for strengthening Taiwan's constitutional democracy. Ma's solemn pledge in his inauguration speech that he would resolve to reestablish a robust tradition of constitutionalism by affirming the authority of the ROC constitution should be seen in this context.

Within the first two years of Ma's presidency, a few positive developments suggested that the legitimacy of the ROC constitution was being enhanced, if not fully consolidated. First, few people questioned the fairness and openness of the previous presidential election. Frank Hsieh, the DPP presidential nominee, delivered a graceful concession speech on election night, which was a marked improvement over the disputed March 2004 election. Next, fewer and fewer political figures across the spectrum were willing to launch open attacks against the ROC constitution after Ma took office. Third, all major democratic institutions had resumed their normal governing function in accordance with the constitution's provisions. Most notably, the Control Yuan was brought back to life with a new slate of members being confirmed and sworn in. Last, the number of highly politicized cases that required a timely ruling by the Council of Grand Justices was substantially reduced.

However, not all signs suggested a smooth journey to the consolidation of Taiwan's constitutional democracy. The indictment of Chen Shui-bian on charges of corruption, extortion, perjury, and obstruction of justice sparked an emotionally charged debate between DPP loyalists and the Pan-Blue camp. The tension ratcheted up with each round of legal battles over the extension of Chen Shui-bian's detention. On the one hand, the former president's loyalists and the pro-DPP media insisted that the prosecution was politically motivated and that Chen's family was being victimized by a KMT-orchestrated political purge. On the other hand, the losing side in each round questioned the independence of the judiciary. Pan-Blue camp loyalists were furious when an allegedly pro-DPP Court of Appeals judge cleared Chen and his family of many counts of corruption charges, and they rejoiced when the High Court sent Chen and his wife to prison on other counts. The Chen Shui-bian loyalists unleashed their grief and anguish by electing Chen's son to the Kaohsiung City Council by a large winning margin in the 2010 election.

The divisions over national identity posed an even greater challenge to Taiwan's young democracy. Witnessing the long-term option of Taiwan's independence being shut off and their electoral foundation eroded by the acceleration of cross-Strait economic integration, the DPP leadership and their followers felt increasingly frustrated, anxious, and powerless under a KMT-dominated political order. With only a quarter of the seats in the legislature, the Pan-Green camp could not raise any meaningful objections to the KMT-initiated legislative proposals to loosen up restrictions on cross-Strait economic and cultural exchanges. Increasingly, the opposition camp resorted to strategies of civil disobedience to register their anger and defiance. The DPP justified its turn to disruptive acts with the allegation that the KMT was cutting deals with Beijing at the expense of Taiwanese sovereignty.

When it came to roll-call votes over cross-Strait bills, the DPP caucus frequently paralyzed the legislative process with such disruptive tactics as using human chains to block the entrance, locking up the LY Speaker in his private chamber, or knocking down the Speaker's microphone and taking away his gavel. The DPP leaders were also increasingly willing to mobilize their die-hard supporters to take to the streets and test the limits of law enforcement agents' patience and tolerance. A few worrisome incidents occurred during Ma Ying-jeou's first term. For instance, a retired People's Republic of China senior official, who had served as the spokesperson for the Taiwan Affairs Office, was chased down by an angry pro-independence mob and pushed to the ground during his private sightseeing tour of Tainan. In a separate instance, a violent clash between an angry pro-independence crowd and riot police erupted at the closing moments of a DPP-organized, large-scale demonstration protesting the first-ever visit by Chen Yunlin, Beijing's top envoy to Taiwan.

Fortunately, incidences of violent confrontation and abuses of police power remained few and far between during Ma Ying-jeou's first term. Nevertheless, it remained to be seen if the resiliency of Taiwan's young democratic regime could hold up equally well if and when cross-Strait negotiations moved beyond economic issues and entered the territory of sensitive political issues.

Notes

1. For an evaluation of Taiwan's semipresidential system, please see Yu-shan Wu, "The ROC's Semi-Presidentialism at Work: Unstable Compromise, Not Cohabitation," *Issues and Studies* 36, no. 5 (2000): 1–40.

2. Jih-wen Lin, "The Politics of Reform in Japan and Taiwan," *Journal of Democracy* 17, no. 2 (2006): 118–131.

3. Yun-han Chu, "Consolidating Democracy in Taiwan: From *Guoshi* to *Guofa* Conference," in *Democratization in Taiwan: Implications for China,* ed. Hung-mao Tien and Steve Yui-sang Tsang (New York: St. Martin's Press, 1998), 23–48.

4. Chen Shui-bian was not directly involved in the negotiation process and later openly announced that he would not be bound by the compromise between the DPP and the KMT.

5. For an analysis of why Taiwan's SNTV system for legislative elections practically renders the threat of a no-confidence vote not credible, see Jih-wen Lin, "Institutionalized Uncertainty and Governance Crisis in Post-Hegemonic Taiwan," *Journal of East Asian Studies* 3, no. 3 (2003): 433–460.

6. There are two remaining caveats, however. First, the commencement dates of the two offices are three months and three weeks apart. If the two elections are synchronized, the presidential election has to be moved up to late January, thus creating a four-month-long interregnum before the inauguration. Second, in theory, the parliament can be dissolved whenever it votes down a sitting cabinet with a vote of no confidence. Under this scenario, the two elections will once again become desynchronized.

7. For a sophisticated elaboration on the justification for a new constitution, see Jiunn-Rong Yeh, "The Second Call for a New Constitution in Taiwan" (paper presented at Taiwan's Constitutional Reform: Domestic Inspiration and External Constraints, Woodrow Wilson International Center for Scholars, Washington, DC, July 21, 2004).

8. For example, see the propositions put forward by the Constitutional Reform Alliance in Taiwan, available at http://blog.roodo.com/21cra_en.

9. Ma Ying-jeou made that pledge in his essay published on ROC's Constitution Day, "Marching Toward a Normal Democratic Society," *China Times,* December 25, 2005.

10. *China Times,* February 17, 2006.

11. Under the current rule, each committee has three rotating chairs (the so-called conveners or convening members); therefore, the majority party (or coalition) does not always steer standing committees. If there were only one chair with a fixed

term, the majority party (or coalition) would have full steering power, much like what has been the case in the US Congress. If this were the case, the president would be obliged to appoint a premier with the support of the majority party (or coalition) in the parliament in order to avoid total paralysis of the executive. This idea was introduced by Shen Fu-hsiung, a former DPP LY member.

12. In late December 1996, President Lee convened a National Development Conference, which brought together government officials, academics, professionals, and representatives of the KMT, the DPP, and independents to examine and debate various proposals for constitutional reform. For the dynamics of the National Development Conference (*Guofa* Conference), see Chu, "Consolidating Democracy in Taiwan."

13. Frank Hsieh is perhaps the only DPP politician who openly announced that DPP followers should try to live with the built-in One China principle of the existing constitution.

14. Cheng-liang Kuo, "To Occupy the Centralist Position, the DPP Has to Give Up Its Radicalism," chinareviewnews.com, January 31, 2012.

15. "DPP in Crisis After Chen's Betrayal," *Liberty Times,* March 6, 2005.

16. Lin, "The Politics of Reform in Japan and Taiwan."

9

Civil Society and the Politics of Engagement

Chang-Ling Huang

As Alexis de Tocqueville stressed in his classic work *Democracy in America,* civil society is good and important for democracy. Robert Putnam has more recently elaborated on this argument, theorizing about and providing evidence for the importance of "social capital" to the civic life that underpins democracy.[1] Through the wide panoply of voluntary associations that make up civil society, citizens cultivate civic cultures, establish behavioral norms, and strengthen communication skills, generating social capital that makes us "better able to govern a just and stable democracy."[2] Building on Putnam's work, empirical studies have repeatedly demonstrated the positive relation between civil society and democracy.[3] Recent cross-sectional studies on third- and fourth-wave democracies have reaffirmed this positive relationship: states that have dense networks of well-organized civil society groups are more likely to protect the political and civil liberties of their citizens and to have better institutional performance.[4]

These empirical studies usually measure the strength of civil society by organizational or membership density. In their exploration of the relationship between civil society and democracy, however, researchers have seldom discussed the source of the density, or the *reason* that people become engaged in civic activities. Putnam treated this as "habits of heart." His apolitical and voluntarist view, however, has been the target of much criticism. The associational life of citizens might indeed lead to more participation in politics and better democracy, but citizen organizations can also be antidemocratic. In short, the effect of civil society cuts both ways: it can either help or hurt democracy, depending on the larger political setting.[5]

One of the most important elements of this larger context is the nature of the state. A democratic civil society and a democratic state are mutually beneficial and are even necessary for the other to exist.[6] As Theda Skocpol pointed out, organized civil society has seldom flourished without both a capable state and inclusive democratic politics.[7] In other words, without a responsive state, however associational it is, a vibrant civil society alone will not ensure democracy.

Taiwan's democratization has commonly been depicted as an election-driven process, because local elections that began in the 1950s helped stabilize the Kuomintang's (KMT's) rule in Taiwan and eventually allowed more liberal forces to take advantage of this institutional mechanism to push for political change.[8] Like other new democracies, elections have been the most prominent aspect of Taiwan's political transformation. Since vote rigging no longer occurs and vote buying is no longer rampant or very effective, impartial observers would agree that interest representation through the electoral mechanism has been fully developed in Taiwan.

Democracy, however, entails more than elections. Equally important are the establishment of the rule of law, the organization and articulation of social interests, and citizen participation and involvement in decision-making processes.[9] In other words, interest representation through elections is only one aspect of democratic practice. For the state to better respond to society's demands and needs, interest representation through nonelectoral means is also important, and this requires arrangements that allow the state to interact regularly and consistently with society.

This chapter describes how, under an institutional mechanism created for nonelectoral interest representation, Taiwanese civil society has engaged with the state to make it more responsive. Although these efforts have not always been successful, the process has made more apparent the distinction between political society and civil society. The challenge to make the state responsive, as this chapter argues, is rooted within civil society itself, especially in its struggle to define the bounds of legitimate civil action. In the following sections, I first briefly describe the features that characterized Taiwan's civil society during the Chen Shui-bian era. Then I describe three cases of confrontation between the state and civil society during Chen's presidency that involved members of government commissions. After presenting the cases, I discuss the politics of engagement between the state and civil society, showing how the institutions that were created to foster civic engagement in government created challenges for civil society organizations. The chapter concludes on a positive note: although the Democratic Progressive Party (DPP) government might have failed to be a truly progressive government, the additional political space it opened up for civil society was a significant change for Taiwan's democratic institutions. Engaging the state has allowed the progressive segment of civil society to impede, if not prevent, undesirable state policies. Whether the state will take initiatives that will advance democratic or progressive values, however, will depend on changes in the broader political landscape.

The Features of Taiwan's Civil Society

By the time the DPP came to power in May 2000, it had inherited a democratic landscape that had been greatly enriched by the growth of a wide range of civil society organizations, including numerous independent groups devoted to such causes as human rights, labor rights, gender equality, and environmental protection. The activation of Taiwan's civil society began in the late 1970s and early 1980s. The consumer protection movement, feminist publications, and spontaneous and sporadic antipollution protests all emerged around that time. The KMT's long authoritarian rule, however, had largely constrained the activities of civil society. Although social interests began to be articulated, organizational efforts were limited.

This situation changed during Taiwan's gradual transition to democracy. Between 1989 and 1996, the number of civic associations increased by more than an order of magnitude.[10] According to government statistics, in 1999, shortly before the DPP came to power, there were more than 20,000 registered civic associations. Of the three major categories of organizations recorded in these statistics, there were 122 political organizations, 8,249 occupational organizations, and 15,309 social organizations.[11] By contrast, by the end of 2009, the number of civic associations had grown to more than 40,000.[12] In other words, over the eight years of the Chen Shui-bian era, the number of civic associations had roughly doubled. These associations ranged from large-scale charity organizations such as the Buddhist Tzu Chi Foundation and World Vision International, whose reach stretched well beyond Taiwan, to small-scale advocacy organizations that were nevertheless vocal and contentious.

Democratization in Taiwan brought about not only the proliferation but also the institutionalization of civic associations. The number and scale of street protests was reduced after the initial stages of democratization, mainly because more institutional channels were opened for civil society to interact with the state. Literature on the relation between democratization and civil society tends to associate institutionalization with demobilization, with some arguing that leftist parties often abandon their allies in civil society and pursue a demobilization strategy once they make significant gains in elections.[13] In Taiwan, however, the opposite pattern occurred: because local elections had existed even under authoritarian rule, members of the DPP were familiar with the election game even before they organized themselves as a political party or built alliances with civil society groups.

Before the onset of democratization in the late 1980s, there were debates among the prodemocracy forces between the "social movement line" and the "election line." As had been true in the experience of other newly democratized countries, the distinction between civil society and political society was not clear under authoritarian rule or during the transition. Before taking over the government in 2000, the DPP adopted some aspects of both the social movement line and the election line, with its members getting involved in the social movements and trying to raise the profile of social movement demands in election campaigns. The relation between the DPP and the social movement organizations throughout the 1990s was therefore largely symbiotic. Thus, when challenging the ruling KMT, the DPP and the social movement organizations were structurally bound together.

Civil society, of course, consists not only of social movement organizations, but also of noncontentious civic associations. In fact, in terms of scale and numbers, most organizations in Taiwan's civil society were not obviously political and were, instead, based on common occupational, religious, leisure, or charity ties. Democratization, however, is a continuous process with transforming power: the distinction between social movement organizations and non–social movement organizations is not always clear. A civil association's decision to engage in political actions or social advocacy depends not only on the nature of the organization but also on the issues that concern its members—and those issues can change as the political environment evolves. As is shown in the following sections, confrontations between the state and civil society during the Chen Shui-bian era were also a reflection of confrontations between different segments of civil society.

Civil Society and the State During the Chen Shui-Bian Era: Three Cases of Confrontation

Three separate protests, occurring between 2005 and 2007, illustrate how the state-society relationship changed under President Chen. The protests did not involve large numbers of citizens and did not always take place on the street. They did, however, involve unusual actors—the civic members of government commissions (that is, representatives from civil society). These protests created or reemphasized the distinction between political and civil society.

In May 2005, civic members of the Cabinet Commission on the Promotion of Human Rights—among them the president's national policy adviser, Peter Huang—demanded that the cabinet stop the soon-to-be-implemented policy of requiring fingerprints for the state ID card. Huang and Premier Frank Hsieh had a heated debate over the issue during the commission's meeting. Huang, along with eleven other civic members, threatened to resign if the government insisted on implementing the policy.[14] Soon after the media reported the dispute, the spokesperson of the cabinet and the deputy minister of interior both said the fingerprint requirement for state IDs would be implemented in July 2005, as scheduled. They also claimed that this policy would help reduce crime rates. Huang, on the other hand, formed an activist group, called Citizens' Alliance Against the Fingerprint Requirement, which worked with social movement organizations. He wrote op-ed pieces opposing the policy, held press conferences to express his opinions, and persuaded lesislators from the ruling DPP to request an injunction from the Council of Grand Justices, Taiwan's Constitutional Court. Within a week of the news report, the government's position changed, and it expressed a willingness to stop the requirement if the Council of Grand Justices found the policy unconstitutional. On June 19, the justices declared the policy unconstitutional, and the fingerprint requirement was dropped.[15]

In October 2006, four civic members of the Cabinet Commission on the Promotion of Women's Rights resigned to protest the cabinet's decision to submit a revised Health and Reproduction Law to the Legislative Yuan for legislative deliberation. The bill imposed a three-day waiting period for women who sought an abortion. After the commission members resigned, they held press conferences with other feminist activists and severely criticized the government for ignoring women's rights.[16] The cabinet minister who was in charge of the revision told the press that the revised bill was already submitted to the Legislative Yuan for deliberation, so anyone not satisfied with the revision could lobby the legislature's members. The minister's words further outraged the commission's civic members, and all of them, including the ones who had not resigned, signed a document, published as an op-ed piece in a major newspaper, criticizing the government's policy.[17] Although antiabortion legislators pushed hard for the bill to be put on the legislative agenda, the media's coverage of the protest resignation and the press conferences allowed feminists to convince political parties not to move forward with such a highly controversial bill. The bill was therefore not put on the agenda.

In July 2007, two civic members of the Environmental Impact Assessment Commission refused to attend the commission's regular meeting. Instead, they put on headbands bearing the words "Environmental Impact Assessment Is Dead" and sat in front of the Environmental Protection Agency (EPA) building to protest. Another civic member of the commission, in support of the protest, tore up a copy of the Environmental Impact Assessment Law and condemned the government for ignoring the law and simplemindedly protecting development interests.[18] Among the major development projects that the government pushed for but that were opposed by these commission members was the construction of the Su-Hua Highway, a highway passing through Su-ao and Hualien along the scenic, but environmentally fragile, area of eastern Taiwan. The media reported that the commission had blocked major development cases and that the president had privately inquired about when the term of the current commission would end.[19] A few days after the sit-in protest, the term of the commission ended as scheduled. Soon after that, the EPA released the list of newly appointed Environmental Impact Assessment Commission members; none of the three protesting members was reappointed.[20] As for the Su-Hua Highway, the case was pending. The new commission cited procedural reasons and did not make any conclusive decision on the case under the DPP government. The construction of the highway, as discussed below, finally began, after several rounds of policy changes between 2008 and 2010, under the KMT government.

These cases shared several similarities. First, these commissions consisted of both bureaucrats and civil society representatives, and the protests took place because at least some civil society members were upset by government policies. Second, the civil society representatives who resigned or protested all had backgrounds in social movement organizations that were friendly toward, or supportive of, the DPP before or even after it became the ruling party. Third, all three commissions were engaged in policy areas in which the DPP government actively sought to distinguish itself from the conservative KMT, adopting slogans that emphasized the party's distinct commitment to reform, such as "Building the Nation on Human Rights Protection," "Equal Power for Men and Women," and "Environmental Protection Comes First."

The protests attracted media attention because it was unprecedented for members of government commissions to publicly confront the government. Among the three commissions, only the Commission on the Promotion of Human Rights was established after the DPP had come to power in 2000; the other two had been established under the KMT in the mid- to late-1990s. While the civic commission members were upset by the government's policy, government leaders were no doubt annoyed by their actions. The civil society representatives criticized the government for betraying its own values, while government officials probably wondered why inviting friends and allies into the commissions had resulted in such embarrassment. To understand the institutional and democratic implications of the confrontation between the commission members and the government, we first have to discuss the politics of engagement.

The Politics of Engagement

The politics of engagement between civil society and the state began in the mid-1990s, when the DPP won control of the Taipei City government. Although the KMT government at the national level had a long history of including civil society representatives in government commissions, especially commissions on economic affairs, these members tended to be scholars and experts. Members of nongovernmental organizations (NGOs), except those from organizations that had been sanctioned by the government since the authoritarian period, were seldom invited to serve on government commissions. After Chen Shui-bian became mayor of Taipei in 1995, however, the city government established various commissions made up of representatives from both civil society organizations and the city bureaucracy. For the first time, many social activists were brought in to serve on government commissions, working alongside government bureaucrats.

There are competing views about what constitutes "civil society" in practice. Diamond's oft-cited definition for *civil society* is "the realm of organized social life that is open, voluntary, self-generating, at least partially self-supporting, [and] autonomous from the state."[21] In Taiwan, civic organizations involved in social issues are usually categorized into two groups: social movement and social welfare organizations. The former tend to emphasize advocacy and challenging of the status quo. The latter focus more on providing direct assistance to those in need. The difference between the two is not always clear, since many organizations engage in advocacy and provide social assistance at the same time. Nevertheless, social movement organizations are usually more contentious than social welfare organizations. When Chen Shui-bian brought in activists from movement organizations to the city government commissions, contentious politics experienced tremendous changes. Activists who used to protest on the street now had a dual relation with the government. They fought against and worked with the government at the same time, and often the same people who fought each other on some occasions, coexisted in the commissions and worked together on others. From the promotion of gender equality to the renovation of public space, the Taipei City government between 1994 and 1998 created a partnership with civil society in many policy areas.

Two highly controversial policies adopted by the city government raised questions about the wisdom of such civil society–bureaucracy partnerships. One was Mayor Chen's decision to abolish the licenses of sex workers and criminalize prostitution in Taipei, which not only triggered debate about the relationship between the state and the feminist movement but also eventually led to a schism within the feminist movement itself.[22] The other was the destruction of a slum near a major commercial area to make way for a city park. The project's execution antagonized urban planners and scholars who had supported the mayor and advocated greater participation in the planning process. Although these two cases negatively affected relations between the DPP city government and the social movement sector, the institutional changes survived Chen Shui-bian's electoral defeat in 1998. The government practice of putting members of social organizations, not just scholars and experts, on government commissions persisted in the city government.

The composition of many commissions established by the Taipei City government under the DPP was broken into halves or thirds: on some, government bureaucrats and civil society representatives held an equal number of seats, and on others, government bureaucrats, scholars and experts, and NGO representatives each held one-third. The mayor chaired many of the commissions. There were usually term limits and rotation requirements for civil society members, including for scholars, experts, and NGO representatives. The term limit was typically two to three years, and the turnover requirement required one-third to one-half of civil society members to be replaced each term. The rules clearly displayed an objective of increasing participation in government and representation in decisionmaking. These rules later became widely adopted by government commissions at various levels, under both the KMT and the DPP. For example, when the Commission on Sustainable Development and the Commission on the Promotion of Women's Rights were established at the cabinet level in 1997, both followed the same rules. Although there were some exceptions, in general, a majority of commission representatives were civil society members. Not only did newly created government commissions include NGO representatives, but existing commissions were also reformed to allow greater civic participation.[23]

Although both the Taipei City government under the DPP and the national government under the KMT in the mid-1990s interacted more closely with civil society through government commissions, there was an essential difference. Commissions under the KMT tended, in general, to be advisory, while under the DPP, they became more participatory. The difference between the two was the source of the confrontations highlighted earlier. Once the DPP assumed power at the national level, it facilitated the institutional transformation of Taiwan's democracy.

A good example illustrating the significant changes of the roles and functions of commissions under the DPP government is the Cabinet Commission on the Promotion of Women's Rights (CPWR). The CPWR was established in 1997 after strong demands from women's organizations.[24] The composition followed the one-third each rule, and the term of the members was two years. Between 1997 and 2001, the commission had seventeen members and held commission meetings once every three to four months. Most of the gender scholars and feminist activists who served on the commission had credentials in the gender community, and the commission's role was largely advisory.

In March 2001, when the third term of the commission began and the DPP was already in power, the statute of the commission was revised. Feminists who were close to the DPP and had experience in working with the Taipei City government under Chen Shui-bian demanded that the commission be enlarged to accommodate more representatives from women's organizations. The number of commission members increased to twenty-seven, and, without replacing those gender scholars and representatives of women's organizations appointed by the KMT government, several additional feminists were added to the commission. Those who joined at that time tended to have extensive experience in the feminist movement. Their political vision was of a DPP government that would use its authority to actively promote gender equality. Their concept of the commission was as a participatory body under which the state and civil society would share power and jointly make policy decisions. These seasoned feminists' vision of an activist commission made bureaucrats and other commission members uncomfortable, and yet serious conflicts did not occur frequently due to the commission's structure: it held meetings only once every three to four months, confining disagreements to those time intervals, and the large number of members made it impossible for the commission to exercise much real policy influence.

When the commission's fourth term began in 2003, things began to change rapidly, however, and an activist commission gradually emerged. First, all the nonbureaucratic commission members formerly appointed by the KMT were replaced. Second, the commission's organization was altered once again: it was divided into four sections, each responsible for a different policy area. In addition to the formal commission meetings, chaired by the premier and held three to four times a year, they also held premeetings, chaired by the minister of the interior, several weeks before the formal meetings. In addition, various other ministries held special meetings with sections of the commission to discuss specific policy issues. In this new institutional environment, feminists quickly pushed to institute gender mainstreaming within the government.[25] The commission's assertiveness inevitably led to bureaucrats' complaints and to clashes between the bureaucrats and the civil society commission members: bureaucrats insisted that commission members' roles were advisory, while commission members from civil society thought their roles were to ensure that the government made and implemented gender-friendly policies. The clash of views over the roles and functions of the committees eventually led to confrontation between the government and the commission members about abortion rights.

The Conflict over Abortion

Taiwanese women have had implicit abortion rights since enactment of the Eugenics and Health Law in 1984. The law, for the first time in Taiwan's history, listed conditions under which a woman could obtain a legal abortion—rape, incest, or life-threatening health risks to the mother. As is evident in the law's name, in the early 1980s, the predominant concern within the government was not about women's health but about population quality and economic competitiveness. Although their numbers were small, feminists exploited the state's conservative ideology to lobby for a safer environment for abortion. Putting aside discourses that emphasized women's rights, they instead argued that unwanted pregnancies would affect population quality. The law eventually was interpreted to allow a woman to obtain a legal abortion if she could provide medical evidence that the pregnancy would affect her well-being. This clause was so vague that it effectively made abortion legal.

For years afterward, religious organizations were upset by this quasi-legalization of abortion and wanted to change it. In the early 2000s, social and political changes presented them with an opportunity. On the social side, Taiwan's birthrate had been gradually decreasing, and after 2000, it fell to one of the lowest in the world, raising additional concerns about the high rates of abortion on the island. On the political side, in 2003, a new minister was appointed to head the Department of Health, under which there was an Advisory Commission on Eugenics and Health. The new minister was Catholic and appointed a Catholic priest and three other experts with Catholic backgrounds to be commission members. Just like the feminists who used government commissions to promote gender equality, the Catholic members treated the commission within the Department of Health as an important arena to promote a pro-life agenda. Within two years, the commission drafted a revised version of the Eugenics and Health Law and renamed it the Reproduction and Health Law. The new draft law required a six-day waiting period and a consultation session for any woman wanting to have an abortion.

When the civil society members of the CPWR learned of the draft, they strongly opposed the waiting period and consultation requirement. They argued that the draft regulations were a violation of women's rights. For about a year and a half, a seesaw battle between religious and feminist activists was fought in the cabinet-level CPWR and the Department of Health's Advisory Commission on Eugenics and Health. The CPWR argued that laws drafted by the Department of Health should not violate the basic principles established by the CPWR, since the Department of Health was a subordinate unit of the cabinet. Members of the Advisory Commission on Eugenics and Health, however, thought their decisions should be respected and that civil society members of the CPWR should not dictate national policies.

The dispute between these two commissions actually reflected a fundamental difference between two distinct segments of civil society. The draft of the revised law was supposed to be submitted to a meeting of the full cabinet in fall 2005, but it was blocked for almost a year by the civil society members of the CPWR, who made it clear to the premier, who was also the chair of the CPWR, that women's organizations would not accept the draft. In the meantime, religious activists successfully mobilized Buddhist organizations to support the pro-life cause. Unlike Catholic churches, Buddhist organizations were large and influential in Taiwan and commanded a great number of believers. Eventually the Department of Health changed the waiting period from six days to three days, submitted the draft to the cabinet, and got it approved. The resignation in protest of the four civil society members of the CPWR basically meant that feminists lost the "battle of commissions" and were forced to fight the religious organizations in the legislature.

As noted earlier, feminists then tried to stop the bill from being placed on the legislative agenda and brought up for consideration there. Because religious organizations enjoyed a significant resource advantage over feminist ones, women's rights activists would have faced a tough fight at that stage to keep it from passing. And yet the feminist groups were able to delay consideration until the end of the legislative term and thus prevent its passage.

When a new legislature was elected in January 2008, the staunchest supporter of the waiting period was not reelected. Most of the newly elected legislators were not eager to take up such huge controversies that potentially would cost them votes either way, and so the bill was not revived. Neither the feminists nor the religious organizations could claim a victory in this battle, and the issue faded from view.

The Environmental Conflict

Human rights and environmental activists shared the feminists' expectation that a DPP government would play an active role in promoting progressive values. As occurred in the abortion rights issue, the Su-Hua Highway project was blocked by the civil society members of a commission—in this case, the Commission on Environmental Impact Assessment (CEIA). The CEIA was established in 1994 following the enactment of the Environmental Impact Assessment (EIA) Law. Civil society representatives on the CEIA had initially been appointed by the minister of the EPA. In 2001, however, this was modified to include a nominating committee made up of both bureaucrats and civil society organizations. The EPA openly solicited nominations, and any social organization could submit recommendations for committee members. Environmental organizations consistently put forward names, though those people were not always appointed because the final decision was at the discretion of the minister. Environmentalists had already begun to approach the EIA review meetings as major battlegrounds, even before the DPP came to power, but there had never before been a major development case that was completely blocked by the committee.[26]

The Su-Hua Highway was an ambitious construction project in a difficult and environmentally sensitive area, and the cost was estimated to be at least US$3.3 billion. The Ministry of Transportation began planning the highway in 1990, with the goal of promoting the economic development of eastern Taiwan. During the 2000 presidential campaign, both Chen Shui-bian and the KMT candidate, Lien Chan, pledged to construct the highway if they were elected. Three days before the presidential election, the first EIA review was completed, and the project received a "conditional pass." After Chen Shui-bian won the presidential election, both he and his premier expressed their determination to press forward with the plan to build the highway.[27] The CEIA, however, returned the first EIA report to the Ministry of Transportation in November 2001, asserting that there was no immediate need to construct the highway. The Ministry of Transportation proceeded with preparation work for the construction anyway and planned to resubmit the EIA report.

Over the next three years, supporters and opponents of this project engaged in extensive mobilization and advocacy efforts. Supporters claimed that Hualien County deserved to enjoy economic prosperity, while opponents charged that the planned highway route crossed too many fault lines and environmentally sensitive areas and that Hualien should seek economic prosperity by adopting an alternative development model. By the time the 2004 presidential election approached, the project had become highly politicized. Both the KMT and DPP politicians claimed that the other side had blocked the project, whereas both had, in reality, taken inconsistent positions on this issue.[28] At one time, the premier even indicated that he hoped that the Hualien County government would decide the controversy.[29]

After Chen Shui-bian won reelection in March 2004, a coalition of environmental organizations demanded that the government cancel the highway project once and for all and use the money for other infrastructure projects in Hualien.[30] In 2005, a scholar and longtime environmentalist was appointed as the minister of the EPA, and many environmental activists became civil society representatives on the CEIA. One of the first things the new commission members did was to undertake site visits along the planned route of the Su-Hua Highway. Over the next two years, these members not only objected to the construction of the highway but also had repeated run-ins with the Chen Shui-bian administration, including signing open letters condemning the government for putting development before the environment. The commission meetings became the most important institutional battleground for environmentalists: whenever they were held, a wide array of environmental activists attended to record the meetings, posting their observations and comments on blogs and electronic bulletin boards.[31] Although the most vocal environmentalists on the commission were not reappointed when their terms expired in July 2007, the fight to stop the highway still continued.

In April 2008, shortly after Ma Ying-jeou's victory in the March election, but before Chen Shui-bian's term had ended, the CEIA held another special meeting to review the Su-Hua Highway case. Both supporters and opponents attended the meetings, and both sides rallied for their cause outside the EPA building. In the end, the commission members again refused to approve the project and returned the case to the Ministry of Transportation. In July, the new KMT government proposed to build a "replacement highway," which was billed as a plan to improve the existing highway between Su-ao and Hualien, rather than constructing an entirely new freeway.[32] The government's plan was strongly opposed by environmentalists, who argued that the government was trying to confuse people with the name change, and that as long as freeway standards were adopted for the road, the environmental impact would be like building a new highway.

Facing this strong opposition, the Ma administration instructed the Ministry of Transportation to come up with a plan that would reduce the environmental impact. At the same time, the KMT was facing electoral pressure: local elections were held at the end of 2009, and in Hualien County, a former KMT politician ran for county executive on a pro-highway platform and defeated the KMT's official candidate in a landslide. Shortly after the local elections, the Ma administration proposed a scaled-down version of its earlier plan, which the media nicknamed the "improved highway." Opposition from environmental organizations persisted, but it was not nearly as fierce as it had been previously. In October 2010, a section of the existing highway built along the face of a cliff collapsed during a typhoon, killing more than 20 people, including a number of tourists from China. The tragedy turned the tide in the debate: despite remaining opposition from environmental organizations, within a month, the CEIA gave a conditional pass for the construction plan of the "improved highway."

Conflict over the Fingerprint Requirement

In comparison to the abortion rights and Su-Hua Highway controversies, the case of the fingerprint requirement for the state IDs appears relatively straightforward, because human rights activists did not encounter any countermobilization. The fingerprint requirement policy was based on Article 8 of the Household Registration Law, a legacy of the authoritarian era mandating that all households be registered with the state and that each citizen be issued a state ID number listed at their household of record. When children reached the age of fourteen, they were required to apply for a state ID card containing a state ID number and other basic identifying information. Between 1996 and 1997, several high-profile violent crimes occurred, prompting politicians in 1998 to pass a revision of the Household Registration Law, requiring all state ID card applicants to be fingerprinted. The Ministry of Interior had long planned to introduce a new version of the state ID card to combat counterfeiting, because the cards were widely used by both government and the private sector as the most important proof of identification. The ministry decided to implement the fingerprint requirement at the same time that it rolled out the replacement ID cards, as well as to create a national fingerprint database. The government argued that the fingerprint requirement would help reduce crime rates, and public opinion polls repeatedly showed popular support for the policy.

The Commission on the Protection of Human Rights was established in 2001, with rules of representation and term lengths similar to those of the other commissions. When the commission's civil society members learned that the government planned to introduce the fingerprint requirement on July 1, 2005, the same day that the new state ID cards were to be issued, they demanded the government stop the policy. They argued that the fingerprint requirement was unconstitutional and a violation of citizens' rights: it would contribute little to reducing crime rates but would carry great risks of identity theft for citizens. When the commission members rallied support from the social movement sector, the premier explained that the government was implementing the policy based on the law passed by the legislature. Activists, if not satisfied, should direct their energy to lobbying legislators.[33] DPP legislators maintained that the fingerprint requirement was important for reducing crime rates. The opposition parties, however, wanted the controversy to be resolved by poll results.[34] Eventually the DPP legislative caucus agreed to submit a petition to the Council of Grand Justices for constitutional interpretation, and the government agreed to temporarily suspend the policy until the Court made the decision. When the grand justices declared the fingerprint requirement unconstitutional and issued an injunction, the DPP party whip emphasized that DPP lawmakers supported the fingerprint requirement policy but had to abide by the decision made by the Court.[35]

The three cases reviewed above demonstrate the politics of engagement. Democratization opens up political space for civil society to challenge and to engage the state. Democracy, however, does not define civil society, whose interests and capacity for action can vary widely by issue. The abortion rights case illustrates how heterogeneous civil society actors can be: religious and women's organizations, though holding opposing views, took advantage of the same institutional mechanism. They both wanted to make the state respond to their demands, but their interests and values about abortion could not have been more different. The state, as much as possible, avoided taking sides. The controversy over the fingerprint requirement was resolved because it was relatively easy for the state to accept the view of civil society actors. It was a much bigger challenge, however, for the state ultimately to decide which views best reflected the "public interest," which is why the political fate of abortion rights remains undetermined, and why the Su-Hua Highway project went through several rounds of policy revisions.

Despite the limitation of the commission mechanism, under DPP rule, the progressive segment of civil society still took seriously the political space that the mechanism offered. For the organizationally weak progressive forces in Taiwan, engaging the state allowed them more opportunities and resources to push for change. However, the main civil society actors in the political process are sometimes, if not always, transformed as well, since every benefit has its cost and different institutions incur different transaction costs.

The Challenge of Governance

The paradox of the state is that it is "simultaneously apart from society and a part of society."[36] The reverse is also true. Civil society has become not just apart from the state but also a part of the state. By the end of the Chen Shui-bian era, the engagement between the two had become an important element of Taiwan's democracy. By the end of 2007, for instance, at the cabinet and minister levels, there were 522 government commissions, which included civil society representatives, and innumerable local government commissions.[37] Although there were high-profile confrontations, these commissions usually served as a bridge between the state and civil society. Their institutional boundaries remain unclear, however: whether these commissions are advisory, participatory, or real decisionmaking bodies depends on many factors, including the government's and society's attitudes toward the commissions.

There is no doubt that, along with democratization, Taiwan's governance structure has profoundly changed. The challenges of the new governance structure are similar to those documented by the public governance literature: accountability and representation[38] and the contestation between politics and professionalism.[39]

For civil society, engaging the state provides a nonelectoral form of political participation. Although quite a bit of comparative research has focused on quasi-autonomous nongovernmental organizations, nonmajoritarian institutions, nondepartmental public bodies, and board governance, the interaction of nonelectoral representative bodies such as government commissions with elected representative institutions remains a topic for exploration in Taiwan. The corporatist framework presented by Philippe Schmitter years ago would not fit Taiwan's experience, because civic organizations—perhaps with the exception of large religious organizations—tend to be small, dispersed, and diversified.[40] The highly decentralized structure of nonstate actors has made it difficult, if not completely impossible, to create vertical linkages between organizations. Coalitions of civic organizations tend to be ad hoc and temporary for specific policy goals.

The greatest challenge for civil society in its engagement with the government is still the huge resource gap between these two. According to a survey conducted in 2005, more than 70 percent of the nonprofit organizations have fewer than four full-time staff members, and less than 10 percent of these organizations have an annual budget over ten million new Taiwan dollars (approximately US$300,000).[41] Although the same survey shows that people who work in the nonprofit sector have more education and greater job satisfaction than those in government or business, the very fact that civic organizations are resource poor creates huge challenges in their relations with the state. In his study of Brazil's public policy management councils, Barth noted that since council members worked on a voluntary basis, "they implicitly have less time to participate in the councils."[42] The same is true in Taiwan. All civil society representatives on government commissions are volunteers. Even for full-time NGO workers, whose organizations are dealing with the policy issues of the commission on which they sit, the time and devotion put into commission work imposes costs on the organization. Such costs are not limited to human or material resources, but can also involve the direction of the organization's development. The civil society members on the government commissions therefore face a dilemma: If they demand more participation, especially if they want to emphasize the importance of sharing decisionmaking power, then they have to devote more time and energy to the unpaid labor of commission work and face the organizational cost that might be incurred. But if they regard their roles in the commissions as advisory, then they have to accept the fact that their advice will not always be followed.

Conclusion: The Politics of Engagement Continues (or Not?)

When Chen Shui-bian assumed the presidency in 2000, civil society, especially the social movement sector, had high expectations for a more open and responsive government. However, the DPP administration's decision in 2001 to continue building the fourth nuclear power plant was the first signal to the social movement sector that its expectations might be unrealistic, if not wrong. As Wu pointed out through a detailed analysis of publications and statements of DPP politicians, social movements were merely an instrument for the DPP during democratization. The party's strategy since the 1980s to "politicize social movements and socialize political movements" successfully built a coalition of forces against the authoritarian KMT. In other words, when the KMT was in power, Taiwan's political and civil societies had to work together to push for greater democracy. Once the KMT was no longer in power, the separation of the civil society from political society finally became apparent.[43] Under DPP rule, confrontations between civil society and the state took on different forms than in the past.

The DPP might have failed to fulfill the expectations of the progressive camp, but the political space and policy influence gained by civil society under DPP rule were nevertheless significant. For the three cases reviewed in this chapter, one might argue that, if the DPP had not abandoned progressive values, the controversies over abortion rights and the Su-Hua Highway would have been resolved in favor of the progressives, at least politically. Though this might be true, one could also ask, what would have happened to abortion rights and the Su-Hua Highway if the DPP were not in power? Few, I think, would argue that the progressive causes would have fared better.

The KMT won the 2008 legislative and presidential elections in a landslide, marking a clear break with the Chen Shui-bian era. Civil society, especially the segment of social movement organizations, has been less willing in general to engage (or less successful in engaging) with the KMT-run state, in part because of the KMT's past performance on progressive issues. After the KMT returned to power, social activists soon discovered that they would not be as influential through government commissions as they were under the DPP rule. The case of the revision of the Assembly and Parade Act is illustrative on this point.

In November 2008, not long after the KMT returned to power, a delegation from the People's Republic of China (PRC) came to Taiwan for negotiations on cross-Strait affairs, a key moment in President Ma Ying-jeou's first term. During their stay, the DPP and pro-independence social organizations initiated large-scale protests against the PRC's Taiwan policies. In their efforts to maintain order and protect Chinese delegates' safety, the police clashed with the protesters and were criticized for employing an unnecessarily heavy-handed response against the demonstrators. The conflict between the protesters and the police led social movement organizations to demand revisions to the Assembly and Parade Act.

President Ma had actually made amending the Assembly and Parade Law one of his campaign promises before he was elected, as the act was a bit of an anachronism. It was enacted in 1988, soon after Taiwan had lifted martial law, and was aimed at restricting assembly and protest activities, rather than protecting civil liberties. As supporters of the KMT had also found fault with the law when they were engaged in political protests during the Chen Shui-bian era, revising it became a plank in the KMT's campaign platform. After the conflict between the protesters and the police in November 2008, the Ma administration began to draft a revised Assembly and Parade Act. However, during the drafting process, the Commission on the Protection of Human Rights was not consulted; when the cabinet submitted the bill to the legislature, it was severely criticized for being "one step forward, two steps backward."

In May 2009, shortly before the legislature was set to deliberate and vote on the bill, several members of the Commission on the Protection of Human Rights wrote an op-ed piece calling for the government to reconsider the bill.[44] That op-ed piece resulted in a negotiation session personally led by President Ma with both social movement activists and the Chief of the Police Bureau.[45] After that session, the KMT party whip in the legislature also met social activists for further discussions and negotiations. The revised bill was not voted on as scheduled, mainly because the KMT and social activists could not reach a consensus on whether an assembly or parade should be required to first notify the police. The social movement organizations wanted the notification to be voluntary, whereas the KMT wanted it to be compulsory. The negotiations stalled in June 2009, and the act remained unrevised.

The process by which revisions to the Assembly and Parade Act were introduced illustrates how little interaction there was under the Ma administration between the cabinet and the Commission on the Protection of Human Rights. Unlike the abortion rights case discussed earlier, members of the Commission on the Protection of Human Rights did not have any opportunity to express their opinions within the government when the revised bill was drafted, and they had to resort to writing an op-ed piece to make their views known.

Although hundreds of government commissions continued to provide a platform for civil society to interact with the state, this governance mechanism could not by itself provide enough political space for social movement organizations, especially those that emerged after 2008, to force government concessions to their demands. Activists from movement organizations either declined or did not receive invitations to participate in many of the relevant government commissions. In addition, while government commissions could provide a forum for policy consultations, they could hardly resolve political disputes between the state and civil society. Particularly after President Ma's second term began in 2012, the central government became the target of waves of social protests over land confiscation, urban renewal, environmental protection, and labor rights. The dissatisfaction toward the Ma government culminated in March 2014 in the Sunflower Movement, in which students and social activists occupied the floor of the Legislative Yuan for three weeks to prevent the government from signing a service trade pact with China.

The Sunflower Movement had a significant impact on Taiwanese politics, as the KMT suffered landslide losses in the local elections at the end of 2014 and the national ones at the beginning of 2016. Although the long-term effects of the Sunflower Movement are not yet known, the greatest consequence will probably be its impact on civil society. While many participants opposed the service trade pact with China for political reasons such as asserting Taiwan's independence, there also were obvious concerns about its effect on Taiwanese society, especially its consequences for economic redistribution. Social movement organizations that participated in the movement emphasized the potential negative impact of the service trade pact, or any trade pact, on Taiwanese society. This new focus also has the potential to strain the old coalition between the DPP and the social movements. Although this coalition appeared to re-emerge during the Sunflower Movement, the social movement organizations made it clear that they would use the same criteria to monitor or challenge the DPP about social concerns over trade pacts, just as they had the KMT.[46] Thus, it remains to be seen whether the distinction between civil society and political society will again become sharper under the new DPP government.

In its relation to the state, Taiwan's civil society has come a long way. During the martial law era, it was repressed, penetrated, or co-opted by the state. But as Taiwan's society and politics changed, elements of civil society became more active and began to challenge the state directly. After 1992, when the legislature was democratically elected for the first time, civil society groups also began to interact with the legislative branch of the government, and by 1995, they were engaging with the executive branch as well—first with the Taipei city government and then with the national government. During the Chen Shui-bian era, the participation of civil society representatives in government policymaking reached new heights. Despite some confrontations between state and civil society actors during this period, overall government commissions held unprecedented influence over decisionmaking on a wide array of issues.

After the KMT returned to power in 2008, the roles of government commissions largely reverted back to advisory and less participatory roles, and waves of social protests emerged again. Whether this pattern changes yet again will depend a great deal on whether the new DPP government under Tsai Ing-wen once again allows more opportunities for civil society, and especially for social movement organizations, to participate in the government's decisionmaking process. One thing, however, is certain: whether on the streets or in government commission meeting rooms, civil society will continue engaging with the state to ensure the continued consolidation of Taiwan's democracy.

Notes

1. Alexis de Tocqueville, *Democracy in America* (New York: Harper and Row, 1966 [1835]); Robert Putnam, *Bowling Alone: The Collapse and Revival of American Community* (New York: Simon and Schuster, 2000).

2. Putnam, *Bowling Alone*, 290.

3. For empirical research that supports the positive relationship between civil society and democracy, see Rollin F. Tusalem, "A Boon or a Bane? The Role of Civil

Society in Third- and Fourth-Wave Democracies," *International Political Science Review* 28, no. 3 (2007): 361–386.

4. Ibid., 364–366.

5. Michael Foley and Bob Edwards, "The Paradox of Civil Society," *Journal of Democracy* 7, no. 3 (1996): 38–52.

6. According to Foley and Edwards, this is what Michael Walzer calls "the paradox of the civil society argument." Ibid., 44.

7. Theda Skocpol, "Unraveling from Above," *American Prospect* 25 (1996): 25.

8. Shelley Rigger, *Politics in Taiwan: Voting for Democracy* (London and New York: Routledge, 1999); Linda Chao and Ramon Myers, "How Elections Promoted Democracy Under Martial Law," in *Elections and Democracy in Greater China,* ed. Larry Diamond and Ramon Myers (Oxford: Oxford University Press, 2001); Christian Schafferer, *The Power of the Ballot Box: Political Development and Election Campaigning in Taiwan* (Lanham, MD: Lexington Books, 2003).

9. As Guillermo O'Donnell pointed out, horizontal accountability is as important as vertical accountability in democracy. See Guillermo O'Donnell, "Horizontal Accountability in New Democracies," *Journal of Democracy* 9, no. 3 (1998): 112–126.

10. Hei-yuan Chiu, "Liberty of Association, Group Participation, and Democracy," in *Rule of Law, Human Rights, and Civil Society,* ed. Hei-yuan Chiu, Chung-hua Ku, and Sechin Y. S. Chien (Taipei: Laureate Press, 2002).

11. Republic of China, *Statistical Year Book of the Interior,* Ministry of Interior, http://sowf.moi.gov.tw/stat/year/list.htm.

12. Republic of China, *2009 Year End Civil Association Overview,* Ministry of Interior, http://www.moi.gov.tw/stat/news_content.aspx?sn=4003.

13. Giuseppe Di Palma, *To Craft Democracy: An Essay on Democratic Transitions* (Berkeley: University of California Press, 1990); Philip Oxhorn, "The Popular Sector Response to an Authoritarian Regime: Shantytown Organizations Since the Military Coup," *Latin American Perspectives* 18, no. 1 (1991): 66–91. Cited in Ming-sho Ho, "Civil Society and Democratic Institutions," in *Analysis of Social Movements in Taiwan and China,* ed. Mao-kuei Chang and Yong-nian Zheng (Taipei: New Naturalism Press, 2003), 42.

14. *United Daily News,* May 17, 2005.

15. *Liberty Times,* June 20, 2005.

16. *China Times,* October 23, 2006.

17. *Liberty Times,* October 24, 2006.

18. *United Daily News,* July 20, 2007.

19. *United Daily News,* July 21, 2007.

20. According to news reports, the two protesting commission members had expressed no interest in continuing to serve on the commission after their terms ended, but the one who tore up the law wanted to remain as a commission member.

21. Larry Diamond, *Developing Democracy: Toward Consolidation* (Baltimore, MD: Johns Hopkins University Press, 1999), 221.

22. The feminist debate on the relationship between the state and the movement was also related to the thorny issue of national identity. Because the DPP proclaimed a different national identity from that of the KMT, there were also discussions about how engaging the state meant engaging in a nation-building agenda. For a more detailed discussion of this issue, see Yu-fen Chang and Mao-kuei Chang, "Examining Taiwan's Opposition Movement and National Question from the Perspective of the Public Prostitute Controversy," in *Analysis of Social Movements in Taiwan and China,* ed. Mao-kuei Chang and Yong-nian Zheng (Taipei: New Naturalism Press, 2003).

23. For example, the Taiwanese government implemented labor insurance in the 1950s. A committee supervised the labor insurance fund. The composition of this committee went through four rounds of reforms. Each time, the reform aimed to increase social representation in the committee. See Dun-yuan Chen, *A Study of the Formation and Operation of the Future National Health Insurance Supervisory Committee* (Taipei: Commissioned Report by the Department of Health, Executive Yuan, 2006).

24. In 1996, Peng Wan-ru, the director of the DPP's Department of Women's Affairs, was murdered. The killing was believed to be a random crime at night and not politically motivated. The killer, however, was never caught. Women's organizations protested against the state's inability to create a safe environment and demanded that the government, at that time still under the rule of the KMT, be more responsive toward women's needs.

25. Gender mainstreaming has become a global feminist strategy since 1995, when it was presented in the platform for action in the United Nation's Fourth World Conference on Women, held in Beijing. The core idea of this strategy is to make sure that gender equality is a mainstream value in a state's policymaking, policy execution, and policy evaluation processes. In other words, this strategy requires that the state become an active agent in promoting gender equality.

26. For example, the Pinnan development project was greatly reduced in scope in the EIA review process. See Ming-sho Ho, "Contested Governance Between Politics and Professionalism in Taiwan," *Journal of Contemporary Asia* 34, no. 2 (2004): 245–248.

27. *United Daily News,* August 27, 2000; *United Daily News,* October 20, 2000.

28. *United Daily News,* January 6, 2004; *United Daily News,* February 11, 2004; *United Daily News*, February 27, 2004.

29. In December 2003, the DPP premier announced that the construction of the freeway would be temporarily suspended and that the government would wait for three months for the Hualien County government and councils to reach a conclusion about whether Hualien wanted this project. *United Evening News,* December 11, 2003.

30. *Minsheng Daily,* April 28, 2004.

31. One commission member, Robin Winkler, an American Taiwanese lawyer and the founder of the environmental organization Wild at Heart Legal Defense Association, posted the minutes and agenda of every commission meeting on the organization's blog during his term.

32. *Liberty Times,* July 7, 2008.

33. *Central News Agency,* May 17, 2005.

34. *Liberty Times,* June 11, 2006.

35. The minister of interior, in addition to reiterating the crime rates argument, cited the United States as an example for the fingerprint requirement to defend the government's position. Human rights activists were outraged and reminded the minister that the United States did not implement this policy toward its own citizens, only toward foreigners. And, even for foreigners, the activists added, the US policy of the fingerprint requirement was criticized in the international human rights community. *China Times,* July 4, 2005.

36. Joel Migdal, *State in Society: Studying How States and Societies Transform and Constitute One Another* (Cambridge, UK: Cambridge University Press, 2001), 263.

37. "Agenda for the 28th Meetings of the Commission on the Promotion of Women's Rights," Ministry of Interior (2008), 90.

38. Chen, *A Study of the Formation and Operation of the Future National Health Insurance Supervisory Committee.*

39. Ho, "Contested Governance Between Politics and Professionalism in Taiwan."

40. Philippe Schmitter, "Still the Century of Corporatism?" *Review of Politics* 36, no. 1 (1974): 85–131.

41. Yu-yuan Kuan, Chao-hsien Leu, and Ching-hsia Cheng, "The Employment of the Third Sector in Taiwan: Survey Results of 2005," *The National Taiwan University Journal of Social Work* 16 (2008): 45–86.

42. Jutta Barth, "Public Policy Management Councils in Brazil: How Far Does Institutionalized Participation Reach?" *Public Administration and Development* 26, no. 3 (2006): 260.

43. Jieh-min Wu, "Disenchantment with the Clausewitzian Action Logic: An Analysis of the Current Trouble of the Social Movement," *Taiwan Sociology* 4 (2002): 159–198.

44. *United Daily News,* May 5, 2009.

45. *United Daily News,* May 11, 2009.

46. An illustrative example was the public statement made by the convener of the Economic Democracy Union, Attorney Lai Chung-chiang. The Economic Democracy Union is an organization formerly known as the Democratic Front Against the Cross-Strait Trade in Services Agreement. On January 22, 2016, right after the DPP won both the presidential and parliamentary elections, Mr. Lai publicly stated on his Facebook page that the pressure should now be exerted on the DPP to stop the negotiation with China regarding cross-strait goods trade pacts.

10

Press Freedom
and the Mass Media

Chien-san Feng

In its second term as ruling party between 2004 and 2008, the Democratic Progressive Party (DPP) government under President Chen Shui-bian was applauded for its commendable record of respecting freedom of the press. Both Reporters Without Borders in Paris and Freedom House in New York, two organizations that have a systematic procedure for evaluating and annually ranking press freedom across countries, found Taiwan's media to be one of the freest in Asia. This record, with only minor downward revision, continued after the Kuomintang (KMT) returned to power in 2008. Press freedom did not, however, help foster the development of a public forum for constructive democratic dialogue.

Why did a freer media during the Chen Shui-bian era fail to enhance the practice of democracy in Taiwan? After the KMT—the ruling party and the dominant communications and media conglomerate for more than half a century—lost the presidential election in 2000, the breakup of its media empire gathered pace, bringing a more diverse structure of media ownership to Taiwan. Nonetheless, this more democratic media environment was more apparent than substantial and produced serious conflicts and clashes between partisan media outlets and the DPP government.

In this chapter, I document, analyze, and interpret how and why there was more press freedom with less corresponding democratic and republican media discourse during the Chen era. In the main, this outcome was the consequence of three factors: the lasting legacy of decades of authoritarian control of television and the press, a regulatory agency with neither the motivation nor the capacity to effectively monitor media, and the deepening partisan divides in society. To provide context for this argument, I start by introducing, in brief, Taiwan's contemporary media landscape in historical perspective; then I lay out the thesis and conclude with a delineation and assessment of ongoing intellectual efforts to defend and expand public broadcasting services as one of the possible remedies for overcoming the democratic deficit in Taiwan's media sector.

Taiwan's Media Landscape

Prior to the mid-1990s, mainstream media in Taiwan either fell under the KMT's direct control or had much closer political and ideological affinities with the KMT than with the DPP. Taiwan's media environment was commonly described as "two newspapers, three networks" (*liangbao santai*)—a pithy phrase that highlighted the industry's concentration and centralization before democratization. The "two newspapers," the *China Times* (CT) and the *United Daily News* (UDN), were created by and remained through the Chen era under the ownership of veteran KMT officers and their families.[1] Excluding their subsidiaries,[2] CT and UDN claimed in 1986 to have daily circulations of 1,200,000 and 1,440,000, respectively, among a population of twenty million. Altogether, over 80 percent of advertising expenditures spent in newspapers were concentrated in CT, UDN, and their sister publications, and between 1979 and 1988, the newspapers were politically important enough that their chairmen were recruited as members of the KMT's Central Standing Committee. In addition, the three networks were all set up by the party-state during the martial law era: the Taiwan Television Company (TTV) was established in 1962; the China TV Company (CTV), in 1969; and the Chinese Television System (CTS), in 1971. From their inception as the sole effective national networks, these three media companies enjoyed a monopoly over television advertising expenditures for more than thirty years; only in the late 1990s did satellite channels, coupled with cable systems, emerge to chip away at their economic rents and political sway.

The two-newspaper, three-network system finally broke down for good in 1996—a watershed year for Taiwan's media environment. Taiwan held its first direct presidential election in March of that year, and the first terrestrial television network founded by DPP figures, Formosa TV Company (FTV), was granted a license and went on the air in 1997. The *Liberty Times* (LT) had become a significant player in the newspaper market as well. Founded in 1992 with investment from a prominent Taiwanese banking and land capitalist, the paper was not much different in its first decade from the CT and UDN in lending its support to the KMT: in 1996, it even printed on its front page a banner declaring itself to be "The Best Newspaper as Endorsed by President Lee."[3] However, with a strong Taiwanese identity and as the only major paper carrying a more pro-independence stance, LT's subsequent political color matched its economic interests well, just as UDN and CT found their brand of identity politics to be commercially beneficial. Between 1996 and 2000, rising Taiwanese identity contributed not only to a change of regime but also to an acceleration in the decline of the formerly dominant media companies. As Tables 10.1 and 10.2 show, media power clearly became more fragmented over this period.

Within eight years, LT grew from a small player in the newspaper market (with 5 percent of total circulation) in 1992 to become, in 2000, the biggest (22.3 percent). Its sales declined in the early 2000s due to an overall decline in readership and to competition from the sensationalist *Apple Daily* (AD). (*Apple Daily*'s owner, Jimmy Lai, was known for his regular China-bashing but also opposed Taiwanese independence.) Yet the circulation gap between LT, which was by the Chen era committed to

Table 10.1 Advertising Income, Circulation, and Political Orientation of Taiwan's Major Newspapers, 1992–2011

		"Deep green" Independent Taiwanese state	**"Light blue"** Confederation of two Chinese states	**"Deep blue"** If unified with China, then referendum needed	**Neutral** Consumerism, sensationalism, China-bashing, but against independent Taiwanese state
		Liberty Times	*China Times*	*United Daily*	*Apple Daily*
1992	% of people reading[a]	5.1	21.9	21.8	
	Ad income[b]	0.36	5.70	5.45	
1996	% of people reading	16.1	18.2	17.4	
	Ad income	1.86	6.20	5.65	
2000	% of people reading	22.3	17.2	17.5	
	Ad income	4.20	4.50	4.42	
2002	% of people reading	19.7	14.1	12.7	Launched
	Ad income	4.08	3.89	3.40	in May 2003
2004	% of people reading	17.6	11.3	12.6	11.9
	Ad income	4.10	3.43	2.95	1.80
2007	% of people reading	16.0	8.3	9.8	15.7
	Ad income	3.80	1.70	1.85	3.30
2011	% of people reading	16.4	5.0	6.6	17.3
	Ad income	3.27	1.32[c]	1.45[c]	2.75

Sources: Calculated and compiled from various issues of *Brain* monthly and *Advertising Magazine* published between 1993 and 2008; *Taiwan* (ROC) *Advertising Yearbook 2011–2012*.
Notes: a. Measured by the question, "Did you read this newspaper yesterday?" b. In billion new Taiwan dollars; US$1 is roughly equivalent to NT$30–34. c. Estimate.

Table 10.2 Dwindling TV Advertising Income and More Twenty-Four-Hour News Channels, 1992–2011

	Terrestrial channels					Satellite channels transmitted via cable systems and related methods				
Year	TTV	CTV Blue	CTS	FTV Green	Subtotal[a]	Subtotal[a]	No. of channels	No. of channels with more than NT$1 billion income	No. of twenty-four-hour news channels	
1992	5.1	4.7	4.5	Launched in June 1997	14.3	Not available	6–7	None	None	Hong Kong–based TVBS started its TV talk show in September 1993, modeled upon existing radio call-in shows
1993	5.1	5.0	5.4		15.5		8–9	None	None	TVBS-N (1995),
1996	4.7	4.4	4.6		13.7		NA	1	1	FTV-N, ET-N, USTV-N
1997	4.8	4.7	4.9	0.8	15.1		130+	1	4	(all 1997), Set-N (1998),
2000	3.4	3.9	3.5	2.7	**13.5**	*17.7*	NA	2	8	ET-NS(1999), Eranews (2000),
2002	1.6	2.3	2.0	2.2	**8.1**	*19.7*	130	None	8	CTiNews (2000).
2004	2.2	1.8	1.7	2.1	**7.8**	*18.6*	131	1	8	In early 2002, there were 59 satellite news-gathering
2007	1.2	1.3	1.0	2.0	**5.5**	*17.3*	142	1	8	vehicles, including 22 from terrestrial TV networks, operating in Taiwan, mainly in the Taipei metropolitan area, which has a population of around six million.
2011	1.1	1.5	1.0	1.4	**5.0**	*21.2*	200+	3	8	

Sources: Commonwealth 251 (2002): 110–150; Government Information Office; calculated and compiled from various issues of *Brain* monthly and *Advertising Magazine* published between 1993 and 2008; *Taiwan (ROC) Advertising Yearbook 2011–2012.*

Note: a. In billion new Taiwan dollars; US$1 is roughly equivalent to NT$30–34.

deep green, pro-independence ideals, and the combined circulation of CT and UDN, the two traditional blue newspapers, narrowed further over the years. In 2000, the gap was 12.4 percent in the blue side's favor; in 2007, the figure had decreased to 2.1 percent; and by 2011, the figure was reversed, with the combined readership of CT and UDN sliding to 11.6 percent of the total, while LT held 16.4 percent of the market. (Another 17.3 percent went to AD.) Another factor behind this narrowing gap was probably the intensified and more frequent conflicts between the DPP government and both CT and UDN, to which I shall return later in this chapter.

The television trends are no less striking, as shown in Table 10.2. While terrestrial TV remains the market leader in most Asian and European countries, Taiwan's three legacy networks of the KMT regime relinquished their lead to the cable and satellite channels in only five or six years: in 2000, their combined advertising income (13.5 billion new Taiwan [NT] dollars) was surpassed for the first time, and in 2002, they all reported their first loss as revenue dropped by 40 percent. Another peculiarity of Taiwan's TV ecology is its abundance of news channels broadcasting twenty-four hours a day, with high percentages of live coverage. The first twenty-four-hour news channel appeared in late 1995; by 1997, there were four; and by 2000, eight such channels existed. The proliferation of satellite news vans responding to every breaking event led journalists to lament as early as 1997 that the situation was "super no good" (*chaoji buhao*). The use of such vans did not encourage reflection or even preparation before reporting; they instead focused on speed, and everything, significant or not, became sensationalized in live broadcasts.[4] By 2002, the leading business monthly *Commonwealth* could no longer contain its frustration, running a cover story lampooning Taiwan's media environment. The headline ran "Stupid Media, You Are Ruining This Country," and the reporter asked rhetorically, "Why do we need eight 24 hour news channels for a society with only 23 million people?"[5] The luxury of press freedom was squandered as Taiwan's increasingly fragmented and competitive commercial media were left with meager resources. The tragic result was that the media increasingly failed to carry out its democratic functions and responsibilities. I further elaborate upon this contention later in this chapter. I then suggest that the development and expansion of public service television could help Taiwan strengthen its media environment.

Confronting the Government at Will

Beginning in the early 1970s, those outside the KMT party-state made use of magazines, the cable television system, newspapers, and illegal radio as outlets to voice their discontent. This confrontation was a product of an undemocratic regime, with marginal media being used to fight back against the mainstream, state-controlled press. During the Chen era, by comparison, the superficially similar opposition to the DPP government that came from UDN, CT, and some TV talk show programs could only have occurred in a more democratic society. The two sides of this tug-of-war game were still not equals, but the power difference between them was greatly reduced. Likewise, although the *Liberty Times* carried more sympathetic and supportive coverage of the DPP government, its relationship with the ruling DPP was not the same as the previous patron-client relationship between the KMT and UDN and CT,[6] both of which became relentless critics of the DPP administration after 2000. Just as is frequently observed in some Western democracies,[7] in Taiwan, some of the major media instead "democratically" supported President Chen's government for both ideological and commercial reasons.

Conflicts between the state and the media during the Chen era can be placed into two broad categories: criminal investigations initiated by prosecutors under the Ministry of Justice or the Judicial Yuan and regulatory actions taken by the Executive Yuan. Among the cases of criminal investigations, three stand out as especially important. The first was on October 3, 2000, when the *China Times Evening News* had its editorial office searched; it was then charged with publishing official state secrets. The second was on March 20, 2002, when the full print run of the weekly news magazine *Next* was confiscated on the grounds that it was putting national security in jeopardy.[8] The third case centered on journalistic privilege for confidential sources: in April 2006, a UDN journalist was fined three consecutive times after refusing to disclose the identity of his sources in defiance of a court injunction.[9]

These cases were especially troubling because they involved physical violence, office searches, confiscations, and fines for what was arguably the legitimate practice of journalism. Nevertheless, the reaction to these incidents was relatively mild compared to the regulatory and programming decisions that had a more partisan subtext, and thus fed a self-serving narrative of political persecution among some segments of the media. One prominent instance occurred in 2003 and involved the show of a popular TV commentator, Sisy Chen. Chen had once been a DPP member and had served as the party's director of communications, but she later left the party and was elected as an independent in the 2001 legislative election. By the time she became a legislator, Chen was hosting a daily talk show TV program that was notable for her strident criticism of the DPP and President Chen. It also had an audience rating between 0.5 percent and 1.0 percent, one of the highest among all talk shows. When it was announced on April 7 that Chen's program would be rescheduled in a different time slot, the UDN openly speculated that the move might have been made as the result of pressure from President Chen or his subordinates. Over the next several weeks, the UDN devoted 24,000 square centimeters of column space just to coverage of the Sisy Chen "scandal"—forty times that of the *China Times*, and ten times more than the *Liberty Times*, which itself devoted most of that space to a rebuttal of UDN criticism.

A much more worrisome development during the Chen era was the changes in government public relations efforts, particularly the practice of paying media outlets to place stories favorable to the Chen administration. It had been a long-standing practice for various government branches to purchase media space or time as part of public relations campaigns, but these agencies had typically acted without any central coordination. That changed in 2003, when Arthur Iap, the director of the Government Information Office (GIO), decided to centralize negotiations with media outlets and try to use the government's bargaining power to get a better deal. Iap also borrowed the commercial strategy of paying for product placement: clients would pay media companies to edit their messages into whatever media content was suitable and available—be it daily news, documentary, situation comedy, drama, or entertainment shows. This practice violated not only professional ethnics but also national law: under Taiwan's Broadcasting Act, it was illegal to blur the differences between advertising and nonadvertising content.[10] Yet the GIO, which was also responsible for media regulation, was taking the lead in breaking the law. What is interesting, however, is not just that the government's unethical—and, in the case of broadcasting, illegal—behavior was exposed and criticized, but also the way the Pan-Blue media reported it. Although the UDN and CT editorial pages led the attack against the GIO for its product placement strategy, they did not inform their readers that they had actually received the most money from the government's product placement budget.[11]

Two interpretations of the contradictory behavior of UDN and CT are possible. It may have been the result of a separation between editorial policy and advertising interests. If this was the case, the coexistence of the use of product placement with editorial criticism of the practice is an indicator of this separation. It is more likely, however, that their constant criticism reflected less a watchdog function than their own ideologically driven hypocrisy.

Another example of partisanship clouding the judgment of media outlets occurred in mid-April 2003, when the Chen administration announced an initiative to assess the quality of Taiwan's independent media. The initiative involved two separate research projects. One was an industry survey intended to provide basic statistics about newspapers. The other was an evaluation of press performance as measured against a set of common standards of professionalism. Neither should have been particularly controversial. Media organizations in most democratic countries regularly conduct surveys to gather information on market trends and consumer preferences, and most press organizations have established either an independent ombudsman or a complaints bureau to receive and respond to criticism of reporting. At the time of the initiative, however, Taiwan's media had not adopted such practices, so the GIO was breaking new ground by promoting greater transparency and professionalism of the media as a whole. The controversy arose when the GIO chose the Foundation for the Advancement of Media Excellence (FAME) to conduct the evaluation. Although FAME was officially a nonpartisan, nongovernmental organization, it was widely perceived to be sympathetic to the DPP.

The UDN and CT responded to the announcement with intense, relentlessly hostile coverage of the initiative and of FAME's alleged links to the Chen administration. As Table 10.3 shows, UDN and CT together published twenty-two separate editorial pieces, including ten written by their own journalists or editors. The editorial staffs at both papers apparently viewed this exercise as a trial run for the GIO: if the media did not counterattack quickly and forcefully, the DPP government would soon come up with additional measures to limit editorial freedom. By contrast, the LT again aligned itself with the DPP and lamented the UDN's and CT's "abuse" of press freedom.

Most journalists not employed by one of these three papers, as well as most communications scholars, viewed the response from UDN and

Table 10.3 Segmentation of the News Market by Party Affiliation, 2003

	United Daily News		*China Times*		*Liberty Times*		Total	
	Number of comments[a]	All items (cm^2)[b]	Number of comments	All items (cm^2)	Number of comments	All items (cm^2)	Number of comments	All items (cm^2)
Sisy Chen	1	23,800	0	500	0	1,900	1	26,200
Product placement	5	5,200	1	3,500	0	100	6	8,800
Media assessment	8	12,000	14	12,600	1	5,700	23	30,300

Source: Author's calculations.

Notes: a. Up to seven days after the event was first reported, including bylined or anonymous editorials but excluding pure news and letters to the editor. b. Up to seven days after the event was reported, all news and comments.

CT as wildly inappropriate. Several wrote critical commentaries that appeared in *Media Watch,* a bimonthly periodical that had been published by the Association of Taiwan Journalists since 1997.[12] These critics noted that, even if FAME concluded in its report that the UDN and CT fell short of some standard of professionalism, the GIO had no tools to compel the two papers to change their practices: the only law providing for meaningful regulation of the press, the Publication Act, had been abolished in 1999 and had not been replaced. Nor was it likely that FAME's assessment would attract much attention from readers: certainly neither UDN nor CT would bother to publish the results, and even if LT carried a report, the two papers' target audience would be likely to discount it due to LT's reputation for "greenness," if they even saw it at all. In sum, it is hard to see how either the industry survey or the media assessment could have been part of a state conspiracy to subvert press freedom.

The fears expressed by UDN's and CT's editorial writers of a "chilling effect" on the press were, to be blunt, illogical, not well-reasoned, and without evidence. Their disproportionately strident reaction to the initiative was probably motivated by a combination of partisan and market considerations: the market for news in Taiwan during this era of intense competition became increasingly segmented, with newspapers forced to appeal to and reinforce the political beliefs of their core readership. This pressure created a dynamic in which editors were constantly manufacturing political controversies to maintain readership—all in the name of "democracy" and the public's "right to know." Nevertheless, the attacks from UDN and CT had the practical effect of forcing the GIO to end financial support for FAME's media quality initiative.[13]

In July 2005, another political thunderbolt hit the media when the GIO followed the recommendation of the Satellite Television Review Commission and refused to renew broadcast licenses for seven of the sixty-nine satellite TV channels. These channels either had too high a proportion of sexual content in their programming or did not meet their broadcast obligations as stipulated in their contracts with the GIO. This was the first time that any satellite channel had been forced to discontinue operations because of a government decision rather than market pressures, and a heated debate ensued in both the press and academia. This time opinions were more balanced between concerns about media freedom and the appropriate regulatory power of the state, though GIO was generally faulted for its failure to inform the industry of the impending action earlier.[14]

As if this were a cloud presaging a storm, three months later, the new GIO director, Pasuya Yao, announced an investigation into the ownership structure of TVBS to determine if it had any Chinese shareholders.

Because it invoked the politically explosive "China factor," the investigation ignited a much bigger controversy: TVBS was widely perceived to be blue-leaning, and its *2100 All People Talk* program had been the most popular political talk show on television since its inception ten years earlier.[15] LT, UDN, and CT all covered the controversy in predictably partisan ways, each catering to the dominant political views among its readership. But more dramatically, on November 2, 2005, the UDN ran a lengthy editorial that was striking for its endorsement of active resistance against state attempts to regulate the media. This astonishing text is a good illustration of the kind of emotional appeals and bombastic language that characterized the partisan green-blue divide during the Chen era and is therefore worth quoting at some length:

> The GIO has dispatched a special envoy to TVBS, . . . demanding that it disclose its "capital structure." . . . In response, that energetic and popular supporter of TVBS, the People's First Party, has announced that if the government revokes the license, it will lead millions of people to take to the streets. . . . We believe this should be the last resort. . . . If [TVBS's] license is revoked, then to save "press freedom from being ridden over roughshod," we should opt to "lend more loyal support to press freedom." . . . Every media organization should participate using its institutional name, and each media worker using his own name; all teachers and students of communication disciplines, and all those readers willing to support press freedom . . . should either participate through practical action or spiritual support in this peaceful but firm "campaign to save press freedom." . . . Step One, find an alternative outlet so that if TVBS is forced to close, the "2100 All People Talk" can remain on air. . . . Step Two, . . . this "talk" can be held in an open public space such as Ketagalan Boulevard [in front of the Presidential Hall], and transmitted live. . . . This will create the impression that this is a "free media campaign." . . . If the DPP still either bans or tramples [the talk show], then street demonstrations cannot be avoided. However, even if we take this issue to the street, . . . we media people and the audience must take the lead, and political parties should be excluded. . . . Press freedom is a paramount constitutional value, and if the GIO revokes TVBS's license, we media people and the audience are in fact privileged to take a stand in support of the constitution. Will this occasion present itself? Let's borrow from an answer to [GIO director] Pasuya Yao: "Don't talk nonsense, it's showdown time!"[16]

Such provocative rhetoric is no less stunning than the war of words between media tycoons Ted Turner and Rupert Murdoch, in which Turner called Murdoch "crazy and dangerous" and was called a "son of a bitch" in return.[17]

The UDN and other like-minded media outlets may have been sincere in their belief that press freedom was retreating or under severe and constant threat during the Chen era. But this same media landscape looked very different from the perspective of the established democracies, where press-monitoring organizations held much more positive views of trends in press freedom in Taiwan. For instance, according to the Paris-based Reporters Without Borders, among the 200 or so countries surveyed, Taiwan's press freedom ranking registered steady improvement during the Chen years: from 61st place in 2003 and 2004, it increased to 60 in 2005, 51 in 2006, 43 in 2007, and 32 in 2008. Freedom House, based in New York, recorded a similar trend: from 2004 to 2009, Taiwan ranked 49, 44, 35, 33, and 32, respectively, and for the last three of those years, Taiwan's press freedom was ranked the best in Asia.[18] Another testament to Taiwan's liberal media environment during this period was its underground radio scene, which had flourished since the 1990s. In 1997, the government set up a special police task force to monitor and confiscate these "free radio" facilities, but it had limited success in stopping illegal radio broadcasts throughout the Chen era.[19] In 2006, for instance, the National Communications Commission (NCC) reported 110 seizures of illegal radio broadcasting equipment, and 116 in 2007, but another 100 or more continued to broadcast at least occasionally.[20] Illegal radio stations were only reduced substantially beginning in 2009, after Ma Ying-jeou assumed the presidency and the KMT regained control of the central government.

In a surprising turn, in 2009, the Ma administration itself ended up in an unexpected confrontation with the Pan-Blue *China Times,* suggesting that the conflict between media outlets and the government was not just a matter of partisan politics. Less than six months into Ma's first term, the family running CT and its subsidiary outlets sold their media businesses to Tsai Eng-meng, the chairman of Want Want China and one of the wealthiest men in Taiwan. Want Want Group was a food manufacturer that employed more than 50,000 people and earned 90 percent of its revenue in mainland China. Tsai's obvious economic interests in China raised suspicions that the *China Times* would take a more decidedly pro-Beijing slant in its news coverage; Tsai did little to dispel these worries, at one point remarking in an interview with the *Washington Post* that he "can't wait for Taiwan's unification with China."[21]

Despite the Ma administration's focus on improving cross-Strait relations and its China-friendly rhetoric, Tsai quickly ran into trouble with the NCC. Because the CT group had control over five different TV channels accounting for 10 percent of the total market, in addition to two newspapers and several magazines, NCC approval was required for the transfer of ownership to take place. Although the commission approved the sale, it also attached a number of stringent requirements that Tsai had to meet. In June 2009, he responded by running a half-page ad on the cover of the CT, criticizing the decision and displaying "wanted" head shots of three NCC commissioners. Tsai argued that the conditions placed on the sale were illegal and threatened "dangerous consequences" for the commissioners if the decision was not revoked.

In the end, the NCC did alter its decision to permit Tsai's full ownership of the CT group, but it continued to foil his plans for further expansion of his media empire. In July 2012, the NCC approved Tsai's purchase of fully one-third of Taiwan's cable system, but only on the condition that he divest his news channels. Tsai refused, and the sale was blocked. Four months later, other news outlets revealed that Tsai was part of a group attempting to take control of *Apple Daily,* despite his initial public denials.[22] The news that the island's most popular independent daily newspaper, formerly a fierce critic of Beijing, might fall under Tsai's sway led to a popular outcry, and many students, academics, and journalists joined a campaign against the sale.[23] Partly as a response to this campaign, the NCC drafted a comprehensive law regulating media mergers in February 2013; if passed, it would have prevented Tsai's purchase of *Apple Daily.* In response, Tsai had CT run a conspicuous article on March 27, 2013, titled "The Ma Administration Is Violating Due Process; We Refuse to Endure Another Humiliation." Tsai continued his public criticism of the NCC; on June 20, for instance, the CT ran a front-page advertisement accusing the NCC of unfairly discriminating against the Want Want China Times Group. But in the end, Tsai never managed to win approval for the takeover of *Apple Daily,* and it has remained independent throughout the Ma era.

Media Freedom with Dwindling Resources

If press freedom in Taiwan under DPP rule increased, then what sort of freedom was it? Since 1994, Freedom House has deployed three indicators to capture different aspects of press freedom. In addition to the legal and political aspects, there is also a less-recognized economic element necessary to make effective use of press freedom. As *The Economist* explains, "In many countries, the chief barrier to free expression is no longer censorship. It is cash. Good journalism costs money, so poor countries, especially if they are small, struggle to produce it."[24] The emphasis of Freedom House and *The Economist* on the relationship among censorship, economic resources, and press freedom is significant, and it points to a major problem area in Taiwan's media environment. Press freedom without the corresponding resources to finance high-quality media operations will not produce the media environment that a mature democracy should aspire to. High-quality public television in Taiwan could go a long way toward improving this environment.

Although Taiwan has a sizable population and a relatively high gross domestic product per capita, its media remain resource poor in comparison to other countries at a similar level of development. In particular, resources to support good journalism have historically been undersupplied, as Tables 10.1 and 10.2 show. Before the mid-1990s, the mainstream media—in particular, the "two newspaper, three station" operations—were highly profitable, and yet this profitability was mainly the result of rents paid by the KMT government to ensure the political loyalty of those media outlets. Media profits during this period were channeled not into producing high-quality (and expensive) journalism but instead toward preventing dissident voices from being heard.

By the time Chen Shui-bian won the presidential election in 2000, Taiwan's media market had already become extremely competitive, which eventually led to hundreds of layoffs at the old mainstream media companies and a decline in the overall quality of reporting. For instance, from 2005 to 2006, the CT and UDN groups each closed a subsidiary.[25] In late 2008, the CT group itself announced that it would sell all its assets, and it was reported that the remaining two big dailies, LT and AD, were losing money and planning to cut their labor force further.[26] The television sector did not fare any better. As Table 10.2 shows, the four big terrestrial channels together accounted for less than 25 percent of market share in 2007, and 19 percent in 2011, and they had not turned a profit since at least 2002. In contrast, in Hong Kong, TVB alone held 80 percent of the television market, while South Korea's four television companies together grabbed a similar share of their market.

In an ironic twist, during the Chen era, Taiwan's private media enjoyed more freedom to report than ever before but fewer resources to make use of it; as a result, they failed to fill their democratic role in many ways. The media in Taiwan did not provide an adequate check on power or produce informative, reliable news coverage, and the cutthroat competition for viewers made people working in the industry slaves to ratings. One of the most devastating criticisms of the changes in this system came from within. A few months before the DPP won the presidential election, on December 1, 1999, Cheng Shumin, the chief executive officer of the KMT's media conglomerate China Television Company, bought a half-page advertisement in many daily newspapers to vent her anger at what Taiwan's media had become. She attacked the narrow-minded focus on commercial ratings, asserting that the accumulated effect of a focus on profits over anything else had, over the years, created an industry whose workers were "foolish, idiotic, and hysterical."

The private sector should not bear all the blame for the decline in Taiwan's media environment, however; by its absence, the state also contributed to the poor quality of reporting and lack of service to the public interest. Among high- and middle-income countries, Taiwan's support for public broadcasting is at the bottom of the list. As Table 10.4 shows, in 2006, government support for broadcasting ranged from NT$3,925 per person per year in Norway to NT$39 in Taiwan. By contrast, the United States, which is an outlier among the developed democracies, spent NT$269 per person, and even the supposedly libertarian territory of Hong Kong spent NT$70, almost twice the figure for Taiwan. It is probably not a coincidence that both the United States and Hong Kong had created public broadcasting services by 1968, whereas Taiwan's equivalent was launched only in 1998.

As a publicly owned entity, public television ideally can and should supply a space where direct state control and profit considerations are reduced to a minimum—or at least to an acceptable level. Western European countries, which pioneered the use of public television, have been its historical champions and still promote the concept worldwide. Since a more neoliberal ethos took hold in the 1980s, most formerly nationalized industries in Europe were privatized, but public broadcasting has been a key exception. To date, only one major public network, TF1 in France, has been taken out of the public sector and placed in private hands, while many more new public broadcasting channels have been launched over the past twenty years. By comparison, Taiwan is a latecomer to public broadcasting. The KMT government proposed a public TV station in the early 1980s but did not begin preparations for a full channel until 1991; it took another seven years before public TV service was up and running. By this time, as the power structure of Taiwan's society had grown increasingly diversified, the KMT was more reluctant to construct a network that was large enough to act as an effective counterbalance to commercial broadcasting forces. The annual budget allocated to public TV was reduced by more than half. A new political coalition was clearly

Table 10.4 Per Capita State Spending on Public Service Television by Country (in new Taiwan dollars), 2006

	Norway	Denmark	UK	Japan	S. Korea	Hong Kong	Poland	Turkey	S. Africa	USA	Taiwan
NT$	3,925	3,487	3,376	1,417	389	269	154	78	73	70	39

Source: Compiled from Fei-fei Wang et al., *For Our Common Good: Public Service Broadcasting in the 21st Century* (Taipei: Public Television Foundation, 2007).

Note: Figures for Norway, Denmark, Poland, Turkey, and the United States are for 2004 or 2005.

needed to give public broadcasting a chance to expand its role. However, after the change in government came, the promise of a greater role for public broadcasting was only partially fulfilled.

Expanding Public Service Television as a Remedy?

In a number of countries in recent years, academics and intellectuals have called for various media reforms, including an extended emphasis on defending and expanding public broadcasting. These campaigns have been waged through canvassing or lobbying politicians or via "preaching" in their classrooms and the media.[27] In Taiwan, the media reform movement, in a broad sense, can be traced back to the late 1950s. The most fearless challengers were dissident media outlets, which gathered considerable attention and momentum in the 1980s but gradually died out toward the end of the 1990s. It was only during the Chen Shui-bian era that the movement coalesced into a more organized campaign with a lasting impact on media reform centered upon public television.

The campaign by academics did not create but rather took advantage of opportunities opened up by the 2000 presidential election. Among the five candidates, Chen Shui-bian was the only one to prepare a set of fifteen public policies before the election, including "A Blueprint for a Citizens' Media Policy."[28] With the benefit of hindsight, this blueprint was significant for two reasons. It may have been the first comprehensive proposal for reforming Taiwan's media structure put forward by any politician. In the mid-1990s, the DPP occasionally put forward progressive ideas about how the media needed to be reformed, and key people in the party, such as Chen and Frank Hsieh, gave nominal or substantial support to them. More important, though, Chen won the election. Without his victory, the DPP's media blueprint would have been, at best, a historical document. Together with students and journalists, academics seized this unexpected opportunity to advocate for expansion of the public role in the media industry. In its far-reaching analysis of media policy, the policy document contended,

> One arresting feature of Taiwan's terrestrial and cable broadcasting is their exclusive reliance upon advertising for their finance. . . . These channels exist in an intensively competitive market and perform poorly. . . . An appropriate policy for Taiwan Television Company (TTV) and Chinese Television Service (CTS), two major players in the TV market and partly owned by the state, is for them to enter into voluntary cooperation and arrange different program genres in the same time slots, so that they can jointly provide audiences with better service. For such an ideal

to be realized, a good policy should therefore, contrary to what has been commonly advocated, increase, not reduce the government's shares in TTV and CTS.[29]

Beginning in 1995, a movement calling itself the Oust the Party-Government-Military Campaign had sought to privatize all three terrestrial television networks. However, within this campaign, there was, from the very beginning, a dissenting argument that the more democracy-enhancing strategy would be to take at least two of these three channels into full public ownership, rather than to privatize them completely. With Chen's victory, this marginal view suddenly became mainstream. The team writing the blueprint was aware that rallying support for public broadcasting would not be an easy task. Among the fifteen groups that wrote Chen's preelection policy documents, the only group that reconvened and consolidated immediately after the election was the one responsible for the media manifesto. In a short period, they launched the Campaign for Citizens' Television (CCTV) and won the endorsement of more than a hundred scholars in the field of communications, as well as that of students and journalists. CCTV opted for a strategy of appealing to professional reason, rather than popular appeal, and the most conspicuous and ambitious of the blueprint's recommendations was to make TTV and CTS public assets. Before they dissolved themselves two and a half years later, CCTV tried every possible means to take advantage of the historic moment to get their message across, publishing more than a hundred newspaper or magazine articles and circulating several pamphlets and reports with official proposed budgets for the new service. Altogether, the movement lobbied over thirty legislators and other high-raking officials across party lines and delivered dozens of public speeches in support of the proposal.[30]

The response from the Chen administration and the legislature, however, was muted; government officials paid only lip service to the demands, and no reforms were in the works. Thus, CCTV decided that more assertive action needed to be taken. On October 10, 2002—the National Day of the Republic of China—the campaign took out a half-page advertisement in the *China Times,* paid for with NT$150,000 in member donations. The text declared, "We Have No More Patience! CCTV Condemns President Chen and the Executive Yuan for Their Slow Progress in Carrying Out Media Reforms!" The rest of the advertisement documented what CCTV had completed over the previous two years and frankly admitted that the movement had limited capacity to achieve meaningful reform on its own. In the end, CCTV committed itself to coming back and waging another campaign for media reform in due course.

On May 4, 2003, the original founders of CCTV set up the Campaign for Media Reform (CMR), with more communications scholars, students, journalists, and intellectuals from other disciplines joining the ranks. In addition to the original objective of expanding public service television, CMR broadened its activities to include hosting a weekly program on a national radio network, setting up its own website,[31] and actively monitoring and commenting on media practices and policies. After years of effort, CCTV, CMR, and Media Watch Taiwan had successfully managed to provide a different rhetorical framework for discussing television reform.

One conspicuous achievement of this movement was that the appeal to privatize government-held media companies became much less prominent. In the 1990s, privatization of all terrestrial television networks was the only legitimate objective of reforms, but as a result of the CCTV campaign, taking either TTV or CTS into public ownership became a serious policy option on the table in the Chen administration, and discussion of expanding the scale of public service television began to appear more frequently in newspaper forums. The first news to reflect this change came in October 2001, when the GIO confirmed that both TTV and CTS would not be privatized; instead, the government would buy back private shares. In June 2004, using language similar to that of the CMR, GIO officially started to promote the idea of "energetic and efficient public service television." One year later, in August 2005, the Executive Yuan swiftly and unexpectedly proclaimed that it would provide an extra NT$9.2 billion for public television in 2007 and 2008, subject to approval by the Legislative Yuan. This proposal turned out to be too good to be true; the abrupt announcement of a major policy change had not been preceded by discussions with legislators, and the funding increase never won approval in the Legislative Yuan. Even the CMR opposed it in principle.[32]

Nevertheless, in January 2006, a new media act came into effect that created a new Taiwan Broadcasting System (TBS), the first public service television corporation. All government shares of CTS were transferred to TBS, and the station officially started operations in July 2006. By January 2007, TBS had taken over management of several other government-sponsored channels, including Hakka TV, Indigenous TV, and Macro-TV for Overseas Chinese. By 2012, when it switched to digital transmission, TBS had ten channels under its management. With a combined annual revenue of approximately NT$4 billion—half from advertising or private donations and another half from the state budget—TBS has, since the end of the Chen era, become one of the biggest television corporations in Taiwan. Compared to the other established public television companies listed in Table 10.4, though, TBS is still tiny.

During the presidency of Ma Ying-jeou, TBS suffered for at least three years from internal conflicts over its management, before its board of governors finally elected a new chairperson in July 2013.[33] As Taiwan nears the end of the Ma era, it remains to be seen whether TBS will ultimately develop into a positive force for improvement in Taiwan's television environment. At the least, grassroots support for a strong, robust TBS has grown substantially since the Chen Shui-bian years.[34]

Conclusion

Press freedom does not come free; it does not exist in a vacuum. An independent press requires corresponding resources and necessarily rests on a material base. Public broadcasting is an institutional arrangement that at once promotes freedom and provides resources. Although it is not the only way to reinforce press freedom, without state support for public broadcasting, it is difficult to see many other promising options for improving Taiwan's media environment and strengthening its democracy.

The KMT state began preparations for a public television service in 1991 and launched the so-called "small but beautiful" Public Television Service in 1998. Acting at least partly out of political expedience, the DPP proposed before the 2000 election that this service be greatly expanded. Subsequent developments moved quite beyond the Chen administration's control and expectations, and politicians in both major camps gradually lost interest in realizing this original plan in full. At this juncture, a collection of academics, students, and journalists banded together to wage a campaign in support of public broadcasting. The result was the birth of the Taiwan Broadcasting Service in 2006.

The TBS is still in its infancy, and there is no guarantee that it will grow up tall and strong. Absent robust social democratic traditions and faced with fierce divides over national identity and partisan politics, neither the KMT nor the DPP have been especially enthusiastic about lending support to an expanded TBS. The Taiwanese state itself deserves much of the blame for the underdeveloped state of public broadcasting and the lowest-common-denominator quality of most broadcast media today. For a long time after the KMT withdrew to Taiwan, the state failed to develop a thoughtful media policy: it had no laws to regulate the TV and film industry until the Broadcasting Act was enacted in 1975 and the Film Act, in 1983. By comparison, in South Korea, the corresponding laws and regulations were introduced in the 1950s and 1960s. Without the meaningful deliberation and debate to accompany the formulation of laws and policies that only a professional, independent press can provide, short-term political calculations tend to take priority over long-term strategic plans, and the capacity of bureaucrats to develop and implement consistent, welfare-enhancing regulations is weakened. What is worse, in the 1990s, when technological advancements demanded wiser and more effective responses, there was frequent turnover of GIO directors: Taiwan had six between 1990 and 2000; and the DPP government had eight directors in eight years.

It is an open question whether TBS will finally emerge as a full-blown media institution enjoying economies of scale, a professional staff, and political independence. In addition to its potential impact on state planning and its capacity to implement sensible communication policy, the continued development of public broadcasting presents a significant opportunity to aid the consolidation of Taiwan's democracy.[35] Given the stakes, more popular and intellectual participation in this process will be indispensable.

Notes

1. The CT and its subsidiary were sold to the Want Want Group in May 2009.

2. CT also runs the *Commercial Times,* while UDN operates the *Economic Daily.* In 1988, both papers launched evening counterparts, though CT's was closed in October 2005. UDN's *Livelihood Daily,* which began publishing in 1978 and focused on coverage of sports, medicine, and leisure activities with a peak circulation of 500,000 copies a day, stopped operations in November 2006.

3. *Liberty Times,* August 7, 1996.

4. See the special September 1997 issue of the bimonthly *Media Watch,* edited and published by the Association of Taiwan Journalists.

5. *Tianxia Zazhi [Commonwealth],* April 2002.

6. Chin-Chuan Lee, "Sparking a Fire: The Press and the Ferment of Democratic Change in Taiwan," *Journalism Monographs* 138 (April 1993); Chin-Chuan Lee, "Weiquan zhuyi guojia yu dianshi: Taiwan yu Nanhan zhi bijiao" [Authoritarian states and television: A comparative study between Taiwan and South Korea], *Mass Communication Research* 85 (October 2010): 1–30.

7. Of course Silvio Berlusconi, newly elected for the third time as Italian prime minister in April 2008, and Rupert Murdoch, the chairperson of News UK, are notorious for their "wise" cooperation with the (incoming) government in exchange for business interests, and the French system is full of stories of close cooperation between media and state interests. See *The Economist,* April 3, 2004.

8. The second conflict, in particular, generated widespread criticism from society. See "Xinwen ziyou yu guojia anquan" [Press freedom and national security], *Taiwan: A Radical Quarterly in Social Studies* 46 (June 2002): 251–272

9. See *UDN,* April 25, 2006. The *Taiwan Law Journal* 63 (November 2006) published a special issue on the case; for a more recent case, see *China Times,* April 23, 2008.

10. In the United States, the private sector can legally purchase product placement in media outlets, but the practice is forbidden in the public sector. It should also

be noted that the US government has been guilty of at least occasional violations of this rule. See *The Economist,* February 5, 2005.

11. *Cai Xun [Wealth Magazine]*, April 2003.

12. *Media Watch,* May 2003.

13. FAME eventually found other private resources to continue the evaluations; between June 2005 and March 2008, it published twenty-nine reports on media matters on its website, and between 2009 and 2013, it made available more than forty more. Relevant information was initially available at http://www.bdf.org.tw/fame /epaper.php and after 2009 at http://www.feja.org.tw/modules/news007/index.php? storytopic=52&start=0, accessed October 2013.

14. *Taiwan Law Journal* published five articles in September 2005 on this issue. One year earlier, CHOI-FM radio in Canada had its license revoked, and its listeners took their objections to the street, demanding a proper legal appeal. See *The Economist,* August 7, 2004. Some of the Taiwanese satellite companies did get the GIO's licensing decision overturned on appeal.

15. Di Wei, "Xin zheng-mei guanxi pipan: cong TVBS shijian tanqi" [New media politics: A comment on the TVBS episode], *Taiwan: A Radical Quarterly in Social Studies* 60 (December 2005): iii–viii.

16. *United Daily News,* November 2, 2005, A2.

17. *The Guardian,* October 10, 1996, 20, and October 14, 1996, 14; *Independent on Sunday,* November 24, 1996, 15.

18 The ratings are available at http://www.rsf.org and http://freedomhouse.org.

19. For a report, see http://www.legco.gov.hk/yr05-06/chinese/panels/itb/papers /itb0311cb1-1035-3c.pdf; *Apple Daily (HK),* January 22, 2008.

20. Annual report submitted by the National Communications Council to the Executive Yuan. The contrast with the so-called laissez-faire environment of Hong Kong is instructive: the first illegal radio station there went on the air only in 2007 and operated only sporadically thereafter.

21. Andrew Higgins, "Tycoon Prods Taiwan Closer to China," *Washington Post,* January 20, 2012, at http://www.washingtonpost.com/world/tycoon-prods-taiwan -closer-to-china/2012/01/20/gIQAhswmFQ_story.html.

22. "Newspapers in Taiwan: Lai Takes His Leave," *The Economist,* December 1, 2012.

23. Ming-Yeh Tsai Rawnsley, "Anti-Media Monopoly Explained," *Taipei Times,* February 4, 2013, 8; "Press Freedom in Taiwan: Keeping the Doctor Away," *The Economist,* April 6, 2013.

24. *The Economist,* December 12, 2004; for an excellent discussion on the relationship among media, markets, democracy, and liberal ideas, see Owen Fiss, *Liberalism Divided: Freedom of Speech and the Many Uses of State Power* (Boulder, CO: Westview Press, 1996), and Edwin Baker, *Media Markets and Democracy* (New York: Cambridge University Press, 2002).

25. See note 2.

26. *Win Weekly,* December 12, 2008.

27. For American experiences, see Robert McChesney, *The Problem of Media: Communication Politics of 21st Century America* (New York: Monthly Review, 2002); for other English-speaking countries, see Robert A. Hackett, *Remaking Media: The Struggle to Democratize Public Communication* (London: Routledge, 2006), and Robert A. Hackett and William K. Carroll, "Critical Social Movements and Media Reform," *Media Development* 51, no. 1 (2004): 14–19; for Thailand, see Ubonrat Siriyuvasak, "Regulation, Reform, and the Question of Democratising the Broadcast Media in Thailand," *Javonst/Public* 8, no. 2 (2001): 89–108, and Ubonrat Siriyu-vasak, "Thailand's Media: Politics and Money Versus Media," in *Asia Media Report:*

A Crisis Within (a report on media trends in Asia, produced and coordinated by Inter Press Service Asia-Pacific), 166–185; for South Korea, see Dong-sub Han, "The Middle Classes, Ideological Intention, and Resurrection of a Progressive Newspaper," *International Communication Gazette* 62, no. 1 (2000): 61–74; Yung-Ho Im, "The Media, Civil Society, and New Social Movements in Korea, 1985–89," in *Asian Cultural Studies,* ed. Kuan-hsin Chen (London: Routledge, 1998), 330–351, and Lih-yun Lin, "Weiquanzhuyi guojia yu dianshi: Taiwan yu Nanhan zhi bijiao" [Authoritarian states and television: A comparative study between Taiwan and South Korea], *Mass Communication Research* 85 (Fall 2005): 1–30.

28. This author organized a team to prepare this blueprint.

29. *Chen Shui-bian's Media Policy Blueprint for a Civil Society,* 2000, election booklet.

30. Lih-yun Lin, "Zuo er yan, qi er xing: 'wumeng' de shijian" [The translation of knowledge into action: Campaign for citizens' TV], *Taiwan: A Radical Quarterly in Social Studies* 50 (June 2003): 145–170.

31. The website is available at http://twmedia.org.

32. My analysis can be accessed at http://www3.nccu.edu.tw/~jsfeng/ptv2006a.doc.

33. "Taiwan Politics: Ma the Bumbler, a Former Heart-Throb Loses His Shine," *The Economist,* November 17, 2012.

34. On January 1 and 3, 2009, two demonstrations with more than 3,000 participants defending and demanding an expansion of TBS were held in Taiwan's two biggest cities, Taipei and Kaohsiung; the main organizers included Media Watch Taiwan and CMR. See full-page coverage in the *Liberty Times* the following day.

35. In 2006, Taiwan's National Communications Commission was created. Unlike the GIO director, its commissioners' tenure, independence, and professional capacity were protected and guaranteed by law. The Department of Cultural Affairs was created in May 2012 when Ma started his second term, and it assumed the GIO's remaining responsibilities. The GIO was abolished at the same time.

11

Restructuring
State-Business Relations

*James W. Y. Wang, Shang-mao Chen,
and Cheng-tian Kuo*

Since the government lifted martial law in 1987, the Taiwanese "democratic miracle" has been both enchanting and embarrassing to liberal democrats. It has been enchanting because the Taiwanese have weathered the end of one-party rule and two transfers of power without as much violence and chaos as occurred in most other transitional democracies. It has been embarrassing, however, because Taiwan's per capita gross national product (GNP) growth rates started falling steadily over this period, from 10.97 percent in 1987 to 5.38 percent in 2000, with an average annual rate of 5.65 percent. Even worse, the first transfer of power produced the first negative growth rate in Taiwan's post–World War II history: the economy shrank by –2.3 percent in 2001. From 2002 to 2007, Taiwan's economic growth rates hovered between 3.67 and 6.19 percent, with an average of 5.20 percent.[1] Gone were the double-digit growth rates of the predemocratization years. The signing of the Economic Cooperation Framework Agreement (ECFA) with the People's Republic of China (PRC) in 2010 coincided with a temporary jump in Taiwan's economic growth rate from –1.81 to 10.76 percent. Yet, in 2012, the growth rate fell to 1.32 percent, with an average of only 4.00 percent growth over President Ma Ying-jeou's first term.

The Taiwanese case thus seems to lend support to the "no easy choice" thesis that there is a necessary trade-off between democratization and economic growth.[2] Some proponents of the developmental-state model of economic growth and of "Asian values" have argued that democratization will deprive Asia's autonomous-authoritarian developmental states of their capacity to sustain economic development; they point to Taiwan's performance during its transition to democracy as an example.[3]

However, the claim that there is a necessary trade-off between democracy and development stands in contrast to modernization theory and contradicts other recent empirical findings. Modernization theory's "compatibility thesis" argues that democracy may promote economic development over the long term, because democracy (1) increases the supply of social welfare (education, health, nutrition, and so on), which contributes to the rise of productivity; (2) promotes more efficient resource allocation by restricting monopolies and oligopolies; (3) protects property rights; and (4) enhances the quality of public policies by promoting transparency and accountability.[4] The experiences of Western democracies and statistical findings by (neo-)modernization theorists appear to support this argument.[5]

Recent work on democratic governance offers an answer to the seeming inconsistency between the trade-off and compatibility theses.[6] The literature on democratic governance suggests that economic growth in new democracies is contingent upon the strengthening of the capacity and political autonomy of democracy-augmenting institutions, such as the judiciary, election commissions, anticorruption agencies, human rights commissions, ombudsman systems, accounting offices, central banks, and security exchange commissions. Although not included in the common definition of *democracy,* each of these institutions can have a significant impact on political and economic performance.

This chapter builds on these theories of democratic governance but also incorporates the strategic-choice theory of democratization.[7] During democratization, political elites interact with one another and choose different constitutional, legal, and political strategies to maximize their short-term or long-term interests. In this chapter we argue that constitutional ambiguity, a strong but unaccountable state, and strategic choices of political leaders explain both the transformation of institutional relations between the state and business since 1987 in Taiwan and the poor economic performance of more recent years. After seven constitutional revisions from 1990 to 2004, the Taiwanese constitutional system provided for an exceptionally powerful presidential office, without equivalent political accountability, and a weak Executive Yuan, which nonetheless had to shoulder major political responsibilities. From 1990 to 2008, this constitutional ambiguity created a large space for corruption and diverted the attention of top public officials from economic development to maximizing their short-term personal interests. The inheritance of a strong state from the preceding authoritarian regime, along with expanded political control by the presidential office over state-controlled banks and enterprises, contributed to the rise of party-state capitalism under the Kuomintang (KMT) and clientelistic capitalism under the Democratic Progressive Party (DPP).

Under pressure from the changes wrought by democratization and economic liberalization, Taiwanese political elites chose different constitutional, legal, and political strategies to maximize their own interests at the expense of Taiwan's economic development. When President Ma Yingjeou won the election in 2008, he took advantage of this constitutional ambiguity, the strong state, and a large single-party majority to try to reinvigorate a rationalist bureaucracy, create a more predictable economic environment for business, and reduce state intervention in the economy. However, it is debatable whether free markets alone are the best way to encourage economic development during global economic recessions, such as the one that hit shortly after President Ma took office. As a consequence of his strategy, Taiwan's economy probably underperformed in relation to other Organisation for Economic Co-operation and Development (OECD) countries, such as the United States, Japan, and South Korea, which boosted their economies with expansionary fiscal and financial policies.

The following sections of this chapter trace the transformation of state-business relations from 1949 to the present: the state corporatism of 1949–1987, the party-state capitalism of 1987–2000, the realignment of state-business relations of 2000–2004, the clientelist capitalism of 2004–2008, and the free market capitalism of 2008–2012. The relative emphasis of this chapter is on developments after 2000. The chapter concludes with a proposition for corresponding institutional reforms.

The Transformation of State-Business Relations During Taiwan's Transition to Democracy

The existence of a "developmental state" has been vital to the "economic miracles" of East Asian countries such as Japan, South Korea, Taiwan, Hong Kong, Singapore, and China.[8] As big institutions in economic development, the Asian states moved from an initially passive role of interest aggregation and policy implementation to a pivotal role of promoting national competitiveness.[9] These developmental states were characterized by an enlightened political leadership that was committed to economic development and a strong economic bureaucracy staffed by competent technocrats and politically insulated from protectionist business groups. Under the governed interdependence of the developmental state, businesses had no choice but to follow the state's developmental strategies to increase their global competitiveness.[10]

But what happened to these developmental states after they underwent democratization and subsequent leadership changes? How did businesses react to the "new game in town"—democracy? And what was the impact of this new state-business relationship on economic development? We argue that constitutional reform, bureaucratic accountability, and the strategic choices of political leaders are the keys to answering these questions. Democratic constitutional reforms diffused the political power of the developmental state and complicated coordination between different branches of government and between the state and business. But constitutional reforms also enhanced the political power of the head of state due to his newly found democratic legitimacy.[11]

Under these circumstances, the accountability and efficiency of the rational bureaucracy established by the developmental state leadership can decline if the new democratic leader fails to shield it from clientelistic business influence. The "democratization of corruption" is a common phenomenon among new democracies: the legal and political uncertainty associated with democratic reforms often enhances the political influence of bureaucrats due to their civil service expertise and longevity.[12] Without corresponding institutional reforms to increase bureaucratic accountability and transparency, their increased political power can lead to increased corruption. Leaders also react in different ways to similar challenges: the idiosyncratic personalities and capacities of political leaders may lead them to adopt divergent strategies.

Political leaders with strong support from political parties and from the majority of the electorate are better positioned to initiate major economic reforms, while those without strong, stable political constituencies might instead choose to maximize their short-term political interests at the expense of long-term economic development. Proliberalization political coalitions are likely to be associated with the former, while protectionist clientelist relations are more commonly associated with the latter. These strategic choices are made more complicated when the idiosyncratic personalities and capacities of political leaders are taken into consideration.[13] Aggressive political leaders can overextend their structural power and stumble into political and economic crises, while conservative political leaders might underuse their structural power and miss opportunities for political and economic reforms.

How did businesses respond to democratization in the Asian developmental states? These states had either transformed a segment of the traditional landed class into export-oriented business sectors (as in the cases of Japan and South Korea) or simply created new export-oriented business sectors out of nothing (as in the cases of Hong Kong, Singapore, and Taiwan). The export sector's stellar performance gave export-oriented businesses a political advantage in the formulation of national economic policies before the transition to democracy, and it facilitated a virtuous cycle of business influence and economic development. The landed class and the protected business sectors (such as real estate, construction, banking, insurance, stock trading, public enterprises, local transportation, and services) served only as auxiliary arms to the export sector.[14]

However, the transition to democracy generated political uncertainty and disrupted the old state-business relations. As politicians eagerly looked for campaign financial resources and grassroots support when meaningful elections were introduced and became more competitive, the landed class and protected businesses provided convenient and reliable political allies. They had cultivated stable personal networks in the localities with their business partners and customers, which could easily be tapped for campaign funding and votes.[15] In return, elected politicians would provide subsidies and special favors to their business supporters. The export business sectors thus began to lose favor with political elites. During the transition to democracy, export-oriented businesses continued to exert significant pressure on the government to promote free trade through their taxes, campaign contributions, and networks of company employees. However, having most of their business partners and customers overseas, they could contribute many fewer votes than could the landed class and the protected business sectors.

Therefore, the postdevelopmental state has aimed to maximize its votes by adopting economic policies that are politically, but not necessarily economically, optimal.[16] In the early stages of the transition to democracy, the political influence of the landed class and the protected business sectors was likely to overshadow national politics and result in economic stagnation. To promote free market policies, then, elected political leaders in these states needed (but have not necessarily been able) to revive their alliances with the export business sector.[17] This revival has depended on idiosyncratic factors in each case—both the political leaders and the choice of export businesses to voice or to exit. The rise of China has added another complicating factor: export businesses in these postdevelopmental states may increasingly find the exit strategy of moving production to the PRC more attractive.

In some of the East Asian developmental state cases, the landed class and the protected business sectors were not necessarily harmful to economic development, provided the capacity of the state was not degraded during the transition to democracy. After all, the landed class and the protected business sector had previously served as auxiliary arms to economic development. Yet, scholars have found that rampant corruption in some East Asian cases undermined the state's accountability and capacity during the transition to democracy.[18] To counter this decline, a central challenge for young democracies in postdevelopmental states is to restore or establish new institutions of accountability and capacity, such as anti-corruption agencies, ombudsmen, transparency laws, conflict-of-interest laws, and central banks and financial regulatory commissions with strong political autonomy.

The next section applies this theoretical framework to analyze the restructuring of state-business relations in Taiwan during the transition to democracy. The analysis is summarized in the schematic shown in Figure 11.1.

The Road to 2000:
From State Corporatism to Party-State Capitalism

After World War II, when the defeated KMT state retreated to Taiwan, its political economy was largely inherited. Politically, the KMT state exploited its strategic position in the East Asian security framework maintained by the United States. Through a brutal clampdown on political dissidents in the tragic massacre of February 28, 1947, and the ensuing

Figure 11.1 Regime Shifts in Taiwan's Political Economy

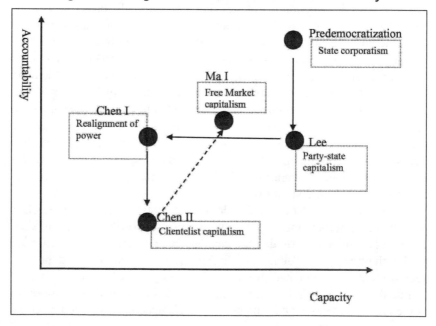

white terror period, the KMT maintained a repressive, autocratic regime. Economically, this left the KMT state in a privileged position to distribute US aid, trade quotas, and imported materials to local elites. In addition, the KMT government converted Japanese conglomerates of the colonial regime into state-owned enterprises. Consequently, the state-owned and para-state enterprises of the postwar era held command of the "strategic heights" of the economy, forming a near monopoly of upstream economic resources in the sectors of finance, public utility, and most capital-intensive industries.

The Republic of China (ROC) constitution laid out a framework for a state that was supposed to be both capable and accountable to its leaders, and on Taiwan, the KMT largely succeeded in fulfilling this vision. The government had vertical and horizontal lines of accountability. Strongman Chiang Kai-shek was highly skilled at using the intelligence and security agencies to consolidate his rule after the retreat to Taiwan: a strict and sophisticated intragovernmental monitoring mechanism was established that effectively reduced corruption during this period. After the purge of corrupt officials from 1950 to 1952, the KMT regime also began recruiting local college students into the bureaucracy and established a meritocracy. Local political leaders and governments were held at least somewhat accountable through regular, contested elections.[19]

In addition to these institutions of vertical accountability, various procedures to ensure horizontal accountability were also put in place. During the long period of authoritarian rule under the KMT, the state-party relationship acted as an informal check on political leaders. The Control Yuan acted as a kind of ombudsman to monitor officials in the Executive Yuan, and the Legislative Yuan's approval was required to adopt new budgets and legislation. The resulting state was highly capable, with strong regulatory power over taxation, licensing, and industrial regulation and distributive power exercised through various governmental funds and para-state enterprises that influenced business decisions through joint ventures and stock transactions. Even today, after two changes in ruling party, the regulatory and administrative power of the Taiwanese state has remained relatively strong. But the transition to democracy took a toll on the government's internal accountability. As a result, Taiwan's economic development entered turbulent territory.

The death of President Chiang Ching-kuo in early 1988 was a critical juncture in the evolution of the political system.[20] The post-Chiang struggle inside the KMT opened up space for a transition to democracy. In the presidential election of 1990, the last to be determined by a vote in the National Assembly rather than a direct popular election, the "mainstream faction" led by Chiang's successor Lee Teng-hui allied with local factional leaders to defeat the "nonmainstream" faction led by the old guard of mainlander elites. At the same time, Lee initiated various constitutional reforms, which had the effect of expanding presidential powers without increasing the president's accountability to other branches. Over time, the five-power system laid out in the original Sun Yat-sen–inspired constitution evolved into a semipresidential system in which the president had all the political power without corresponding accountability, while the premier had all the political accountability without holding actual power. With both constitutional and political power concentrated in the hands of President Lee, the Legislative Yuan and Control Yuan gradually lost the ability to effectively monitor and check the Executive Yuan.[21]

These constitutional reforms, and the changes in interests of political elites that they induced, transformed state-business relations. The conventional party-state machinery and its sponsored businesses tended to be affiliated with the nonmainstream faction in the KMT. President Lee, however, mobilized local capitalists and local factions, mainly of the majority Hoklo ethnicity, to build a counterweight to the mainlander political and business elites. This top-down reform subtly transformed the old state-corporatist arrangements. President Lee established a new ruling coalition by placing his protégés in critical positions within the old state-business networks; the "arm's length" distance between state and business was no longer maintained. As a consequence, clientelism and "black gold"—the combination of organized crime and political corruption—expanded in the wake of the transition to democracy.

These economic reforms began in sync with political liberalization, as the imperative to win elections reoriented the interests of incumbent KMT members.[22] First, the KMT expanded its business interests to be able to meet the party's rising campaign expenses. The Business Management Committee (BMC) was created in August 1993 to coordinate the expansion of party enterprises. By 1994, the KMT had invested in 104 firms divided into ten special categories and administered by seven holding companies.[23] By the end of 1998, the total assets held by KMT enterprises amounted to US$200 billion, ranking the party as the fifth-largest conglomerate in Taiwan. Through various holding companies, the KMT also gained control of four banks: the Medium Business Bank of Kaohsiung, the China Development Industrial Bank, Fanya Bank, and Bank Sinopac.[24] In 1999, the China Development Industrial Bank, which was the holding company for the KMT's enterprises, ranked first among Taiwan's 150 financial institutions, in terms of both net profit rate (before tax) and return on assets.[25]

These party conglomerates became increasingly important to the KMT because of the rising campaign expenses faced by the party. Starting in about 1990, elections began to turn on the party's ability to distribute money and mobilize voters for its candidates. Constitutional reforms eventually made all the major institutions of the central government directly elected by Taiwanese, culminating with the first direct election of the president in 1996. Not surprisingly, in response to rapidly escalating campaign costs, the KMT tried to restructure its relationship with businesses to shore up its electoral advantages. A marriage of convenience occurred as the KMT colluded with leading business groups and expanded the scope of its economic interests. Various conglomerates, including the Core Pacific Group, the Ruentex Group, the Zhang-yi Group, the Shin Kong Group, the Hung-Kuo Group, Formosa Plastics, and the Koos Group, cooperated with the KMT to earn extra benefits.[26]

The mutually reinforcing relationship between the KMT and business also had a major impact on the financial sector. In the late 1980s, deregulation of the banking and security sectors, the inflow of hot money from abroad, and stock market bubbles encouraged greater financial leveraging by conglomerates. Two important deregulatory policies followed. First, in 1989, the securities market was liberalized. Foreseeing this as a good opportunity to acquire additional financial leverage, local factions and conglomerates established their own securities firms to take advantage of the economic bubbles of the early 1990s, and by the end of 1990, 350 new securities firms had entered the market.[27] Second, in 1991, the Ministry of Finance lifted the ban on private banks and issued licenses to fifteen new ones. Virtually all the conglomerates with strong political ties to the KMT were granted permission to open new banks. As a result, the deregulation of the securities and banking industries opened new channels for conglomerates to acquire capital. In return, these conglomerates, which acquired access to privileged government information about the financial markets, became big campaign contributors to the KMT.

Ultimately, the relationship between the KMT and business became institutionalized. The KMT Business Management Committee met once every two months to coordinate investment strategies with conglomerates. The KMT also reserved more seats inside the top party decision-making organ, the Central Standing Committee, to co-opt businesspeople. In addition, the KMT helped businesspeople win seats in the legislature. Finally, President Lee maintained personal contacts with business leaders to form his own individual networks.

As a result, the postdevelopmental state lost much of its political autonomy, and its commitment to sustainable, long-term economic development weakened. But its administrative power to serve and control conglomerates was not diminished. The state was still equipped with various institutions and policy instruments to influence the behavior and economic opportunities of conglomerates.[28] For instance, the Ministry of Economic Affairs had jurisdiction over state-controlled enterprises, which could be used to form joint ventures, conduct stock transactions, establish cooperative projects, and be sold (privatized) to conglomerates. The Ministry of Finance supervised the Central Bank, state-controlled banks, and the Taiwan Stock Exchange Corporation (the Taiwanese counterpart to the New York Stock Exchange). It could also investigate uncooperative conglomerates for tax violations. The Council of Labor Affairs handled the Labor Insurance Fund, the Labor Pension Fund, and the Civil Servant Pension Fund and could also harass conglomerates by investigating their workplace safety and labor contracts. The Ministry of Transportation managed the Postal Savings Fund, and the Executive Yuan had direct control over allocation of the Development Fund. Together, these policy instruments constituted formidable sticks and carrots that could be wielded against all conglomerates in Taiwan.[29]

Most notable among these policy instruments were state-controlled companies (banks and enterprises). The old term *state-owned companies* no longer adequately described the new forms these companies took in the 1990s. After the Privatization Law was revised in 1991, previously state-owned companies were classified as private companies if the state's share of stock ownership fell below 50 percent.[30] In most "privatized" companies, however, the state continued to hold the largest share (up to 49 percent) of stock ownership, so that it had the right to appoint the president and general manager of these companies and retain the most influence over the boards of directors and trustees. After "privatization," these state-controlled companies were no longer subject to the supervision of the legislature and became powerful political instruments of President Lee. They offered high salaries and bonuses to political loyalists, whom the president could appoint as company presidents, general managers, directors, and trustees. They also helped President Lee cultivate personal political networks with other politicians and business leaders by allocating lucrative government procurement projects, joint-venture opportunities, easy access to loans, cross-shareholding, and insider information in various financial markets. These state-controlled companies were further authorized to establish subsidiaries to channel funds and profits to political clients, thus circumventing the monitoring of parent company boards of directors and trustees.

These institutional alliances among the ruling party, KMT enterprises, conglomerates, and the state led to an increasingly institutionalized form of corrupt party-state capitalism.[31] In response, in 2000, the DPP ran in part on an anticorruption platform and won the presidential election. Many Taiwanese voters were fed up with rampant corruption under KMT rule and placed their hopes for economic and political reforms in the DPP.

2000–2004: The Realignment of State-Business Relations

The presidential election of 2000 marked a watershed in state-business relations in Taiwan. Thanks to a split within the KMT, the DPP's Chen Shui-bian won the presidential election with 39.3 percent of the total votes, ahead of James Soong's 36.8 percent and Lien Chan's 23.1 percent. However, the fact that Chen did not win the election by a simple majority generated tremendous political uncertainty in state-business relationships. The Chen administration placed a high priority on weakening the close collusion between the KMT and leading businesses that had grown up during the Lee era. But the KMT persistently defended its interests, relying on a loose Pan-Blue majority in the legislature and sympathizers in the lower echelon of the state bureaucracy in the hope that they would get everything back to "normal" in four years. The business community was totally confused. Should and could they maintain their close ties with the KMT? Or should they switch their political allegiance to the DPP? This uncertainty among business elites in the first year of DPP rule contributed to the first negative growth rate of per capita GNP in Taiwan's postwar economic history.

After Chen Shui-bian came into office, his first priority was to destroy the KMT party-state networks without undermining the capacity of the state. In the state and para-state sectors, the DPP government eventually replaced more than 7,000 appointed positions with DPP supporters. These positions included presidents, general managers, boards of directors, and boards of trustees in state-controlled companies. The change of management in some state-controlled companies brought immediate improvements in efficiency. For instance, in 2002, the Chinese Petroleum Corporation, Taiwan Power Company, Taiwan Sugar Corporation, TAIYEN, and the China Shipbuilding Industry Corporation all reported substantial profit growth. But the DPP also received criticism for being a halfhearted reformer of state-business ties. In addition to the changes in company personnel came changes among political and business actors who wanted to have access to government procurement projects, joint ventures, easy loans, and insider information in financial markets provided by these state-controlled companies. At the same time, the DPP government declared that the KMT enterprises and properties obtained during the authoritarian period were "illegal assets" and started legal procedures to confiscate them.

As a consequence, KMT enterprises suffered tremendously from the loss of business opportunities within the state-controlled companies and conglomerates. One local report found that in 2001, five of the seven KMT holding companies had suffered losses of at least US$40 million after tax. In terms of pretax ranking of the 100 biggest business groups in Taiwan, the KMT's business group tumbled from thirteenth in 1999 to ninety-ninth in 2001. Needless to say, the KMT business group kept performing poorly under DPP rule and became a liability to the party. The KMT sold most of these assets at fire-sale prices over the following years.

The DPP government also realized that it needed business support for both political support and economic development. The DPP had traditionally had a tense relationship with the business community and repeatedly criticized businesses for being a part of the corrupt system of party-state capitalism under the KMT. The business community's refusal to invest new capital during the recession of 2000–2001, however, helped demonstrate their displeasure toward the new government's "antibusiness" measures, such as the suspension of the construction of the fourth nuclear power plant. The government belatedly moved to repair its relationship with business in order to revitalize the economy. President Chen acknowledged past tensions with the business community and attempted to engineer a new state-business network. He formed an alliance with some export-oriented conglomerates by enlisting them as presidential advisers. The shipping business giant Evergreen, Taiwan Semiconductor Manufacturing Company, Acer, and the Qimei petrochemical conglomerate all became major supporters of the new government.

In July 2001, President Chen held an Economic Development Advisory Conference to solicit business ideas about how to build a new economy that would not rely on the old KMT-dominated networks. Several probusiness policies were put forward: relaxing President Lee's "no haste, be patient" policy toward trade with the PRC, introducing liberalization measures related to the impending entry to the World Trade Organization, weakening environmental and labor protections, and excluding foreign labor from minimum wage regulations. However, President Chen later reneged on these promises due to pressure from environmental groups, labor unions, and supporters of Taiwanese independence.[32] In September of the same year, Chen announced a policy of "active liberalization, effective regulation," the intent of which was to restrain cross-Strait trade, which further irritated Taiwan's business community.

At the same time, economic bureaucrats became distracted from a focus on long-term, sustainable economic development due to the political uncertainty surrounding the top leadership. President Chen viewed much of the bureaucracy with suspicion or hostility, and he insisted on political correctness in the recruitment of decisionmakers within the state structure. This strategy resulted in frequent changes of premiers, ministers, deputy ministers, and bureau chiefs. In particular, the prestigious Council for Economic Planning and Development no longer held the pivotal position as the lead development agency that it had enjoyed under KMT rule. The appointment of three new CEPD chairs in six years worsened the incoherence of economic policymaking. As a result, higher-level bureaucrats preoccupied themselves with cultivating good relationships with the presidential office, and middle-level bureaucrats stayed busy performing cut-and-paste modifications to existing programs to meet the demands of new administrative heads or looked for more lucrative jobs in private companies.[33]

The major battlefield between the DPP government and the KMT was in the legislature. Although the KMT lost the presidential election in 2000, it still led a loosely organized majority coalition in the legislature, including the KMT (66 seats), the People First Party (PFP; 45 seats), the New Party (1 seat), and several independent legislators. The Pan-Blue camp together controlled just short of a majority of the 225 seats in the Legislative Yuan, but the ten independent legislators mostly allied with the Pan-Blue camp. In the 2001 election, the DPP increased its seat share and became the largest party in the legislature, winning 89 seats. But even with support from its ally, the Taiwan Solidarity Union, the DPP still fell short of a majority, and the party's attempt to lure some KMT and independent legislators to join the DPP backfired, provoking vehement objections from the Pan-Blue camp and retaliation in the legislature. The political back-and-forth of this maneuvering by both sides resulted in sudden changes in proposed reforms and ultimately contributed to the expansion of corruption at the individual level.

In addition to the obstacles the Chen administration encountered in the legislature, it also faced resistance from the KMT-entrenched bureaucracy. The ideological conflict between the new government and professional bureaucrats resulted in coordination problems in decisionmaking and implementation. In many cases, Pan-Blue legislators used leaks from bureaucrats to criticize incumbent DPP ministers. For instance, in late 2000, Premier Chang Chun-hsiung announced the discontinuation of the construction of the fourth nuclear power plant, which was one of President Chen's campaign promises to environmentalist groups. This decision immediately triggered bitter criticism from pronuclear legislators and the business community. During the ensuing controversy, bureaucrats in the Ministry of Economic Affairs, the Atomic Energy Council, and the state-owned Taiwan Power Company quietly provided information to KMT legislators and the general public that supported continuing construction of the plant. Eventually, the DPP administration had to concede to the pronuclear alliance and restart the project.[34]

Another example of the Chen administration's battles against entrenched KMT networks was its attempt to reform the financial departments of the farmers' and fishermen's associations. The long-term relationship between the KMT and local factions had enabled local politicians to expand credit through these local financial institutions without following standard credit-checking procedures. Foreseeing the emergence of a domestic financial crisis and in an attempt to undermine the KMT's political constituencies, the DPP government decided to restructure the credit departments of these associations. But the radical reform package of the "2-5-8 financial agenda" announced by President Chen received strong criticism.[35] On November 23, 2002, the farmers' and fishermen's associations mobilized more than 100,000 members to the streets in protest. The political pressure forced the chair of the Council of Agriculture to resign and blocked the reform initiative. However, the Chen administration resumed the financial reform effort later and was able to penetrate this KMT stronghold by replacing local factional members with DPP supporters in some local financial institutions.

By comparison, the state-business relationship changed substantially after the DPP took power. Without a legislative majority, the Chen administration struggled to get new initiatives passed, and the interminable struggle between the legislative and executive branches of the government weakened state capacity. Even though President Chen shared with Lee Teng-hui an overriding interest in getting reelected, he also worked hard to dismantle the old party-state regime that had developed under President Lee and to cultivate a new kind of political economy to replace it. All these efforts made Chen's control over the bureaucracy relatively unchecked in his second term. Before the 2004 presidential election, President Chen had fully exploited the campaign resources of state-controlled companies by placing his personal supporters on their management teams. But after 2004, political loyalty, patronage, and DPP factional affiliation— instead of technical expertise—became the ultimate criteria for choosing people to appoint to these state-controlled companies.[36]

2004 to 2008: The Emergence of Clientelist Capitalism

Among the third-wave democracies, voters were usually willing to tolerate poor economic performance under the new government for a period of several months to several years.[37] In Taiwan, President Chen was fortunate to be given another chance in 2004 to complete his unfinished reforms, despite the lackluster economic growth during his first term and despite running against a joint slate of the KMT's Lien Chan and PFP's James Soong. President Chen won the election by a tiny margin of 0.2 percent of the total votes over the KMT-PFP ticket, leading to a period of constitutional and political ambiguity about his legitimacy. The defeated Pan-Blue camp refused to recognize the election results, blaming the defeat instead on President Chen's alleged orchestration of an assassination attempt on the day before the election. The Pan-Blue camp subsequently staged all-night sit-ins and filed several lawsuits against the result. Even though the Supreme Court finally turned down the appeal, the government was paralyzed for several months.

The reelection of President Chen also worsened cross-Strait relations. Upon his inauguration for a second term, President Chen shook up his team of presidential advisers, replacing a number of leaders of export-oriented conglomerates with supporters of Taiwanese independence and businesspeople in protected sectors of the economy, such as real estate, construction, and finance.[38] Less than a year later, the PRC passed an Anti-Secession Law that would provide a legal basis to invade Taiwan should the Chen administration declare independence. This law provoked widespread fury in Taiwan and further encouraged the development of Taiwanese nationalism. The alliance of President Chen and Taiwanese nationalists pushed the DPP toward a more extreme independence position and served to divert domestic criticisms of Chen and the party when corruption scandals broke out.

Taiwan's business community was dismayed at President Chen's inclination toward independence, fearing that it would hurt their business relations with the Chinese. In the 2004 presidential election, President Chen introduced a "defensive" plebiscite to be held along with the presidential election. The earlier draft of the Referendum Law that Chen had used to announce the vote included the option of calling a plebiscite on independence that would certainly have triggered a serious crisis in the Taiwan Strait. But under American pressure, the draft was watered down to a more innocuous version, and during the election, the plebiscite failed when it fell well short of the turnout requirement due to a boycott by Pan-Blue supporters.

In February 2005, the president of one of Taiwan's largest semiconductor manufacturers, United Microelectronics Corporation, was prosecuted for investing in a Chinese semiconductor company without prior government approval. In the following month, the former presidential adviser to President Chen and president of the petrochemical exporter Qimei announced his retirement after he came out in support of a One

China policy and against Taiwanese independence. His investments in the PRC had been targeted by Chinese officials because of his role as an adviser to President Chen. In January 2006, the DPP government changed the restrictive cross-Strait policy of "active liberalization, effective regulation" to that of an even more restrictive "active regulation, effective liberalization."

The most dangerous move by the Chen administration was the introduction of a plebiscite on entering the United Nations, to be held concurrently with the 2008 presidential election. The Beijing government had signaled that the plebiscite was tantamount to a formal declaration of independence and that, if it passed, the PRC would have no choice but to react according to the Anti-Secession Law. The Taiwanese and foreign business communities in Taiwan strongly condemned the plebiscite. Ultimately, as in 2004, the plebiscite failed when only 36 percent of the electorate cast a vote, far below the required turnout.

At the constitutional level, the monitoring branch of the government, the Control Yuan, was indefinitely suspended at the end of 2004 when a list of nominees sent by President Chen to the Legislative Yuan was blocked by the Pan-Blue coalition. With no new members to replace those whose terms had expired, the Control Yuan stopped functioning after February 2005. By the end of 2007, more than 40,000 uninvestigated complaints of government corruption and wrongdoing had piled up without action.[39] The suspension of the Control Yuan was an additional factor that allowed individual-level government corruption to spread during President Chen's second term.

By contrast, the Legislative Yuan remained a check on the executive through the end of President Chen's second term. Chen's reelection victory had led the DPP to miscalculate its own political strength: in an effort to win a majority and end Pan-Blue obstruction, the party over-nominated candidates for the legislative election in December 2004 and fell short. The Pan-Blue camp instead consolidated their control over the Legislative Yuan, and the KMT began a political resurgence, taking seats from both the DPP and the PFP and once again becoming the largest party in the legislature. In addition, in 2005, Taipei mayor Ma Ying-jeou won the chairmanship of the KMT, defeating Wang Jin-pyng, the Speaker of the Legislative Yuan. The victory marked something of a symbolic break with the KMT's corrupt past, as Wang had close ties to local factions and had been a central figure during the party's "black gold" politics heyday.

Nevertheless, the combination of constitutional ambiguity, the suspension of the Control Yuan, the radicalization of the Taiwan independence movement, and the expansion of political patronage in state-owned companies all led to a flood of corruption in President Chen's second term. Indeed, as the core of the administration, the presidential office also became the core of corruption. In 2006, the supreme prosecutor's office filed a high-profile corruption lawsuit against several of President Chen's family members and closest aides, which the Taiwanese media dubbed "one wife" (the first lady), "two secretaries" (general secretaries of the presidential office), and "three professionals" (a lawyer, an accountant, and a doctor to the first family). (President Chen enjoyed legal immunity according to the constitution.) The DPP's corruption then extended from the core to the Executive Yuan, the legislature, and state-controlled companies. In fact, state-controlled companies were almost always the accessories to corruption scandals due to their far-reaching and intensive involvement in business activities.

The corruption case against President Chen's aides and family triggered repeated recall motions in the Legislative Yuan. The attempts to impeach the president were defeated because the revised constitution required a two-thirds majority in the legislature to pass, and President Chen and his supporters successfully appealed to Taiwanese nationalism to persuade Pan-Green legislators that his downfall would be equivalent to the end of the independence dream. The general public was not persuaded, however, and President Chen's popularity plummeted. The subsequent "Million Voices Against Corruption" street demonstrations in August 2006, led by former DPP chair Shih Ming-teh and joined by the Pan-Blue camp, posed a direct challenge to the DPP's mandate to govern. The DPP responded by adopting a more radical pro-independence campaign strategy in the legislative election of January 2008; it failed miserably. Taiwanese voters hammered the last nail into the DPP coffin by giving Ma Ying-jeou 58 percent of the vote in the presidential election that March.

After 2008: Free Market Capitalism

In the 2008 presidential election, Ma Ying-jeou won a landslide victory against the DPP candidate Frank Hsieh, and the KMT captured a huge majority in the legislature. The newly inaugurated President Ma thus stood in a strong position to change the economic policy direction set by his predecessors. The KMT's historic rapprochement with the Chinese Communist Party in 2005, in which then-KMT chair Lien Chan visited the mainland, was used as the starting point for drafting a new framework for cross-Strait relations. President Ma followed a largely neoliberal blueprint of dismantling political barriers and economic restrictions to accelerate bilateral economic integration. He also sought to sign preferential trade agreements with major trade partners as a way to reinvigorate Taiwan's flagging economy. During Ma's presidency, Taiwan signed the ECFA with the PRC, resumed the Trade and Investment Framework Agreement (TIFA) talks with the United States, signed an investment liberalization agreement with Japan,[40] and reached free trade agreements with Singapore[41] and New Zealand.[42] Considered together, these agreements substantially improved the prospects for Taiwan's integration into the regional economy.

The second transfer of power marked not only the end of an era of fierce partisan confrontation but also the return of the KMT's political-economic agenda. As the chair of the KMT and with a large majority in the Legislative Yuan, President Ma had unusually concentrated political authority with which to blaze a new trail for Taiwan's economy. By building on the KMT's reconciliation with Beijing, which started with cross-party talks in 2005, Ma was able to pursue closer economic ties with the PRC. The ban on the "three links"—direct commercial, postal, and transportation links with the Chinese mainland—was lifted; investment restrictions on capital from the PRC were removed; and additional negotiations to institutionalize other aspects of cross-Strait relations were initiated. In a nutshell, the Ma administration's development strategy was to revitalize Taiwan's economy by hitching it to China's economic growth engine through closer cross-Strait links.

President Ma's initiatives to revamp relations with China and state-business relations within Taiwan were grounded upon four preconditions. The first was the state's capacity to confront the impact of the global financial crisis that grew out of the 2008 subprime loan market collapse in the United States. Despite Taiwan's relatively successful experience weathering the Asian financial crisis, the state's capacity to handle a financial crisis in a more liberalized market was uncertain. The second precondition was a crackdown on clientelism. President Ma considered rampant corruption to be a key factor crippling governance in Chen Shui-bian's second term, and he was thus obliged to reestablish bureaucratic accountability to restore the public's confidence in the government. The third was improving the professionalism and independence of policymakers. After the transition to democracy, business leaders had become a principal source of campaign donations and enjoyed disproportionate and growing influence over policy that could affect their private interests. To improve the quality of policymaking, professionalism and independence from business interests had to be reemphasized. The fourth precondition was economic liberalization. Ma's economic advisers believed that the legacies of the developmental state, including the continuing role of state-owned companies, national stabilization funds, administrative economic guidance, and political interference in economic policymaking, had hindered Taiwan's economic growth after the transition to democracy. In the Ma administration's view, Taiwan needed to bring its respect for free market practices up to global standards. Close links with the Chinese market and preferential trade agreements would help remove barriers to trade and eventually improve Taiwan's international competitiveness.

At its heart, Ma Ying-jeou's economic policy sought to build a rational bureaucracy that would support and respect free markets. Political appointees to key ministerial positions were either leading academics or career bureaucrats with extensive policy experience. The administration's policy guidelines were drafted based on professional advice; the influence of political considerations in the policymaking process, such as the balance of power between intraparty factions and the interests of business groups, was kept to a minimum. President Ma attempted to position the state as the regulator of the market based on the rule of law—a significant departure from the KMT's traditional embrace of the developmental state. In fact, this was arguably the first time that the Taiwanese government had attempted to promote economic development through a neoliberal, free market approach.

Beginning in the early 1990s, Taiwan implemented a series of market reforms. The state-owned companies were privatized. The financial sector was deregulated. Domestic markets were liberalized. Most restrictions on foreign direct investment were eliminated. Taiwan was regularly ranked as one of the most competitive countries in the world in the Global Competitiveness Report. In the context of this series of reforms, President Ma viewed closer economic partnership with the PRC as a kind of "last mile" reform that would complete this transformation and boost Taiwan's economy further. Thus, as soon as he was inaugurated, Ma made improving cross-Strait relations his top policy priority.

Starting in 2009, and with the support of old-guard KMT members and major business and industrial leaders, the Ma administration began a series of negotiations on preferential trade agreements (PTAs) across the Taiwan Strait. These negotiations were conducted by two semiofficial government bodies—the Straits Exchange Foundation on the Taiwanese side and the Association for Relations Across the Taiwan Straits on the PRC side. During the fourth round of meetings in December 2009, the two sides agreed on the agenda and basic framework for prospective PTA talks. After additional rounds of negotiations, the ECFA was signed on June 29, 2010, in Chongqing, China.

ECFA was widely heralded as a major milestone in cross-Strait relations, not only paving the way for greater institutionalization of the bilateral relationship, but also creating many new opportunities for Taiwanese businesses. An "early harvest" list of economic concessions was established that resembled the Framework Agreement on Comprehensive Economic Co-operation of ASEAN+3 (Association of Southeast Asian Nations, plus China, Japan, and Korea). Taiwan's main export sectors to China's market, including petrochemicals, machinery, textiles, and auto parts, were the biggest beneficiaries. From February 2011 to August 2012, Taiwan and the PRC continued negotiations on the Cross-Strait Service Trade Agreement (CSSTA), reaching a consensus after eight rounds of talks. CSSTA, which was aimed at further institutionalization of bilateral relations in the service sectors, specified changes in the permitted scopes, scales, and interests of service-sector exchange across the Taiwan Strait. The Ma administration agreed to sixty-four commitments to open segments of the domestic market, and the Beijing government agreed to eighty. Limitations on foreign ownership, the scope of foreign businesses, and trade were drastically revised or eliminated. Taiwan's e-businesses, information technology industry, online game providers, financial industry, environmental protection industry, and logistics and transport industries were expected to enjoy substantial benefits from the agreement. During Ma's presidency, Taiwan also resumed TIFA talks with the United States and signed a bilateral investment agreement with Japan, a free trade pact with Singapore, and an economic cooperation agreement with New Zealand. In addition, several airports and ports were designated as pilot "free trade zones." President Ma argued that this pursuit of greater integration into regional markets was important for Taiwan to avoid economic marginalization over the long term.

ECFA had a significant impact on cross-Strait economic integration. Yet the cleavage between the export coalitions and import coalitions in domestic politics did not disappear, but only deepened. As the main beneficiaries of cross-Strait agreements, the export-oriented business groups gained more reliable access to China's markets and substantially expanded the scale of their businesses there. During President Ma's campaign for reelection in 2012, Taiwan's business magnates jointly and publicly endorsed the KMT's trade policy. By contrast, business leaders in the import-oriented sectors felt greater uncertainty about the future. They accused Ma's pro–big business positions and ECFA of contributing to a broader economic slowdown, a widening income gap, wage stagnation, and an increasing concentration of wealth. Taiwan's increasing economic reliance on markets in the PRC also raised concerns about national security. Although the opposition DPP by and large accepted the reality that Taiwan's long-term economic growth depended on the cross-Strait economic relationship, they nevertheless repeatedly criticized President Ma's neglect of small and medium enterprises and raised questions about ECFA's effectiveness in boosting the economy.

Conclusion

In the final issue of "President A-Bian's Electronic Newsletter" (*A-Bian zongtong dianzibao*) published on May 15, 2008, President Chen defended his policies over the previous eight years by referencing Samuel Huntington and Joan Nelson's book *No Easy Choice*. Facing numerous dilemmas, he argued, he had always chosen democracy, transitional justice, and Taiwanese nationalism. But over what? He did not say.[43] Indeed, the previous analysis demonstrates that the relationship between democratization and economic development in Taiwan has been more complicated than either pessimists or optimists predicted. Against the expectations of the liberal optimist, annual growth rates in Taiwan declined after martial law was lifted in 1987, and the downward trend has continued to the present. Thus, this outcome seems to lend support to Huntington's "no easy choice" thesis—that is, there is a necessary trade-off between democracy and economic growth. The neoliberal economic development strategy that President Ma pursued has yet to deliver a clear uptick in economic growth. However, the literature on democratic transparency and accountability reminds us that the intermediate variables linking democratization and economic development are transparency and accountability institutions. Twenty years after the lifting of martial law, Taiwan's democracy is still in need of institution building and reforms in several areas of state-business relations.

First, at the constitutional level, the transparency and accountability of the presidential office need to be strengthened. As Lord Acton famously said, "Power tends to corrupt; absolute power corrupts absolutely." The current constitutional ambiguity that resulted from seven half-baked amendments provides for a powerful president without corresponding accountability to other branches of government, as well as a politically vulnerable and unstable Executive Yuan. Taiwan's young democracy cannot count on the personal integrity of Ma Ying-jeou alone, however valuable that might be, to ensure that presidential power is not abused. Either through a Supreme Court reinterpretation, a constitutional revision, or self-restraint on the part of the president, major decisionmakers in the presidential office should be made accountable to the legislature. The requirement for impeaching or recalling the president should also be lowered. In addition, President Ma's steps to revive the Control Yuan will help improve the accountability of public officials.

Second, at the state level, extensive reforms of state-controlled companies are urgently needed. The KMT's party-state capitalism could not have led to so much systemic corruption without the existence of these state-controlled companies. The DPP could not have so rapidly destroyed the KMT's system of state-business relations without the help of these state-controlled companies. And these very same state-controlled companies enabled the DPP to build up its own clientelist system of state-business relations as fast as it had destroyed the KMT's. The legislature should revise the Public Enterprise Law to reduce government ownership in state-controlled companies to that of a minority shareholder, thus removing the government's power to appoint the management teams of these companies.

Third, the power of business associations should be strengthened. Scholars have consistently found a positive correlation between corporatism and economic development around the world.[44] Others have argued that state corporatism was a major factor behind Taiwan's economic success.[45] However, President Ma has continued to seek economic advice from individual business leaders instead of business associations—a repeat of the approaches of President Lee and President Chen to state-business relations—and the bias is obvious. The Taiwanese government would do well to restore corporatist consultation with business associations and to better incorporate these associations into the policy-making process—as well as into implementation—including more delegation of monitoring and enforcement authority.

Fourth, financial liberalization should be continued to increase the scale and competition of Taiwan's financial markets, which have been a major arena for corruption. More important, the presence of more foreign actors will weaken the cozy relationships that have persisted among the ruling party, conglomerates, local factions, and the state. In the face of greater foreign competition, domestic crony capitalism will be more difficult to sustain. Financial liberalization here refers not only to the liberalization of capital flows, which most Asian countries did before 1997, but also to the encouragement of foreign financial institutions to establish branches in Taiwan and to engage in the same business activities as their Taiwanese counterparts. New laws that guarantee neutral treatment of foreign financial institutions are certainly in order.

Fifth, the cross-Strait relationship needs careful handling. Presidents Lee and Chen devoted much of their time and attention to placating the Taiwanese independence movement, which contributed not only to the rise of a separate Taiwanese identity but also to increased tensions across the Strait.[46] Unnecessary restrictions on cross-Strait trade and investment were imposed on Taiwanese businesses, which urgently sought to establish stronger links to global production networks. As President Ma remakes cross-Strait relations on the principle of "neither independence nor unification," both sides of the Taiwan Strait should continue to engage in productive dialogue to construct a more pragmatic relationship.

Sixth, the issue of reverse brain drain deserves more attention. Taiwan's wage stagnation after the signing of ECFA has not only led to the outflow of talent but also eroded Taiwan's ability to attract world-class managers from abroad. Human capital is vital to Taiwan's global competitiveness. To raise incomes, the government should take action to strategically boost the economy, reduce corporate income tax rates to raise real salaries, and allow corporations to deduct the cost of labor insurance.[47] The goal should be to raise the income levels of the middle class quickly.

In sum, Taiwan is at a critical juncture: it needs to reverse the negative relationship between democratization and economic development. The Ma administration's commitment to remake itself as a "self-restraining state"[48] has been successful in avoiding the emergence of a new type of crony capitalism. But it is time to launch a strategy of social corporatism to help regain Taiwan's economic momentum.

Notes

1. National Statistics of Republic of China, at 2001 constant prices in various years.
2. Samuel P. Huntington and Joan M. Nelson, *No Easy Choice: Political Participation in Developing Countries* (Cambridge, MA: Harvard University Press, 1976).
3. For the developmental-state views of Taiwan's economic development, see Thomas Gold, *State and Society in the Taiwan Miracle* (Armonk, NY: M. E. Sharpe, 1986); Robert Wade, *Governing the Market: Economic Theory and the Role of Government in East Asian Industrialization* (Princeton, NJ: Princeton University Press, 1990); Fareed Zakaria, "A Conversation with Lee Kwan Yew," *Foreign Affairs* 72, no. 2 (March/April 1994): 109–126; Cheng-tian Kuo, *Global Competitiveness and Industrial Growth in Taiwan and the Philippines* (Pittsburgh, PA: University of Pittsburgh Press, 1995); and Steve Chan, Cal Clark, and Danny Lam, *Beyond the Developmental State: East Asia's Political Economies Reconsidered* (New York: St. Martin's Press, 1998).
4. Jagdish Bhagwati, "The New Thinking on Development," *Journal of Democracy* 6, no. 4 (1995): 54.
5. Seymour Martin Lipset, "Some Social Requisites of Democracy: Economic Development and Political Legitimacy," *American Political Science Review* 53, no. 1 (1959): 69–105; Seymour Martin Lipset, "The Social Requisites of Democracy Revisited: 1993 Presidential Address," *American Sociological Review* 59, no. 1 (1994): 1–22.
6. The representative works on democratic governance include Adam Przeworski, Susan C. Stokes, and Bernard Manin, eds., *Democracy, Accountability, and Representation* (New York: Cambridge University Press, 1999); Andreas Schedler, Larry Diamond, and Marc Plattner, eds., *The Self-Restraining State: Power and Accountability in New Democracies* (Boulder, CO: Lynne Rienner, 1999); and Larry Diamond, *Developing Democracy: Toward Consolidation* (Baltimore, MD: Johns Hopkins University Press, 1999).
7. Guillermo O'Donnell, Philippe C. Schmitter, and Laurence Whitehead, eds., *Transitions from Authoritarian Rule: Prospects for Democracy* (Baltimore, MD: Johns Hopkins University Press, 1986).
8. Mohammad Shahid Alam, *Governments and Markets in Economic Development Strategies: Lessons from Korea, Taiwan, and Japan* (New York: Praeger, 1989);

Alice H. Amsden, *Asia's Next Giant: South Korea and Late Industrialization* (New York: Oxford University Press, 1989); Chan, Clark, and Lam, *Beyond the Developmental State*; Peter B. Evans, Dietrich Rueschemeyer, and Theda Skocpol, eds., *Bringing the State Back In* (New York: Cambridge University Press, 1985); Chalmers Johnson, *MITI and the Japanese Miracle: The Growth of Industrial Policy, 1925–1975* (Stanford, CA: Stanford University Press, 1982); Chung-in Moon and Rashemi Prasad, "Beyond the Developmental State: Networks Politics, and Institutions," *Governance* 7, no. 4 (1994): 360–386; Ziya Onis, "The Logic of the Developmentalist State," *Comparative Politics* 24, no. 1 (1991): 109–121; Wade, *Governing the Market*; Gordon White, *Developmental States in East Asia* (New York: St. Martin's Press, 1988); and Meredith Woo-Cumings, "Back to Basics: Ideology, Nationalism, and Asian Values in East Asia," in *Economic Nationalism in a Globalizing World,* ed. Eric Helleiner and Andreas Pickel (Ithaca, NY: Cornell University Press, 2005), 91–117.

9. Linda Weiss, *The Myth of the Powerless State: Governing the Economy in a Global Era* (Cambridge, UK: Polity, 1998); Linda Weiss and Elizabeth Thurbon, "Is the State Being 'Transformed' by Globalisation?," in *States in the Global Economy: Bringing Domestic Institutions Back In,* ed. Linda Weiss (Cambridge, UK: Cambridge University Press, 2003), 298–316; and Linda Weiss and Elizabeth Thurbon, "'Where There's a Will, There's a Way': Governing the Market in Times of Uncertainty," *Issues and Studies* 40, no. 1 (2004): 61–72.

10. Stephan Haggard, "Institutions and Growth in East Asia," *Studies in Comparative International Development* 38, no. 4 (2004): 53–81; Wade, *Governing the Market*; and Weiss, *The Myth of the Powerless State*.

11. Kathleen Bawn, "Political Decisions About Bureaucratic Accountability: Interests, Institutions, and Prospects for Reform," in *Reinventing Government and the Problem of Bureaucracy,* ed. Gary Libecap (Greenwich, CT: JAI Press, 1996); Kathleen Bawn, "Choosing Strategies to Control the Bureaucracy: Statutory Constraints, Oversight, and the Committee System," *Journal of Law, Economics and Organization* 13, no. 1 (1997): 101–126.

12. Juan J. Linz and Alfred C. Stepan, *Problems of Democratic Transition and Consolidation: Southern Europe, South America, and Post-Communist Europe* (Baltimore, MD: Johns Hopkins University Press, 1996); Michael T. Rock, "Corruption and Democracy" (DESA Working Paper no. 55, UN Department of Economic and Social Affairs, August 2007), 1–18; David C. Kang, *Crony Capitalism: Corruption and Development in South Korea and the Philippines* (New York: Cambridge University Press, 2002).

13. Adam Przeworski, *Democracy and the Market: Political and Economic Reforms in Eastern Europe and Latin America* (Cambridge, UK: Cambridge University Press, 1991); and T. J. Cheng and Stephan Haggard, eds., *Political Change in Taiwan* (Boulder, CO: Lynne Rienner).

14. Stephan Haggard, Sylvia Maxfield, and Ben Ross Schneider, "Theories of Business and Business-State Relations," in *Business and the State in Developing Countries,* ed. Sylvia Maxfield and Ben Ross Schneider (Ithaca, NY: Cornell University Press, 1997).

15. Yun-han Chu, "The Realignment of Business-Government Relations and Regime Transition in Taiwan," in *Business and Government in Industrialising Asia,* ed. Andrew MacIntyre (St. Leonards, Australia: Allen and Unwin, 1994), 113–141.

16. Karl Marx, *The Eighteenth Brumaire of Louis Bonaparte* (New York: International Publishers, 1963).

17. Peter Gourevitch, *Politics in Hard Times: Comparative Responses to International Economic Crises* (Ithaca, NY: Cornell University Press, 1986).

18. See MacIntyre, *Business and Government in Industrializing Asia* (note 15); Tim Lindsey and Howard Dick, eds., *Corruption in Asia: Rethinking the Governance Paradigm* (Sydney: The Federation Press, 2002); and Kang, *Crony Capitalism*.

19. Yun-han Chu, *Crafting Democracy in Taiwan* (Taipei: Institute for National Policy Research, 1992).

20. For more on the way elections changed Taiwanese politics, see Shelley Rigger, *Politics in Taiwan: Voting for Democracy* (New York: Routledge, 1999).

21. See the chapters in Wen-cheng Lin, ed., *Xianzheng Gaige Yu Guojia Fazhan* [Constitutional reform and national development: The experience of Taiwan constitutional reform in 2005] (Taipei: Taiwan Foundation for Democracy, 2005).

22. Shang-mao Chen and Cheng-tian Kuo, "Democratization and Financial Reform in Taiwan" (paper presented at the Conference on Democracy and Human Rights in Greater China, Hong Kong, December 13, 2003); and Cheng-tian Kuo, Shangmao Chen, and Zonghao Huang, "From Asian Miracle to Asian Debacle: Capital Institutions and Reforms in Taiwan" (paper presented at the Annual Meeting of the American Political Science Association, Atlanta, GA, September 2–5, 1999).

23. The seven holding companies are (1) Central Investment Holding Company: financial, petrochemical, and general enterprises; (2) Kuang-Hwa Investment Holding Company: gas and technology enterprises; (3) Chi-Sheng Industrial Company: construction and land development; (4) Jen-Hwa Investment Holding Company: special projects; (5) Kingdom Holding Company: insurance; (6) Asia Pacific Holdings: overseas enterprises; and (7) Hua Hsia Investment Holding Company: communications.

24. *Shangye Zhoukan* [*Business Weekly*] 605 (1999): 84–111.

25. *Shangye Zhoukan* 603 (1999): 76–131.

26. Tsung-hao Huang, "State-Business Relations in Taiwan Since 1949," *Issues and Studies* 43, no. 4 (2004): 35–71.

27. Shang-mao Chen, "Taiwan, Taiguo yu Malaixiya jinrong gaige de zhengzhi jingji fenxi: Zhidu touminghua yu wenze" [The politics of financial reform in Taiwan, Thailand, and Malaysia: Institutional transparency and accountability] (PhD dissertation, National Chengchi University, Taiwan, 2004).

28. Cheng-tian Kuo, "Taiwan's Distorted Democracy in Comparative Perspective," *Journal of Asian and African Studies* 35, no. 1 (2000): 85–111.

29. In 2007, the four major funds, plus the National Stabilization Fund, had an estimated worth of over US$100 billion. See http://magazine.sina.com/chinatimes weekly/1570/2008-03-25/ba49882.shtml, accessed May 20, 2008.

30. http://www.get.com.tw/goldensun/distribute/intro2.html, accessed May 20, 2008.

31. Qingxi Zhang, *Jiexi Jingji Longduan* [Analysis of monopoly] (Taipei: Qianwei, 1993).

32. James W. Y. Wang, "The Political Economy of Collective Labour Legislation in Taiwan," *Journal of Current Chinese Affairs* 39, no. 3 (2010): 51–85.

33. Hwei-luan Poong, Cheng-tian Kuo, S. Philip Hsu, Hung-Hwei Liu, and James W. Y. Wang, "Networking Governance of e-Taiwan Policy," in *Rethinking New International Order in East Asia: US, China, and Taiwan*, ed. I. Yuan (Taipei: Institute of International Relations, National Chengchi University, 2005), 185–226.

34. Ming-sho Ho, "Weakened State and Social Movement: The Paradox of Taiwanese Environmental Politics After the Power Transfer," *Journal of Contemporary China* 14, no. 43 (2005): 339–352.

35. The "2-5-8 financial agenda" in 2002 was to reduce the average nonperforming loan ratio (NPLR) to less than 5 percent and raise the average capital adequacy ratio to 8 percent within two years. The NPLR for domestic banks, which had once

reached a record high of 8.09 percent, was lowered to 2.83 percent by August 31, 2005.

36. "Guo Qingjiang Dictated, Silenced Board of Directors," *United Daily News,* May 19, 2008, A13.

37. Diamond, *Developing Democracy.*

38. A similar collection of independence supporters and protected-sector capitalists were enlisted as advisers to the Executive Yuan in September 2004. See "35 Advisers to the Executive Yuan Announced," *United Daily News,* September 8, 2004.

39. "Control Yuan Members Unfilled, More Than 40,000 Cases Accumulated," *United Daily News,* October 8, 2007.

40. Taiwan signed this investment agreement with Japan on September 22, 2011. The full title of the bilateral investment agreement was the Arrangement Between the Association of East Asian Relations and the Interchange Association for the Mutual Cooperation on the Liberalization, Promotion, and Protection of Investment.

41. Taiwan reached a free trade pact with Singapore on November 7, 2013. The full title of this pact was the Agreement Between Singapore and the Separate Customs Territory of Taiwan, Penghu, Kinmen, and Matsu on Economic Partnership.

42. Taiwan concluded an economic cooperation agreement with New Zealand on July 10, 2013. The full title of this agreement was the Agreement Between New Zealand and the Separate Customs Territory of Taiwan, Penghu, Kinmen, and Matsu on Economic Cooperation.

43. A-Bian is President Chen's nickname. See http://atchinese.com/2008-12-03-08-52-05/2008-12-03-09-40-51/50185, accessed on December 16, 2014.

44. John R. Freeman, *Democracy and Markets: The Politics of Mixed Economies* (Ithaca, NY: Cornell University Press, 1989).

45. Kuo, *Global Competitiveness and Industrial Growth in Taiwan and the Philippines*; Weiss, *The Myth of the Powerless State.*

46. "Taiwan Identity, Hardworking Accomplishments in Eight Years," *Liberty Times,* May 16, 2008.

47. Annalee Saxenian, "Transnational Communities and the Evolution of Global Production Networks: The Cases of Taiwan, China, and India," *Industry and Innovation* 9, no. 3 (2002): 183–202; Oded Stark and David E. Bloom, "The New Economics of Labor Migration," *The American Economic Review* 75, no. 2 (1985): 173–178.

48. Schedler, Diamond, and Plattner, *The Self-Restraining State.*

12

Democratic Progressive Party Clientelism: A Failed Political Project

Chin-Shou Wang

When the Democratic Progressive Party (DPP) won the 2000 presidential election, it also won the opportunity to build its own clientelist system of political support to replace the Kuomintang's (KMT's). However, the DPP failed in its attempt to construct a new system of clientelism to help it win elections during the eight years of Chen Shui-bian's presidency. This failure was one reason for the DPP's defeat in the 2008 presidential election. When it was in control of state resources, the DPP tried to learn the skills that the KMT had used to rule Taiwan for five decades. Yet in 2008, the DPP was unable to rely on clientelist networks to mobilize voters at the local level. Moreover, the pursuit of clientelism came at a political cost to the DPP, transforming it from a relatively clean political party to a significantly corrupt one.

This chapter explores why the DPP did not succeed in building its own clientelist system. I advance two arguments. First, corruption did not take hold at the time of the handover of power in 2000; instead, the seeds of DPP corruption were sown as far back as the 1990s, when many local elites defected from the KMT to the DPP and brought with them corrupt patterns of behavior. Second, the many political conditions that had underpinned the KMT's authoritarian system of patronage were fundamentally different after Taiwan's transition to democracy. These changing conditions not only led to the breakdown of clientelism under the KMT but also prevented the DPP from constructing its own patronage system to replace it. Five factors were involved in the breakdown of clientelism in Taiwan: (1) the appearance of opposition parties and their victories in some executive races, (2) competition among local elites for office and patronage, (3) the decline in effective state coercion, (4) the depoliticization of the intelligence apparatus, and (5) the increasing freedom of the press.

The appearance of opposition parties gave local elites and voters an alternative to the authoritarian party, and the opposition parties' control over some local executive positions weakened the resource-exchange relationship between the authoritarian party and local elites and voters. The competition among local political elites, in turn, weakened their vote-brokerage organizations and undermined their ability to mobilize voters during elections. The decline in effective state coercion made it more and more difficult for the KMT (and later the DPP) to punish local elites who defied the party's dictates, to protect illegal activities, and to mask corruption. The depoliticization of the intelligence apparatus weakened the authoritarian-era KMT's ability to understand the ecology of local politics, making it more difficult for the party to control and mobilize its clients. Finally, with the help of the other changes, freedom of the press allowed corruption to become a salient political issue during elections. Hence, clientelism was a high-cost political strategy; by the beginning of the Chen Shui-bian era, Taiwan's political parties had to pay a high price for using it to win votes.

In this chapter, I briefly discuss the breakdown of the KMT's clientelist system. I then describe the processes that characterized local elites' defection from the KMT to the DPP. Finally, I consider why the DPP could not successfully craft its own clientelist system, even when it controlled state resources from the president's office.

The Breakdown of the KMT's Clientelist System

Although clientelism under the KMT began to change in the years before martial law was lifted in 1987, it was not fundamentally transformed until the beginning of the transition to democracy. Few people could see fundamental changes within the KMT's electoral networks, and the golden age of the KMT's clientelist system came and went without much notice. That the KMT remained in power after the transition to democracy has hindered efforts to conceptualize the changes in the system. In a path-breaking study, Nai-teh Wu argued that the KMT used clientelism to maintain a viable and durable authoritarian regime in a strange and hostile island.[1] Wu's study and others that followed treated clientelism as an independent variable and the KMT's stable authoritarian regime as the dependent variable. But there is no good reason to believe that causality ran in only one direction: in Taiwan, clientelism and the authoritarian regime strengthened each other.

As I have argued elsewhere,[2] five factors contributed to the effectiveness of clientelism as practiced by the KMT during the martial law era. First, the lack of a viable opposition party prevented the defection of the KMT's clientelist elites and voters to alternatives. Second, the absence of intrafactional electoral competition helped the system maintain a strong organizational structure with a high capacity for electoral mobilization. Third, political control over the judiciary was an essential element. Without an independent judiciary to offer some protection against politically motivated prosecution, the KMT could effectively threaten and punish its politicians for defying the party's wishes. Fourth, the KMT built an extensive intelligence apparatus that penetrated local political networks, allowing the party to collect sensitive information and monitor its clients. Finally, the KMT paid a very low political cost for using clientelism as a ruling and mobilization strategy because of restrictions on the media. Without a free press, there was little or no opportunity for citizens to learn about the negative consequences of clientelism on society—in particular, local politicians' corrupt activities. As Carolyn Warner argued in the context of France and Italy, "Only where a party can construct an effective monitoring system is clientelism a feasible and efficient strategy for winning votes; only where the voters have no alternative to the party is the vote exchange rational for the voter."[3]

As Taiwan transitioned to democracy, these five factors supporting the KMT's system of clientelism underwent fundamental change, which eventually led to the system's collapse. First, the emergence of viable opposition parties gave both voters and political elites alternatives to the KMT. Some mainlanders who had previously been among the KMT's core supporters were instead attracted to the New Party after it was founded in 1993. The decrease in the number of reliable supporters diminished the political resources available to the KMT to control local factions and undercut its ability to equalize votes among its nominees under the single nontransferable vote (SNTV) electoral system.

In addition to the New Party, the *Tangwai* (Outside the Party) movement and its successor, the DPP, posed a more immediate threat to the KMT's system of clientelism. Both attracted many local political elites, from village and ward vote brokers (*tiau-a-ka*) to whole factions, who often joined the DPP because of political ideology or personal interest. Depending on the circumstances, they tended either to take the initiative in defecting from the KMT or to receive strategic DPP appeals encouraging them to switch sides.

The immediate political consequence of the emergence of viable opposition parties was a breakdown in the proper functioning of three of the KMT's strategies for controlling local politicians: the so-called parachute approach to nominations, the use of divide-and-rule and checks-and-balances tactics to prevent cross-factional coalitions from forming against the party, and the use of rules to require frequent turnover among the ranks of local officeholders. At the same time, the victories of opposition candidates in some executive races meant that the KMT could no longer depend on these positions to distribute resources in exchange for the political loyalty of local elites. The ruling party's monopoly on political and economic resources was broken.

Second, new political offices were opened to direct election, creating additional competition among local elites and providing them with additional opportunities to access state resources, as they were no longer limited to the local government level. At the same time, the introduction of additional elections had an unintentional effect on the organizational structure of local factions. After 1992, Legislative Yuan seats became much more important in relation to those of the Taiwan Provincial Assembly, which had been one of the two main sources of patronage during the authoritarian period. Every local faction was often forced to support more than two candidates, and under the SNTV system, running more than two candidates from the same faction would typically cause a split in the local faction and often lead to its defeat.[4]

Third, Taiwan's judiciary became more independent, mainly through the efforts of reformist judges and prosecutors. As Weitseng Chen and Chia-Shin Hsu describe in Chapter 7 of this volume, the KMT found it more and more difficult to control the judiciary in politically sensitive cases. When it tried to interfere, the party faced varying degrees of resistance from the reformists. A more independent judiciary had several political consequences for the KMT's system of clientelism. It undermined one of the KMT's chief strategies for controlling local elites—that is, using legal prosecution to punish party mavericks. Without the threat of serious punishment, discontented local politicians could defect from the KMT without paying much of a price. In addition, a more independent judiciary made it difficult for the KMT to shield its politicians' corruption and vote buying from legal scrutiny.[5]

Fourth, during the transition to democracy, there was a great deal of progress in civil-military relations and a depoliticization of the intelligence apparatus in Taiwan, as Yi-suo Tzeng details in Chapter 13. By the end of the Chen Shui-bian era, the military and the intelligence apparatus were almost completely removed from the political arena. Almost all arms of the intelligence apparatus ceased conducting any kind of political investigations. Even the Bureau of Investigation, an extremely powerful and important organization during the martial law era, became more independent and nonpartisan toward the end of the KMT's reign. Without the high-quality intelligence that these agencies had previously provided it, the KMT could no longer cheaply and easily monitor its local elites.

Finally, clientelism was never a cheap strategy for mobilizing voters, and it became more and more costly during the transition to democracy. As the KMT fought to win increasingly competitive elections, the ruling party became synonymous with what was known in Taiwan as "black gold" (*heijin*)—the combination of political corruption and organized crime. Several political and social factors made the emergence of black gold an electoral issue. The indictment of corrupt politicians by reformist prosecutors helped the public understand the seriousness of clientelist corruption. Without censorship, the press could expose the clientelist elites' corruption and their transactions with the KMT. The DPP also wielded the specter of black gold politics as a political weapon to attack the KMT in election campaigns.

In Taiwan, authoritarianism, not elections and democracy, under-pinned the KMT's clientelist system, and the transition to democracy helped break down this system. But there is at least one area in which Taiwan's experience is similar to other third-wave democracies: clientelist elites exploited more of the state's resources after democratization. Most studies of clientelism and democratization emphasize the importance of resource distribution for maintaining patronage networks, and thus they ignore or downplay the importance of other dimensions, including coercion, information, organizational structure, and costs. These issues are important for the strength, maintenance, and breakdown of clientelism. Thus, the progress of judicial independence, the depoliticization of the intelligence apparatus, and the freedom of the press may have made the developmental path of Taiwan's postdemocratization clientelism different from the corresponding paths of some of the other new democracies.

The DPP and Local Elites
Before the 2000 Presidential Election

There is a widespread belief in Taiwan that the DPP started to become cor-rupt only after it won the 2000 presidential election and gained the ability to exploit central government resources. This argument ignores a crucial historical fact: the DPP had maintained long-standing relationships with local elites, some of whom were extraordinarily corrupt. In fact, many local KMT politicians had already joined the DPP before Chen Shui-bian won the 2000 presidential election. In this section, I track the origins of corruption in the DPP back to the authoritarian period, considering how the relationship among the DPP, KMT, and local elites changed over time.

One reason for the KMT's successful development of its clientelist system was that the party monopolized political and economic resources. Locally elected KMT politicians acted as intermediaries and were a crucial channel through which many Taiwanese were able to reach government resources. At the same time, voters and local politicians who were not happy with the KMT had no alternative but to join or support in the ballot booth. More important, many local politicians who did not agree with the KMT found that the party's powerful and extensive reach forced them to withdraw from politics or to join local factions. Local factions, in their own right, often had to accept the arrangements set up by the KMT. Without a real opposition party, there was no tool that local factions could use as leverage in negotiations with the KMT.

From the Tangwai to the DPP

Nevertheless, defection from the KMT was possible. Four types of actors could potentially defect: voters, brokers, elites, and factions. These types of actors differed in their importance and appeal to potential supporters. Whereas the New Party only indirectly affected the KMT's system of clientelism, the DPP posed a direct challenge. Most leaders and activists of the local factions were native Taiwanese (*benshengren*) and were more likely to be attracted to the DPP for ethnic and ideological reasons. In addition, unlike the New Party, the DPP could and did win elections for executive positions. These victories weakened the resource exchange and distribution networks of the KMT's system of clientelism. In this section, I discuss how the DPP, and before it the Tangwai, offered a real alternative for local factions that were not satisfied with the KMT.

With no viable opposition party around, politicians who opposed the KMT's rule in Taiwan had few good choices. They could attempt to organize a small clandestine group to attempt to overthrow the KMT, but this strategy was too risky and costly for most politicians. One of the safer ways to take part in politics was to join a local faction.[6] Although local factions were a part of the KMT's networks and its vote machine, there are many examples of political dissidents who joined. For example, one dissident faction member noted that he did not express his political views toward the KMT or mention his family history during the authoritarian period. His uncle had been the principal of a high school before losing his life at the hands of KMT forces in the February 28 Incident.[7] With the appearance of the DPP, this dissident defected from the local faction and became a DPP member, later becoming the chairperson of the township party branch.[8] As one KMT party official commented on this phenomenon,

> Before the emergence of the Tangwai movement, if a local faction wanted to resist the KMT, they could not find an alliance, because there was no other political party competing with the KMT. What they could do was engage in passive resistance. However, the situation totally changed after the DPP was formed. If local factions were not content, they just simply defected to the DPP.[9]

These anti-KMT members of local factions were not an obvious threat to the KMT regime. They did not organize themselves into independent political units; they just hid within the local factions. Instead, the significant challenge to the KMT came from the Tangwai movement, which grew out of a diverse collection of anti-KMT activists and politicians in the 1970s. The Tangwai differed in many ways from dissidents in the local factions. Although some Tangwai members were from local factions, they were more powerful and independent than non-KMT factional members. More important, the Tangwai operated as a quasi-political party, offering voters a meaningful alternative to the KMT at election time. To counter KMT demands to support a certain set of candidates, local factions could use the Tangwai as a weapon in a tactical alliance against the KMT and rival local factions.

The emergence of the Tangwai undermined two of the KMT's strategies for controlling local elites: the practice of "parachuting" outside KMT candidates into local elections to weaken local factional control over political offices, and the use of divide-and-rule and checks-and-balances tactics to keep factions loyal to the party. In the 1968 county executive elections, for instance, the KMT nominated three nonfactional "parachute" candidates, and all of them won their respective elections. In the following elections in 1972, the KMT nominated fourteen nonfactional candidates, with the same result. But in the next county-executive elections held in 1977, the Tangwai had emerged as a political force at the local level. When the KMT nominated seventeen nonfactional candidates and only three factional ones, the party experienced its worst electoral performance ever, losing four county-executive races.[10] One reason for the KMT's electoral failure was that local factions did not turn out voters for the KMT's parachute candidates and, in some cases, even covertly supported the Tangwai candidates.[11] What made the 1977 elections different from those of 1968 and 1972 was not the local factions' discontent toward the KMT, but the appearance of the Tangwai. The rise of a viable opposition movement undercut the KMT's parachute strategy.

After its poor performance in the 1977 elections, the KMT decided to nominate more local-faction candidates in the next election. However, the appearance and success of the opposition movement motivated many local factions to begin to resist the KMT's divide-and-rule and checks-and-balances tactics, because local factions could support the Tangwai rather than a rival faction's candidates without suffering political consequences. Before the emergence of the Tangwai, the KMT had maintained its regime, in part, by exploiting divisions between factions, enforcing a system of factional rotation in key elected offices in return for access to patronage. Once the Tangwai appeared, however, factionalism became a dilemma for the KMT: it incentivized local politicians to support or cooperate with the opposition candidates unless the ruling party provided additional benefits. The KMT had to work harder than ever in campaigns to "integrate" these rival local factions into mobilized votes for the KMT candidates.[12]

Reasons for Defection

Whereas the relationship between the Tangwai and the local factions may have been a temporary, tactical alliance, the DPP's cooperation with local factions took on a more permanent form in many cases. During the martial law era, the KMT could still impose a high political cost on local factions that joined the Tangwai; thus, their support for the opposition movement was strategic and conditional. But once the DPP was formally founded in September 1986 as the successor to the Tangwai and as the transition to democracy began to gather speed, many members of local factions openly switched to the new opposition party. Local politicians typically decided to join the DPP for one of two reasons: ideology or personal interest. Many local elites with an anti-KMT orientation switched to the opposition party soon after it was founded.[13] Some of them had had long-running conflicts with the KMT that dated to well before the DPP was established. For example, in a township in Changhua County in the 1970s, one general manager of the Farmers' Association found that the KMT was no longer nominating him for elected positions. He defected to the DPP immediately after the party's founding and then became the chairperson of its local branch.[14]

Once the DPP had been established and had consolidated the anti-KMT vote behind it, local politicians began to join the party for another reason: the DPP offered them a new niche in which to advance their political careers. In its early days, DPP members were more closely allied with national elites and intellectuals, and its local branches were almost empty, if they existed at all. By contrast, the KMT's local organizations were overcrowded. Thus, the political opportunities offered by the DPP were attractive to many ambitious politicians. Three related but distinct personal interests pushed local elites to defect from the KMT: party nominations, party reputation, and resource exchanges. Of course, some local politicians may have defected to the DPP for different combinations of these three reasons.

The first reason behind some local politicians' defection was that they were unable to acquire the KMT's nomination to run in elections. As one interviewee, an important member of a local faction, frankly admitted, "No matter how long I stayed in the KMT, I would never be nominated. I joined the DPP because I wanted to get the DPP's nomination."[15] He switched to the DPP not long before the election, and as the opposition party's nominee, he ran and defeated the KMT candidate, becoming the most powerful DPP member in town. Similar cases occurred in other towns.[16]

The second reason was that local politicians wanted to exploit the DPP's reputation.[17] When the party was first founded, it had built a valuable party brand associated with clean politics and a strong Taiwanese identity. Thus, joining the DPP could help a local politician improve a tarnished reputation or give him or her a new public image. At the same time, local politicians who received the DPP's nomination could count on winning the votes of the DPP's core loyalists. In some cases, DPP membership could save local politicians money that would otherwise have been spent buying votes;[18] compared to the KMT, the DPP was less dependent on financial handouts to mobilize supporters, because, in many areas, more voters had a strong identification with the DPP than the KMT.[19] The DPP also had a much better success rate in central elections than in local elections; therefore, some local politicians joined the DPP to try to win the support of such voters. For example, a former KMT party official was forced to retire because of a financial scandal within the party. After he retired, he joined a township-level local faction. He ran as an independent candidate for the position of mayor but lost the election. When he tried a second time, he joined the DPP four months before the beginning of the campaign and ran as a DPP candidate.[20] Only a few local DPP activists disagreed with his joining the party.[21] With the support of the DPP and a local faction, he won the election. However, this politician did not change his character too much even after he joined the DPP. Several interviewees said that he had asked for a commission of 20 percent for almost all public construction projects under the township government.[22]

Clientelism Under the DPP

Although the KMT's system of clientelism broke down as Taiwan democratized, the DPP appeared to many scholars and politicians to be well-positioned to build its own system, particularly after Chen Shui-bian became president and the party gained access to central government resources. This section discusses the DPP's experience in interacting with the KMT's local elites and then presents an argument for why the DPP's attempt to build a clientelist system of its own ultimately failed.

One of the ironies of Taiwan's transition to democracy is that the KMT's system of clientelism actually helped shape the opposition into a more viable electoral organization. Many local elites joined the Tangwai not to overthrow the KMT but to compete with the KMT's own preferred candidates, and like their opponents, they adopted a similar strategy: providing benefits and services to voters. Thus, local elites who joined the opposition helped deradicalize it.[23] This strategy of recruiting more pragmatic local politicians was criticized in the 1980s by the younger, activist generation of the opposition movement, who rarely had a deep engagement in local politics. After the DPP's disappointing performance in the 1991 National Assembly election, however, the party, under the leadership of its chair, Hsu Hsin-Liang, began to reach out to local elites, exploiting the internal conflicts and factionalism of the KMT's political networks to make a play for their support. At the same time, some DPP members won administrative positions, including several county executives, which blocked some of the resource exchanges that had kept the KMT's system intact and which also allowed the party to provide some favors for its own supporters. The DPP pursued two political strategies to compete with the KMT's factional networks: "wooing defectors" and "encircling the center from the localities." Under these two political strategies, more and more local elites entered the DPP, and some DPP politicians, learning a lesson from earlier failures in the management of resource distribution, developed greater skills in maintaining clientelist relationships with their own supporters.

The biggest change in the clientelist system came after the 2000 presidential election. It was the first time that the DPP had gained access to the state's resources on a grand scale and exerted control over the state apparatus, including the military, the intelligence services, and the prosecutorial system. Not long after Chen Shui-bian won the presidential election, a county-level faction, the Lin faction of Chiayi County, defected from the KMT to the DPP. This defection helped the DPP win the Chiayi County executive election in 2001. As a consequence, many scholars and practitioners expected that the DPP would be able to re-create the KMT's system of clientelism. For instance, shortly before the 2004 Taiwanese presidential election, leading political scientist Yun-han Chu wrote an article in *China Times,* stating,

What the leaders of the Pan-Blue [the KMT, the People First Party, and the New Party] worry about most is that if the DPP stays in power, it will successfully and totally control the military, intelligence apparatus, judiciary, prosecution, and investigation system. In the meantime, the DPP can use administrative resources and judicial means to threaten and lure local factions in order to eradicate the foundation of the KMT on the local level.[24]

Chu's opinion was widely shared—many scholars and politicians commenting on this subject made similar arguments at the time. However, most observers generally ignored both the importance of the five factors that underpinned clientelism during the authoritarian period and the fundamental changes that followed as Taiwan's transition to democracy began.

Ruling Party Alternatives

The first factor concerns the political party alternatives to the DPP. When the DPP could not satisfy its own local clientelist networks, they could, and did, defect from the party at election time. In addition, surprisingly few local elites switched sides to join the DPP after the 2000 presidential election, despite its newfound control over state resources; the case of the Lin faction of Chiayi County turned out to be an exception rather than a trend.

Why did so few local elites defect from the KMT to the DPP? First, by the beginning of the Chen Shui-bian era, most localities already had some established local politicians in the DPP camp. Thus, if non-DPP elites defected to the DPP, they would have to compete with local DPP politicians for positions of power, and DPP supporters might not necessarily welcome the defectors. Second, the DPP's electoral base did not increase much following the 2000 presidential election, even though it won control of the national executive. In fact, DPP candidates still performed relatively poorly in local elections. Thus, joining the DPP would not necessarily help local elites win office.

The Lin faction case is instructive on these points because it was so exceptional. First, at the time, the DPP was electorally weak in Chiayi County, so the Lin faction could seize control of the DPP leadership there with relative ease. Second, the rival Huang faction controlled most of the county's local political resources. The DPP and the Lin faction could not defeat the KMT and the Huang faction in an election if they did not cooperate with each other. Third, many county-level factions around the island were collapsing at the time. However, the Lin faction still had a strong organizational structure, and its leaders could compel factional members to switch to the DPP. In other cases, the leaders of weakened local factions did not have sufficiently strong authority with which to force their members to join the party. In addition, no matter how many local elites joined the DPP, the party still had difficulty preventing their defection at election time. Unlike the KMT during the authoritarian period, the DPP did not have any means to coerce local factions to fall in line and support the party's nominees. As a consequence, local elites would not hesitate to abandon the DPP if the party could not satisfy their personal and political demands. Alternative political parties, including the Taiwan Solidarity Union, had political ideologies that were very close to that of the DPP, and factions could easily defect to them instead.

Factional Organization

The organizational structure of clientelism is important in three distinct but related respects: resource distribution, internal control, and electoral mobilization. First, resource distribution is an essential of clientelism. Without the ability to target material benefits to supporters and withhold them from others, clientelist structures cannot function well. Political elites have to build an extensive organizational network to make sure that benefits can be delivered to the lowest levels of their patronage system. Therefore, the more stable and extensive a brokerage organization is, the better it can help facilitate the distribution of benefits and ensure a reliable base of support for candidates at election time.

Second, the strong organizational structure of clientelism requires some mechanism of internal control in order to discipline and mobilize local elites. The more elites are incorporated into the organization, the fewer alternative power centers political parties will have to deal with in their efforts to mobilize support for their candidates. By eliminating the need to interact directly with most local politicians, political parties can more easily control their local bases of support.

Third, a stronger organizational structure of clientelism has a higher capacity for electoral mobilization. For instance, one study found that when one controlled for the level of urbanization, turnout in elections in factional townships was 8 percent higher than it was in nonfactional townships in 1980s Taiwan.[25] This big difference is attributable to the fact that local factions controlled a certain number of vote brokers in their organizations who could turn out large numbers of voters to the polls. Therefore, unlike nonfactional candidates, factional candidates did not need to spend much time and resources on appealing to individual voters. In addition to having a higher capacity for electoral mobilization, a stronger organizational structure of clientelism also had a higher capacity to equalize votes—an important consideration under the SNTV system in place for council and legislative elections.

Ultimately, the DPP was unable to develop an effective clientelist organization incorporating local factions into the party's electoral base and was never able to move past the level of exchanges with individual local politicians. Unlike in the old, stable KMT system, DPP politicians had to compete with each other for nominations and votes, hindering the party's efforts to build a strong organization that could credibly enforce clientelist bargains. In addition, the collapse of local factions was well under way by the time Chen Shui-bian came into office, making it a very time- and resource-intensive process for the DPP to build a political machine that incorporated local elites.

Nevertheless, Chen Shui-bian and the DPP carried out a "cutthroat war" as they tried to recruit local elites to join the party. President Chen himself spent considerable time, energy, and resources to meet local politicians in person, targeting not only county-level but also township-level and village-level local elites. This initiative ultimately failed: because Chen's time and energy were limited, it was impossible for him to build a clientelistic organization based on his own personal networks. Thus, without the benefit of strong factional organizations, the DPP struggled to deliver resources to local elites and mobilize voters.

Judicial Reform

Most scholars and politicians have ignored the effects of judicial reform on the breakdown of clientelism in Taiwan. The court system has been independent from political parties for some time. Some of my interviewees even asserted that the court system had become *too* independent and arbitrary and lacked proper institutional oversight by elected officials.[26]

The prosecutorial system is even more complicated than the court system. Prosecutors in Taiwan have an ambiguous status that is in some ways similar to that of judges. Prosecutors are independent from political parties but are under the control of the Ministry of Justice, whose leader is appointed by the president.

The DPP government never developed an adequate strategy to deal with the threat to the party from prosecutors. DPP politicians were not fully aware of the prosecutorial system's changes over the previous decade, and they did not understand the history of the conflicts between the KMT and reform-minded Ministry of Justice prosecutors. In addition, after his election, Chen Shui-bian named a maverick DPP politician, Chen Ding-nan, as the minister of justice. Chen Ding-nan was appointed to the role primarily because President Chen wanted to bolster his own reputation as a supporter of judicial reform. Like many KMT politicians, President Chen apparently did not believe that the prosecutorial system would be much of a threat to his administration or to the DPP's efforts to build a clientelist network of its own. After becoming minister, however, Chen Ding-nan remained fiercely independent of the party, which was unable to exercise much influence over him. Although three other DPP members were appointed as deputy ministers at the same time, their tenures were very short, and not one of them played an important role in prosecutorial affairs.

To make matters worse for the DPP, the party and Chen Ding-nan himself did not have particularly good relations with many of the reform-minded prosecutors. Although Chen Ding-nan promoted two members of the Prosecutors' Reform Association to district attorney, he relied much more on administrative prosecutors who had been hired and promoted during the KMT period. Chen Ding-nan did not consult with the Prosecutors' Reform Association on his hiring decisions or on practices within the ministry, and the key Ministry of Justice staff did not include any members of the association or anyone with experience in the prosecutorial reform movement. Because the DPP government and Chen Ding-nan did not understand the political environment within the prosecutorial system, the old-guard administrative prosecutors were able to exercise great influence over the affairs of the ministry, including the transfer and promotion of prosecutors.

The prosecutorial system became both more independent and more powerful than ever before during the Chen Shui-bian era. Nevertheless, this historic achievement came despite, not because of, promises by President Chen and the DPP to reform the justice and prosecutorial systems. After taking power, the DPP wanted not so much to reform the prosecutorial system as to control it. Indeed, President Chen himself tried to resist implementing several reforms, and he appointed a notorious conservative to the position of prosecutor general. But he had no long-term plan to deal with the prosecutorial system's threat to the DPP's efforts to build its own patronage networks. In short, the DPP did little to facilitate prosecutorial reform, even as many DPP politicians were being investigated on corruption charges.

Instead, the uncertainty generated by intense political competition forced the DPP and President Chen to take a shorter-term view of their interests. Beginning shortly after he took office, President Chen faced impeachment attempts initiated by the Pan-Blue camp in the legislature. Because the DPP still held only a minority of the seats in the Legislative Yuan, the most important objective for President Chen and the DPP was, from their perspective, to stay in power for at least a one-term presidency, rather than to fulfill political promises of reform. To maintain their power, the DPP, following in the KMT's steps, continually tried—but failed—to control the prosecutorial system.

The younger generations of prosecutors took the rule of law seriously, and the prosecutorial system became much more independent. And yet most politicians at the time still regarded prosecutors as doing the bidding of political parties and politicians. As a consequence, the DPP wasted an opportunity to work with reform-minded prosecutors to reform the judicial and prosecutorial systems, and it was caught by surprise when party members faced criminal prosecutions. In one striking incident, a DPP mayor was indicted on charges of corruption by a prosecutor shortly after Chen Shui-bian took office, despite the prosecutor's pro-DPP political background and despite the role the prosecutor's father had played as a campaign adviser to the indicted DPP mayor. This case was not exceptional. Several other Pan-Green county executives were also indicted on charges of corruption after the 2000 presidential election. In short, there is no evidence to demonstrate that the DPP could successfully control the prosecutorial system, much less the courts, when it was in power.

The Intelligence Apparatus

Few studies of clientelism have discussed the role of information in the relationship between patrons and clients. One reason for this is that the issue was not a serious concern in the indigenous and peasant societies in which anthropologists developed these theories. However, the issue of information is more serious in contemporary modern societies because of the complexity and the much larger scale of operations of clientelist systems. Clientelism exists not only in small and simple communities; it is also a means for controlling and mobilizing modern political parties and politicians.

Carolyn Warner argued that information and monitoring are acute problems in clientelist relationships.[27] In contemporary societies, face-to-face interaction is not enough to overcome information and monitoring problems. Patrons must find another way to uncover clientelist elites' hidden information and actions so that they can control and mobilize their brokers and clients.

One way the KMT mitigated these information and monitoring problems was by building an extensive intelligence apparatus that penetrated local elite networks. It played more than just an information-gathering role, however; like the judiciary, the intelligence services were part of the means of coercion that the KMT used to control and threaten local elites and dissidents. But the intelligence apparatus was mostly depoliticized during the transition to democracy, and it ceased to play a regular role in domestic surveillance. Thus, when Chen Shui-bian took office, he had less intelligence on local politics available to him than all his predecessors did, and he had far less ability to act on that intelligence to threaten or punish local elites who did not cooperate with the DPP.

Partisan politics contributed to this change. The DPP faced a harder task in trying to control the intelligence apparatus than KMT President Lee Teng-hui did.[28] Most intelligence officers were sympathetic to the KMT and its allies, whereas many DPP members viewed those officers with suspicion. Facing political pressure from the DPP, the Bureau of Investigation was forced to adopt a position of political neutrality after the 2000 presidential election and was stripped of most of its political investigation functions.[29] When the DPP then tried to use the bureau to conduct political investigations, some of the investigators who were sympathetic to the Pan-Blue camp leaked information about these investigations to the KMT.[30] Two interviewees who expressed different political standpoints nevertheless expressed the same view on this specific matter: the DPP did not understand the intelligence apparatus well and was not able to fully control the Bureau of Investigation.[31]

In his groundbreaking study of civil-military relations during the Lee Teng-hui and Chen Shui-bian eras, Yi-suo Tzeng argued that they followed "a general trend toward civil control and apolitical military, with the control pattern starting to transform into classic professionalism in both the armed forces and intelligence apparatus."[32] Although the reform of the security apparatus did not progress as far as the DPP's public statements would imply, Chen did not alter the general trend toward greater civilian control and apolitical professionalism. As Tzeng concluded, "The majority of the career officers and agents have developed a sense of political neutrality and the rule of law in carrying out the orders from the higher authority even if the higher echelon of the agency has been politicized."[33] In short, there is no evidence that the DPP was able to manipulate the intelligence apparatus effectively enough to aid its clientelist project.

The Cost of Clientelism

Most studies of clientelism emphasize that patronage is a useful organizational and vote-getting strategy for political parties, while at the same time ignoring the variety of costs associated with using patronage.[34] Katz and Mair summarized the issue thusly:

In short, the state, which is invaded by the parties, and the rules of which are determined by the parties, becomes a fount of resources through which these parties not only help to ensure their own survival, but through which they can also enhance their capacity to resist challenges from newly mobilized alternatives.[35]

In a similar vein, Wu Nai-teh compared four types of interest intermediation (populism, clientelism, corporatism, and pluralism) with three dimensions (the mobilization capacity of ruling elites, pressure of nonelites on elites, and access of intermediate elites), and argued that populism is closest to the ideal strategy for incumbent leaders because of the high capacity for mobilization and the low levels of accountability that it offers. Wu went on to say, "Populism, however, is not an institution the ruling elites can adopt at their own will."[36] Steven Levitsky's study of Peronism in Argentina is consistent with Wu's argument. According to Levitsky, "At the base level, PJ [Peronist Party] politicians used their access to public office to build patronage-based support networks at the margins of the unions." Indeed, an Argentine clientelist politician once claimed, "We beat the union. We took the party from them."[37] To these researchers and practitioners, clientelism is a vote-winning strategy.

Although some researchers have noted the negative consequences of clientelism,[38] they have tended to focus on the socioeconomic and political externalities of patronage, rather than on the parties that used it. Carolyn M. Warner's study is an exception.[39] She contended that "patronage is not a cost-free and consistently optimal strategy" for office-seeking parties.[40] The costs of patronage as a mobilization strategy include losing voters who do not benefit from patronage, losing control over members and activists, disillusioning and alienating those who act from principle and idealism, reducing autonomy and strategic flexibility, and increasing internal conflict. Over the long run, these costs can undermine a party's vote-winning capacity.

Like the KMT, the DPP had to pay a political price for using clientelism. Partisan competition and a free media made it impossible for Taiwan's political actors to hide clientelist transactions during the Chen Shui-bian era. The cost to the DPP was the loss of its idealism and its clean party image. For example, in the 2003 supplementary Hualien County executive election, the media reported on ministers' visits and expensive banquets held with local elites. Even the DPP's clientelist transactions with local elites, then, could not escape media scrutiny. Clientelism may have been useful for building new bases of support among local factions, but there was a broader loss of voter support that the DPP failed to anticipate: intellectuals and the urban middle class in

Taiwan tended to disapprove of the new connections between the DPP and corrupt local elites, and many chose, on this issue alone, not to support the DPP in national elections.

Ultimately, this factor as much as any other made clientelist mobilization a poor strategy for the DPP to adopt in trying to rule Taiwan: the party was unable to craft a mechanism to distribute resources through clientelist networks but still bore the high reputational costs of media exposure of corrupt practices. The KMT had faced the same problem in an earlier era. Before the transition to democracy began, the activities of the KMT clientelist elites were limited to Taiwan provincial- and county-government levels. When the national level was opened up to political competition, clientelist elites could attempt to influence the KMT and central government policies and had greater access to central government resources. As a consequence, the KMT faced a classic "common-pool resources" problem.[41] As in the case of the Liberal Democratic Party in Japan, the KMT was forced to restrain its legislators' resource extraction to levels optimal for the party as a whole; otherwise, the party would not have been able to carry out effective public policies or to weather the more negative consequences of patronage.[42] But as long as the KMT could exclude clientelist elites from engaging in national politics, it could easily adopt efficient welfare-maximizing policies at the central government level.

In contrast, Chen Shui-bian not only distributed many political and economic resources but also infringed on the policymaking process to further short-term political goals. This caused two problems for the DPP's nascent clientelist system. First, the DPP could not efficiently and widely distribute political and economic resources among its clients, because Chen Shui-bian himself determined most distributions of resources. Second, the DPP government struggled to design and carry out welfare-maximizing policies at the central government level. The disillusionment of voters with the DPP stemmed in part from President Chen's adverse interference with DPP government personnel and policies.

Conclusion

The DPP's overall clientelist project was a political failure. The party's control of central government resources in the presidential office did not guarantee the establishment of a successful clientelist operation: resources, it turned out, were just one of many dimensions of the clientelist system that the KMT had built in Taiwan. After the transition to democracy, no political party, including the KMT and the DPP, could use clientelism effectively and successfully. The DPP and Chen Shui-bian never seriously thought through how to build an effective clientelist system under democratic conditions. Although it is possible, in such circumstances, for a single politician to build his or her individual personal clientelist network, it is almost impossible to rule a country through a single individual's personal clientelist network. The clientelist system that existed under the KMT was not Chiang Kai-shek's or Chiang Ching-kuo's personal network; rather, it was a broad, stable, institutionalized, and party-based system. As Wu wrote, clientelism "was created deliberately on an extensive scale, to an intensive degree and operating bureaucratically in a relatively modern society by a rather sophisticated ruling group for a very clear political purpose."[43] Thus, it was impossible to build a functional DPP clientelist system by relying solely on Chen Shui-bian's personal efforts and relationships.

If clientelism as a mobilization-and-control strategy proved ineffective, why did Chen Shui-bian and the DPP still use it? There are at least three possible explanations. First, the KMT's long rule in Taiwan led many DPP politicians to regard clientelism as an effective political strategy. Second, DPP politicians failed to realize that the mechanisms supporting KMT clientelism had changed. Third, there were no other effective electoral strategies available to the DPP; the DPP had no choice but to attempt to rely on clientelism.

Clientelism played a key role in the development of Taiwanese politics. It helped the KMT consolidate its authoritarian regime, and it allowed the KMT to retain power for thirteen years after the beginning of democratization. But the legacy of clientelism still haunts Taiwan's democracy. Whereas the golden age of the KMT's system of clientelism has passed, that of the DPP's system of clientelism never arrived.

Notes

1. Nai-teh Wu, "The Politics of a Regime Patronage System: Mobilization and Control Within an Authoritarian Regime" (PhD diss., Department of Political Science, University of Chicago, Chicago, IL, 1987).

2. Chin-shou Wang, "Democratization and the Breakdown of Clientelism in Taiwan, 1987–2001" (PhD diss., Department of Sociology, University of North Carolina at Chapel Hill, 2004).

3. Carolyn M. Warner, "Mass Parties and Clientelism in France and Italy," in *Clientelism, Interests, and Democratic Representation: The European Experience in Historical and Comparative Perspective*, ed. Simona Piattoni (New York: Cambridge University Press, 2001), 125–126.

4. Chin-shou Wang, "The Openness of Political Market and the Breakdown of Local Factions," [In Chinese.] *Journal of Electoral Studies* 14, no. 2 (November 2007): 25–51.

5. Chin-shou Wang, "Judicial Independence Reform and the Breakdown of the Kuomintang's Clientelism," [In Chinese.] *Taiwanese Political Science Review* 10, no. 1 (June 2006): 103–162.

6. This section draws extensively from interviews I conducted during my field-work. These claims were stated by Interviewee 63, Interviewee 114, and Interviewee 121. Also see Ching-yi Wang, "The History of Development of Local Factions in Tai-Chung County: The Case of County Magistrate and Taiwan Provincial Assembly Elections, 1951–1987" (master's thesis, Department of History, National Taiwan Normal University, Taipei, 1994), 195–196.

7. Interviewee 121.

8. I heard of several similar cases during my fieldwork (Interviewee 77, Interviewee 87, Interviewee 108, and Interviewee 114). The most extreme case was that of one political prisoner (Interviewee 63) who had become the leader of a local faction. Another local figure (Interviewee 106) had been elected to a position in the KMT Central Standing Committee but still held strong anti-KMT views.

9. Interviewee 34.

10. The Tangwai and independents also won twenty-one seats in the Taiwan Provincial Assembly in the same election.

11. Ming-tong Chen, *Factional Politics and Taiwan's Political Change* (Taipei: Yueh-Tan Press, 1995), 182–185.

12. For information on how the KMT integrated the local factions, refer to the following case study of the 1993 elections: Chin-shou Wang, "The Making and Operation of a Kuomintang Candidate's Vote-Buying Machine: A Case Study of the 1993 Feng-Mang County Magistrate Election," [In Chinese.] *Taiwanese Political Science Review* 2 (December 1997): 3–62.

13. Interviewee 46, Interviewee 50, Interviewee 63, Interviewee 64, Interviewee 104, and Interviewee 121.

14. Yung-mao Chao and Chiung-wen Huang, "The Characteristic Change of Farmer Association Factions Around the Transformation of Taiwanese Authoritarian Regime: A Case Study of Sheilin Township from 1970 to 1990," [In Chinese.] *Taiwanese Journal of Political Science* 13 (December 2000): 165–200.

15. Interviewee 104.

16. Interviewee 67 and Interviewee 121.

17. Interviewee 11, Interviewee 15, Interviewee 16, Interviewee 96, Interviewee 104, Interviewee 105, Interviewee 110, Interviewee 111, and Interviewee 121.

18. Interviewee 121. An important case that illustrates this point was in the 2001 elections, when the leader of Chiayi County's Lin faction, Chen Ming-wen, defected from the KMT to the DPP and ran as the DPP candidate for county executive. One interviewee (Interviewee 120) said that Chen might have saved millions of dollars, as he had not needed to buy the votes of the DPP's hard-core supporters.

19. However, more DPP candidates recently have resorted to vote buying to mobilize voters.

20. Interviewee 24.

21. Interviewee 45.

22. Interviewee 22, Interviewee 34, Interviewee 44, and Interviewee 53.

23. Chia-lung Lin, "Paths to Democracy: Taiwan in Comparative Perspective" (PhD diss., Department of Political Science, Yale University, 1998), 154–155.

24. Yun-han Chu, "The Historic Choice of Taiwanese Voters," *China Times,* March 15, 2004.

25. Mao-kuei Chang and Chun-chieh Chen, "The Relations Among Modernization, Local Factions, and the Turn Out Rate of Local Elections," in *The Papers of the Conference on Voting Behavior and Electoral Culture,* ed. Chinese Political Science Association (Taipei: Chinese Political Science Association, 1986), 487–519.

26. Interviewee 98 and Interviewee 126.

27. Warner, "Mass Parties and Clientelism in France and Italy," 125.

28. Interviewee 70 and Interviewee 72.

29. Interviewee 68, Interviewee 72, and Interviewee 78.

30. In the 2001 elections, some intelligence agents still conducted political investigations. This action was reported by newspapers. One interviewee said that the political investigations had been conducted by some individual investigators, and not under the orders of the Bureau of Investigation (Interviewee 78). However, I was not able to verify this statement.

31. Interviewee 70 and Interviewee 72.

32. Yi-suo Tzeng, "Civil-Military Relations in Democratizing Taiwan, 1986–2007" (PhD diss., Department of Political Science and International Affairs, George Washington University, 2009), 148.

33. Ibid., 198.

34. Carolyn M. Warner, "Political Parties and the Opportunity Costs of Patronage," *Party Politics* 3, no. 4 (October 1997): 533–548.

35. Richard S. Katz and Peter Mair, "Changing Models of Party Organization and Party Democracy: The Emergence of the Cartel Party," *Party Politics* 1, no. 1 (January 1995): 5–28.

36. Wu, "The Politics of a Regime Patronage System," 38.

37. Steven Robert Levitsky, *Transforming Labor-Based Parties in Latin America: Argentine Peronism in Comparative Perspective* (Cambridge, UK: Cambridge University Press, 2003), 107.

38. Judith Chubb, *Patronage, Power, and Poverty in Southern Italy: A Tale of Two Cities* (Cambridge, UK: Cambridge University Press, 1982); Scott P. Mainwaring, *Rethinking Party System in the Third Wave of Democratization: The Case of Brazil* (Stanford, CA: Stanford University Press, 1999).

39. However, it is a pity that Warner's paper is meant to be suggestive, not definitive, and does not contain many empirical studies; see Warner, "Political Parties and the Opportunity Costs of Patronage," 534. For a short discussion of the cost of machine politics under Peronism in Argentina, refer to Levitsky, *Transforming Labor-Based Parties in Latin America*, 209–210.

40. Warner, "Political Parties and the Opportunity Costs of Patronage," 544.

41. Elinor Ostrom, *Governing the Commons: The Evolution of Institutions for Collective Action* (Cambridge, UK: Cambridge University Press, 1990).

42. J. Mark Ramseyer and Frances McCall Rosenbluth, *Japan's Political Marketplace* (Cambridge, MA: Harvard University Press, 1993), 12.

43. Wu, "The Politics of a Regime Patronage System," 12.

13

Depoliticizing Taiwan's Security Apparatus

Yisuo Tzeng

When Chen Shui-bian first took office in 2000, one of the most important unresolved challenges facing Taiwan's young democracy was the deepening of civilian control over the national security apparatus. By the end of President Chen's second term eight years later, this challenge had been at least partially resolved: Chen's final appointments to director of the National Security Bureau and minister of defense were both civilians, breaking a long precedent of military officers serving in those roles. Yet, in the eyes of many Democratic Progressive Party (DPP) members, this achievement paled in comparison to the unfinished task of establishing the political neutrality of the armed forces and intelligence agencies. The opposition Kuomintang (KMT) and People First Party (PFP) held similar fears but from the opposite perspective: at the end of Chen's second term, both major parties in the Pan-Blue camp remained deeply suspicious that the DPP had frequently manipulated the security apparatus for partisan gain.

This perceptual gap had an antecedent in confrontations before the DPP had come to power in 2000—but at that time, the roles were reversed. The Republic of China (ROC) military and intelligence agencies began as revolutionary forces in mainland China, and they had been subordinate to KMT party control for several decades on Taiwan. As a consequence, at the time of the first transfer of power in 2000, many DPP members were distrustful of the security forces, suspecting that they remained politically loyal to the outgoing KMT. Thus, for the DPP, fostering the political neutrality of the military and intelligence agencies was a top priority.

This chapter considers how and to what degree this vision of a democratically controlled, professional, nonpartisan security apparatus was realized during the Chen Shui-bian era. My central contention is that the legacy of KMT party control over the security forces presented a different kind of challenge for democratic consolidation in Taiwan than that faced by many other young democracies. The conventional concerns surrounding civilian-military relations are about establishing the primacy of civilian over military leadership and delegitimizing the idea of the military as an independent actor in domestic politics. Yet in Taiwan, these principles were already firmly embedded in the culture of the security forces. As in most parties organized along Leninist lines, the KMT's dense hierarchical party structure and system of political indoctrination had ensured that the military and intelligence agencies, though highly professionalized, were also fully subordinate to the party's top leadership. Instead, similar to many post-Soviet countries with a history of party-rather than state-controlled armies, the greatest obstacle to the consolidation of democratic civil-military relations has been the manipulation of the security apparatus for partisan ends by civilian politicians—both by KMT administrations and under Chen Shui-bian. Establishing civilian control over the military is typically seen as an important step toward democratic consolidation, but in this chapter I argue that the effect has run in the opposite direction in Taiwan: the deepening commitment of the security forces to the principle of partisan neutrality has followed, rather than led, broader democratic consolidation.

In what follows, I discuss the process by which Taiwan's armed forces and intelligence services have been transformed from politicized forces under ruling party control into apolitical, noninterventionist institutions. I first present a brief conceptualization of democratic civil-military relations in Taiwan. Based on this conceptual framework, the subsequent sections provide an empirical examination of the challenges in depoliticizing the armed forces, followed by a parallel examination of changes in the intelligence services. The chapter concludes by describing the theoretical and policy implications of the findings and suggesting questions for future research.

Recasting Depoliticization in Democratic Civil-Military Relations

In studying young democracies undergoing democratic consolidation, students of civil-military relations usually focus on the establishment and deepening of civilian control over the security forces rather than on the spread of belief in the principle of political neutrality. One influential perspective on the meaning of a "democratically controlled" military is that of Morris Janowitz, who suggested that the armed forces are democratic when they comply with the will of the majority of society. Samuel Huntington drew an additional useful distinction when he differentiated between objective and subjective control of the military. Under objective civilian control, the armed forces comply with directions from democratically elected executive and parliamentary bodies but retain professional autonomy. Under subjective control, by contrast, the military pledges loyalty only to a certain segment of society. In Huntington's terms, control by a Janowitzian "social majority" and control by a ruling political party like the KMT are kinds of subjective control and, therefore, fall short of a fully democratic civilian-military relationship.[1]

Most theories of democratic civil-military relations identify military nonintervention into politics as a necessary, but not sufficient, condition for the implementation of civilian control.[2] Because Taiwan is now a consolidating democracy, and its history of civil-military relations is mostly free of coup attempts or periods of praetorian tutelage, this literature leads one to expect that the deepening of civilian control over the security apparatus should have proceeded relatively smoothly after the transfer of power to the DPP.

Yet that has not quite been the case in Taiwan, where challenges related to "nationalization" (*guojiahua*) and partisan neutrality have occurred in parallel with those of civilian control. Although civilian politicians eventually assumed the positions of minister of defense and National Security Bureau (NSB) director, President Chen continued throughout his presidency to place a higher priority on nationalizing and depoliticizing the armed forces than on strengthening formal civilian control. That emphasis, combined with the fact that Taiwan's history bears little resemblance to countries with a legacy of praetorian tutelage operating under the shadow of repeated military coup attempts, suggests that the traditional concern about reducing military intervention in domestic politics during transitions to democracy was not central in this case.

Absent this concern, what aspects of civil-military relations have been relevant to democratic consolidation in Taiwan? The emphasis of President Chen and others on the importance of depoliticizing the armed forces is a reminder that Taiwan's security sector has been under Leninist party control since its creation. It also suggests that the proper comparison is with postcommunist experiences. In addition to sharing the same need to move from partisan to nationalized civilian control of the security apparatus, the postcommunist cases also suggest that manipulation of the armed forces and intelligence services by civilian authorities for partisan ends can be a serious problem. Given how politically divided Taiwan's society was during the Chen Shui-bian era, it is useful to consider how the partisan transfer of power affected efforts to depoliticize the military. From theories of democratic civil-military relations and from the experiences of the postcommunist world, we know that external threat perceptions, the specific process through which democratization unfolded, and party-army traditions were all important factors in the promotion of civilian control in Taiwan.

First, the existential threat posed by China has decisively shaped Taiwan's external security environment. Michael Desch argued that the existence of external threats leads to an outward defense posture, which in turn facilitates civilian control and stable civil-military relations.[3] The emphasis on an outward-oriented mission and shared civil-military perceptions of the threat to the state and nation is consistent with Huntington's concept of classic professionalism, in which upholding political neutrality is the most effective way for the security sector to prevent civilian interference, retain its autonomy, and achieve objective control.[4]

Another feature important to Taiwan's civil-military relations is the legacy left by decades of one-party control. On the one hand, certain elements of the party-army legacy, such as the tradition of civilian supremacy, have helped smooth the transition from party control to professionalized nonpartisan civilian control.[5] On the other hand, other military traditions, such as the emphasis on ideological correctness and loyalty to a supreme leader, are more negative. Moreover, the traditional party-army ethos reflected a form of Janowitzian professionalism,[6] in which the armed forces were obligated to work to further the interests of the masses.[7] This doctrine contributed to a legacy of subjective civilian control that hindered the establishment of a fully nonpartisan, depoliticized, professional military.

Finally, democratization typically proceeds hand in hand with increased scrutiny of the armed forces by a newly empowered legislature and an increasingly vibrant and active civil society, and the institutionalization of oversight by these bodies[8] helps deepen democratic professionalism and civilian control.[9] At the same time, as democracy becomes the only game in town, these institutions tend to push for military accountability not just to the executive branch but also to parliament and other representatives of society.[10] As a consequence, the security apparatus may increasingly have to report to multiple principals. Although this may, at first glance, appear to create greater limits on the military, it can actually create more space than before for military officers to maneuver by pitting principals against each other. Nevertheless, while security-sector actors no doubt make use of these new democratic institutions to push for their own organizational interests, these institutions also provide a way for the security forces to retain their professional autonomy and preserve their own political neutrality. Thus, the strengthening of civil society and legislative oversight actually provides a useful check on civilian political interference in the security sectors.

This discussion highlights several issues in Taiwan's civil military relations that warrant closer examination. For one, because China's hostility was widely perceived to pose a threat to Taiwan's survival, debates over how to address that threat inevitably became linked to the ongoing partisan battles and political divisions that characterized the Chen Shuibian era. The confrontations between the Pan-Green and Pan-Blue camps over the appropriate response to the China threat hindered efforts to depoliticize the armed forces. Another unresolved issue was how far "nationalization" of the military should proceed: although there was agreement about the removal of KMT party cells from the security apparatus and a shifting of loyalty to the nation-state, there was less consensus about ending the tradition of devotion to a supreme leader. Also of interest is the way in which the security establishment adapted to a changing political landscape and a more divided and polarized society. Finally, it is important to consider to what degree the security forces were able to carve out niches of professional expertise and to respond to political demands in ways that conformed to democratic norms.

Military Nationalization:
The Armed Forces Under the Two Defense Acts

The principle of military nationalization, or *jundui guojiahua,* requires that the armed forces obey the constitution and go beyond personal, regional, and partisan attachments to pledge allegiance solely to the nation-state. Given the military's party-army tradition and the mutual distrust between the armed forces and DPP over identity issues, Chen Shuibian's victory in the presidential election in March 2000 raised concerns about the military's loyalty to the newly elected administration. To address these worries, the chief of the general staff, General Tang Yeouming, following President Lee Teng-hui's advice, ordered the political commissar system to issue a videotape, recorded in advance, swearing the armed forces' allegiance to the newly elected government. This was a critical move to clear doubts about where the military placed its loyalty. In addition, General Tang convened the top brass at Yangmingshan to address military officers' suspicions about the DPP's pro-independence leanings. The emphasis on the military's loyalty to a constitutionally legitimate regime rather than to the outgoing ruling party helped dispel the threat of military intervention and reinforced the nationalization of the armed forces.[11] Finally, the quick removal of the KMT party cells, epitomized by the termination of partisan activities within the armed forces, ushered in a new phase of military nationalization and depoliticization at the beginning of Chen Shui-bian's presidency.

Tang Yeou-ming was not the only general urged by President Lee to help smooth the transition process. Under President Lee's recommendation, the outgoing defense minister, Tang Fei, also a retired general, accepted President Chen's request to serve as the first premier in the Chen administration. The appointment of Tang Fei has parallels with an earlier episode in which President Lee promoted the then-military strongman Hau Pei-tsun to premier as a way to strip him of military commanding authority. Yet President Chen's appointment of Tang Fei was not a replay of the Hau case for two reasons. First and most obviously, Tang Fei was no strongman in the eyes of either civilians or the military. Second, and more important, Tang Fei's appointment signaled not his removal from military power but rather the skillful employment of military traditions in a way that both upheld civilian supremacy and created a counterbalance to General Tang Yeou-ming within the military.

Competition between Tang Fei and Tang Yeou-ming was manifested in the making and implementation of Taiwan's two defense acts: the National Defense Law (NDL) and the Ministry of National Defense Organization Law. Passed in January 2000 by the Legislative Yuan, these two acts provided for a reorganization of defense agencies and formalized civilian control over the armed forces. The military's supreme commanding authority was switched from the chief of the general staff in the General Staff Headquarters (GSH) to the hands of the defense minister in the Ministry of National Defense (MND), a post for civilians rather than those in uniform. The defense minister now reports directly to the president, thereby ensuring a single chain of command. Moreover, the defense minister is required to accept oversight by the Legislative Yuan, in contrast to the prior system in which the GSH chief of general staff supervised everything other than administrative affairs and was free from parliamentary monitoring. In the making of the defense acts during Lee Teng-hui's presidency, Tang Fei tacitly supported the legislature's push to integrate the dual tracks into one, and he sent his subordinates to organize a study group that produced the MND's draft version of the legislation. By contrast, Tang Yeou-ming resisted the legislation, and GSH staff participated in the study group with great reluctance.[12] Yet Tang Yeou-ming shifted his stance as soon as he assumed the position of defense minister early in Chen's tenure and demanded that his successor as chief of the general staff stay out of what was now the MND's domain.

The two defense acts marked an important milestone in Taiwan's efforts to institutionalize civilian control over the armed forces. To deepen de facto civilian leadership, the defense acts specified that at least one-third of the staff positions in the MND were to be filled by civilians, and of the two vice defense minister positions, one was always to be assigned to a civilian politician appointed by President Chen. In practice, however, a shortage of civilian staff was commonplace during the Chen administration. The first civilian defense minister came only at the very end of Chen's term and under awkward circumstances. The defense minister Lee Tien-yu, a retired military general believed to be close to President Chen, was forced to resign less than three months before the end of Chen's second term to take responsibility for a controversial investment in a defense industrial corporation. The appointment of a civilian defense minister, in and of itself, came as a surprise to DPP security experts,[13] and the appointment of Dr. Michael Tsai as the defense minister for the final three months of the Chen administration hardly qualified as a major step toward civilian control over the armed forces.

The shortfall of civilian staff in the MND occurred for a variety of reasons. Some ascribed it to the shortage of civilian defense expertise and civilians' poor understanding of military subculture.[14] Both of these problems are typical of embryonic civilian control in young democracies, and, more often than not, both come as a result of military resistance and civilian reluctance. The long-term absence of civilian defense ministers is an obvious case in point. Many observers expected President Chen to appoint a civilian defense minister at the beginning of his second term. Yet resistance from the military persisted. For instance, the defense minister Chen actually chose, Lee Jye, did not hesitate to make his objections to a civilian appointee known in public. But military resistance is simply business as usual. An equally important factor at play is the top leader's political will—or lack thereof. As insiders pointed out, President Chen considered himself to be the best civilian defense expert in the ruling party and therefore had few, if any, incentives to select a civilian to lead the MND.[15]

A second, though rarely noted, problem was the personalized, "chieftain-style" nature of leadership in the barracks, which led to sudden shifts in policy and in the division of organizational responsibilities whenever there was a change in defense minister. For instance, because of his rivalry with Tang Fei, Tang Yeou-ming quickly reorganized the military hierarchy when he became defense minister, hindering efforts to institutionalize the reforms mandated by the defense laws.[16] Even under the best conditions, reform efforts were likely to increase not only rivalries between different departments and agencies but also uncertainty over the division of responsibilities. For example, the responsibility for assessing force structure and determining resource allocations was traditionally shared between the Strategic Planning Department (SPD), the Integrated Assessment Office (IAO), and the Human Resources Department (HRD). Rather than reassigning tasks and streamlining coordination, however, the MND maintained these overlapping responsibilities and interpreted the defense acts in ways that furthered its own short-term interests. The defense minister's preferences continued to dictate which offices were assigned which missions; tasks could still be transferred between different offices of the MND or, worse, simply be assigned directly to the GSH, in blatant disregard of the regulations specified in the two defense laws. It is well known that responsibility for strategic planning followed Lieutenant General Lin Ching-jing when he transferred from the SPD to the IAO. What is less well known is that, several years after the defense laws came into effect, the first general staff department of the GSH resumed control of human resources management, a job that was supposed to be handled by the HRD at the ministry level.[17]

The Politics of Depoliticization

The chieftain-style command tradition and the strong norm of civilian supremacy have together sustained a strongly personalized pattern of decisionmaking on the civilian side of the defense ministry, on issues ranging from political allegiance, to military indoctrination, to doctrinal shifts, to procurement contestations, and, finally, to personnel selection. The personalization of far-ranging organizational decisions in a military that serves a democratic yet divided society is concerning, and it raises questions about whether the reform process has gone off track. One of the main reforms mandated by the two defense laws was the depoliticization of the military. In this section, I briefly discuss the politics of depoliticization in Taiwan, considering whether the mode of control of the armed forces has merely switched from one kind of subjective civilian control to another, or whether it has already moved most of the way toward objective control.

Given the intense partisan divisions that characterize politics in Taiwan, the partisan affiliations of and political participation by those in uniform is obviously a sensitive issue. Because the majority of military officers identified more closely with the KMT, or at least the Pan-Blue camp, mutual suspicions between the military and the DPP administration remained strong during President Chen's first term. Responding to this sensitivity and in accordance with the National Defense Law, the MND initially banned any participation in political activities by on-duty military personnel. In a further effort to prevent political clashes and electoral competition between the Pan-Green and Pan-Blue camps from spilling over into the military itself, the MND then began enforcing a policy of partisan neutrality among all enlisted personnel at all times.

Nevertheless, the March 19, 2004, gunshot incident, in which President Chen and Vice President Annette Lu were lightly wounded by bullets fired by a mysterious assailant from a crowd lining their parade route, ignited a political firestorm of accusations that quickly engulfed the security forces. In response to the attempted assassination, the DPP government activated an emergency national security protocol that placed security forces on high alert. Because the shooting took place the day before the election, this action had the effect of keeping many troops in the barracks and preventing them from going to the polls. President Chen's final margin of victory in the election was tiny, which contributed to Pan-Blue suspicions that the mysterious assassination attempt was staged as part of a plot to aid the president's reelection campaign. Tang Yeou-ming, the defense minister, was rumored to have collaborated with retired KMT generals to coordinate a wave of resignations by the top brass in protest of such a conspiracy. President Chen responded by accusing Tang Yeou-ming and the KMT of staging a "soft coup" attempt. Making things worse, in the process of the subsequent court trial against Tang Yeou-ming, his successor, Lee Jye, was called to testify, and he chose to stand with President Chen. As a result, the protocol for national security emergencies during national elections became a highly politicized and extremely sensitive issue.

After the controversy surrounding the shooting incident subsided, the MND further tightened restrictions on the military's political participation. All active-duty military officers and soldiers were forbidden from participating in any kind of political activities, including taking part in political discussions online, either at work or after work. The DPP vice defense ministers attempted to set an example by not participating in party meetings and election rallies. In addition, the non-DPP defense ministers who had retired from the military to take up the post went the extra mile by not only abstaining from political activities but also renouncing their KMT party membership. While these steps were encouraging from the perspective of civilian control, they did the right thing for the wrong reasons: they abstained from politics mostly because they still thought of themselves as military officers who ought to uphold political neutrality, rather than as civilians holding a nonpartisan position.[18]

The MND responded to concerns that such strict regulation would strip the military of their right to political participation by arguing that it was all but impossible to distinguish working hours from after hours, since military personnel were on call twenty-four hours a day and seven days a week.[19] This was an odd explanation, but it was surprisingly acceptable to many officers, who simply hoped to retain political neutrality in their profession. The MND, in fact, implemented the requirements thoroughly, imposing punishments in several cases of officer participation in anti–Chen Shui-bian rallies and the 2008 presidential election campaign.

The attempted shifts in the military's formal ethos also became swept up in the fierce conflicts between the Pan-Green and Pan-Blue camps over identity politics. The MND found itself caught in a dilemma. On one side, many members of the ruling DPP advocated for greater "Taiwanization" and pushed hard to have the armed forces formally identify with "Taiwan" rather than the "Republic of China." On the other side, legislators from the Pan-Blue camp criticized military officials for "appeasing" the partisan demands of the DPP government and violating their constitutional mandate to protect the Republic of China. Faced with these conflicting pressures, the MND eventually developed a nuanced position, stating that the mission of the armed forces was to protect those living on the island of Taiwan. In this way, the MND struck a balance between the two competing national identities by drawing on Janowitz's concept of social responsibility and obscuring the nation's political and geographic identities.[20] By and large, politicization of this kind originated externally from civilian politicians instead of from inside the barracks. It is worth noting that before the competing positions held by the Pan-Green and Pan-Blue camps gradually converged toward the equation of Taiwan with the Republic of China, the armed forces were quite successful in keeping this highly sensitive and politicized controversy from undermining military cohesiveness. Moreover, by the end of Chen Shui-bian's presidency, the armed forces had embraced the order to discard the Sun Yat-sen ideology of the Three Principles of the People and loyalty to a supreme leader, thereby simplifying the formal military ethos to a combination of honor, responsibility, and loyalty to the nation-state.

In addition to the sensitive issue of military ideology, seemingly mundane changes in military doctrine also became flashpoints in the identity-driven contestation that characterized the Chen Shui-bian era. The attempt to shift to a more offensive force posture by prioritizing "effective deterrence" over "firm defense" raised concerns from both the United States and the opposition camp about the DPP government's intentions and its possible antagonistic effects on China. In response, the US government reportedly blocked the export of critical parts for an indigenous cruise missile under development at the Military Armaments Bureau–affiliated Chung-Shan Institute of Science and Technology. Yet this strategic turn was not really a new direction. Historically, offensive measures have always been a component of Taiwan's military posture. Although the KMT regime changed strategy to prioritize defense of the island in the mid-1960s, military research and development (R&D) and procurement of offensive and deterrent weaponry continued throughout the Chiang Kai-shek, Chiang Ching-kuo, and Lee Teng-hui eras. From this perspective, neither the supposed strategic reorientation nor the emphasis on procurement and military R&D were a significant change for the armed forces.

As far as civil-military relations and, in particular, depoliticization issues are concerned, the key questions are who made the decision to go offensive and what role did the armed forces play in this turn of strategic direction, to the extent there was one? The SPD and IAO took no initiative in advanced planning but instead simply took orders from the defense minister, who in turn took directives either from the military meetings with the president or from the National Security Council under the president's authorization. Although the switch to an offensive strategy aligned with the corporate interests of certain elements within the armed forces, corporate interests were less of a driving force than military indoctrination that required the armed forces to prepare for the worst and fight when ordered to. Thus, incorporating offensive action into strategic plans was one of the requirements of professionalism. Debatable as it may be, the military hardly crossed the line of political neutrality by merely following the strategic shift and making necessary changes to official doctrine.

Most civilians and military officials agree that what most divides civilian politicians and civil society is not the existence of the threat posed by China but determining the best approach to tackling the China threat. During the eight years of Chen Shui-bian's presidency, the opposition Pan-Blue camp saw China's rise as presenting a mixture of threats and opportunities; thus, they advocated minimizing the threats while maximizing the opportunities by reducing unnecessary provocations and improving cross-Strait communication. Given its status quo posture, the Pan-Blue camp viewed the DPP's shift to a more offensive strategic plan as provocative and unnecessary, calculated either to further the DPP's hidden independence agenda or to aid its election campaigns.

As a consequence, the debates over procurement budgets for US arms packages, which had not attracted much opposition before the Chen era, increasingly led to highly politicized confrontations in the Legislative Yuan (LY). The Pan-Blue camp's majority in the legislature allowed it to block a large special budget for weapons procurement from the United States and prevent its passage. In response, the DPP resorted to calling a referendum on the issue to coincide with the 2004 presidential election; this action, however, was motivated more by identity politics and electoral considerations than by genuine concern about the arms package. The referendum failed because the threshold for passage required the participation of an absolute majority of all registered voters; a Pan-Blue boycott of the referendum ensured that it fell far short of the turnout requirement. Ironically, part of the arms package was later approved by the LY as the result of a consensus reached between the US government and the KMT, thereby ushering in a gradual bipartisan convergence of positions on procurement issues.

In general, the military played a passive-aggressive role in the battles over the procurement budget. The MND was initially most upset about the skyrocketing price of the arms package, and its advocacy was limited because of these financial concerns. As a form of silent protest, Tang Yeou-ming kept the revised proposal in the MND rather than sending it back to the LY. In Chen Shui-bian's second term, however, Lee Jye was promoted as defense minister and pressured by the president to do whatever it took to get the procurement budget passed in the LY. Instead of beginning with a bipartisan public hearing or debate in the LY, however, the military's political commissar system became involved in a public relations (PR) campaign, which quickly triggered accusations of impropriety. In addition, some high-ranking military officers, under pressure from the president and defense minister, also began lobbying Pan-Blue legislators. Yet both the PR campaign and the lobbying efforts yielded very limited success, all at the cost of the military's becoming embroiled in domestic political conflicts. The military's complaints about unreasonably high prices for weapons, which were based on professional expertise, were less credible to the Pan-Green camp precisely because of the legacy of subjective, partisan control under the KMT regime.

Nevertheless, there was a silver lining in the storm over depoliticization: democratic norms gradually took root within the military. The bargaining process over the arms package offered the armed forces a great opportunity to learn to exert their influence in democratic ways, either through a PR campaign or through lobbying in the LY. Moreover, although the legislature's defense oversight capabilities grew only slowly, by the end of the Chen era, the leaking of insider information to the media, legislators, and nongovernmental organization watchdogs helped serve as an additional check on subjective control.

Most unauthorized information released from the military involved human rights violations, procurement controversies, or personnel promotions. Although leaks about procurement usually occurred because of conflicts between rival companies competing for arms contracts, those involving high-ranking personnel decisions often had to do with institutional regulations and the professional background of officers. For instance, President Chen was criticized for violating personnel regulations and norms by fast-tracking the promotion of officers in the so-called A-Bian Family faction.[21] The most prominent instance of this was his appointment of ethnic Taiwanese officers to lead the presidential guard and their subsequent rapid ascension through the ranks. At the beginning of his presidency, President Chen favored ethnic Taiwanese generals for most key positions, including the chief of the general staff, general service commanders, and chief of the presidential guards. And yet Chen was not really departing from precedent with these appointments. The promotion of ethnic Taiwanese over mainlander generals was an unstated policy dating back to the late Chiang Ching-kuo era, and all presidents since Chiang Kai-shek had practiced the accelerated promotion of chiefs of the presidential guard. President Chen appears to have taken advantage of this tradition to strengthen his control over the armed forces.

More problematic is that institutionalized personnel practices were weakened when particular generals gained promotions because of their personal connections to the president, rather than because of career experience and performance. Once the regulations on term and tenure limitations were bent to allow the promotion of specific generals with close ties to the president, those officers most eager for promotions were incentivized to take more partisan stances and to seek out opportunities to demonstrate their political correctness. While there may have been a few instances of this kind of behavior at the beginning of the Chiang Ching-kuo and Lee Teng-hui presidencies, promotion of politically demonstrative officers had become common by the end of President Chen's second term, weakening the military's professionalism.

The most serious criticism levied by military officers against President Chen was that he undermined the nationalization project through his personnel and promotion policies. The formal rules and informal norms of tenure and promotion, which were developed in part to enhance civilian control over the military, also provided the president a means to build a faction of ambitious officers within the armed forces who were principally loyal to him. When Chen was later sentenced to jail for embezzlement, there were numerous accusations that officers had secured early promotions by bribing the president; however, the MND's internal investigations found no confirmation.[22]

In fact, the real problem in President Chen's relations with the military was not that his personnel decisions contributed to a subculture of cronyism but that he continued the legacy of subjective political control, using whatever means were most convenient to strengthen his own authority over the armed forces. In the end, civilian control that sustains or exacerbates the politicization of the military hinders, rather than helps, the broader process of democratic consolidation.

Intelligence Institutionalization: Depoliticization and Securitization

At the beginning of Chen Shui-bian's first term, the challenge of intelligence reform was framed as a need to "institutionalize" (*fazhihua*) the intelligence services rather than "nationalize" (*guojiahua*) them. Yet even at the end of the Chen era, there was no consensus among political elites in Taiwan about *how* intelligence gathering and security planning should be institutionalized.[23] The main point of contention was the degree to which the intelligence services should be accountable not only to the president but also to other democratic institutions, particularly the legislature.

The Debate over Depoliticization

Under the Chen administration, there were two approaches to reform of Taiwan's intelligence services. The first emphasized the depoliticization of the security apparatus, in parallel with an effort to foster a nonpartisan, fully professional military. Given the security state's fearsome history as the KMT's primary instrument for political repression, revamping the intelligence-gathering mission to focus on foreign rather than domestic threats was a chief concern of the DPP. A national security account scandal within the NSB that made headlines at the beginning of Chen's first term added pressure to increase transparency in the intelligence services and strengthen their legal and legislative oversight.

One approach was to institutionalize formal oversight of the intelligence and security agencies by other branches of government, especially the Legislative Yuan. The Intelligence Working Regulation Laws (IWRLs) that govern the security apparatus stipulate that the NSB should coordinate and manage the intelligence operations of the Investigative Bureau under the Justice Ministry, the Military Intelligence Bureau under the MND, the Coast Guard Administration, the Military Police Command under the MND, and the Police Administration under the Interior Ministry. Under Taiwan's dual-executive system, the Executive Yuan is accountable to both the Legislative Yuan and the president. Therefore, those security agencies under the Executive Yuan are also subject to formal oversight by the LY. While the NSB is under the direction of the president, it is still obliged to report to the LY, because the NSB is the leading intelligence service that coordinates and directs all other security and intelligence agencies.

The other approach centered on the provision of legal authority for intelligence activities, with much less attention paid to democratic accountability and depoliticization. This approach characterized changes to the National Security Council (NSC), which successfully resisted attempts by the legislature to monitor its activities. By law, the NSC is a presidential advisory body. As such, NSC advisers argued that they were political appointees accountable only to the president and therefore exempt from legislative oversight. At the end of President Chen's first term, a new NSC Organization Law was adopted, expanding the NSC's official research capacity. In addition to civilian national security advisers, the NSC now includes research staff from the civil service, as well as military and intelligence officers.

Although the NSC under Chen had no capacity to collect and analyze intelligence, the national security advisers and the research staff in the NSC still directed intelligence collection and received compiled intelligence reports. The NSC drew on this intelligence and information to draft strategic plans and policy directives for the president's reference. This advisory role, along with the NSC's affiliation with the Office of the President rather than the Executive Yuan, meant that it remained beyond the reach of the Legislative Yuan.

The comparison of the NSC with the NSB is instructive. The NSC coordinated and directed all intelligence services and agencies but claimed an exclusion from legislative oversight. The NSB enjoyed a leading position in the intelligence community, but it was a nonpartisan body subject to monitoring by the LY. In contrast, as the body tasked with serving the president directly, the NSC's reach sprawled into the Executive Yuan, yet it remained unaccountable to the legislature. Nor was the NSC required to be a nonpartisan body: its policymaking orientation ensured that it was closely associated with the presidential administration's political goals. As an organization created to bridge the dual executive structures specified in the ROC constitution, the NSC, in essence, existed in an underinstitutionalized legal gray area.

Given the tiny size of the NSC's personnel and budget, its institutional influence appeared, on the surface, to be no match for the Investigative Bureau in the Ministry of Justice or the Military Intelligence Bureau. Yet there is more than meets the eye here. Each and every NSC appointee, the secretary-general included, was a political appointee. During the Chen administration, this essentially meant that the NSC's influence waxed and waned depending on the personal influence of individual security advisers with the president. The NSC's operations also varied with the preferences and personality of the NSC secretary-general. In the beginning, each adviser reported directly to President Chen, bypassing the secretary-general. Reprising its role in the Lee Teng-hui administration, the NSC's initial focus under Chen was on crisis management and secret diplomacy. However, the NSC's reach and mission expanded considerably under President Chen to include strategic defense planning and diplomatic outreach, all justified under the guise of national security. Thus, the legislative expansion of the NSC's formal role and resources actually reinforced its tendency toward secrecy and contributed further to the politicization of intelligence.

A Mixed Picture of Depoliticization

The model of an apolitical intelligence apparatus demands strict political neutrality during all parts of the intelligence cycle, from collection, to analysis, to distribution of intelligence. It is inappropriate for the intelligence agencies to attempt to influence how end users employ this intelligence while also participating in domestic political conflicts.

The inauguration of President Chen created new problems for intelligence work at all stages of this cycle. It was widely rumored, for instance, that military intelligence lost contact with agents deployed or recruited in the mainland because those agents distrusted the DPP administration's pro-independence leanings and became disillusioned with their mission. Responding to this wave of agent defections, the Military Intelligence Bureau resorted to a greater reliance on Taiwanese businesspeople for information. The lack of professional training and ethics among these new agents severely limited the bureau's intelligence-gathering successes. Yet these defections merely continued a long decline in the quality of intelligence provided by Military Intelligence Bureau agents. One can trace this decline all the way back to the Chiang Ching-kuo presidency, as the capacity of first-generation agents left behind after 1949 gradually withered away. The public release of highly sensitive intelligence about China's missile exercises during the 1996 presidential campaign, which led to the exposure of high-level sources in the Chinese Communist Party, contributed to another wave of intelligence losses. Given these circumstances, even military intelligence officers themselves cast doubt on the effectiveness of the remaining human intelligence in China that was available to the Chen administration.[24]

Because of the mutual suspicion between the opposition parties and the intelligence community, the NSB made it a standard practice to swear political neutrality during election campaigns and to brief both presidential candidates about the latest intelligence on Taiwan's national security environment. This briefing was, in fact, an exemplary model of nonpartisan analysis and distribution of intelligence, and it helped the intelligence services to demonstrate their organizational commitment to a democratic and apolitical mind-set. Nevertheless, partisan suspicions about the collection, distribution, and employment of intelligence remained. Eavesdropping by the Investigative Bureau of the Ministry of Justice and by the Police Administration for counterintelligence and law enforcement purposes continued to raise concerns about the selective use of information gathered this way for the ruling party's benefit. For the entirety of Chen Shui-bian's presidency, Pan-Blue legislators and politicians regularly voiced suspicions that their phones were wiretapped—much as DPP politicians had done during the previous KMT regime.[25]

Compounding these suspicions, in 2005, President Chen accused PFP chair James Soong of holding a secret meeting in the United States with Chen Yunlin, the chair of China's Association for Relations Across the Taiwan Straits. President Chen implied that his accusation was grounded in national intelligence reports, though it later turned out that the claim was based on inaccurate intelligence collected by the Investigative Bureau, which merely cited a newspaper report. The incident was a good demonstration of how the bureau's intelligence gathering, analysis, distribution, and final use remained politicized under President Chen. It was also a serious blow to the Investigative Bureau's reputation and further eroded opposition confidence in the bureau's political neutrality.

The Soong-Chen incident was especially damaging because the Investigative Bureau's strong suit had long been domestic electoral politics, not international political surveillance. Its involvement in partisan conflict in the James Soong case increased concern among the Pan-Blue opposition that the bureau was engaged in domestic intelligence gathering for the ruling DPP's advantage. With a dense network of local posts and agents and their related connections and informants, the Investigative Bureau had a systematic mechanism for forecasting election vote totals that was second to none—one that the KMT itself had built up and relied on during its long time in power. In one of the many ironies of this era, the Pan-Blue parties began to question whether this information was now being circulated and used exclusively by the DPP, putting them at an electoral disadvantage. The Investigative Bureau openly denied the accusations and only admitted that the election forecasts had been, in accordance with the IWRL, distributed to relevant agencies for their reference. But whether the NSB turned the election forecasts over to President Chen was actually beyond the Investigative Bureau's control.[26] From this perspective, by following the dictates of the IWRL, the bureau found a middle way to balance between the competing goals of remaining nonpartisan while still being accountable to elected civilian authorities.

During the Chen administration, the NSB and the Investigative Bureau were the two agencies most frequently criticized for their surveillance and eavesdropping practices. High-level officials from both bureaus denied any illegal wiretapping both in public and in interviews with this author. Typically, the police and prosecution investigators were the ones equipped to carry out such missions, and the NSB was not directly in charge of wiretapping implementation. By law, all eavesdropping had to be approved by the agency's director and authorized by either prosecutors or judges; otherwise, such activity was a felony. Both the NSB and the Investigative Bureau insisted that their security ethics placed the highest priority on abiding by the law. As one NSB vice director unequivocally stated, "No public servants are willing to break the law and risk their pensions in executing illegal operations for their supervisors."[27]

In addition to the agencies in charge of internal security, one cannot help but question whether foreign intelligence bodies of the MND became involved in domestic intelligence operations. The MND's Military Intelligence Bureau and the Office for Electronic and Information Development possessed an enormous capacity to tap into phone lines, cell phones, and electronic signals originating as far away as Xinjiang in the Chinese mainland. The Military Intelligence Bureau's monitoring equipment was inherited from the Taiwan Garrison Command after the end of the martial law years, and its capabilities were upgraded in President Chen's second term.[28] The Office of Electronic Technology in the Military Intelligence Bureau was believed to have inherited the Garrison Command's responsibility for wiretapping domestic politicians and security officers. Apart from phone lines and cell phones, the Office for Electronic and Information Development reportedly competed with the NSB, the Investigative Bureau, and the Police Administration in electronic warfare, and it probably conducted Internet surveillance and espionage as well. The Office for Electronic and Information Development claimed that its mission was solely to monitor mainland China's military tactical intelligence, and the Military Intelligence Bureau denied accusations of domestic spying using similar logic;[29] yet some intelligence officers within the intelligence community cast doubt on these claims and suggested otherwise.[30]

During Defense Minister Lee Jye's tenure, the political commissar system's internal inspection and counterintelligence missions were replaced by a newly established Center for United Surveillance—a team that comprised, in large part, members of the Counterintelligence General Platoon. Yet the center's claim to expertise in counterintelligence was challenged when the intelligence office of the Coast Guard Administration (CGA), which was previously under the Garrison Command, exposed espionage inside the MND's Office for Electronic and Information Development. The MND was notified by the NSB after the CGA

reported the leak. In addition, amid the partisan battle over the arms procurement package, several legislators blamed the wiretapping installed by
the Center for United Surveillance for leaks of sensitive information from
their offices. Lee Jye's successor, General Lee Tien-yu, who had experience as the political warfare commander of the air force, acknowledged
the center's poor performance and decided to disband it, returning the
inspection and counterintelligence missions back to the political commissar system.

Securitization

As identity conflicts and partisan politics have become obstacles to
depoliticizing the security forces, one strategy has been to raise the
specter of external security threats as a way to foster domestic unity. Yet
when those threats emanate primarily from China, the same politicized
identity issues also come into play. Thus, during the later years of the
Chen Shui-bian era, the security forces pursued a strategy of hyping a
diverse array of nontraditional national security threats beyond the cross-
Strait military balance. This approach of "securitizing" nonmilitary issues
produced a marriage of convenience between the NSC and the armed
forces. As such, it benefited both the military's corporate interest in
upgrading capabilities and readiness and the NSC's desire to expand its
policy reach deeper into foreign affairs and defense.

The employment of health diplomacy is one example. In responding to
the avian bird flu crisis of 2005–2006, the NSC skillfully applied the concept of "comprehensive security" to strengthen its control over domestic
crisis management mechanisms, while at the same time using a human
security justification to push for Taiwan to join the World Health Organization. Another example is the NSC-led Yu Shan Political-Military exercises,
war games that started with the premise of a surprise Chinese "decapitation
strike" aimed at eliminating Taiwan's political and military leadership.
Although certain details of the scenario were widely ridiculed by military
officers as unrealistic or impractical, the security adviser in charge insisted
that the drills be taken seriously as a good training exercise.[31]

Both the NSC's National Security White Paper and the MND's
National Defense White Paper emphasized that the greatest security
threat to Taiwan was from a surprise decapitation strike by China. Nevertheless, the armed forces and certain elements of the internal security
forces took advantage of the NSC's discussion of terrorist threats to justify an expansion of rapid-response special forces, including enlargement
of special ops forces among the military police, paratroopers, the marines,
the CGA, the national police force, and, most strikingly, the military

police garrison responsible for guarding the Presidential Hall, the capital, and national airports. In addition, with the impetus provided by the National Defense Education Act, the MND's civilian vice minister pushed to incorporate a "multiple threats" doctrine, emphasizing preparation for comprehensive mobilization of the security forces into tours, diplomatic and military exchanges, public speeches, and even boot camps.

Conclusion

This chapter has examined the evolving challenges of civil-military relations during Chen Shui-bian's presidency. Deeply divisive identity conflicts and partisan struggles combined to hinder the depoliticization of the security apparatus. Faced with these mounting political pressures, the armed forces and the intelligence services tended to respond by hyping security threats in an attempt to transcend partisan divides.

There is some reason for concern about this process of "depoliticization through securitization." The strategy of using external threats to foster domestic unity raises the specter of a police state, which is by no means new to Taiwan. The combination of the MND's national defense indoctrination at all levels of society with the NSC's political-military exercises is particularly alarming in light of previous Taiwanese history. These actions have echoes of the comprehensive warfare campaign implemented by the Garrison Command and the political-military joint exercises initiated by the so-called Liu Shao-kang Office in the late Chiang Ching-kuo era. Fortunately, at this point, most observers see little danger of Taiwan returning to a highly militarized police state, as the strengthening of representative institutions and the empowerment of civil society in a democratic Taiwan makes that outcome unlikely.

The bottom line is that the armed forces worked hard after the first transfer of power to find ways to transcend partisan confrontations and identity conflicts, thereby creating the political space and time to improve their own professionalism and readiness. Put simply, the armed forces tried to avoid questions about the circumstances under which they should fight. Instead, they used this breathing room to prepare for the worst fights they were likely to face. Given that Taiwan's armed forces still perceive traditional professionalism and objective control as orthodox, the question of whether the push to securitize nontraditional threats is reinforcing or undermining political neutrality in the armed forces is something to keep an eye on in the future.

Yet it is not at all clear that this emphasis on securitization will persist, especially given trends under the KMT's Ma Ying-jeou. Because the

Ma administration has stressed societal harmony, it is possible that a new pattern of civilian control over the security apparatus is taking root. Agreement on an accommodative national identity in Taiwan's consolidating democracy is likely to enable the development of a consensus on the country's strategic direction. This, in turn, should reduce politically motivated civilian interference with the security forces, and it should help deepen their commitment to the norm of political neutrality. In conclusion, much depends on how far the Ma Ying-jeou administration is ultimately able to go in mending political and social divisions in Taiwan.

Finally, as far as the security forces are concerned, the greatest negative legacy of the Chen era is the damage caused by his personalization of personnel decisions. Fixing this damage requires spelling out more explicitly the new military ethos of loyalty to the nation rather than to the party-state. It could also require restoring the formal term and tenure limits ignored by President Chen. Most promising, however, would be to continue efforts to institutionalize greater civilian participation in the security sector, perhaps aided by formal regulations that explicitly spell out the nonpartisan character of civilian appointees. Deepening the norm of nonpartisan civilian participation in the security apparatus is likely to provide the best way to balance presidential authority against the imperative of maintaining a professionalized and depoliticized military. The ultimate effect of the Ma Ying-jeou administration's policies on this issue is an important topic for future work.

Notes

1. Morris Janowitz, *The Professional Soldier: A Social and Political Portrait* (New York: Free Press, 1960); Samuel Huntington, *The Soldier and the State: The Theory and Politics of Civil-Military Relations* (Cambridge, MA: Harvard University Press, 1957).

2. Felipe Aguero, "Democratic Consolidation and the Military in Southern Europe and Latin America," in *The Politics of Democratic Consolidation: Southern Europe in Comparative Perspective,* ed. Richard Gunther, P. Nikiforos Diamandouros, and Hans-Jurgen Puhle (Baltimore, MD: Johns Hopkins University Press, 1995), 126.

3. Michael C. Desch, *Civilian Control of the Military: The Changing Security Environment* (Baltimore, MD: Johns Hopkins University Press, 1999), 13–14.

4. Michael C. Desch, "Threat Environments and Military Missions," in *Civil-Military Relations and Democracy,* ed. Larry Diamond and Marc F. Plattner (Baltimore, MD: Johns Hopkins University Press, 1996), 13–15.

5. Andrew Cottey, Tim Edmunds, and Anthony Forster, "The Second Generation Problematic: Rethinking Democracy and Civil-Military Relations," *Armed Forces and Society* 29 (Winter 2002): 31–56.

6. Janowitz, *The Professional Soldier,* 427.

7. Alfred Stepan, "The New Professionalism of Internal Warfare and Military Role Expansion," in *Authoritarian Brazil: Origins, Policies, and Future,* ed. Alfred Stepan (New Haven, CT: Yale University Press, 1973), 52.

8. Alfred Stepan, *Rethinking Military Politics: Brazil and the Southern Cone* (Princeton, NJ: Princeton University Press, 1988), 128–136.

9. On democratic professionalism, see Samuel J. Fitch, *The Armed Forces and Democracy in Latin America* (Baltimore, MD: Johns Hopkins University Press, 1998), 175–182.

10. Cottey, Edmunds, and Forster, "The Second Generation Problematic."

11. Interview with a senior political officer (retired) on October 24, 2007. The officer had been an aide of General Tang Yeou-ming present at the Yangmingshan meeting.

12. Retired General Swuai Hua-ming, interview with the author on June 13, 2007. Swuai was the leader and organizer of the study group. Doctor Chen Jing-fu, interview with the author on August 29, 2007.

13. That includes Dr. Michael Tsai himself, based on the author's interview with him in Taichung on August 16, 2007. At that time, he was seeking a party nomination as a candidate for the legislature. In February 2008, Tsai assumed the post of defense minister.

14. Interview with a retired general on May 24, 2007. He became a civilian high-ranking official in charge of MND's human resource affairs in 2004, and later assumed the head of MND's Department of Strategic Planning in 2015.

15. Interviews with two DPP security officials during the summer of 2007.

16. The author owes the idea of "chieftain" to Dr. York Chen.

17. Interview with a retired general and now a civilian high-ranking official in charge of MND's human resource affairs on May 24, 2007.

18. Based on interviews with retired military officers during the summer of 2007.

19. Interviews with Michael Tsai and York Chen during the summer of 2007.

20. General Chang Chiang-wen, interview with the author on November 7, 2007. Chang is a retired major general who once served as political warfare commander in the military policy command.

21. A-Bian is Chen Shui-bian's nickname.

22. See MND's Investigation Report on Anti-Corruption Action at http://www .mnd.gov.tw/UserFiles/File/%E9%80%B1%E5%B9%B4%E5%A0%B1%E5%91%8A %E6%91%98%E8%A6%81%E7%89%880407.pdf.

23. Lee Wen-chung (former DPP legislator), interview with the author on September 13, 2007.

24. Interviews with a senior military officer retired from military intelligence bureau, on June 8, 2007, and September 18, 2007. Interview with a retired military general from the MND's intelligence department, on September 15, 2007.

25. Su Chi, interview with the author on June 15, 2007. Dr. Su Chi was at that time a KMT legislator and later the secretary-general of the NSC during Ma Ying-jeou's presidency.

26. Tsuei Sheng-hsiang, interview with the author on July 23, 2007. Mr. Tsuei was the former vice director of the Investigative Bureau and retired in early 2007.

27. General Tsai De-sheng, interview with the author on July 12, 2007. General Tsai was the vice director of the NSB; the interview was conducted at the NSB headquarters in Yangmingshan.

28. Interview with a senior military officer, on August 10, 2007. The officer was retired from the Military Intelligence Bureau.

29. Feng Hsu, "Military Intelligence Bureau Denied the Use of Upgraded Equipment in Domestic Surveillance," *News Report from Central Agency,* October 11, 2005.

30. Interview with a retired military general who once served in the MND Office for Electronic and Information Development, on November 5, 2007. Interview with a senior military officer retired from the Military Intelligence Bureau, on August 10, 2007. Also see a news report released from a local newspaper in Taiwan regarding a Japanese magazine's interview with a senior military officer retired from the Military Intelligence Bureau, "Pang Da-wei as Whistle Blower," *United News Report,* Taipei, April 17, 2010.

31. York Chen, interview with the author on November 28, 2007. Dr. York Chen was at that time a national security adviser at the NSC. The interview was conducted in the Presidential Hall.

14

Troubled Waters: The Conflict over Cross-Strait Relations

Tse-Kang Leng

Ever since the release of Ye Jianying's nine-point proposal for peaceful reunification in 1981, the People's Republic of China (PRC) has promoted the establishment of the so-called Three Links—direct commercial, postal, and transportation links—as stepping-stones for closer bilateral relations with Taiwan. During the presidencies of Chiang Ching-kuo and Lee Teng-hui in the 1980s and 1990s, the Republic of China regime on Taiwan took a conservative approach toward establishing direct links with the other side of the Taiwan Strait, and little concrete changes were made. But as China's comprehensive power steadily increased, and after Taiwan and the PRC both joined the World Trade Organization (WTO) in 2002, pressure to open direct links rose. The responses of Taiwan's two most recent presidents, Chen Shui-bian of the Democratic Progressive Party (DPP) and Ma Ying-jeou of the Kuomintang (KMT), to this strategic environment—and to the Three Links issue, in particular—have been very different.

This chapter discusses the interplay of Taiwan's domestic politics and drive for integration into the global economy with cross-Strait economic relations. By focusing on continuity and change in Taiwan's Three Links policies, we can develop a better sense of the forces acting on cross-Strait relations. More than any other set of political issues, state policy on the Three Links has been the focal point for clashes between proglobalization and pro-isolationist camps in Taiwan. The establishment of direct commercial, postal, and transportation links between Taiwan and the PRC necessarily preceded other steps toward normalizing the cross-Strait relationship. Thus, the overall stakes were much higher for both proponents and opponents of cross-Strait integration than the seemingly apolitical issues involved, such as allowing direct air flights across the Strait. Examining the debates over the Three Links can also reveal how the forces of globalization have reshaped domestic political coalitions and empowered new subnational actors in Taiwan. Finally, a study of the Three Links exposes something new about the effects of cross-Strait developments on partisan politics—in this case, the political challenges faced and the costs borne not only by the DPP in attempting to resist the establishment of greater economic ties with the PRC, but also by the KMT in attempting to institutionalize cross-Strait exchanges.

Before focusing on current controversies, this chapter returns to the policies of the Chen Shui-bian era and traces the evolution of domestic political dilemmas posed by the Three Links. It also discusses the achievements of the Ma administration in Three Links policy and reviews the many remaining obstacles to the institutionalization of cross-Strait relations. Breakthroughs in the Three Links have enabled Taiwan to benefit from globalization and economic development in the PRC. However, political prudence and democratic inclusiveness are needed for the current Taiwanese leadership to consolidate these gains and strike an appropriate balance between different domestic interests.

Taiwan's Democratic Politics and the Dynamics of Cross-Strait Relations

The evolution of cross-Strait economic relations reflects Taiwan's democratization and the impact of globalization. Globalization brings with it a transformation of sovereignty and state power. As the literature on globalization and global change emphasizes, global networks created by capitalist agents can coexist with the sovereign state for long periods. In other words, the sovereign state will not "disappear" in an age of greater globalization; instead, it will adapt in the face of new environmental constraints. This transformative process creates new actors in both state and society, including within the business community, nongovernmental organizations, grassroots associations, and other quasi-state organizations.

The other side of the coin on global governance and democratization is the rising significance of local government and governance. The process of globalization involves a significant reallocation of economic coordination and steering functions away from the sovereign state, up to the international and down to the regional levels. But deregulation of cross-border economic activity should not be viewed simply as a loss of control by the state. National legal systems remain the main institutional arrangements through which guarantees of contract and property rights are enforced.[1]

In addition to highlighting the forces of decentralization in democracies in the era of globalization, scholars have also emphasized the importance of enhancing participation and improving the distributional outcomes of democratic regimes. For instance, David Held has argued that "cosmopolitan democracy" should lead to the creation of new political institutions that coexist within the state system. These institutions require regional or global initiatives that promote effectiveness and democratic legitimacy. Such arrangements can generate broad avenues of access for civic participation at national and regional levels.[2] Furthermore, as Christine Keating has argued, cosmopolitan democracy and global participation require a refined definition of the nature of "participation" itself.[3]

The nature of distributive justice in modern democracy is encapsulated in Hans Agne's symmetry principle—that is, democracy requires the distribution of the greatest amount of autonomy among the greatest number of people. The rise of a more global world complicates this logic: democracy also requires that people be included in political procedures to the extent that their decision yields the greatest amount of autonomy to the greatest number of people, while accounting for both those who are included and those who are excluded from the national polity, as well as for actions performed both individually and collectively.[4] On the interaction between globalization and democracy, Kathleen Schwartzman has argued that world-system processes are linked to national political dynamics through class conflict. In this view, domestic political structures become part of the evolving transnational fabric of economic relations.[5] As John Ralston Saul has noted, democracy requires a careful acknowledgment of reality and of our limitations, as well as a careful rebalancing of priorities, binding agreements, and the public good at the global level. These practical elements not only enable us to build the democratic nation-states but also will allow us to build stable, fair, citizen-based global arrangements.[6]

In addition to the effects of globalization and democratic change in Taiwan is the rising power of the People's Republic of China over the past two decades. The Taiwanese government's attempts to constrain economic relations with the PRC failed to stop the business community from using its own channels to enter the mainland Chinese market. In the 1990s, Taiwan's "no haste, be patient" policy (*jieji yongren*) led to the failure of strategic plans, such as the Asia Pacific Operations Center project, to transform Taiwan into a regional hub of service industries. Likewise, the Chen Shui-bian administration's approach to cross-Strait relations from 2000 to 2008 reflected the increasing radicalization of the

"Taiwanese independence line" and the prioritization of de jure independence over other goals. President Chen's policies led to the stagnation of cross-Strait economic interaction and aggravated political and military confrontations across the Taiwan Strait. At the same time, the Chen administration's hostility toward the PRC led to greater economic isolation and a steep decline in Taiwan's international competitiveness. Public discontent with Chen's cross-Strait policies rose significantly, particularly during his second term, from 2004 to 2008.

The second transfer of power in 2008 was widely interpreted as a reflection of voters' disdain toward the Chen administration's antiglobalization and anti-China policies. In short, the consequence of the DPP's push for Taiwanese independence under Chen Shui-bian was the further isolation of Taiwan's economic system and the escalation of tension across the Taiwan Strait. Linking Taiwan's liberal political order to independence, in reality, weakened the dynamism of its democracy. Thus, the Ma Ying-jeou administration's top priority upon assuming office was to reverse this economic and political isolation by increasing connections with the PRC. Although successful in his first term, this strategy has, in Ma's second term, encountered stiff political headwinds.

Local Initiatives to Push the Three Links Before 2008

The Three Links issue is closely related to the increasing economic importance of Taiwan's major urban areas, especially the greater Taipei region of northern Taiwan. As a complementary approach to the Sassen/Friedmann tradition of studying the internal social and political structure of global cities, scholars such as Peter Taylor have used quantitative data to analyze the external connections of these cities.[7] Taylor has argued that the relations between "world cities" should be thought of as an interlocking network joined through the everyday business of global service firms. These firms are the catalysts of the process that creates the world city network. To evaluate this claim, Taylor collected data on eighty global service firms and their offices across 315 cities worldwide in two waves in 2000 and 2004. From these data, he determined the "network connectivity" of individual cities, measuring their integration into the world economy. According to Taylor's report, of the four cities of Shanghai, Hong Kong, Beijing, and Taipei, Shanghai had the greatest increase in global connectivity from 2000 to 2004, while Taipei had the greatest decline.[8]

According to a different survey of economic competitiveness in Chinese cities conducted in 2007 by the Chinese Academy of Social Sciences, Taipei ranked second, one place after Hong Kong. Shanghai ranked third.

Taipei's advantages, as indicated in the report, included high-tech development, infrastructure, human resources, and amenities. Hong Kong continued to demonstrate its strength in global financial management and other service-oriented industries, while Shanghai's potential as a major consumer market and its strategic location put it in third place.[9]

The implication of both surveys is that in order for Taiwan to main tain its international competitiveness in global capital and human resources, enhancing the global reach and connectivity of Taipei would be crucial to its future development prospects. One reason that Taipei's international connectivity ranking declined in the early 2000s was the lack of direct air links with the other side of the Taiwan Strait. According to various estimates, lifting the ban on direct air links would save transportation and related costs of more than 3.8 billion new Taiwan (NT) dollars for Taiwanese firms annually.[10] In 2007, an engineer in a major Taiwanese information technology (IT) company in Shanghai indicated that without direct air links, Taiwanese providers of upstream IT raw material and semifinished products had no choice but to move to the Chinese mainland. The major concern for these firms was to provide "just-in-time" services to major IT finished product manufacturers, such as notebook computer original design manufacturing companies, in order to meet the requirements of international brand holders. The establishment of direct air links, he argued, would encourage the semifinished product manufacturers to "keep their roots in Taiwan" and take advantage of these links to transport high value-added goods to China.[11] This argument was contrary to the official policy line under the DPP, which stated that opening direct air links would have a "hollowing out" effect on Taiwanese high-tech industries.

After the KMT's Ma Ying-jeou became mayor of Taipei in 1998, the Taipei administration pushed hard for the establishment of direct air links with mainland Chinese cities, in direct contrast to Chen Shui-bian's approach to the Three Links issues. Ma argued that air links would help make Taipei a "regional springboard," allowing international capital and human resources to enter the global market. Without cross-Strait links, on the other hand, Taipei could only be oriented toward a regional market for domestic consumption.[12] Ma also argued that direct air links should be decoupled from other sensitive political issues in Taiwan, such as the independence-unification question. Thus, the highest priority of the Taipei city administration was to make Taipei "a base of Taiwanese business people for global expansion."[13] Reflecting this vision, Mayor Ma proposed direct air routes between Songshan Airport in Taipei and Hongqiao Airport in Shanghai. This direct route would connect two "domestic" airports in the downtown areas of both cities and shorten total travel time between them from seven to two hours. Under this proposal, Songshan Airport could also add more international connections to other regional airports in places such as Hong Kong and Macau. Taoyuan International Airport, the existing international airport in greater Taipei, could serve as the major hub for longer-distance flights of over two hours, such as flights to Beijing and other mainland Chinese cities.

Ma's successor Hau Lung-pin continued to push the Songshan Airport project and the plan to market Taipei as the center of a region based on a "two-hour economic circle within greater China." To build support for the plan, the Hau administration emphasized Taipei's advantages in high-quality human resources and advanced research institutions and universities, as well as the presence of major scientific-based clusters such as Neihu Technology Park and Nankang Software Park. Hau also stressed Taipei's strategic air-traffic position among the Asia-Pacific economies. In order to expand Taipei's accessibility to international supply chains and service sectors, Hau argued, it was crucial to establish direct air links across the Strait. He also stated that Taipei's drive for direct air links could eventually expand beyond cross-Strait, city-to-city connections.[14] The upgrading and reorientation of Songshan Airport to serve cross-Strait flights would enhance Taipei's role as a pivotal hub for major manufacturing regions in China's southeastern coastal areas, including the booming Yangtze River Delta and Pearl River Delta.

Business associations in Taiwan also raised their voices in support of closer economic interactions with the PRC. For instance, for more than a decade, the Chinese National Federation of Industries (CNFI) consistently promoted the idea of the Three Links and of closer economic ties with the Chinese mainland. In the CNFI's terms, the Taiwanese government needed to adopt a policy of "circulating water" to replace the "birdcage" strategy maintained by the Chen Shui-bian administration. Direct air links would serve to promote circulation. To increase "brain and technology circulation," the CNFI suggested the construction of "double golden triangles" of high-tech development. These golden triangles would incorporate Taipei, Shanghai, Silicon Valley, and Tokyo into Taiwan's grand strategy for innovation and development. In its annual policy report, CNFI also advocated the creation of a Cross-Strait Economic Zone that would promote the free flow of capital, commodities, and human resources. The precondition for such an area, however, was the establishment of direct air transportation. For CNFI, following this economic framework would enable Taiwan to enhance its position as a global logistics center. Such a plan could also transform Taiwan into an attractive base for ethnic Chinese business communities operating around the world.[15]

In addition to the interaction of local governments with central authorities, other nonstate actors with global reach also lobbied and put pressure on the Chen administration to establish the Three Links. Taipei's foreign business community, for instance, consistently promoted the idea of direct air links. Starting in 1996, the American Chamber of Commerce (AmCham) compiled an annual Taiwan White Paper, which every year focused on the importance of regularizing the flow of people, goods and services, and investments across the Taiwan Strait, with special emphasis on the value of direct transportation links for domestic and multinational business efficiency and effectiveness. In 2007, the European Chamber of Commerce in Taipei (ECCT) published a position paper that it called a "road map to renewed prosperity in Taiwan." Among the ten suggested steps for reform, the first priority was to "normalize cross-Straits economic relations" and allow operations of direct cargo flights and sea freight.[16] The ECCT also supported then-candidate Ma Ying-jeou's proposal to expand Taiwan's logistics center capabilities, which included turning Kaohsiung into a free port with direct shipping links to mainland China, as well as the development of the Taoyuan International Air City.[17] Similarly, a former member of the Canadian business community who had been transferred to Shanghai also indicated the importance of direct transportation links to international business activities in Taipei.

Thus, from the perspective of the foreign business community, the Three Links in general and direct air links in particular needed to be separated from the bilateral cross-Strait political context. The establishment of direct air links would upgrade and enhance Taiwan's ability to participate fully in the global economy. Foreign business communities would be able to take advantage of direct air routes and promote Taiwan, in general, and Taipei, in particular, as a commercial and human resource hub in the Asia-Pacific region.[18]

When AmCham's lobbying failed to receive a positive response from the Chen administration, the group argued in its 2007 White Paper,

> Nothing can be said that hasn't been said repeatedly before about how the failure to act on this issue has isolated, constrained, and damaged Taiwan's economy. So on cross-Strait links, the AmCham message to the Taiwanese government remains clear and unequivocal: Just do it![19]

After Ma Ying-jeou's victory in the 2008 presidential election, foreign business associations continued to express their concerns about cross-Strait relations—in particular, the Three Links issues. For instance, Guy Wittich, chief executive officer of the ECCT, argued that the lack of direct business and transportation links had kept many European businesses away from Taiwan and that the European business community held great expectations for the new president to implement direct air links between Taiwan and the PRC.[20] Wittich expected that the direct air links issue would have a "spillover effect," expanding opportunities for the international business community in other sectors as well. In a speech delivered to AmCham at about the same time, Stephen Young, the director of the American Institute in Taiwan (AIT), noted that the US government had long championed closer economic and trade relations between the two sides of the Taiwan Strait. In addition, the US side hoped that direct links would soon be established and made accessible to overseas passengers and carriers, too.[21]

The DPP Administration and the Stalemate over the Three Links

In the early years of the Chen Shui-bian administration, many observers expected the DPP government to achieve a major breakthrough in cross-Strait relations, especially after Taiwan joined the WTO in 2002. The dual accessions of Taiwan and the PRC to the WTO created a paradox: although both sides had not changed their fundamental policies on cross-Strait issues, many of their citizens and firms had managed to create close and mutually beneficial economic relationships with one another. And yet, government policy was hindering, rather than aiding, the development of these relationships. Continued government restrictions prevented managerial and technical professionals from the PRC from flowing into Taiwan and reshaping its employment structure. In addition, limitations on cross-Strait trade, especially on imports from China, prevented Taiwan from fully specializing in sectors in which it had a comparative advantage. The Three Links and closer economic relations were expected to help Taiwan incorporate the Chinese mainland into its strategic regional economic policy. In addition, collaboration between the governments across the Taiwan Strait under the WTO framework could expand to areas such as stabilizing the exchange rate, controlling financial crises, combating financial fraud, and so on. Other manufacturing sectors could also benefit from closer economic links. For instance, since the major automakers in Taiwan and the PRC had formed joint ventures with foreign automakers, the auto industries in Taiwan and the Chinese mainland had been gradually integrated into the global automobile industry. If Taiwan and the PRC could find a solution to their disagreements under the WTO framework, more cross-Strait cooperation between firms in the automobile industry value chain would follow.[22]

For closer economic interaction to occur under the WTO framework, however, the facilitation of direct air, sea, and postal links was the key.

Yet the DPP's politicization of cross-Strait exchanges pushed the economic trends in the opposition direction. The basic premise of the DPP's Three Links policy was that cross-Strait relations posed a potential threat to Taiwan's sovereignty and integrity. During an interview with the *Financial Times* in 2006, President Chen Shui-bian stated bluntly,

> Taiwan is absolutely not China's tributary or border region. This point is very important; this is absolutely basic. We must not for the sake of commercial profit or the convenience of contact give up Taiwan's separate identity. We must insist on Taiwan's own identity, Taiwan first. . . . China's united front tactics attempt to marginalize us, localize us, take away our sovereignty, and bypass our government. These are all changing the status quo, destroying the status quo.[23]

Chen's remarks indicated that direct air links were a "central" issue to his administration, instead of a "local" concern. Refusing the PRC's proposal of direct air links, in Chen's view, was to preserve Taiwan's sovereignty, pride, and integrity.

Beijing's position on the Three Links was released by Vice Premier Qian Qichen in 2003. Qian indicated that the Three Links were a "domestic affair" in nature and that negotiations about direct air links were not the same as state-to-state talks on international air routes. However, since the Three Links were fundamentally about economic cooperation between Taiwan and the PRC, cross-Strait talks on related matters were to be considered technical and commercial in nature, not political. Thus, it was not necessary to explicitly acknowledge the "One China principle" as a precondition for negotiations.[24] Beijing also suggested that before the establishment of direct air links, both sides should expand the existing charter flight services between mainland Chinese and Taiwanese cities and develop a more comprehensive plan to cover major Chinese festivals and weekends. Flight destinations could also be expanded to more coastal cities on the mainland. Based on past practices, the establishment of direct air links could be negotiated by air industry associations on the two sides of the Taiwan Strait. From Beijing's perspective, the "association to association" model was the best way to solve the deadlock without involving too many political controversies.[25]

Despite this outreach, the DPP administration placed the blame for the stalemate in Three Links talks on the PRC. Taiwan's cabinet-level agency for overseeing cross-Strait relations, the Mainland Affairs Council (MAC), appealed to Beijing to stop prioritizing political considerations and to promptly resume negotiations on the many technical matters related to cross-Strait economic and trade exchanges. The MAC chair, Chen Mingtong, claimed that beginning in January 2007, Beijing had unilaterally raised new political obstacles in an attempt to influence Taiwan's election results, preventing both sides from concluding negotiations on opening up tourism in Taiwan to mainland Chinese tourists and on the implementation of passenger and cargo charter flights. However, he also claimed that the hard line taken by the DPP had forced Beijing to abandon the One China principle in negotiating charter flights during Chinese festivals. The DPP's position had also compelled Beijing to face the reality that Taiwanese people wanted to self-identify as Taiwanese and to abandon threats in favor of soft appeals in its Taiwan policy. One of the major achievements of the DPP administration, the MAC asserted, was to force the PRC to accept the principle of "peace and development" as the common language across the Taiwan Strait.[26]

Chen Shui-bian used a similar form of expression to condemn Beijing as the major obstacle in cross-Strait relations. He argued that the PRC had been politicizing the Three Links negotiations because Beijing suspected that the introduction of direct flights would only serve to boost the DPP administration. Chen argued that the root of the problem was that the PRC was bent on marginalizing Taiwan and treating it as a local government, in an attempt to negate Taiwan's authority and its national sovereignty.[27]

The DPP administration's official policy on the direct air links issue was to insist on the precondition that they be recognized as "international routes" before reopening talks. The MAC argued that Beijing had put up many political hurdles to prevent negotiations, such as an insistence on the One China principle and endorsement of the "1992 consensus." Beijing also defined cross-Strait routes as "domestic routes," which was unacceptable to the administration in Taipei. From the MAC perspective, the PRC had transformed the economic issue into a political one, creating the difficulties that prevented the resumption of cross-Strait negotiations. Beijing's attitude was simply unacceptable to the Chen administration.[28]

The Chen administration also rejected Beijing's proposal to reopen the talks using civilian associations from the two sides. The DPP argued that negotiations on air links should be conducted by two sovereign states and that civilian organizations could not replace formal governmental bodies when negotiating issues related to state sovereignty. The PRC's proposal was just a smoke screen that would serve only to undermine Taiwan's sovereignty. The main obstacle for "delinking" direct flights from political issues was in Beijing, not in Taipei. President Chen Shui-bian stated as much in an interview with the *New York Times*:

> Taiwan's relationship with China is a country-to-country relationship. Of course airplanes can fly directly between one country and another, as between Taiwan and the United States and Japan. If Taiwan today were a

full member of the United Nations, there would of course be nothing strange about direct flights between Taiwan and any city in China. Should we not instead be stressing that only if Taiwan is admitted to the UN can it look forward to steady economic growth?[29]

The issue of the distribution of economic gains from cross-Strait interaction was also at the core of the DPP administration's efforts to strengthen its power base in domestic politics. Control over economic exchange with the PRC served as a useful political instrument. President Chen argued that the "health" of national development required maintaining a balance in regional, industrial, and environmental development. In the past, under KMT rule, the major focus of national development had been concentrated on northern Taiwan; the southern, central, and eastern regions were neglected. After the DPP came to power, Chen noted, it had focused on achieving balanced development for all regions and areas of Taiwan.[30] This distributional concern also extended to Taiwan's international economic status. As the DPP theorist Lin Cho-shui argued, direct air links and closer economic relations with the PRC would deepen Taiwan's dependence on the mainland Chinese market. From the Asia Pacific Operations Center in 1995 to the proposal of a Chinese common market during Ma's 2008 presidential campaign, by contrast, the KMT's strategy was to rely on the PRC to upgrade Taiwan's industrial level. According to the DPP, by establishing the Three Links, Taiwan would become a service hub integrated with the manufacturing capacities of the mainland. In that situation, nonservice sectors in Taiwan would be sacrificed. The KMT, in this view, was willing to sacrifice Taiwan's economic autonomy and impede the island's development into a global high-tech and manufacturing center for the sake of closer cross-Strait relations.[31]

As the MAC chair Chen Ming-tong argued in a presentation to the DPP's Central Standing Committee in 2008, the ultimate goal of cross-Strait economic integration was to realize "de facto unification" and sacrifice Taiwan's sovereignty, democracy, and peace. It would also deepen social divides, leading to economic and political polarization similar to that seen in Latin American countries. Economic integration would benefit only capitalists, without improving the welfare of the general public. It would harm regional development, deepen the urban-rural divide, and distort the income distribution in Taiwan. In addition, the PRC's "floating population" and surplus labor force would flood into Taiwan and negatively affect social stability and safety. Chen asserted,

According to estimates, under the Common Market framework, 1.7 million mainland Chinese laborers would move to Taiwan. They would occupy parks, stations, and public spaces. They would downgrade our quality of life. We would never feel comfortable to let our children play in the parks. Women would feel threatened if they came home late at night.[32]

To sum up, during the Chen Shui-bian era of 2000–2008, the Three Links issue and its potential impacts became tied both to fears of the PRC's penetration of Taiwan's economy and to worries about the negative effects of greater globalization on Taiwan. As a consequence, few concrete changes occurred in cross-Strait relations during this period.

Searching for a Breakthrough at the Top

In contrast to the DPP's policies, Ma Ying-jeou's solution to the challenge of establishing direct air links was to classify them as "cross-Strait lines" (*liang'an xian*). They were to be considered neither international nor domestic routes. This effort to bypass the sensitive sovereignty issue included a return to the "1992 Consensus" formula for cross-Strait negotiations based on an understanding of "one China with separate interpretations."[33]

In addition to its focus on opening direct air links across the Taiwan Strait, starting with weekend charter flights, the KMT also promised to cultivate international backing for greater cross-Strait exchanges. Ma Ying-jeou signaled that he would strive to allow foreigners to board direct flights. He argued that, since those flights would be characterized as "cross-Strait flights" and not "domestic flights" or "international flights," there was no reason foreigners should not be welcomed on board. At the same time, he stressed that while it pursued direct transportation links with the Chinese mainland, his administration would also seek to expand ties with the world, particularly the Asia-Pacific region, by negotiating and signing free trade agreements or other economic cooperation pacts.[34]

To pave the way for talks on opening direct air links, Ma sought to create a more favorable political environment that would help break the ice between Taiwan and the PRC. He objected to the DPP's interpretation of the "status quo" as an independent Taiwan. The status quo across the Taiwan Strait, in Ma's words, was summed up by the "Three Noes": no unification, no independence, and no use of military force. Under this Three Noes formula, Ma hoped to return Taiwan to the pre-1995 period, when it had enjoyed rapid economic growth, political stability, moderate cross-Strait relations, a strong national defense, and enhanced international status.[35] He argued that, for the past ten years, governments on both sides of the Taiwan Strait had been working to undermine the Three Noes and threatening the status quo. At the same time, Ma stated that his precondition for reopening talks was that they be based on principles of dignity, equality, reciprocity, and finding commonality among differences. He also demanded that the PRC dismantle missiles aimed at Taiwan, hold military exchanges, and set up bilateral military confidence-building measures.[36]

Ma Ying-jeou's proglobalization policy platform reflected the widespread discontent felt toward Chen Shui-bian's isolationism. As Yun-han Chu put it, as a mainlander, Ma felt compelled to soothe the historical grievances of the native Taiwanese. He tried very hard to put the spotlight on the lackluster economy and the huge damage that the DPP's self-imposed economic isolation had done to Taiwan, while avoiding a head-on confrontation with the DPP over national identity. On the eve of the 2008 election, Chu argued, more and more people had lost their appetite for ideologically driven political agendas as worries about their own personal economic situations had grown. Many households had experienced economic setbacks, facing stagnant incomes and diminishing job security amid runaway fuel and food prices.[37]

In addition to attracting broad support among the general public, Ma successfully formed a winning coalition among business interests for the 2008 election. The promised opening of the Three Links served to consolidate such a coalition. During the latter half of the Chen Shui-bian era, leading corporations in both the manufacturing and service sectors had shifted to support pro–Three Links policies. For instance, Stan Shih of the Acer group declined an offer to serve as a senior adviser to President Chen. The Chimei Group and Formosa Group openly opposed Chen's conservative approach to the Three Links. The Evergreen Group turned sharply away from its previous support for the DPP and embraced opening to the mainland Chinese market, due to the stagnation of business under the ruling party's policy of constraint. The Fubon Holding Company also withdrew its support for President Chen and became more active in exploring financial and insurance business opportunities on the other side of the Strait.

In his inaugural address, President Ma elaborated on his Three Noes policy, deemphasizing the sovereignty issue and focusing instead on laying the groundwork for increasing exchanges across the Strait. The establishment of direct air links was to serve as a key tool in consolidating and strengthening economic links with China.[38] Ma's remarks demonstrated major differences with the outgoing DPP administration on the sovereignty issue and its connection to the Three Links policy. By not making national identity and sovereignty preconditions for closer economic interaction, Ma reinterpreted the "status quo" across the Taiwan Strait under his Three Noes policy. The essence of Ma's economic development strategy was to tie Taiwan's economy more closely to mainland Chinese and global economic forces, with direct air links as the first step in this process.

Beyond the Three Links:
Domestic Struggles and the Drive for Globalization

When it took office in 2008, the Ma administration regarded the Three Links as stepping-stones toward a re-embrace of globalization through closer engagement with mainland China. Rather than seek to limit economic dependence on the PRC, as the Chen administration had, Ma asserted that deepening the island's ties to the global economy would be a more effective way to protect Taiwan's national security in the face of a rising China. On the PRC side, the calculation was that establishing the Three Links would help promote economic, cultural, and human resource flows between the two sides. From Beijing's perspective, such interaction would eventually lay the foundation for unification.

The first test of the Ma administration's new drive to increase global ties was the effort to expand bilateral air links into regional networks among major East Asian cities. The establishment of the Three Links, especially the air links, resulted in the creation of a "golden loop" among the metropolitan airports of Taipei, Shanghai, Tokyo, and Seoul. The opening of direct cross-Strait flights also served to jump-start Taiwan's negotiations over new air routes with other East Asian countries.

One good example of the subsequent successes created by cross-Strait flights was the air agreement struck between Taiwan and Japan in 2011. The agreement allowed an unlimited number of carriers from both sides to operate scheduled flights between the two countries and an unlimited number of flights between Taiwanese and Japanese destinations outside of Tokyo, the Japanese capital. Most important, the agreement gave both parties "beyond rights," also known as the "fifth freedom" of air transit, which allowed both Taiwanese and Japanese airlines to carry passengers from either country to a second country, and from that country to a third country, and so on. The agreement also lifted all restrictions on the number of carriers operating nonscheduled chartered flights, regardless of whether they were carrying passengers or freight, as well as any restrictions on the number of such flights between the two countries.[39]

The establishment of new air links created opportunities for local governments to capitalize on Taiwan's greater global connectivity. The development of the new "golden loop" routes led to the rejuvenation of

Taipei's outdated Songshan Airport. It also helped transform the surrounding areas into a new service center for the Taipei metropolitan region. In other words, the political thaw at the highest levels in cross-Strait relations helped promote the globalization of Taipei, and the direct links with the other side of the Taiwan Strait became a major pillar of new economic initiatives.

The Ma administration quickly looked to move beyond the establishment of the Three Links toward a more comprehensive and institutionalized set of arrangements to structure cross-Strait economic interaction. The most ambitious were the efforts to sign cross-Strait free trade agreements. Following the KMT's return to power, the two sides of the Taiwan Strait signed more than a dozen separate economic cooperation agreements. Among these, the most prominent was the Economic Cooperation Framework Agreement (ECFA), which was signed in June 2010. The ECFA was a preferential trade agreement that aimed to reduce tariffs and other commercial barriers between the two sides. But the Ma administration also viewed ECFA as a stepping-stone toward greater integration with other regional economies. Because additional rounds of free trade talks at the WTO had been stalled for years, East Asian countries had begun signing dozens of bilateral and multilateral free trade agreements with each other over the past decade. But Taiwan had been unable to conclude any agreements because of pressure on trading partners from the PRC, leaving it as one of two economies in the region—along with North Korea—without a free trade agreement. Signing the ECFA with Beijing, however, would unlock the possibility of agreements with other East Asian countries. Thus, the ECFA played a pivotal role in the Ma administration's grand strategy for strengthening the domestic economy: by improving relations with Beijing and pursuing greater cross-Strait integration, Taiwan would also strengthen its global competitiveness and its links to other regional economies. This greater integration with the global economy, in turn, would compensate for Taiwan's diplomatic isolation and ultimately strengthen its economic security.

For its part, after the DPP returned to the opposition, it maintained its long-standing position against greater economic integration with the PRC. DPP party members raised questions about Ma's "globalization via China" strategy, arguing that it would eventually undermine Taiwan's sovereignty and threaten its democracy. Some trade-related matters, they asserted, such as investment and intellectual property rights protection, could be negotiated separately without rushing to sign the ECFA. In a televised and closely watched debate about ECFA held in 2010 between President Ma and DPP chair Tsai Ing-wen, Tsai raised an additional objection, arguing that a free trade agreement with the PRC would exacerbate an already-growing wealth gap in Taiwan. In addition to accusing the KMT of lacking sincerity in its communications with the Legislative Yuan and the opposition camp on ECFA negotiations, Tsai questioned whether Ma could keep his promise that agricultural imports from China would not overwhelm Taiwanese farmers in the long run. The opposition camp also argued that, as they contended had happened in the case of the Closer Economic Partnership Arrangement (CEPA), signed between the Hong Kong Special Administrative Region and Beijing, the ECFA would eventually lead to the demise of manufacturing industries, a decline in real salaries, a rise in housing costs, and further income inequality in Taiwan.[40]

The establishment of the Three Links and the normalization of other economic exchanges promoted individual interactions across the Strait, as well, especially among tourists and students. From 2008 to 2012, after the opening of Taiwan to tourism from the PRC, mainland Chinese made 7.17 million visits to Taiwan. Although most were in tour groups organized by Chinese travel agencies, about 200,000 visitors from the PRC came as individual travelers in 2012. Mainland tourists accounted for about 30 percent of all visits to Taiwan that year, representing one of the largest single sources of visitors from any country. For mainland Chinese students, Taiwan still has, at the time of this writing, a policy of "Three Restrictions and Six Prohibitions"[41] in place, but, according to the Ma administration, these restrictions will gradually be eased. Taiwan currently only recognizes degrees from forty-one mainland Chinese educational institutions. The goal in the future, however, is for Taiwan to recognize the degrees of all universities and colleges included in the PRC's Project 211, which promotes educational excellence. If this reform is completed, Taiwan will eventually accept degrees from more than a hundred mainland Chinese schools and allow mainland Chinese junior college students to study in Taiwan.[42]

Since the DPP lost control of the presidency in 2008 and returned to the opposition, it has advocated a political approach to cross-Strait relations that stands in clear contrast to the Ma administration's embrace of the 1992 consensus of "one China, different interpretations." From the DPP's viewpoint, Ma's cross-Strait initiatives have come at the expense of downgrading Taiwan's status to that of a "region" under the authority of the PRC. For instance, during her presidential campaign in 2012, Tsai Ing-wen argued that meaningful negotiations between the DPP and Chinese Communist Party (CCP) could be held only if no preconditions were required. Since she became DPP party chair, the real objective of Tsai's approach to cross-Strait relations has been to seek peaceful relations without making unification a precondition. By "acknowledging" Beijing's One China principle, Tsai would replace Ma's endorsement of the "one China, separate interpretations" formula as the basis for cross-Strait interaction with her own party's "Taiwan consensus," which emphasizes the fundamental difference between Taiwan's democratic system and its incompatibility with the authoritarian one-party control of the CCP on the Chinese mainland. The DPP's official position, added to its party platform in 2011, is that the 1992 Consensus was an understanding reached between two authoritarian parties without conferring with the Taiwanese people; thus, a new "Taiwan consensus" should be generated through a democratic process in Taiwan before sitting down at the negotiating table with Beijing. In other words, the 1992 consensus on which cross-Strait negotiations have proceeded during the Ma Ying-jeou era lacks democratic legitimacy and should not be the basis for future agreements.[43]

After Tsai's defeat in the 2012 presidential election, she shifted her focus from cross-Strait relations to domestic affairs. Instead of promoting Taiwan's democracy as the linchpin of an anti-China front, Tsai turned her attention to grassroots empowerment and community-building efforts to build support for the DPP and her political future from the bottom up. In a report published at the end of 2012, Tsai wrote,

> Some said that the hostile environment between political parties impeded political development in Taiwan. Today, one-party rule has led to a confrontation between the state and society, as public opinion can't be heard by the Ma administration. . . .
> To achieve great political and social reforms not only requires negotiation between ruling and opposition parties but also requires the re-empowerment of civil society, so that we can assist and supervise the government to realize reforms. . . . If everyone began the process by paying attention to their communities and expanded that effort to public policies, the action and efforts would converge and ultimately become a power that could change the country.[44]

About a year after Ma Ying-jeou was inaugurated for a second term as president, Taiwan and the PRC signed the Cross-Strait Service Trade Agreement (CSSTA) in June 2013, potentially opening the service sectors on both sides to further cross-Strait interaction. Under the pact, which includes four chapters and twenty-four articles, sixty-four Taiwanese industries would be opened to mainland Chinese investment, while the PRC would open up eighty industries to Taiwan. The Taiwanese industries would include transportation, tourism, and traditional Chinese medicine, while the PRC would open up its finance, retail, electronics, publishing, and travel sectors. Under the agreement, mainland Chinese investors would be allowed to open hotels in Taiwan, and Chinese travel agencies could establish a maximum of three branches in the country and provide services to Taiwanese. However, they would not be allowed to accommodate any foreign tourists, including Chinese. Taiwanese investors would also be allowed to set up travel agencies in China, as well as open restaurants or hotels.

Chinese companies would be allowed to open beauty parlors or hair salons in Taiwan but would only be allowed to employ Taiwanese. Although China would open its publishing industry to Taiwanese investment, Taiwan would allow Chinese companies only to invest in Taiwanese businesses in the printing service industry, with a maximum of 50 percent stock ownership. On financial services, Taiwanese companies would be allowed to invest in security companies in Shanghai, Shenzhen, and Chinese-controlled Fujian Province.[45]

The agreement also appeared to offer several potentially attractive rewards for Taiwan's service providers, giving Taiwan companies competitive advantages over other foreign firms in several sectors. For example, if operating from the mainland's coastal province of Fujian, Taiwan e-commerce firms could own a 55 percent stake in joint ventures with local companies, whereas foreign companies are otherwise prevented from owning more than 50 percent. Similarly, the island's stockbrokers would be allowed to hold 51 percent stakes in joint-venture operations based in Shanghai, Shenzhen, or Fujian, a provision not extended to other overseas investors. Preferential policies were also outlined for the banking, creative, entertainment, and medical sectors.[46]

Nevertheless, domestic objections arose after this new cross-Strait economic pact was signed, and it has since foundered on the shoals of domestic politics. The Ma administration was criticized for not consulting with legislators and industry groups prior to reaching the deal. Critics argued that most of the market liberalizations offered by Beijing had preconditions, whereas most of Taiwan's market openings for mainland companies were unconditional. Taiwan e-commerce ventures would not be allowed to directly offer cross-border services but, instead, would have to set up joint ventures in the PRC's Fujian Province and apply for licenses that would ban content contrary to Chinese policies, such as Beijing's claim that Taiwan is part of Chinese territory. Taiwanese e-commerce enterprises would be forced to take their capital, staff, and know-how to the mainland and to engage in self-censorship. Furthermore, critics charged that the new pact would spark another wave of migration of capital, talent, and know-how to mainland China and thus further push down investment, employment, wages, and consumption in the Taiwanese economy.[47]

The prospects for approval of the CSSTA worsened after it was introduced to the Legislative Yuan in June 2013. Despite the KMT's large majority there, Legislative Yuan Speaker Wang Jin-pyng negotiated a cross-party consensus that the services pact would be subjected to additional scrutiny by legislators and face a time-consuming, line-by-line review. The delay and additional hearings gave the DPP many opportunities to raise objections to the deal and to try to rally public opinion against it. It also put KMT legislators, many of whom had their own concerns about the agreement, in a tough spot. In March 2014, a KMT legislative committee chair attempted, without warning, to discharge the agreement for a floor vote in a procedurally questionable move. The threat of a surprise vote on the agreement sparked a student protest and a three-week occupation of the Legislative Yuan. After the occupation ended, the CSSTA remained stalled in the legislature, and, at the time of this writing, it appears unlikely to be approved before the end of Ma Ying-jeou's second term.

In addition to its efforts to conclude cross-Strait agreements, the Ma administration has also put considerable energy into trying to take advantage of the goodwill that ECFA had earned it in Beijing to expand Taiwan's economic and diplomatic space elsewhere in the region. In August 2010, Taiwan and Singapore announced that the two sides had launched negotiations on a bilateral economic agreement. In contrast to the DPP's insistence during the Chen Shui-bian era on using the name "Taiwan" in international negotiations, the two sides agreed to hold talks following the WTO framework, under which Taiwan is formally known as "Chinese Taipei." In July 2013, Taiwan signed a free trade agreement with New Zealand. Although the Ma administration claimed that "the trade and industrial structures of the two countries strongly complement each other, and that the Economic Cooperation Agreement (ECA) will have a significant complementary effect on their economic development," the scale was weighted in favor of New Zealand's exports over Taiwan's. Given that New Zealand's US$607 million annual agricultural exports to Taiwan made up 20 percent of the total value of its agricultural exports, New Zealand's agricultural sector, especially the dairy industry, was set to reap the most benefits from the deal.

Although the Ma government regarded the agreement with New Zealand as a breakthrough made possible by ECFA, the two sides were, in fact, very prudent in avoiding politically sensitive topics during negotiations. The choice of wording of the title is an example: it was officially called the Agreement Between New Zealand and the Separate Customs Territory of Taiwan, Penghu, Kinmen, and Matsu on Economic Cooperation (ANZTEC), following the formula that Taiwan used to enter the WTO. Furthermore, to avoid ruffling the feathers of the PRC, its second-biggest trading partner and largest export market, New Zealand kept the entire negotiation process as low profile as possible and held the signing ceremony at a local university in Wellington, without the presence of senior officials from either side. A PRC Foreign Ministry spokesperson confirmed in a press conference afterward that Beijing did not object to Taiwan's "nongovernmental business and cultural exchanges," as long as both parties agreed to oppose the creation of "two Chinas" or "one China, one Taiwan."[48]

Following the political-legal approach used for the New Zealand agreement, Taiwan and Singapore finally concluded prolonged negotiations on a free trade agreement in November 2013. This agreement had broader strategic implications for Taiwan, as it opened the way to engage in negotiations with Association of Southeast Asian Nations (ASEAN) countries and strengthened Taiwan's case for joining the proposed Trans-Pacific Partnership (TPP). At the time of the signing, Singapore was Taiwan's fourth-largest export market, with two-way trade worth US$28.2 billion in 2012. The deal would remove all trade barriers between the two economies in phases over the next fifteen years. Although tariff reductions included in the deal were likely to boost Taiwan's gross domestic product by just 0.1 percent by then, the agreement was expected to help Taiwan ink similar pacts with other economies, including Indonesia, India, and the Philippines. The PRC's reaction to the deal was again muted; a spokesperson simply reiterated Beijing's position that it hoped Singapore would abide by the One China policy and deal with its economic ties with Taiwan in a prudent and proper manner.[49]

Conclusion

This chapter has provided a historical review of one of the most controversial issues in cross-Strait relations: economic interactions. The analysis demonstrates that domestic factors in Taiwan's democracy have led to distortionary economic policies. These factors have delayed Taiwan's attempts to create greater linkages to the global economy through engagement with the PRC.

During the Chen administration, the desire to protect Taiwanese sovereignty was the overriding factor in decisions about commercial, postal, and transportation links with the PRC. In addition, the DPP prioritized distributive justice and a reduction in regional economic imbalances in an effort to consolidate an "indigenous" development regime. As a consequence, the DPP policy toward the Three Links was characterized by hesitation and contradictions. The deterioration of relations with Beijing in Chen's second term made the possibility of establishing the Three Links even more remote.

In the 2008 presidential election, public discontent and the desire of the Taiwanese business community to reverse Taiwan's increasing economic isolation helped create a winning coalition for Ma Ying-jeou. The KMT administration under Ma embraced the opportunities that greater integration into the global economy would bring to Taiwan and took a more pragmatic approach toward Three Links policy. New domestic and international actors constructed a complex state-business web of influences to push forward further integration with the PRC and global economies. At the same time, President Ma endeavored to create a more productive cross-Strait political environment by basing Taiwan-PRC relations on the "Three Noes": no unification, no independence, and no use of military force. Nevertheless, while it has successfully promoted greater economic integration with mainland Chinese markets, the Ma administration has also struggled to respond to a widening wealth gap and other domestic governance challenges during his second term.

The Ma administration regards the combination of a new globally oriented economic policy and enhanced economic links to mainland China as significant achievements in upgrading Taiwan's international competitiveness. The reinvigoration of the economy, in this view, will help reinforce Taiwan's autonomy and bolster its confidence in dealing with the PRC. On the domestic front, however, the emergence of new antiglobalization alliances and deepening social divides may generate new sources of instability in Taiwan's young democracy.

The analysis in this chapter also demonstrates the limitations that subnational actors face in achieving breakthroughs on sensitive political issues. The establishment of the Three Links turned out to be just a first step on the way to a more tangled set of domestic and global challenges. To face these challenges, Taiwan would do well to foster greater inclusiveness in the democratic process, helping to build a stronger domestic consensus behind new economic policies. The dramatic improvement in cross-Strait relations since 2008 has helped hitch Taiwan's economy to the growth engine on mainland China. The developments in cross-Strait trade, travel, and communications have forced the opposition camp to focus more on matters such as community building and local empowerment, and the developments are unlikely to be reversed, even if the DPP returns to power in the future.

Nevertheless, thorny issues in cross-Strait relations require careful political calculations in setting domestic priorities. Strengthening institutional capabilities will help rebuild confidence in Taiwan's democracy and allow its leaders to negotiate from a position of greater strength. In the current political environment in Taiwan, the Ma administration has been fighting a two-front economic war on domestic and international soil. Taiwan's drive for greater integration into the global economy ultimately depends on a domestic consensus about how to approach cross-Strait relations. Compromise on cross-Strait issues, in turn, will have to be based on mutual understanding and trust between Taipei and Beijing. The critical function of the Three Links between Taiwan and the PRC has been to help strengthen this understanding.

Notes

1. Saskia Sassen, "Losing Control? The State and the New Geography of Power" (paper presented at the Global Forum on Regional Development Policy, Nagoya, Japan, December 1–4, 1998), 15.
2. David Held, "Democracy and Globalization," in *Re-Imaging Political Community,* ed. Daniele Archibugi (Stanford, CA: Stanford University Press, 1998), 11–27.
3. Christine Keating, "Developmental Democracy and Its Inclusion: Globalization and the Transformation of Participation," *Signs* 29, no. 2 (Winter 2004): 435.
4. Hans Agne, "A Dogma of Democratic Theory and Globalization: Why Politics Need Not Include Everyone It Affects," *European Journal of International Relations* 12, no. 3 (September 2006): 433–458.
5. Kathleen C. Schwartzman, "Globalization and Democracy," *Annual Review of Sociology* 24 (1998): 179.
6. John Ralston Saul, "Globalisation and Democracy" (public lecture given at the University of New South Wales, Sydney, Australia, January 1999).
7. Peter J. Taylor, *World City Network—A Global Urban Analysis* (London: Routledge, 2004).
8. Peter J. Taylor, "Shanghai, Hong Kong, Taipei, and Beijing Within the World City Network: Positions, Trends and Prospects" (paper presented at the Second World Forum for China Studies, Shanghai, September 2, 2006).
9. For a detailed analysis of the ranking, see Pengfei Ni, ed., *Zhongguo Chengshi Jingzhengli Baogao* [Report on the competitiveness of Chinese cities] (Beijing: Shehui Kexue Wenxian Chubanshe, 2007).
10. *Gongshang Shibao,* June 17, 2006, A2.
11. Interview with the author in Songjiang Township, Shanghai, July 12, 2007.
12. Taipei City Administration Press Release, September 26, 2004.
13. Taipei City Administration Press Release, February 11, 2004.
14. Lung-bin Hua, *Message to the Taipei City Council,* March 27, 2007.
15. *Gongzong 2008 Chanye Zhengce Jianyan Shu* [2008 CNFI report of industrial policies], February 3, 2008.
16. European Chamber of Commerce Taipei, "Time to Act! Roadmap to Renewed Prosperity" (ECCT 2007–2008 Position Paper, 2007).
17. ECCT News Release, November 29, 2007.
18. Interview with a Canadian business representative, July 13, 2007.
19. American Chamber of Commerce, *Taiwan White Paper 2007* (Taipei: American Chamber of Commerce, May 2007), 9.
20. *Taipei Times,* March 23, 2008.
21. Remarks by AIT director Stephen M. Young to the 2008 Hsieh Nien Fan of the American Chamber of Commerce in Taipei, April 29, 2008.

22. Julian Chang and Steven Goldstein, eds., *Economic Reform and Cross-Strait Relations: Taiwan and China in the WTO* (Singapore: World Scientific Publishing Company, 2007).

23. "Exclusive Interview: Chen Shui-bian," *Financial Times*, November 2, 2006.

24. *Renmin Ribao*, July 1, 2004.

25. Jia Qinglin, *Message to the Third Cross-Straits Economic and Cultural Forum*, April 28, 2007. Jia was the head of the Chinese People's Political Consultative Conference. *Xinhua Net*, April 28, 2007.

26. Address by Chen Ming-tong at the 2008 New Year's Press Conference, January 8, 2008, Mainland Affairs Council; address by Chen-yuan Tung, February 13, 2008.

27. CNBC Interview with President Chen Shui-bian, Office of the President, September 17, 2007.

28. MAC Regular Press Briefing, October 20, 2006, http://www.mac.gov.tw /english/english/macnews/enews/enews951020.htm.

29. "The *New York Times* Interview with President Chen Shui-bian," Office of the President News Release, October 18, 2007.

30. CNBC Interview with President Chen Shui-bian, Office of the President, September 17, 2007.

31. Cho-shui Lin, "Zili vs. yifu, quanqiu vs. qukuai" [Autonomy vs. dependency, global vs. regional], *Liberty Times*, March 5, 2008.

32. Chen Ming-tong, *A Report to DPP Central Standing Committee*, February 27, 2008.

33. *CNA News*, August 10, 2007.

34. Ma Ying-jeou's Remarks at the International Reception, March 5, 2008.

35. Keynote address at the Confidence Building Measures: Successful Cases and Implications for the Taiwan Straits Conference, January 16, 2008.

36. "A SMART Strategy for National Security" (speech before the Association for Promotion of National Security, February 26, 2008).

37. Yun-han Chu, "Taiwan in 2007: The Waiting Game," *Asian Survey* 48, no. 1 (2008): 127–130.

38. President Ma's Inaugural Address, Office of the President, May 20, 2008, http://www.president.gov.tw/en/.

39. *The China Post*, November 11, 2011, http://www.chinapost.com.tw/taiwan /foreign-affairs/2011/11/11/322617/Taiwan-Japan.htm.

40. Tse-kang Leng, "Coping with China in Hard Times: Taiwan in Global and Domestic Aspects," *Pacific Focus* 26, no. 3 (December 2011): 360–384.

41. This policy refers to the rules provided by the Ministry of Education in Taiwan to regulate students from mainland China. The three restrictions are (1) only certificates or diplomas from top-ranked universities in mainland China will be recognized; (2) the number of Chinese students will be limited to 1 percent of overall local student recruitment; and (3) mainland Chinese students will not be accepted in the research fields of Chinese and Western medicine, pharmacy, national security, and high technology. The six prohibitions are (1) no extra credit will be offered to the mainland students; (2) the process of local student recruitment will not be affected by Chinese student recruitment; (3) no special scholarships will be awarded to mainland students; (4) working off-campus is not permitted; (5) taking tests for professional licenses is not permitted; and (6) working in Taiwan after graduating is not permitted.

42. Ma Ying-jeou, "Gradual Reconciliation in the Cross-Strait Relationship; Expansion of Peace and Prosperity" (speech delivered on February 18, 2013), http:// english.president.gov.tw/Default.aspx?tabid=1124&itemid=29283&rmid=3048.

43. "Tsai Ing-Wen's Remarks at the American Enterprises Institute," September 13, 2011. Released by the Department of Foreign Affairs, DPP; for the full text of the Ten Year Political Platform, refer to http://10.iing.tw/2011/08/blog-post_9219.html.

44. Tsai Ing-wen, "Xie gei 2013 de Taiwan" [A letter to the Taiwan of 2013], December 31, 2012, http://www.thinkingtaiwan.com/public/articles/view/408.

45. *Taipei Times,* June 23, 2013, http://www.taipeitimes.com/News/front/archives /2013/06/22/2003565371.

46. "China/Taiwan: Cross-Strait Services Trade Pact in Limbo," *The Economist* Intelligence Unit, November 15, 2013, http://www.eiu.com/industry/article/109123 9293/chinataiwan-cross-strait-services-trade-pact-in-limbo/2013-11-15.

47. Dennis Engbarth, "Cross-Strait Trade Deal Raises Concerns in Taiwan," *Asia Times,* July 8, 2013, http://www.atimes.com/atimes/China_Business/CBIZ-01-070813 .html.

48. Nicole White, Jieming Chu, and Kaelyn Lowmaster, "ANZTEC and Taiwan's Quest for Economic Integration," August 1, 2013, http://csis.org/publication /anztec-and-taiwans-quest-economic-integration.

49. *Wall Street Journal,* November 7, 2013, http://online.wsj.com/news/articles /SB10001424052702303309504579182900090244112.

Bibliography

Acemoglu, Daron, and James A. Robinson. *Economic Origins of Dictatorship and Democracy.* New York: Cambridge University Press, 2006.

Agne, Hans. "A Dogma of Democratic Theory and Globalization: Why Politics Need Not Include Everyone It Affects." *European Journal of International Relations* 12, no. 3 (2006): 433–458.

Aguero, Felipe. "Democratic Consolidation and the Military in Southern Europe and Latin America." In *The Politics of Democratic Consolidation: Southern Europe in Comparative Perspective,* edited by Richard Gunther, P. Nikiforos Diamandouros, and Hans-Jurgen Puhle. Baltimore, MD: Johns Hopkins University Press, 1995.

Anderson, Christopher J., and Christine A. Guillory. "Political Institutions and Satisfaction with Democracy: A Cross-National Analysis of Consensus and Majoritarian Systems." *American Political Science Review* 91, no. 1 (1997): 66–81.

Anderson, Christopher J., André Blais, Shaun Bowler, Todd Donovan, and Ola Listhaug. *Losers' Consent: Elections and Democratic Legitimacy.* Cambridge, UK: Cambridge University Press, 2005.

Barth, Jutta. "Public Policy Management Councils in Brazil: How Far Does Institutionalized Participation Reach?" *Public Administration and Development* 26, no. 3 (2006): 253–263.

Bawn, Kathleen. "Choosing Strategies to Control the Bureaucracy: Statutory Constraints, Oversight and the Committee System." *Journal of Law, Economics, and Organization* 13, no. 1 (1997): 101–126.

———. "Political Decisions About Bureaucratic Accountability: Interests, Institutions, and Prospects for Reform." In *Reinventing Government and the Problem of Bureaucracy,* edited by Gary D. Libecap. Greenwich, CT: JAI Press, 1996.

Benson, Brett, and Emerson M. S. Niou. "Public Opinion, Foreign Policy, and the Security Balance in the Taiwan Strait." *Security Studies* 14, no. 2 (2005): 1–16.

Chang, Andy G., and T. Y. Wang. "Taiwanese or Chinese? Independence or Unification? An Analysis of Generational Differences in Taiwan." *Journal of Asian and African Studies* 40, no. 1–2 (2005): 29–49.

Chang, Mao-kuei, and Chun-chieh Chen. 1986. "The Relations Among Modernization, Local Factions, and the Turn Out Rate of Local Elections." In *The Papers* of the Conference on Voting Behavior and Electoral Culture, edited by the Chinese Political Science Association, 487–519. Taipei: Chinese Political Science Association, 1986.

Chang, Mao-kuei, and Yong-nian Zheng, eds. *Analysis of Social Movements in Taiwan and China*. Taipei: New Naturalism Press, 2003.

Chao, Chien-min. "Introduction: The DPP in Power." *Journal of Contemporary China* 11, no. 33 (2002): 605–612.

Chao, Linda, and Ramon Myers. "How Elections Promoted Democracy Under Martial Law." In *Elections and Democracy in Greater China*, edited by Larry Diamond and Ramon Myers. Oxford: Oxford University Press, 2001.

Chao, Yung-mao, and Chiung-wen Huang. "The Characteristic Change of Farmer Association Factions Around the Transformation of Taiwanese Authoritarian Regime: A Case Study of Sheilin Township from 1970 to 1990." *Taiwanese Journal of Political Science* 13 (December 2000): 165–200.

Chen, Ming-tong. *Factional Politics and Taiwan's Political Change*. Taipei: Yueh-Tan Press, 1995.

———. "Local Factions and Elections in Taiwan's Democratization." In *Taiwan's Electoral Politics and Democratic Transition: Ruling the Third Wave*, edited by Hung-mao Tien. Armonk, NY: M. E. Sharpe, 1996.

Chen, Weitseng. "Cross the Bridge When There? China-Taiwan Comparison of Rule-of-Law-Without-Democracy Strategy for Transition." Yale Law School Student Scholarship Series, Paper 55, New Haven, CT, 2007.

———. *Law and Economic Miracle: The Interaction Between Economy and Legal System in Taiwan After World War II*. Taipei: Angle Publishing, 2000.

Cheng, Tun-jen, and Yun-han Chu. "State-Business Relations in South Korea and Taiwan." In *Emerging Market Democracies*, edited by Laurence Whitehead, 31–62. Baltimore, MD: Johns Hopkins University Press, 2002.

Chiu, Hei-yuan. "Liberty of Association, Group Participation, and Democracy." In *Rule of Law, Human Rights, and Civil Society*, edited by Hei-yuan Chiu, Chunghua Ku, and Sechin Y. S. Chien. Taipei: Laureate Press, 2002.

Chu, Yun-han. "Consolidating Democracy in Taiwan: From *Guoshi* to *Guofa* Conference." In *Democratization in Taiwan: Implications for China*, edited by Hung-mao Tien and Steve Yui-sang Tsang, 23–48. New York: St. Martin's Press, 1998.

———. "Taiwan in 2007: The Waiting Game." *Asian Survey* 48, no. 1 (2008): 127–130.

———. "Taiwan's Democracy at a Turning Point." *American Journal of Chinese Studies* 11, no. 2 (2005): 901–924.

———. "Taiwan's Politics of Identity: Navigating Between China and the United States." In *Power and Security in Northeast Asia: Shifting Strategies*, edited by Byung-Kook Kim and Anthony Jones. Boulder, CO: Lynne Rienner, 2007.

Chu, Yun-han, and Tse-min Lin. "The Process of Democratic Consolidation in Taiwan: Social Cleavage, Electoral Competition, and the Emerging Party System." In *Taiwan's Electoral Politics and Democratic Transition: Riding the Third Wave*, edited by Hung-mao Tien, 79–104. Armonk, NY: M. E. Sharpe, 1994.

Chubb, Judith. *Patronage, Power, and Poverty in Southern Italy: A Tale of Two Cities*. Cambridge, UK: Cambridge University Press, 1982.

Coleman, John J. "Unified Government, Divided Government, and Party Responsiveness." *American Political Science Review* 93, no. 4 (1999): 821–835.

Cooney, Sean. "The New Taiwan and Its Old Labour Law: Authoritarian Legislation in a Democratized Society." *Comparative Labor Law Journal* 18, no. 1 (1996): 1–61.

Cottey, Andrew, Tim Edmunds, and Anthony Forster. "The Second Generation Problematic: Rethinking Democracy and Civil-Military Relations." *Armed Forces and Society* 29, no. 1 (2002): 31–56.

Cox, Gary W., and Samuel Kernell. "Introduction: Governing a Divided Era." In *The Politics of Divided Government,* edited by Gary W. Cox and Samuel Kernell. Boulder, CO: Westview Press, 1991.

Cutler, N. Lloyd. "Some Reflections About Divided Government." *Presidential Studies Quarterly* 18, no. 3 (1988): 489–490.

Desch, Michael C. *Civilian Control of the Military: The Changing Security Environment.* Baltimore, MD. Johns Hopkins University Press, 1999.

———. 1996. "Threat Environments and Military Missions." In *Civil-Military Relations and Democracy,* edited by Larry Diamond and Marc F. Plattner. Baltimore, MD: Johns Hopkins University Press, 1996.

de Tocqueville, Alexis. *Democracy in America.* New York: Harper and Row, 1966 [1835].

Diamond, Larry. *Developing Democracy: Toward Consolidation.* Baltimore, MD: Johns Hopkins University Press, 1999.

———. *The Spirit of Democracy.* New York: Times Books, 2008.

Diamond, Larry, and Gi-wook Shin. "Introduction." In *New Challenges for Maturing Democracies in Korea and Taiwan,* edited by Larry Diamond and Gi-wook Shin. Stanford, CA: Stanford University Press, 2014.

Di Palma, Giuseppe. *To Craft Democracy: An Essay on Democratic Transitions.* Berkeley: University of California Press, 1990.

Duverger, Maurice. *Political Parties: Their Organization and Activity in the Modern State.* New York: Wiley, 1963.

Edwards, George C. W., III, Andrew Barrett, and Jeffrey Peake. "Legislative Impact of Divided Governmen." *American Journal of Political Science* 41, no. 2 (1997): 545–563.

Elgie, Robert. "What Is Divided Government?" In *Divided Government in Comparative Perspective,* edited by Robert Elgie. Oxford: Oxford University Press, 2001.

Fearon, James D. "Domestic Political Audiences and the Escalation of International Disputes." *American Political Science Review* 88, no. 3 (1994): 577–592.

Fell, Dafydd. "The Evolution and Role of Campaign Issues in Taiwan's 1990s Elections." *Asian Journal of Political Science* 9, no. 1 (2001): 81–94.

———. "Inter-Party Competition in Taiwan Since the 1990s." *China Perspectives* 56 (November/December 2004): 3–13.

———. *Party Politics in Taiwan: Party Change and the Democratic Evolution of Taiwan, 1991–2004.* London: Routledge, 2005.

Fiorina, Morris. *Divided Government.* 2nd ed. Boston: Allyn and Bacon, 1996.

Fiorina, Morris P., Samuel J. Abrams, and Jeremy C. Pope. *Culture War? The Myth of a Polarized America.* New York: Longman, 2006.

Fiorina, Morris, and Matthew Levendusky. 2007. "Disconnected: The Political Class Versus the People." In *Red and Blue Nation? Characteristics and Causes of America's Polarized Politics,* edited by Pietro Nivola and David Brady. Stanford, CA: Hoover Institution and Brookings Institution Press.

Flinders, Matthew. "Volcanic Politics: Executive-Legislative Relations in Britain, 1997–2005." *Australian Journal of Political Science* 41, no. 3 (2006): 385–406.

Foley, Michael, and Bob Edwards. "The Paradox of Civil Society." *Journal of Democracy* 7, no. 3 (1996): 38–52.

Friedman, Barry. "History, Politics, and Judicial Independence." In *Judicial Integrity and Independence,* edited by Andras Sajo and Lorry Rutt Bentch. Leiden, Netherlands: Martinus Nijhoff, 2004.

Ginsberg, Benjamin, and Martin Shefter. *Politics by Other Means.* New York: Basic Books, 1990.

Ginsburg, Thomas. *Judicial Review in New Democracies: Constitutional Courts in Asian Cases.* New York: Cambridge University Press, 2003.

Gourevitch, Peter. *Politics in Hard Times: Comparative Responses to International Economic Crises*. Ithaca, NY: Cornell University Press, 1986.

Hackett, Robert A. *Remaking Media: The Struggle to Democratize Public Communication*. London: Routledge, 2006.

Hackett, Robert A., and William K. Carroll. "Critical Social Movements and Media Reform." *Media Development* 51, no. 1 (2004): 14–19.

Haggard, Stephan. 2004. "Institutions and Growth in East Asia." *Studies in Comparative International Development* 38, no. 4 (2004): 53–81.

Hamer, David. "Parliament and Government: Striking the Balance." In *The House on Capitol Hill: Parliament, Politics, and Power in the National Capital*, edited by Julian Disney and J. R. Nethercote. Annandale, NSW, Australia: Federation Press, 1996.

Han, Dong-sub. "The Middle Classes, Ideological Intention, and Resurrection of a Progressive Newspaper." *International Communication Gazette* 62, no. 1 (2000): 61–74.

Hawang, Shiow-duan. "The Predicament of Minority Government in the Legislative Yuan." [In Chinese.] *Taiwanese Political Science Review* 7, no. 2 (2003): 1–46.

Held, David. "Democracy and Globalization." In *Re-Imaging Political Community*, edited by Daniele Archibugi, 11–27. Stanford, CA: Stanford University Press, 1998.

Ho, Ming-sho. "Taiwan's State and Social Movements Under the DPP Government, 2002–2004." *Journal of East Asian Studies* 5, no. 3 (2005): 401–425.

———. "Weakened State and Social Movement: The Paradox of Taiwanese Environmental Politics After the Power Transfer." *Journal of Contemporary China* 14, no. 43 (2005): 339–352.

Howell, William, Scott Adler, Charles Cameron, and Charles Riemann. "Divided Government and the Legislative Productivity of Congress, 1945–94." *Legislative Studies Quarterly* 25, no. 2 (May 2000): 285–312.

Hsieh, John Fuh-sheng. "National Identity and Taiwan's Mainland Policy." *Journal of Contemporary China* 13, no. 40 (2004): 479–490.

Hsu, Yung-ming, and Chang-ping Lin. "'Nanfang zhengzhi' de zai jianyan: zongtong xuanpiao de fenliang huigui fenxi" [Re-examining "Southern Politics" in Taiwan]. *Journal of Electoral Studies* 16, no. 1 (2009): 1–35.

Hsu, Yung-ming, Chia-hung Tsai, and Hsiu-tin Huang. "Referendum: New Motivation to Forge Taiwan's National Identity." [In Chinese.] *Taiwan Democracy Quarterly* 2, no. 1 (2005): 51–74.

Huang, Chi. "Dimensions of Taiwanese/Chinese Identity and National Identity in Taiwan: A Latent Class Analysis." *Journal of Asian and African Studies* 40, no. 1–2 (2005): 51–70.

Huntington, Samuel. *The Soldier and the State: The Theory and Politics of Civil-Military Relations*. Cambridge, MA: Harvard University Press, 1957.

Huntington, Samuel P., and Joan M. Nelson. *No Easy Choice: Political Participation in Developing Countries*. Cambridge, MA: Harvard University Press, 1976.

Im, Yung-Ho. "The Media, Civil Society, and New Social Movements in Korea, 1985–89." In *Asian Cultural Studies*, edited by Kuan-hsin Chen, 330–351. London: Routledge, 1998.

Janowitz, Morris. *The Professional Soldier: A Social and Political Portrait*. New York: The Free Press, 1960.

Jenson, Jane, Martin Papillon, Paul G. Thomas, and Vincent Lemieux. *Modernizing Governance: A Preliminary Exploration*. Ottawa: Canadian Centre for Management Development, 2000.

Jones, Charles. *The Presidency in a Separated System*. 2nd ed. Washington, DC: Brookings Institution Press, 2005.

Kang, David C. *Crony Capitalism: Corruption and Development in South Korea and the Philippines*. Cambridge, UK: Cambridge University Press, 2002.

Katz, Richard S., and Peter Mair. "Changing Models of Party Organization and Party Democracy: The Emergence of the Cartel Party." *Party Politics* 1, no. 1 (1995): 5–28.

Kaufman-Winn, Jane, and Tang-chi Yeh. "Advocating Democracy: The Role of Lawyers in Taiwan's Political Transformation." *Law and Social Inquiry* 20, no. 2 (1995): 561–599.

Keating, Christine. "Developmental Democracy and Its Inclusion: Globalization and the Transformation of Participation." *Signs* 29, no. 2 (Winter 2004): 417–437.

Kelly, Q. Sean. "Punctuated Change and the Era of Divided Government." In *New Perspective on American Politics,* edited by C. Lawrence Dodd and Calvin Jillson, 162–190. Washington, DC: CQ Press, 1994.

Kuan, Yu-yuan, Chao-hsien Leu, and Ching-hsia Cheng. "The Employment of the Third Sector in Taiwan: Survey Results of 2005." *The National Taiwan University Journal of Social Work* 16 (2008): 45–86.

Kuo, Cheng-tian. "Taiwan's Distorted Democracy in Comparative Perspective." *Journal of Asian and African Studies* 35, no. 1 (2000): 85–111.

Lee, Chin-chuan. "Sparking a Fire: The Press and the Ferment of Democratic Change in Taiwan." *Journalism Monographs* 138 (1993).

Lee Teng-hui. *Xinshihdai taiwanren* [A new era of Taiwanese]. Taipei: Quncehui, 2005.

Leng, Tse-kang. "Coping with China in Hard Times: Taiwan in Global and Domestic Aspects." *Pacific Focus* 26, no. 3 (2011): 360–384.

Levitsky, Steven. *Transforming Labor-Based Parties in Latin America: Argentine Peronism in Comparative Perspective*. Cambridge, UK: Cambridge University Press, 2003.

Lin, Chia-lung. 1998. "Paths to Democracy: Taiwan in Comparative Perspective." PhD diss., Department of Political Science, Yale University, 1998.

Lin, Jih-wen. "The Institutional Context of President Chen's Cross-Strait Messages." *Issues and Studies* 44, no. 1 (2008): 1–31.

———. "Institutionalized Uncertainty and Governance Crisis in Post-Hegemonic Taiwan." *Journal of East Asian Studies* 3, no. 3 (2003): 433–460.

———. "The Politics of Reform in Japan and Taiwan." *Journal of Democracy* 17, no. 2 (2006): 118–131.

Lin, Lih-yun. "Weiquanzhuyi guojia yu dianshi: Taiwan yu Nanhan zhi bijiao" [Authoritarian states and television: A comparative study between Taiwan and South Korea]. *Mass Communication Research* 85 (Fall 2005): 1–30.

———. "Zuo er yan, qi er xing: 'wumeng' de shijian" [The translation of knowledge into action: Campaign for citizens' TV]. *Taiwan: A Radical Quarterly in Social Studies* 50 (June 2003): 145–170.

Linz, Juan J., and Alfred C. Stepan. *Problems of Democratic Transition and Consolidation: Southern Europe, South America, and Post-Communist Europe*. Baltimore, MD: Johns Hopkins University Press, 1996.

Lipset, Seymour Martin. "The Social Requisites of Democracy Revisited: 1993 Presidential Address." *American Sociological Review* 59, no. 1 (1994): 1–22.

———. "Some Social Requisites of Democracy: Economic Development and Political Legitimacy." *American Political Science Review* 53, no. 1 (1959): 69–105.

Liu, Heng-wen. "A Study of the Judges and Prosecutors in Postwar Taiwan: An Observation Focused on Their Training Culture." [In Chinese.] *Journal of Humanities and Social Sciences* 40, no. 1 (2002): 125–182.

Mainwaring, Scott P. *Rethinking Party System in the Third Wave of Democratization: The Case of Brazil*. Stanford, CA: Stanford University Press, 1999.

Marx, Karl. *The Eighteenth Brumaire of Louis Bonaparte*. New York: International Publishers, 1963.

Mayhew, David R. *Divided We Govern: Party Control, Lawmaking, and Investigations, 1946–2002*. New Haven, CT: Yale University Press, 2005.

O'Donnell, Guillermo. "Horizontal Accountability: The Legal Institutionalization of Mistrust." In *Democratic Accountability in Latin America*, edited by Scott Mainwaring and Christopher Welna, 34–54. New York: Oxford University Press, 2003.

Ostrom, Elinor. *Governing the Commons: The Evolution of Institutions for Collective Action*. Cambridge, UK: Cambridge University Press, 1990.

Oxhorn, Philip. "The Popular Sector Response to an Authoritarian Regime: Shantytown Organizations Since the Military Coup." *Latin American Perspectives* 18, no. 1 (1991): 66–91.

Poong, Hwei-luan, Cheng-tian Kuo, S. Philip Hsu, Hung-Hwei Liu, and James W. Y. Wang. "Networking Governance of e-Taiwan Policy." In *Rethinking New International Order in East Asia: US, China, and Taiwan*, edited by I. Yuan, 185–226. Taipei: Institute of International Relations, National Chengchi University, 2005.

Przeworski, Adam. "Democracy and Economic Development." In *The Evolution of Political Knowledge: Democracy, Autonomy, and Conflict in Comparative and International Politics*, edited by Edward D. Mansfield and Richard Sisson. Columbus: The Ohio State University Press, 2004.

———. *Democracy and the Market: Political and Economic Reforms in Eastern Europe and Latin America*. Cambridge, UK: Cambridge University Press, 1991.

Putnam, Robert. *Bowling Alone: The Collapse and Revival of American Community*. New York: Simon and Schuster, 2000.

Pye, Lucian. *Asian Power and Politics: The Cultural Dimensions of Authority*. Cambridge, MA: Belknap Press, 1985.

Ramseyer, J. Mark, and Frances McCall Rosenbluth. *Japan's Political Marketplace*. Cambridge, MA: Harvard University Press, 1993.

Reilly, Benjamin. "Democratization and Electoral Reform in the Asia-Pacific Region." *Comparative Political Studies* 40, no. 11 (2007): 1350–1371.

Rigger, Shelley. *Politics in Taiwan: Voting for Democracy*. New York: Routledge, 1999.

———. *Taiwan's Rising Rationalism: Generations, Politics, and "Taiwanese Nationalism."* Washington, DC: East-West Center, 2006.

Rock, Michael T. "Corruption and Democracy." DESA Working Paper no. 55, Department of Economic and Social Affairs, United Nations Secretariat, New York, August 2007.

Ross, Robert. "Explaining Taiwan's Revisionist Diplomacy." *Journal of Contemporary China* 15, no. 48 (2006): 443–458.

Schafferer, Christian. *The Power of the Ballot Box: Political Development and Election Campaigning in Taiwan*. Lanham, MD: Lexington Books, 2003.

Schattschneider, E. E. *The Semi-Sovereign People: A Realist's View of Democracy in America*. New York: Holt, Reinhart and Winston, 1960.

Schubert, Gunter. "Taiwan's Political Parties and National Identity: The Rise of an Overarching Consensus." *Asian Survey* 44, no. 4 (2004): 534–554.

Schwartzman, Kathleen C. "Globalization and Democracy." *Annual Review of Sociology* 24 (1998): 159–181.

Sheng, Shing-Yuan. "The Influence of the Legislative Branch and the Executive Branch in the Process of Lawmaking: A Comparison of Unified and Divided

Governments." [In Chinese.] *Taiwanese Political Science Review* 7, no. 2 (2003): 51–106.

———. "Issues, Political Cleavage, and Party Competition in Taiwan: From the Angles of the Elites and the Public." Paper presented at the Annual Meeting of the American Political Science Association, Chicago, IL, August 30–September 2, 2007.

Shyu, Huo-yan. "Partisan Territorial Lines Redrawn in Taiwan: A Comparison of the Electoral Bases of the DPP, KMT, and PFP." [In Chinese.] *Soochow Journal of Political Science* 14 (March 2003): 83–134.

Skocpol, Theda. "Unraveling from Above." *American Prospect* 25 (1996): 20–24.

Stepan, Alfred. "The New Professionalism of Internal Warfare and Military Role Expansion." In *Authoritarian Brazil: Origins, Policies, and Future,* edited by Alfred Stepan. New Haven, CT: Yale University Press, 1973.

———. *Rethinking Military Politics: Brazil and the Southern Cone.* Princeton, NJ: Princeton University Press, 1988.

Sundquist, L. James. "Needed: A Political Theory for the New Era of Coalition Government in the United States." *Political Science Quarterly* 103 (Winter 1988): 613–635.

Tan, Alexander C. "Transformation of the Kuomintang Party in Taiwan." *Democratization* 9, no. 3 (2002): 157–158.

Taylor, Peter J. *World City Network—A Global Urban Analysis.* London: Routledge, 2004.

Tsai, Chia-hung. "Policy-Making, Local Factions, and Candidate Coordination in Single Non-Transferable Voting: A Case Study of Taiwan." *Party Politics* 11, no. 1 (2007): 59–77.

Tsai, Chia-hung, Yung-ming Hsu, and Hsiu-tin Huang. "Liangji hua zhengzhi: jieshi Taiwan 2004 zongtong daxuan" [Bi-polarizing the politics: Explaining the 2004 presidential election in Taiwan]. *Journal of Electoral Studies* 14, no. 1 (2006): 1–31.

Tusalem, Rollin F. "A Boon or a Bane? The Role of Civil Society in Third- and Fourth-Wave Democracies." *International Political Science Review* 28, no. 3 (2007): 361–386.

Tzeng, Yi-suo. "Civil-Military Relations in Democratizing Taiwan, 1986–2007." PhD diss., Department of Political Science and International Affairs, George Washington University, 2009.

Wade, Robert. *Governing the Market: Economic Theory and the Role of Government in East Asian Industrialization.* Princeton, NJ: Princeton University Press, 1990.

Wang, Ching-yi. "The History of Development of Local Factions in Tai-Chung County: The Case of County Magistrate and Taiwan Provincial Assembly Elections, 1951–1987." [In Chinese.] Master's thesis, Department of History, National Taiwan Normal University, 1994.

Wang, Chin-shou. "Democratization and the Breakdown of Clientelism in Taiwan, 1987–2001." PhD diss., Department of Sociology, University of North Carolina at Chapel Hill, 2004.

———. "Judicial Independence Reform and the Breakdown of the Kuomintang's Clientelism." [In Chinese.] *Taiwanese Political Science Review* 10, no. 1 (June 2006): 103–162.

Wang, James W. Y. "The Political Economy of Collective Labour Legislation in Taiwan." *Journal of Current Chinese Affairs* 39, no. 3 (2010): 51–85.

Warner, Carolyn M. "Mass Parties and Clientelism in France and Italy." In *Clientelism, Interests, and Democratic Representation: The European Experience in Historical and Comparative Perspective,* edited by Simona Piattoni. New York: Cambridge University Press, 2001.

———. "Political Parties and the Opportunity Costs of Patronage." *Party Politics* 3, no. 4 (1997): 533–548.

Wei, Di. "Xin zheng-mei guanxi pipan: cong TVBS shijian tanqi" [New media politics: A comment on the TVBS episode]. *Taiwan: A Radical Quarterly in Social Studies* 60 (2005): iii–viii.

Weiss, Linda. *The Myth of the Powerless State: Governing the Economy in a Global Era.* Cambridge, UK: Polity Press, 1998.

Weiss, Linda, and Elizabeth Thurbon. "Is the State Being 'Transformed' by Globalisation?" In *States in the Global Economy: Bringing Domestic Institutions Back In,* edited by Linda Weiss, 298–316. Cambridge, UK: Cambridge University, 2003.

Woo-Cumings, Meredith. "Back to Basics: Ideology, Nationalism, and Asian Values in East Asia." In *Economic Nationalism in a Globalizing World,* edited by Eric Helleiner and Andreas Pickel, 91–117. Ithaca, NY: Cornell University Press, 2005.

Wu, Chung-li. "Local Factions and the Kuomintang in Taiwan's Electoral Politics." *International Relations of the Asia Pacific* 3, no. 1 (2003): 89–111.

Wu, Chung-li, and Chang-chih Lin. "The Executive-Legislative Interactions at the Central Government Level Before and After the 2000 Presidential Election in Taiwan: An Examination of the Fourth Nuclear Power Plant Controversy and the Lawmaking Process." [In Chinese.] *Theory and Policy* 16, no. 1 (2002): 73–98.

Wu, Jieh-min. "Disenchantment with the Clausewitzian Action Logic: An Analysis of the Current Trouble of the Social Movement." [In Chinese.] *The Taiwanese Journal of Sociology* 4 (2002): 159–198.

Wu, Nai-teh. "Identity Conflicts and Political Trust." [In Chinese.] *The Taiwanese Journal of Sociology* 4 (December 2002): 75–118.

———. "The Politics of a Regime Patronage System: Mobilization and Control Within an Authoritarian Regime." PhD diss., Department of Political Science, University of Chicago, 1987.

Wu, Yu-shan. "The ROC's Semi-Presidentialism at Work: Unstable Compromise, Not Cohabitation." *Issues and Studies* 36, no. 5 (2000): 1–40.

"Xinwen ziyou yu guojia anquan" [Press freedom and national security]. *Taiwan: A Radical Quarterly in Social Studies* 46 (June 2002): 251–272.

Yang, Wan-ying. "Party Cooperation and Conflict Under Divided Government: The Fourth Term Legislative Yuan." [In Chinese.] *Soochow Journal of Political Science* 16 (2003): 49–95.

The Contributors

Yu-tzung Chang is professor of political science and associate dean of the College of Social Science at National Taiwan University. His research expertise is in comparative democratization, the political economy of east Asia, and social science research methodology

Shang-mao Chen is professor and chair of the Department of Public Affairs at Fo Guang University in Yilan County, Taiwan. His research interests are in the comparative political economy of Asia and the relationship between democratization and economic development.

Wei tseng Chen is assistant professor at National University of Singapore Faculty of Law and deputy director of the Center for Asian Legal Studies. He specializes in comparative Asian law with an emphasis on property, financial institutions and authoritarian rule of law development.

Yun-han Chu is professor of political science at National Taiwan University, research fellow at Academia Sinica's Institute of Political Science, and president of the Chiang Ching-kuo Foundation. Dr. Chu's research and teaching career has focused on the political economy of East Asian newly industrialized countries, democratization, and comparative mass political behavior.

Larry Diamond is senior fellow at the Hoover Institution and at the Freeman Spogli Institute for International Studies, where he is a faculty affiliate at the Center on Democracy, Development, and the Rule of Law (CDDRL). At CDDRL, he directs the programs on Arab Reform and

Democracy, Liberation Technology, and Taiwan Democracy. He is also founding coeditor of the *Journal of Democracy* and senior consultant to the International Forum for Democratic Studies of the National Endowment for Democracy.

Chien-san Feng is professor of journalism in the College of Communication, National Chengchi University, Taipei. His expertise is in the political economy of communications, comparative media studies, and the history of film and policy.

Shiow-duan Hawang is professor of political science at Soochow University, Taipei. Dr. Hawang is a leading expert on executive-legislative relations and legislative organization in Taiwan.

Chang-Ling Huang is associate professor of political science at National Taiwan University. She is a leading scholar on civil society and social movements in Taiwan.

Min-Hua Huang is associate professor of political science at National Taiwan University, Taipei. His research interests include cross-national public opinion research, democratization, Asian politics, and political methodology.

Jimmy Chia-shin Hsu is associate research professor at the Institutum Iurisprudentiae at Academia Sinica, Taiwan. His research interests are in legal theory, constitutional law, freedom of speech, and democratization and the public sphere.

Cheng-tian Kuo is distinguished professor of political science and a faculty affiliate of the Graduate Institute of Religious Studies at National Chengchi University. He is also a member of the Advisory Committee on Religious Affairs in the Ministry of the Interior. Dr. Kuo is a leading expert on religion and politics in Taiwan.

Tse-Kang Leng is professor of political science and a faculty affiliate of the International MBA Program at National Chengchi University, as well as research fellow in the Institute of Political Science at Academia Sinica, Taiwan.

Jih-wen Lin is a research fellow at the Institute of Political Science at Academia Sinica, Taiwan, and professor of political science at National Chengchi University, National Taiwan University, and National Sun Yat-

Sen University. His research interests include East Asian politics, comparative institutional design, and formal modeling.

Shelley Rigger is the Brown Professor of East Asian Politics at Davidson College in Davidson, North Carolina. She is the author two books on Taiwan's domestic politics, *Politics in Taiwan: Voting for Democracy* and *From Opposition to Power: Taiwan's Democratic Progressive Party.*

Kharis Templeman is program manager of the Taiwan Democracy Project in the Center on Democracy, Development, and the Rule of Law at Stanford University. His current research interests include one-party dominance, constitutional design in divided societies, and party competition in new democracies.

Yisuo Tzeng is currently head of the research division at Taiwan Takechi Foundation, a non-profit organization affiliated with Taiwan's Ministry of Economic Affairs. He also lectures on international economic strategy at Tamkang University's Graduate Institute of International Affairs and Strategic Studies as an adjunct assistant professor.

Chin-Shou Wang is professor of political science and a faculty affiliate of the Graduate Institute of Political Economy at National Cheng Kung University, Taiwan. His research interests are in judicial politics, law and society, political sociology, social movements, and qualitative research methods.

James W. Y. Wang is adjunct assistant professor at National Central University, Chungli, Taiwan. He was previously assistant professor of public affairs at Fo Guang University, Taiwan.

Eric Chen-hua Yu is associate research fellow at the Election Study Center and associate professor of political science at National Cheng Chi University, Taiwan. His research interests include public opinion, electoral politics, survey research and quantitative methods.

Index

About the Book

When Chen Shui-bian, Taiwan's first non-Kuomintang president, left office in 2008, his tenure was widely considered a disappointment. More recent events, however, suggest the need for a reassessment of this crucial period in Taiwan's political development. Taiwan's Democracy Challenged provides that assessment, considering key facets of both the progress toward and the obstacles to democratic consolidation during the Chen Shui-bian era.

Yun-han Chu is professor of political science at National Taiwan University, distinguished research fellow at the Institute of Political Science at Academia Sinica, and president of the Chiang Ching-kuo Foundation. **Larry Diamond** is senior fellow at the Freeman Spogli Institute for International Studies and the Hoover Institution, Stanford University. **Kharis Templeman** is research associate at the Spogli Institute's Center on Democracy, Development, and the Rule of Law and also manages the institute's Taiwan Democracy Program.